ALITA
Battle Angel
ALITA™
Last Order™
ANGEL'S VISION

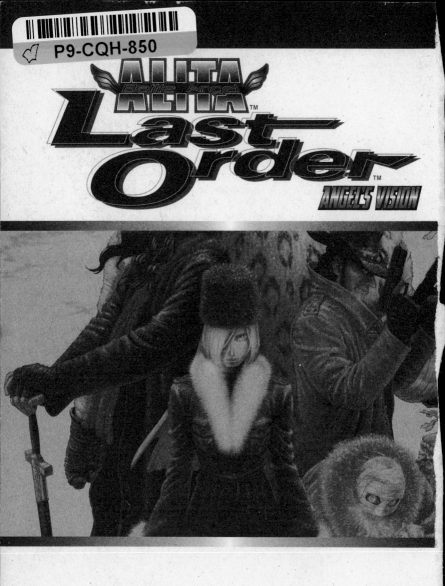

STORY & ART BY YUKITO KISHIRO

BATTLE ANGEL ALITA, VOLS. 1~9

In the near future…the world is divided into the dominated and the dominators. Tiphares, a floating artificial utopia, rules the Scrapyard, the surface, absolutely. But no one knows when or why this floating city was made—or by whom.

Ido, a Tipharean cyber-doctor and denizen of the Scrapyard, finds the head of a cyborg in a pile of rubble, and miraculously rebuilds her. She awakens with no memories, and Ido names her "Alita." Slowly, the harsh life of the Scrapyard stirs the fighting spirit within her, and she begins her path to self-discovery, living as a Hunter-Warrior, or bounty-hunter.

Alita meets and falls in love with Hugo, a boy who idolizes Tiphares. When she loses Hugo, she is heartbroken. Out of desperation, she turns to the pro sport world of Motor Ball, where she competes against the mighty Jashugan.

In a battle with a vicious cyborg named Zapan, whose body was revamped by evil genius Desty Nova, Alita loses Ido—her only family. Even her own life hangs by a thread.

The Tipharean organization G.I.B. presents Alita with a new path, and she chooses to live the life of a TUNED, a Tipharean agent, so that she can search for Nova, who holds the key to Ido's regeneration.

In the process, Alita becomes acquainted with Figure, a mercenary, and recovers the human soul she almost lost. Still, many seem to stand in her way: Kaos, Nova's son and a master of psychometry; Den, Kaos's alter-ego and the leader of the masses that oppose Tiphares; Koyomi, one of Den's groupies; the TUNED AR series, replicas of—and replacements for—Alita. Bitter battles ensue, and Lou, the operator who serves as backup support for the TUNED system, is ultimately relieved of duty. Only then is the shocking truth revealed: Tipharean adults have all had their brains replaced by bio-chips!

Alita resists the hacking of her brain and defeats Nova. It seems as if she has finally won, but a surprising trap awaits her as she makes her way back to Figure—Nova has regenerated himself through nano-technology. Alita is consumed in an explosion, and her brain is taken to Tiphares…

BATTLE ANGEL ALITA: LAST ORDER, VOLS. 1~7

Nova resurrects Alita and gives her the ultimate Imaginos body. Upheaval and bloodshed rule Tiphares as its citizens descend into madness after Nova's bio-chip revelation. Jim, the young genius Nova has chosen as his successor, succumbs to despair and activates his monster robot Sachumodo.

In the depths of Tiphares, Alita finds Lou's body—a mere shell without her brain bio-chip. Alita decides to ride to Ketheres with Nova and his escort, the TUNED AR series, but Nova is captured by Aga Mbadi, Hitechnolat Minister and LADDER Assistant Chairman. Alita and company are jettisoned into space.

Ping, the infamous hacker, saves them all—with an able assist from Queen Limeira of the Mars Kingdom Parliament. Alita finds refuge in the space colony Leviathan I, and decides to participate in the Zenith of Things Tournament (Z.O.T.T.), in which the winning team is falsely promised a commonwealth, while awaiting her chance to steal Lou's brain.

In the first round, Alita's team, the Space Angels, defeat the Guntrolls, the Stellar Nursery Society team led by Caerula Sanguis. This proves to be a fateful reunion for the two. Caerula entrusts Alita with a mysterious computer program named Fata Morgana.

In the second round, Alita leaves the battle with the Starship Cult up to Sechs, Elf, and Zwolf, while she infiltrates Ketheres on her own. Happening upon Tzyk, her former Panzer Kunst instructor, Alita finally regains her lost memories during the ensuing battle. Meanwhile, thanks to Sechs, the Space Angels defeat the Starship Cult, and advance to the next phase…

ALITA

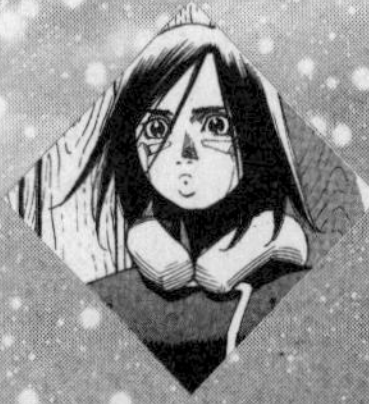

Our heroine was born on Mars and is the master of the cyborg martial art known as the "Panzer Kunst."

PING WU

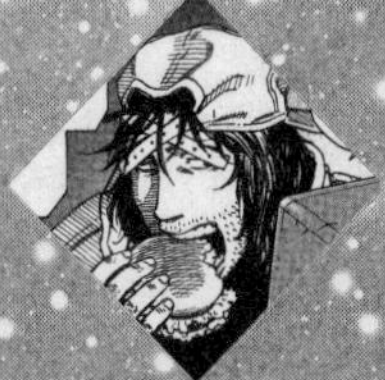

This former infamous hacker is now Alita's partner in crime...

GHOST (PAYNE)

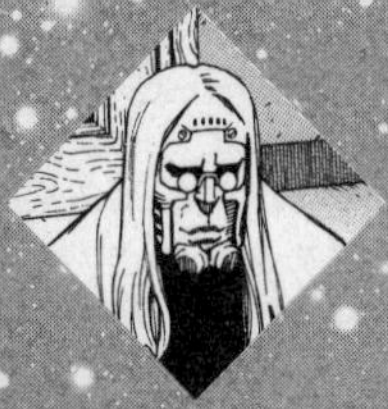

Defeated by Alita, Colonel Payne's ghost now haunts her.

VILMA

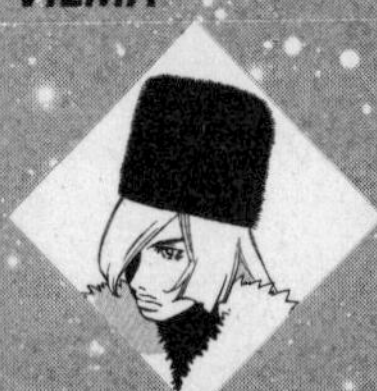

Later known as Caerula Sanguis.

VICTOR

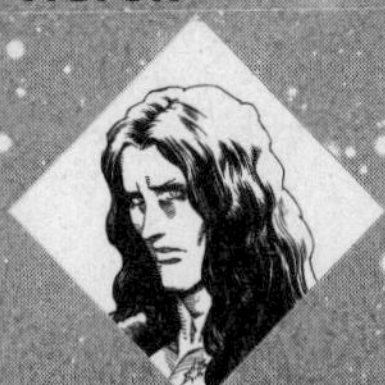

Vilma's lover.

JOHN

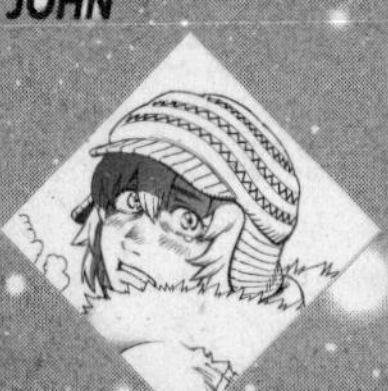

The son of the shelter leader.

BATTLE ANGEL ALITA:
LAST ORDER VOL. 8
Angel's Vision
VIZ Media Edition

Story & Art by
Yukito Kishiro

English Adaptation by
Fred Burke

Translation/Lillian Olsen
Touch-up & Lettering/Primary Graphix: John Hunt
Cover Design/Mark Schumann
Graphic Design/Mark Schumann
Editor/Annette Roman

Managing Editor/Annette Roman
Editorial Director/Elizabeth Kawasaki
Editor in Chief/Alvin Lu
Sr. Director of Acquisitions/Rika Inouye
Sr. VP of Marketing/Liza Coppola
Exec. VP of Sales & Marketing/John Easum
Publisher/Hyoe Narita

Printed in the U.S.A.

Published by VIZ Media, LLC
P.O. Box 77064
San Francisco, CA 94107

10 9 8 7 6 5 4 3 2 1
First printing, December 2006

www.viz.com
store.viz.com

CONTENTS

Phase 44: Point of No Return

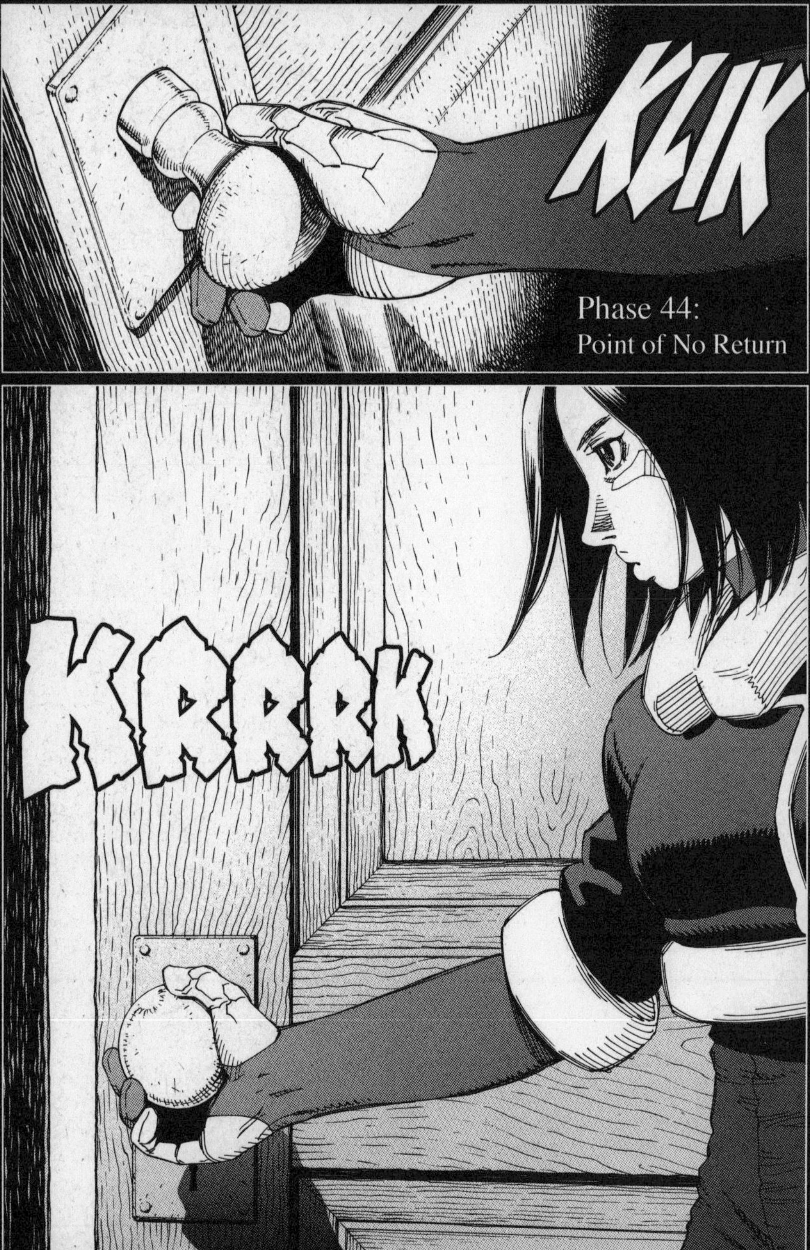
KLIK
KRRRK

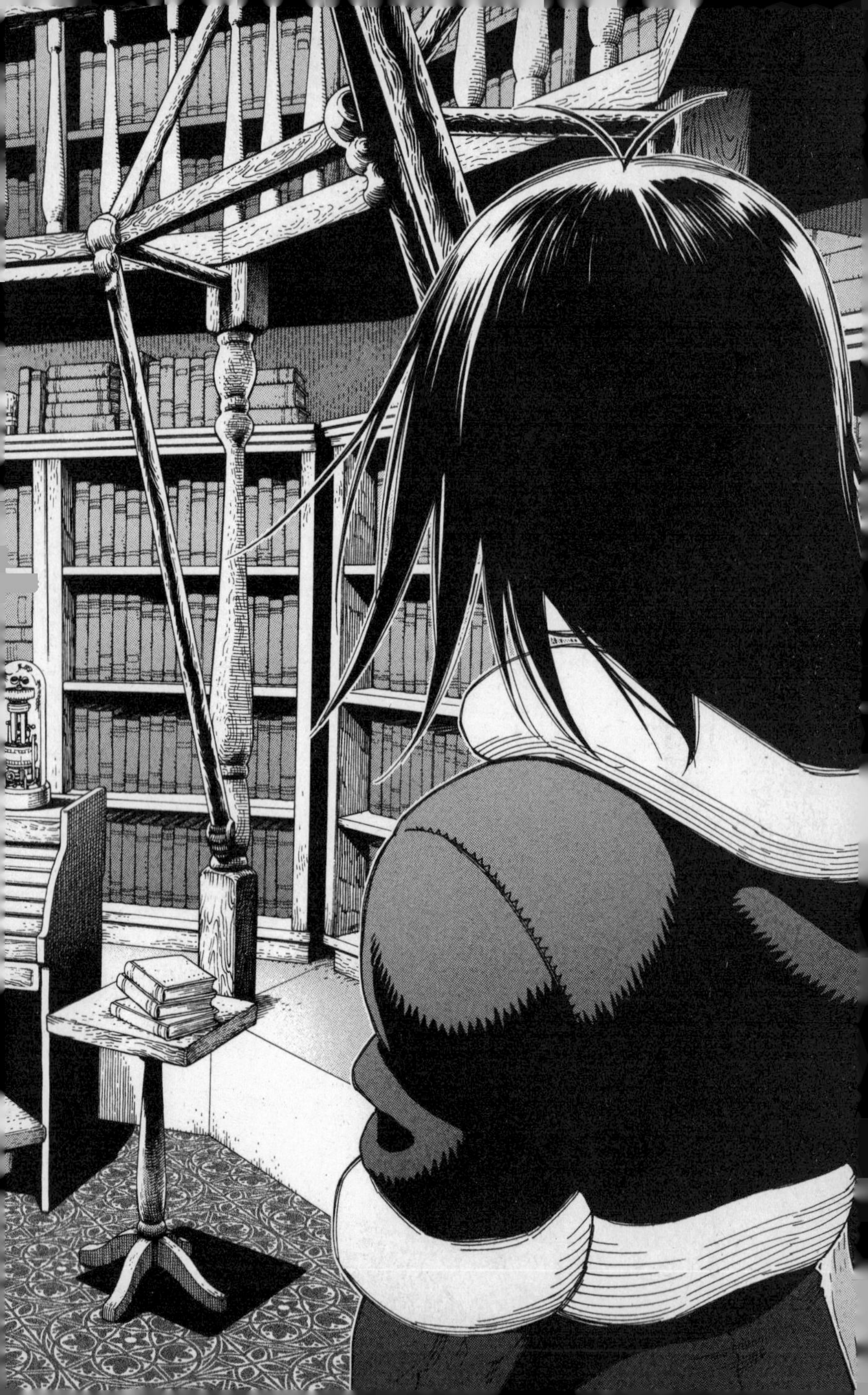

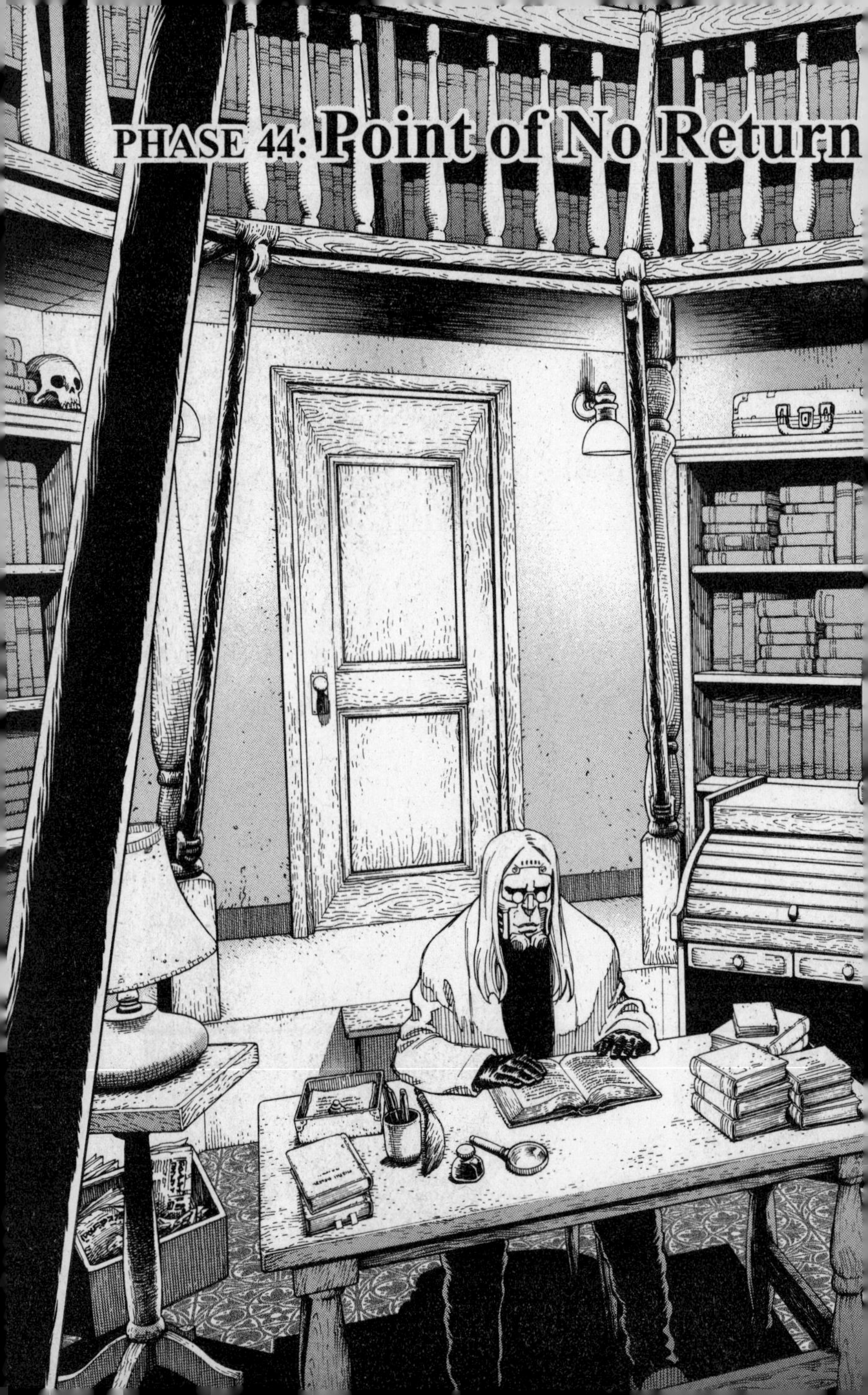
PHASE 44: Point of No Return

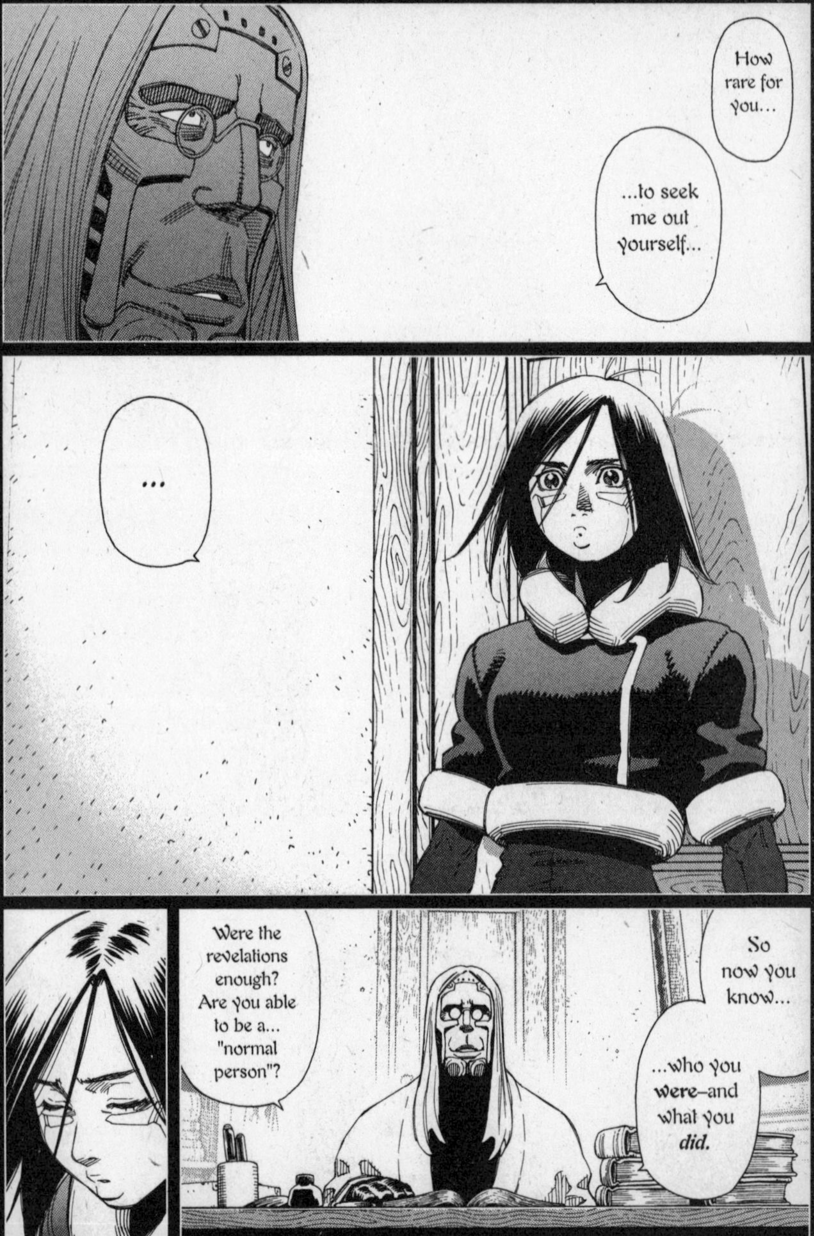
How rare for you...
...to seek me out yourself...
...
So now you know...
...who you were–and what you *did.*
Were the revelations enough? Are you able to be a... "normal person"?

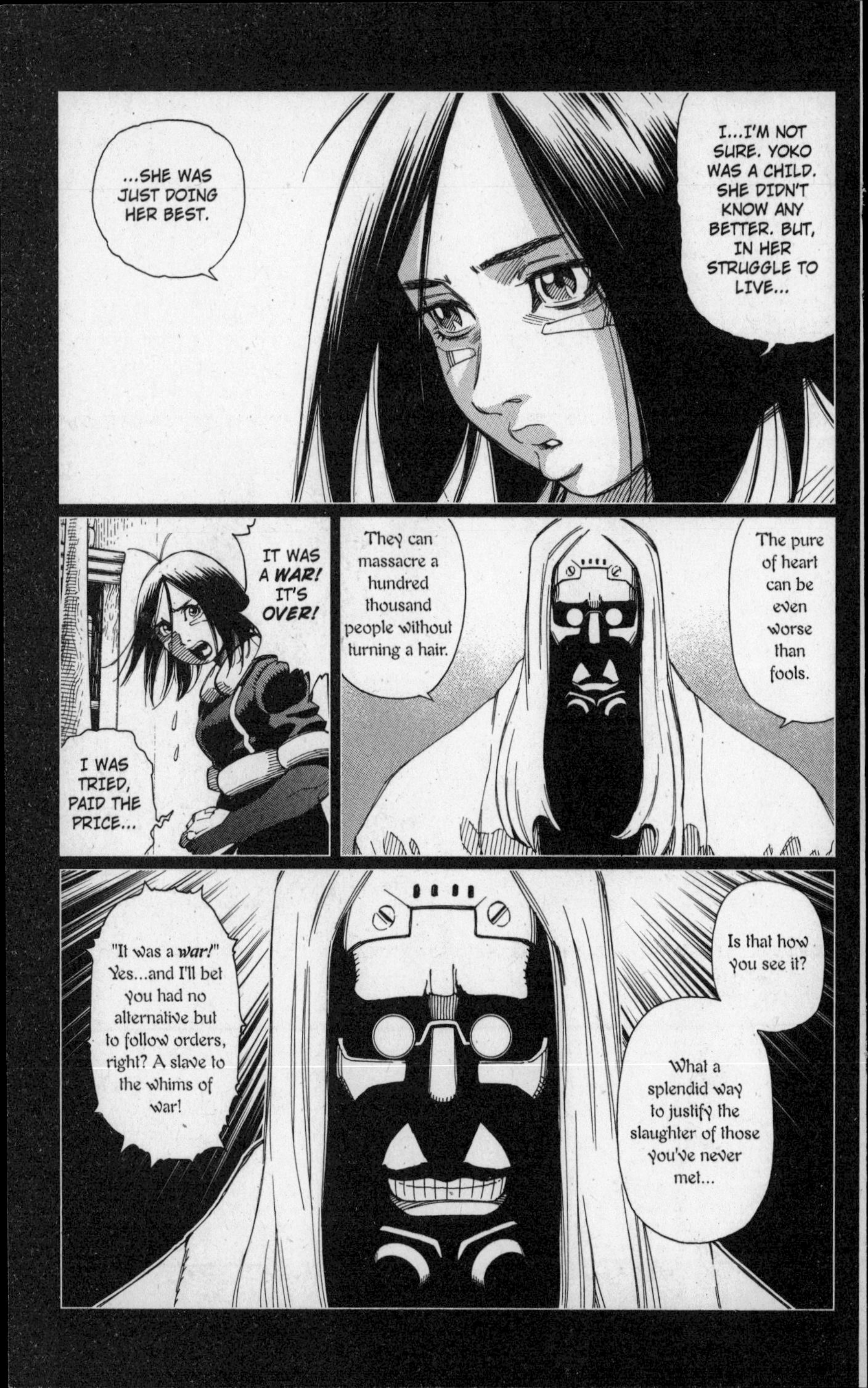
I...I'M NOT SURE. YOKO WAS A CHILD. SHE DIDN'T KNOW ANY BETTER. BUT, IN HER STRUGGLE TO LIVE...
...SHE WAS JUST DOING HER BEST.
The pure of heart can be even worse than fools.
They can massacre a hundred thousand people without turning a hair.
IT WAS A *WAR!* IT'S *OVER!*
I WAS TRIED, PAID THE PRICE...
"It was a *war!*" Yes...and I'll bet you had no alternative but to follow orders, right? A slave to the whims of war!
Is that how you see it?
What a splendid way to justify the slaughter of those you've never met...

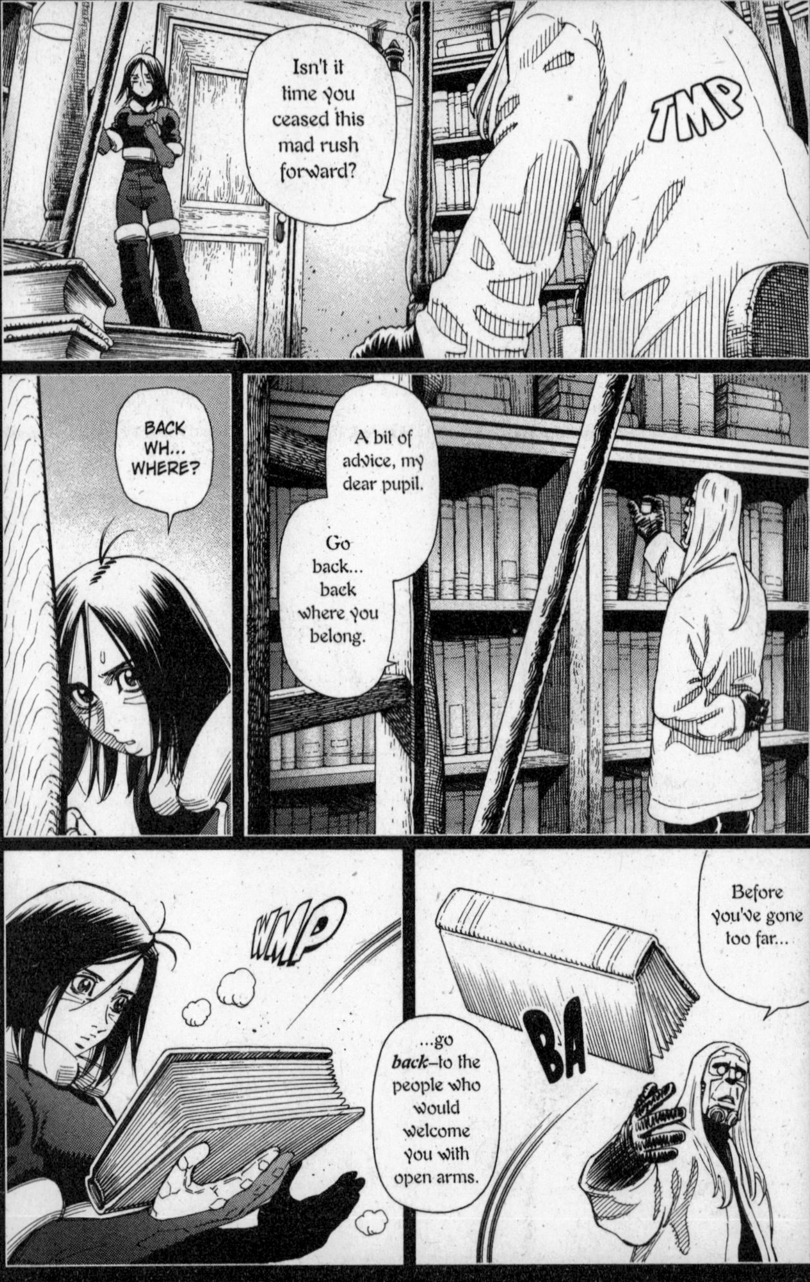
TMP
Isn't it time you ceased this mad rush forward?
A bit of advice, my dear pupil.
Go back... back where you belong.
BACK WH... WHERE?
Before you've gone too far...
BA
...go *back*—to the people who would welcome you with open arms.
WMP

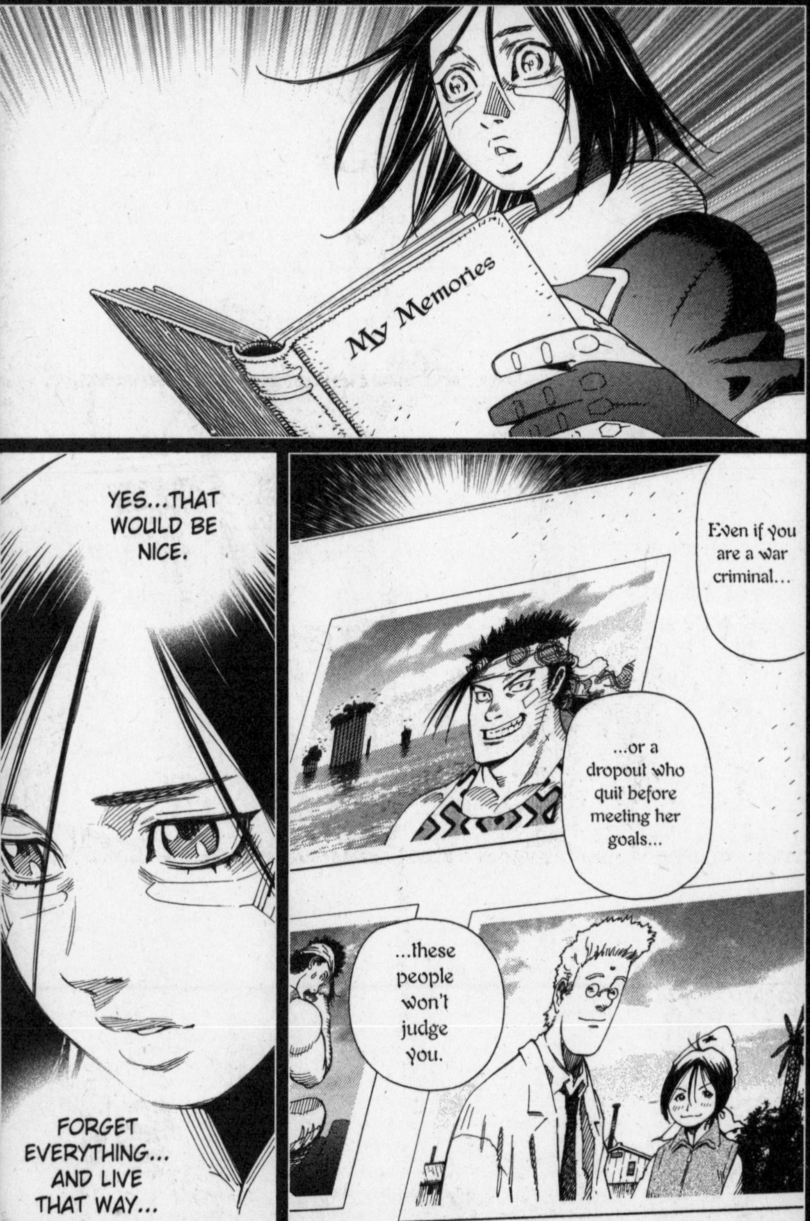
My Memories
Even if you are a war criminal...
...or a dropout who quit before meeting her goals...
...these people won't judge you.
YES...THAT WOULD BE NICE.
FORGET EVERYTHING... AND LIVE THAT WAY...

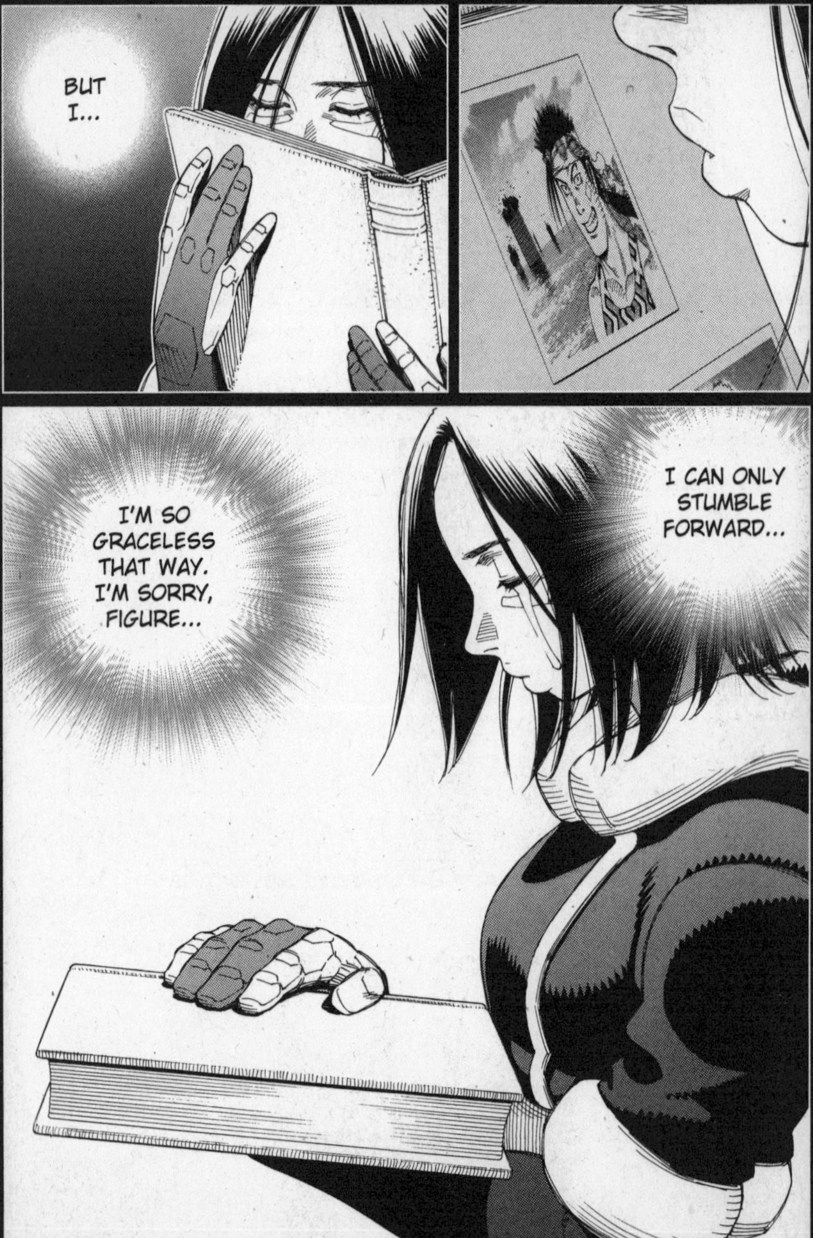
BUT I...
I CAN ONLY STUMBLE FORWARD...
I'M SO GRACELESS THAT WAY. I'M SORRY, FIGURE...

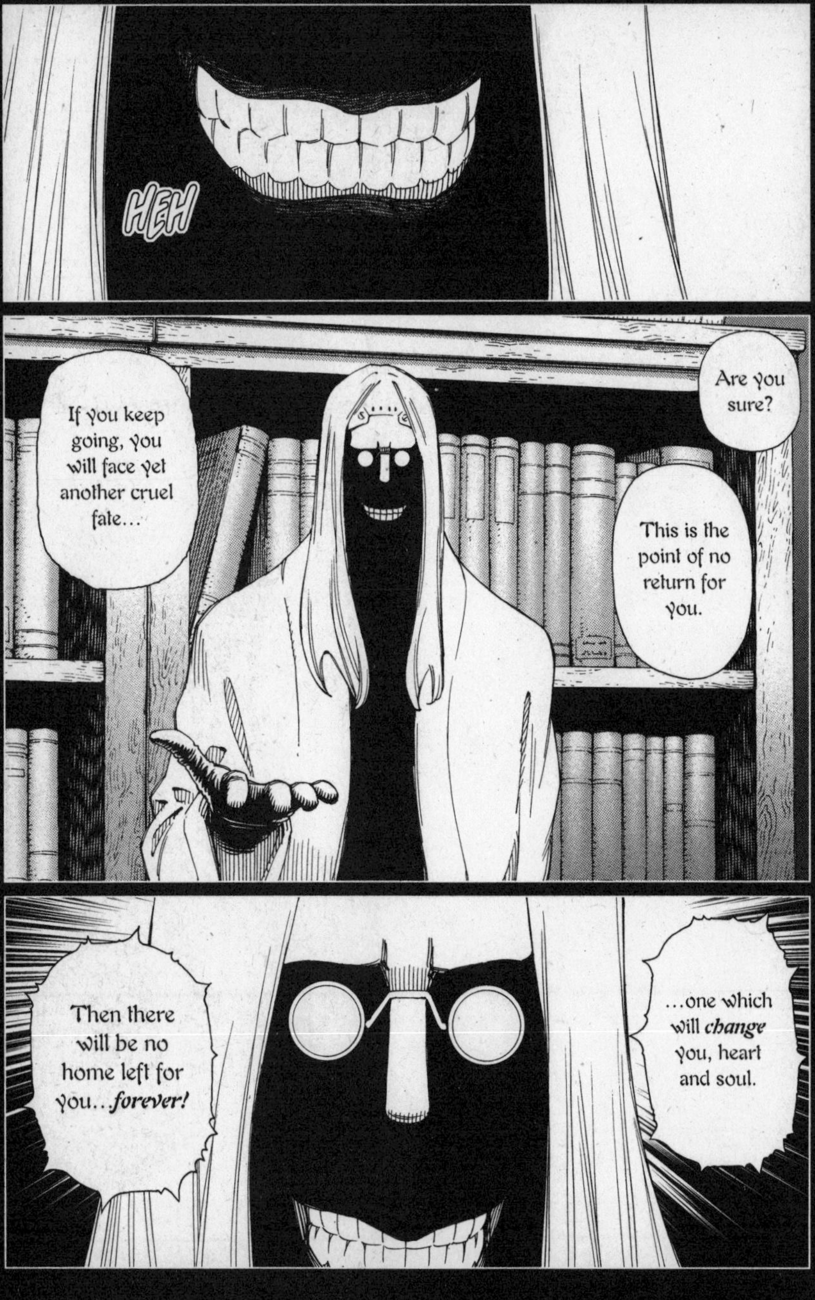
HEH
Are you sure?
This is the point of no return for you.
If you keep going, you will face yet another cruel fate...
...one which will *change* you, heart and soul.
Then there will be no home left for you...*forever!*

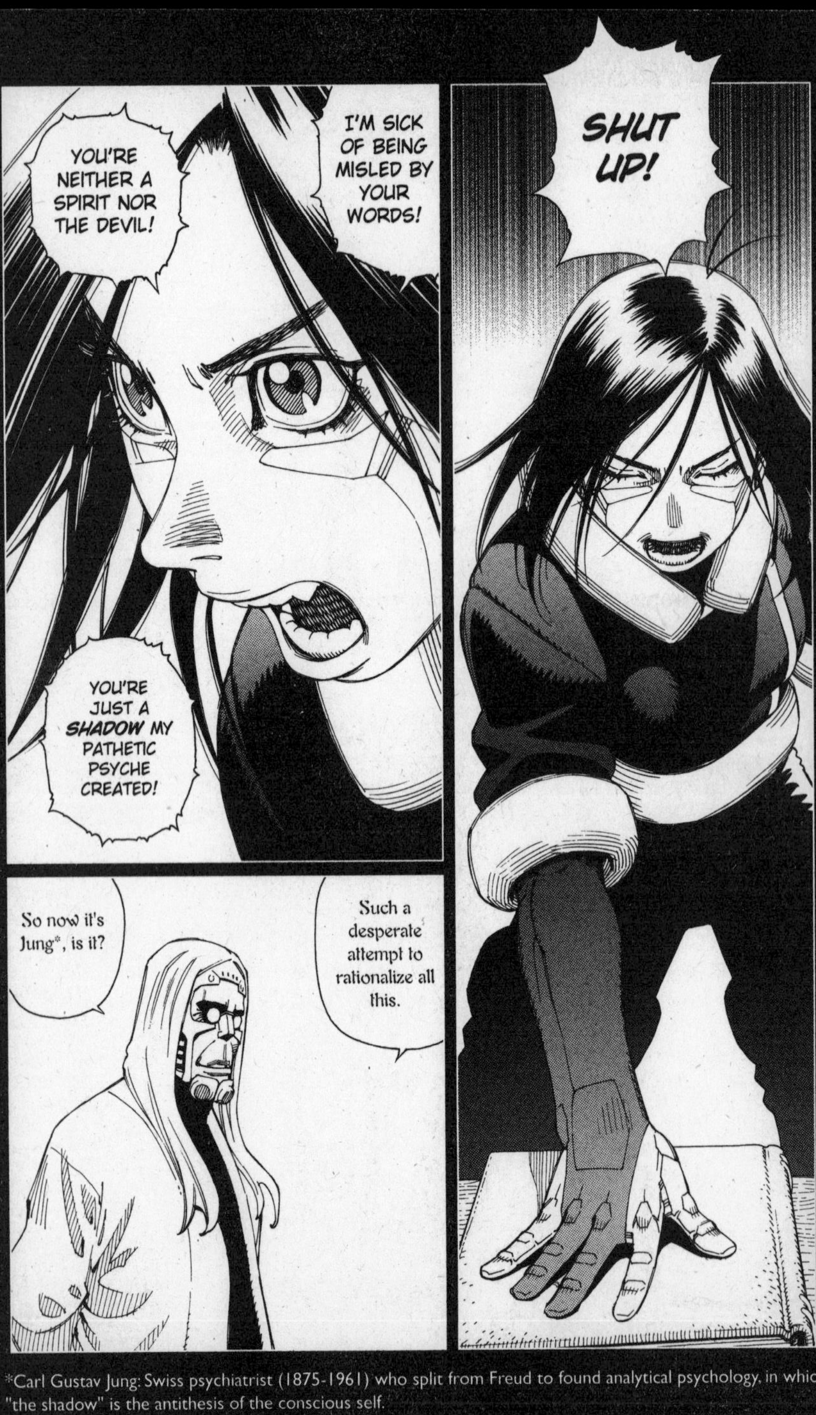
SHUT UP!
I'M SICK OF BEING MISLED BY YOUR WORDS!
YOU'RE NEITHER A SPIRIT NOR THE DEVIL!
YOU'RE JUST A SHADOW MY PATHETIC PSYCHE CREATED!
Such a desperate attempt to rationalize all this.
So now it's Jung*, is it?

*Carl Gustav Jung: Swiss psychiatrist (1875-1961) who split from Freud to found analytical psychology, in which "the shadow" is the antithesis of the conscious self.

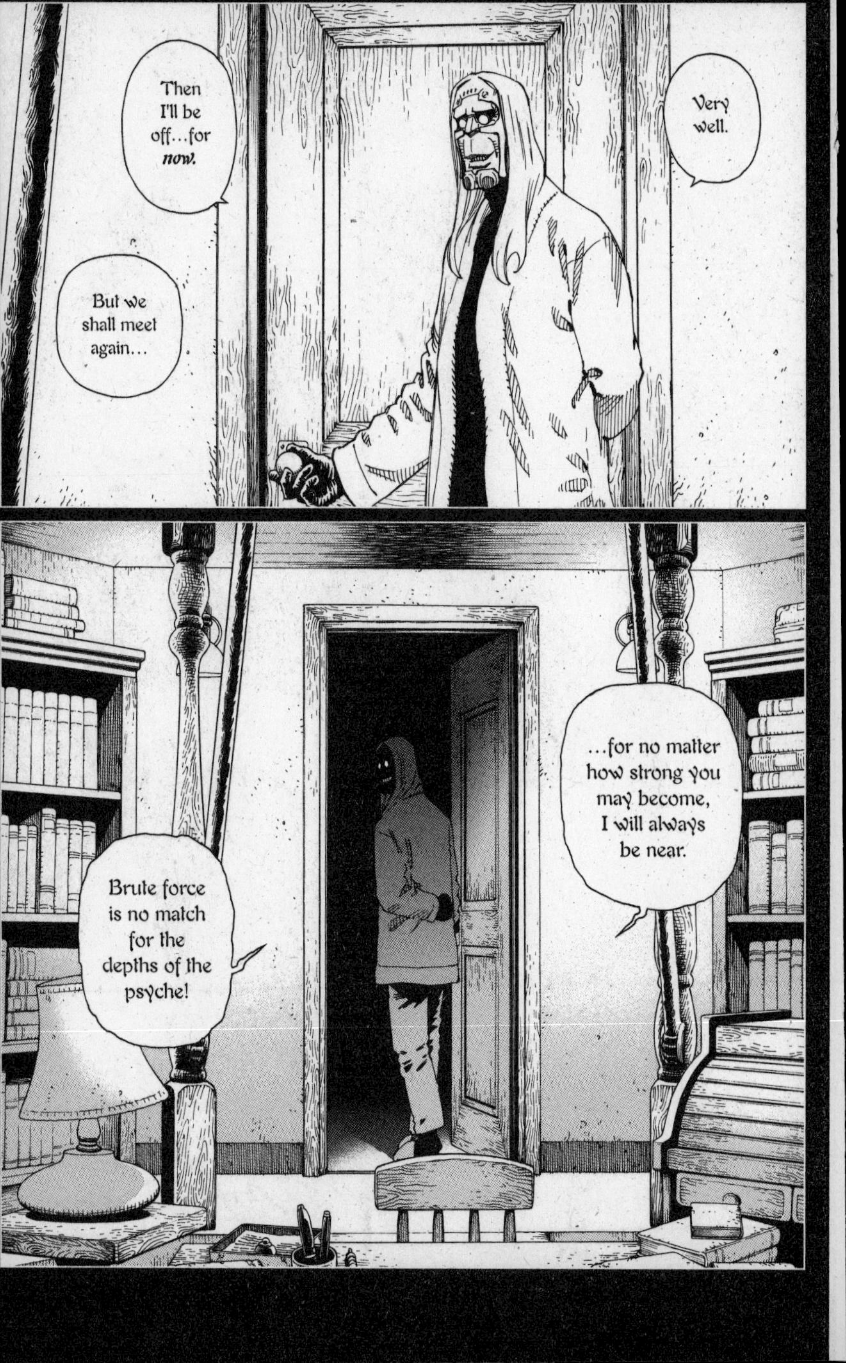
Very well.
Then I'll be off…for *now.*
But we shall meet again…
…for no matter how strong you may become, I will always be near.
Brute force is no match for the depths of the psyche!

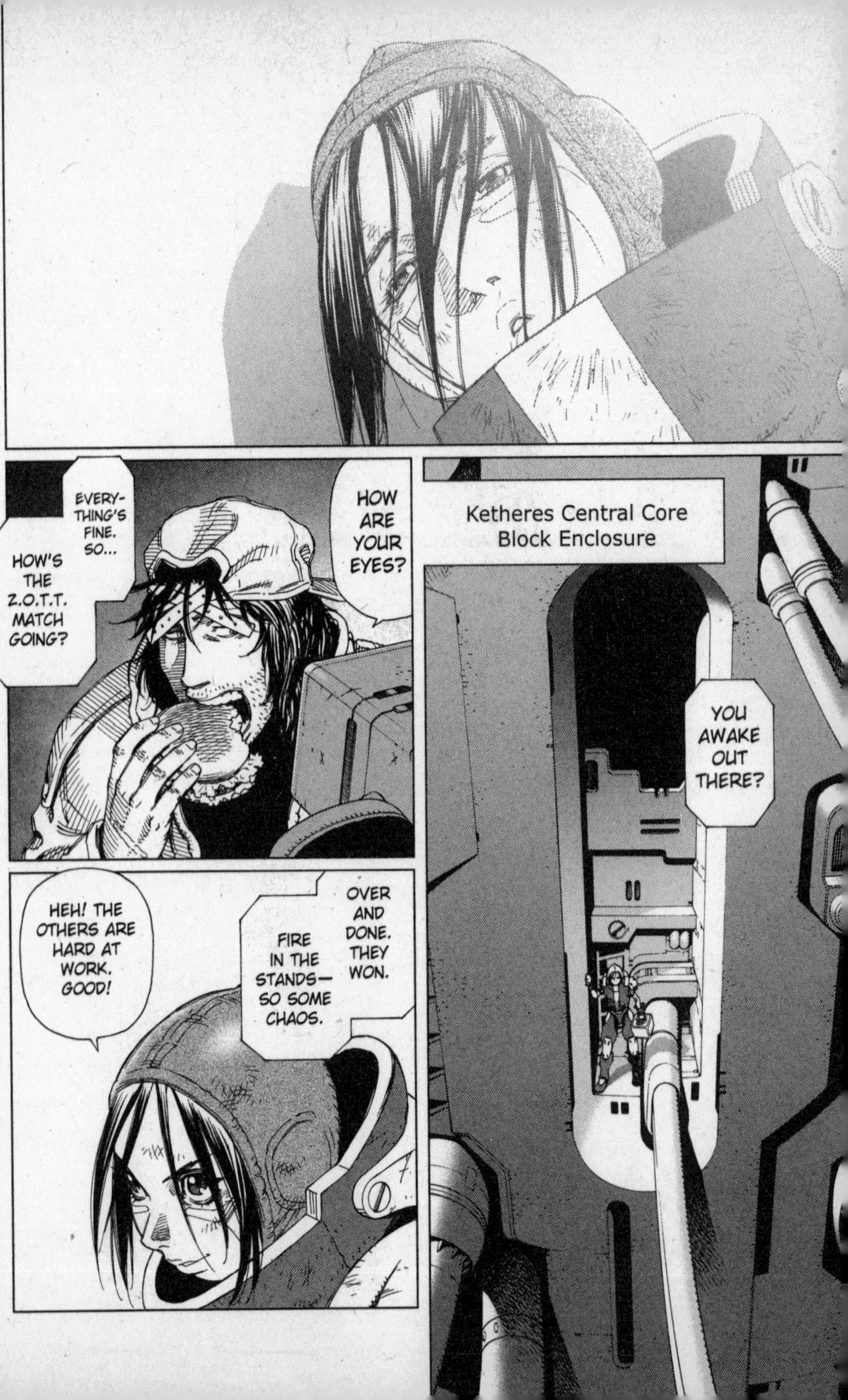
Ketheres Central Core Block Enclosure
YOU AWAKE OUT THERE?
HOW ARE YOUR EYES?
EVERY-THING'S FINE. SO...
HOW'S THE Z.O.T.T. MATCH GOING?
OVER AND DONE. THEY WON.
FIRE IN THE STANDS— SO SOME CHAOS.
HEH! THE OTHERS ARE HARD AT WORK. GOOD!

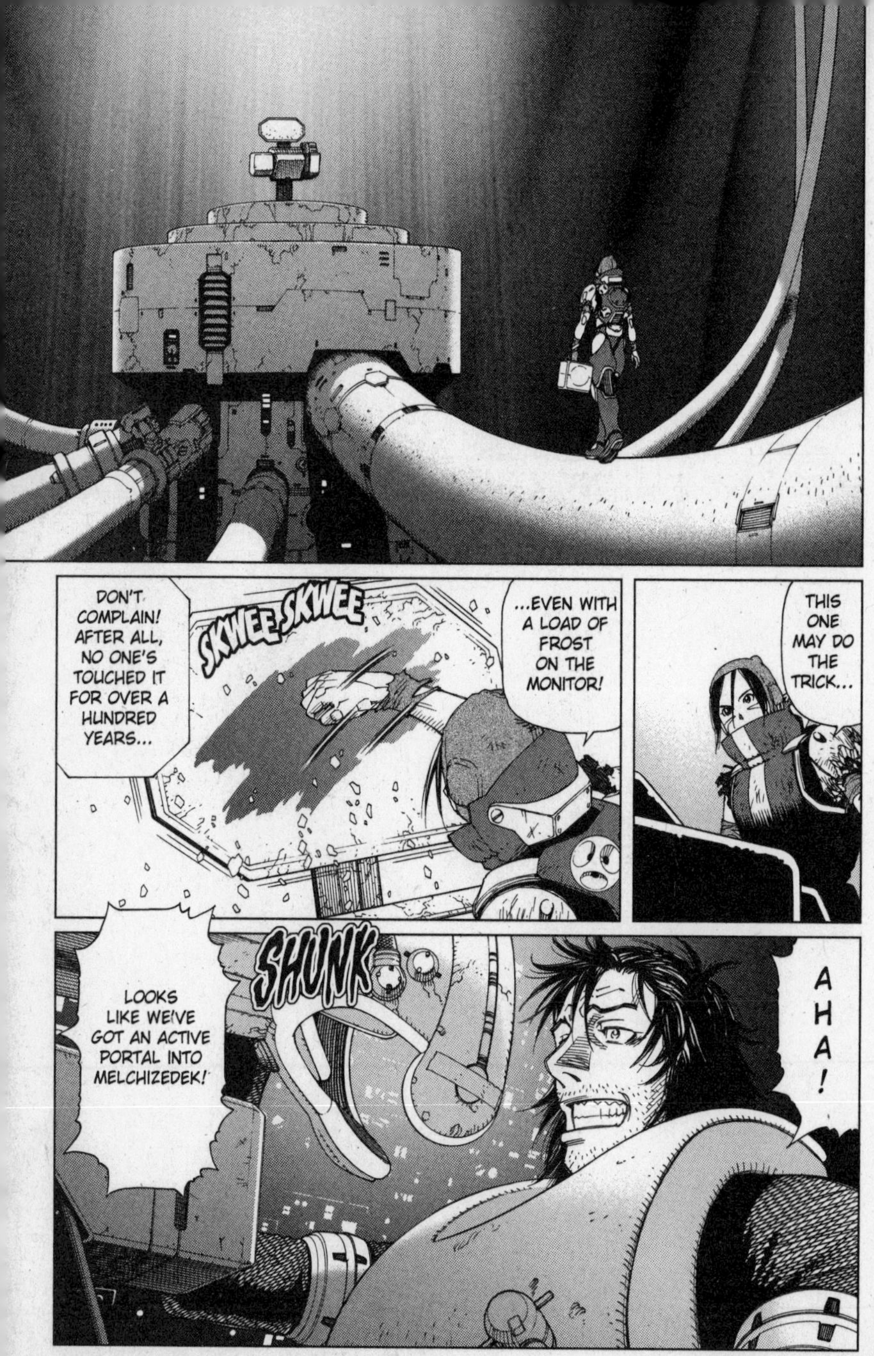
THIS ONE MAY DO THE TRICK...
...EVEN WITH A LOAD OF FROST ON THE MONITOR!
SKWEE SKWEE
DON'T COMPLAIN! AFTER ALL, NO ONE'S TOUCHED IT FOR OVER A HUNDRED YEARS...
AHA!
SHUNK
LOOKS LIKE WE'VE GOT AN ACTIVE PORTAL INTO MELCHIZEDEK!

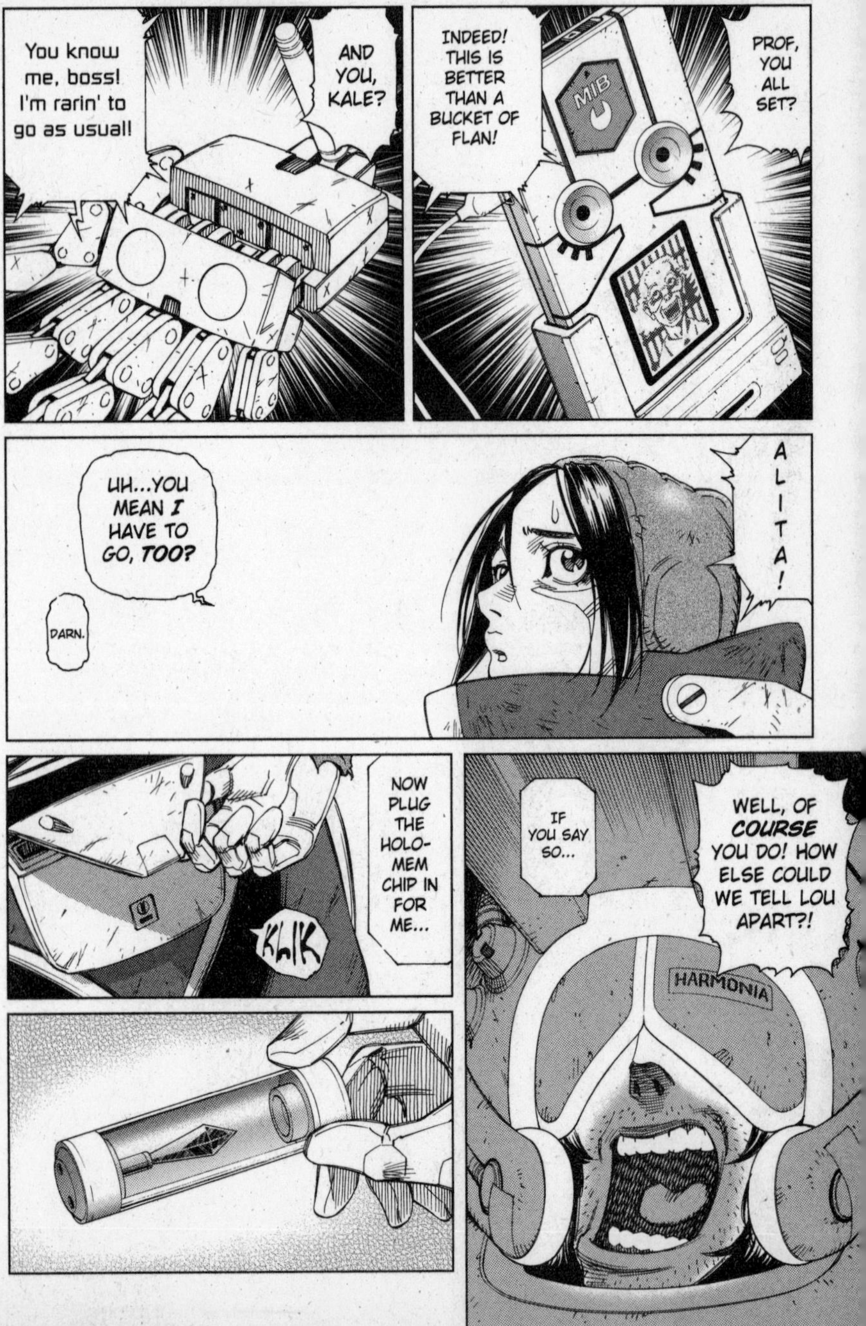
PROF, YOU ALL SET?
INDEED! THIS IS BETTER THAN A BUCKET OF FLAN!
MIB
AND YOU, KALE?
You know me, boss! I'm rarin' to go as usual!
ALITA!
UH...YOU MEAN *I* HAVE TO GO, *TOO?*
DARN.
WELL, OF *COURSE* YOU DO! HOW ELSE COULD WE TELL LOU APART?!
IF YOU SAY SO...
HARMONIA
NOW PLUG THE HOLO-MEM CHIP IN FOR ME...
KLIK

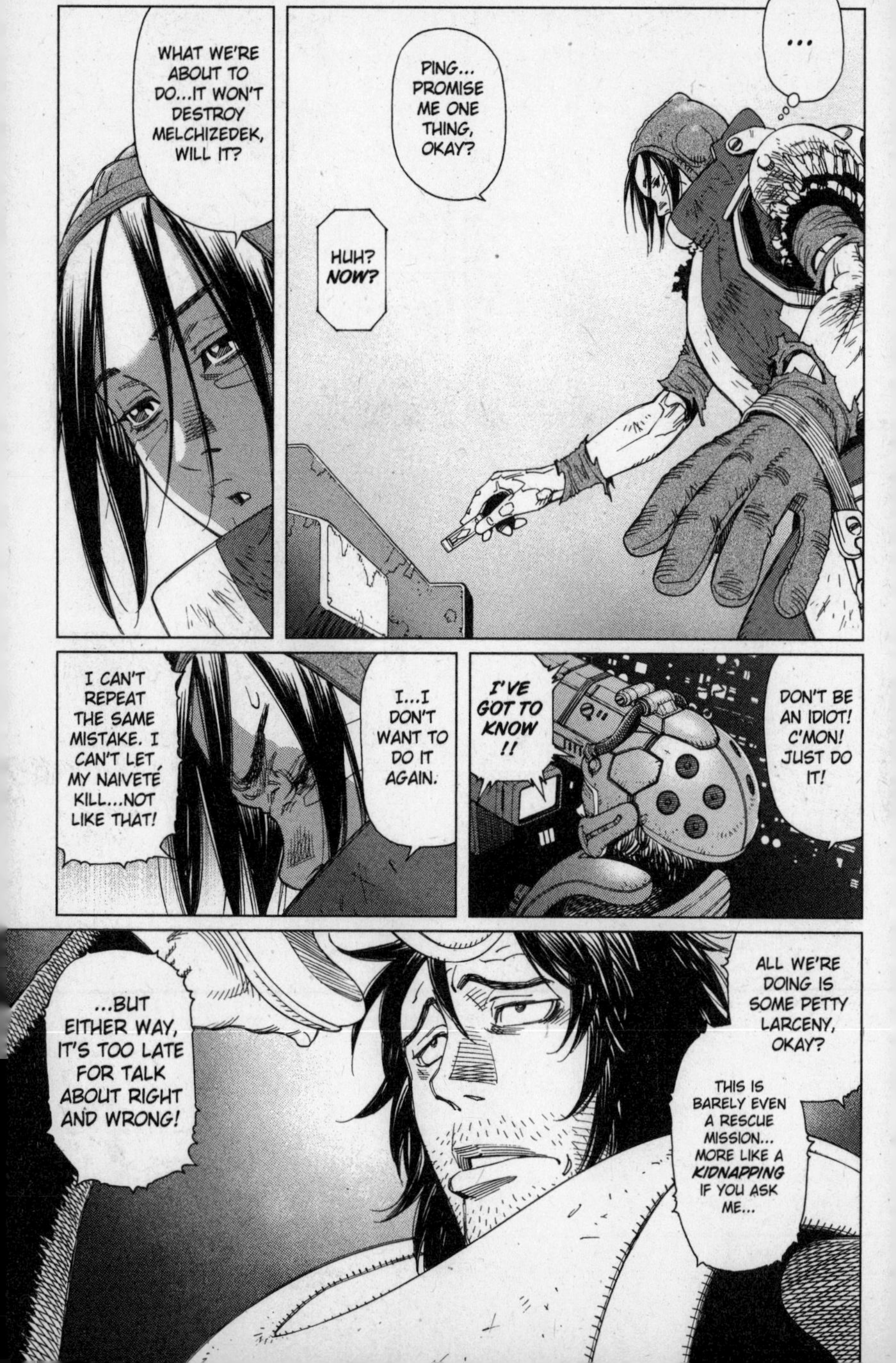
...
PING... PROMISE ME ONE THING, OKAY?
HUH? *NOW?*
WHAT WE'RE ABOUT TO DO...IT WON'T DESTROY MELCHIZEDEK, WILL IT?
DON'T BE AN IDIOT! C'MON! JUST DO IT!
I'VE GOT TO KNOW !!
I...I DON'T WANT TO DO IT AGAIN.
I CAN'T REPEAT THE SAME MISTAKE. I CAN'T LET MY NAIVETÉ KILL...NOT LIKE THAT!
ALL WE'RE DOING IS SOME PETTY LARCENY, OKAY?
THIS IS BARELY EVEN A RESCUE MISSION... MORE LIKE A *KIDNAPPING* IF YOU ASK ME...
...BUT EITHER WAY, IT'S TOO LATE FOR TALK ABOUT RIGHT AND WRONG!

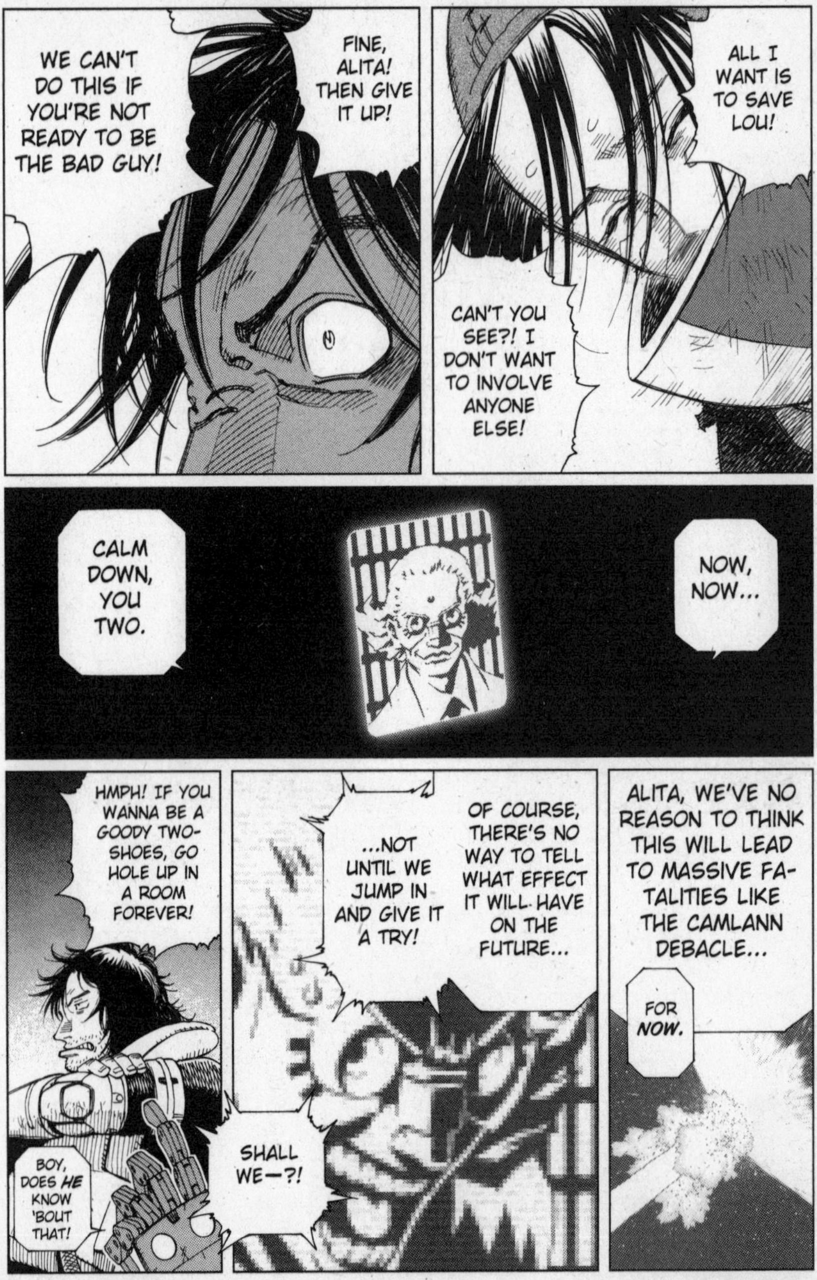
ALL I WANT IS TO SAVE LOU!
CAN'T YOU SEE?! I DON'T WANT TO INVOLVE ANYONE ELSE!
FINE, ALITA! THEN GIVE IT UP!
WE CAN'T DO THIS IF YOU'RE NOT READY TO BE THE BAD GUY!
NOW, NOW...
CALM DOWN, YOU TWO.
ALITA, WE'VE NO REASON TO THINK THIS WILL LEAD TO MASSIVE FATALITIES LIKE THE CAMLANN DEBACLE...
FOR *NOW.*
OF COURSE, THERE'S NO WAY TO TELL WHAT EFFECT IT WILL HAVE ON THE FUTURE...
...NOT UNTIL WE JUMP IN AND GIVE IT A TRY!
SHALL WE—?!
HMPH! IF YOU WANNA BE A GOODY TWO-SHOES, GO HOLE UP IN A ROOM FOREVER!
BOY, DOES *HE* KNOW 'BOUT THAT!

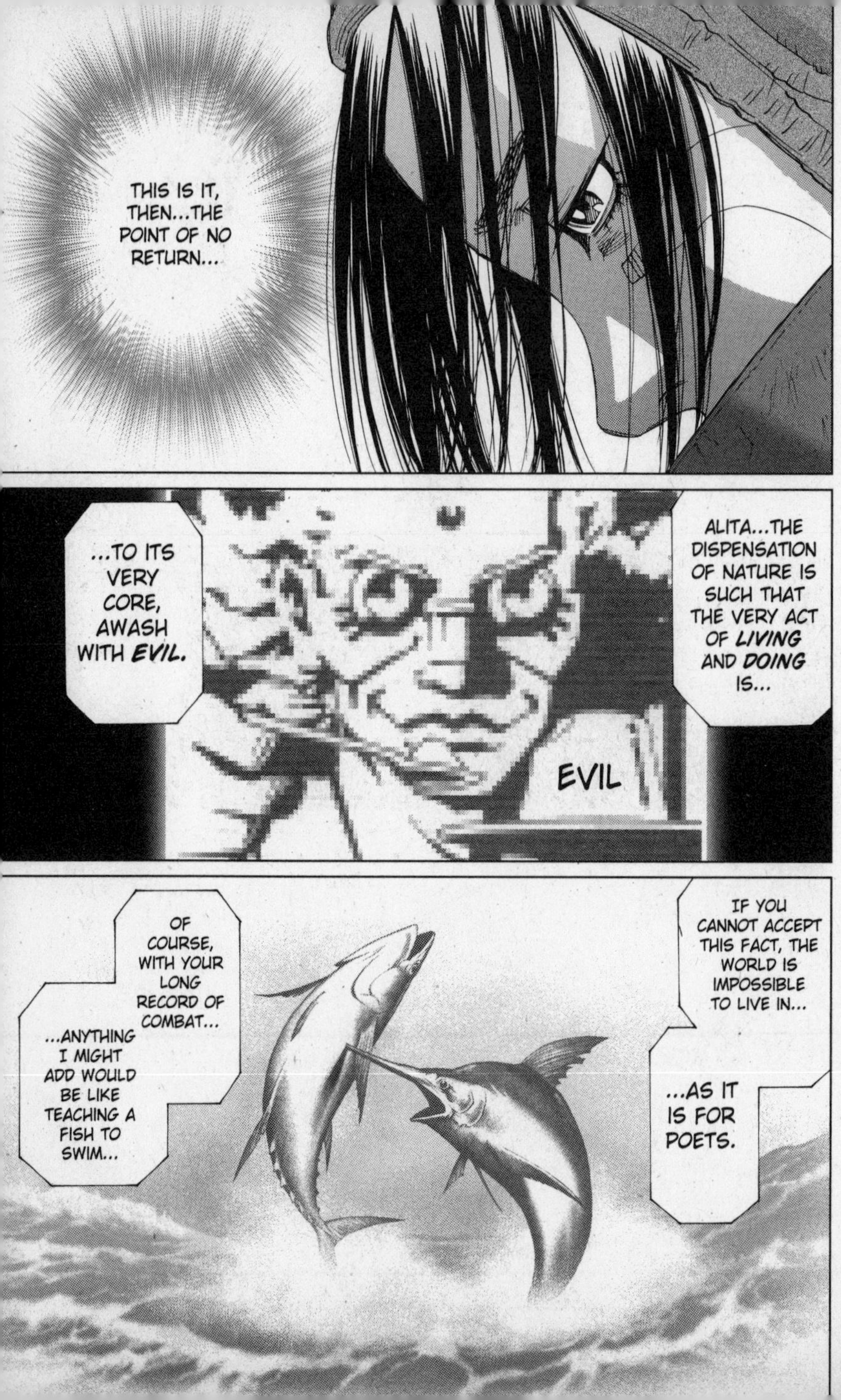
THIS IS IT, THEN...THE POINT OF NO RETURN...
ALITA...THE DISPENSATION OF NATURE IS SUCH THAT THE VERY ACT OF *LIVING* AND *DOING* IS...
EVIL
...TO ITS VERY CORE, AWASH WITH *EVIL.*
IF YOU CANNOT ACCEPT THIS FACT, THE WORLD IS IMPOSSIBLE TO LIVE IN...
...AS IT IS FOR POETS.
OF COURSE, WITH YOUR LONG RECORD OF COMBAT...
...ANYTHING I MIGHT ADD WOULD BE LIKE TEACHING A FISH TO SWIM...

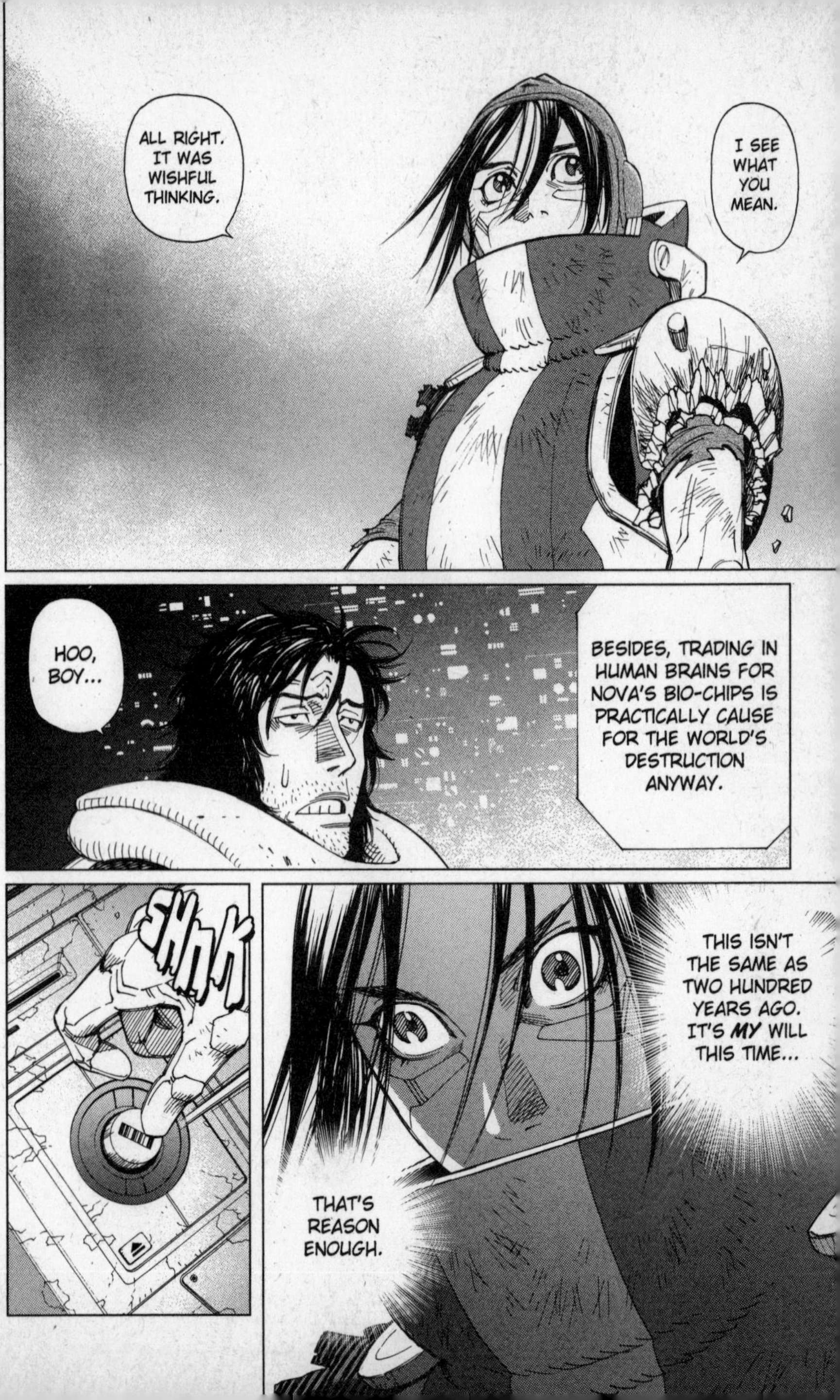
I SEE WHAT YOU MEAN.
ALL RIGHT. IT WAS WISHFUL THINKING.
BESIDES, TRADING IN HUMAN BRAINS FOR NOVA'S BIO-CHIPS IS PRACTICALLY CAUSE FOR THE WORLD'S DESTRUCTION ANYWAY.
HOO, BOY...
THIS ISN'T THE SAME AS TWO HUNDRED YEARS AGO. IT'S *MY* WILL THIS TIME...
THAT'S REASON ENOUGH.
SHNK

LET'S JACK IN!

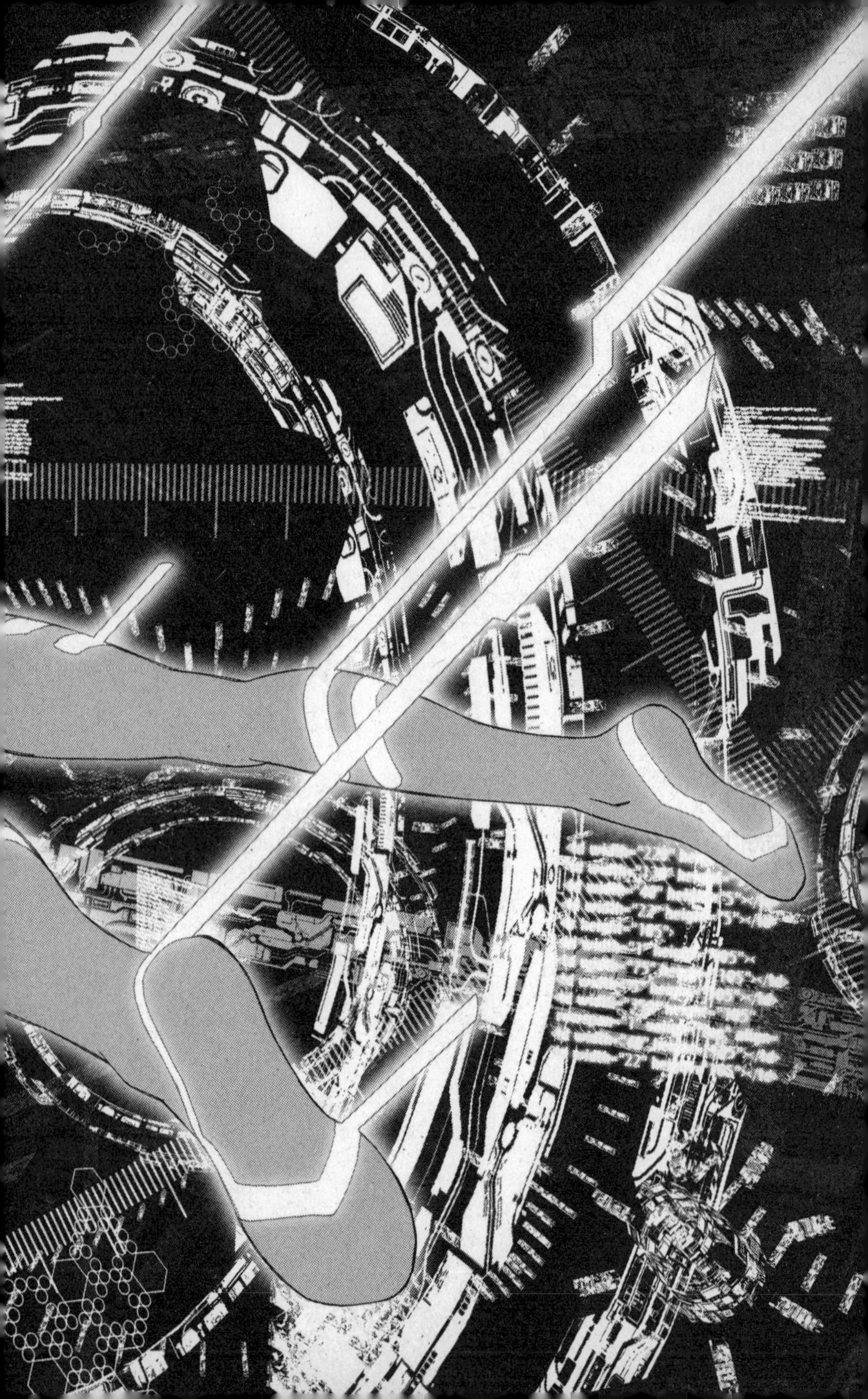

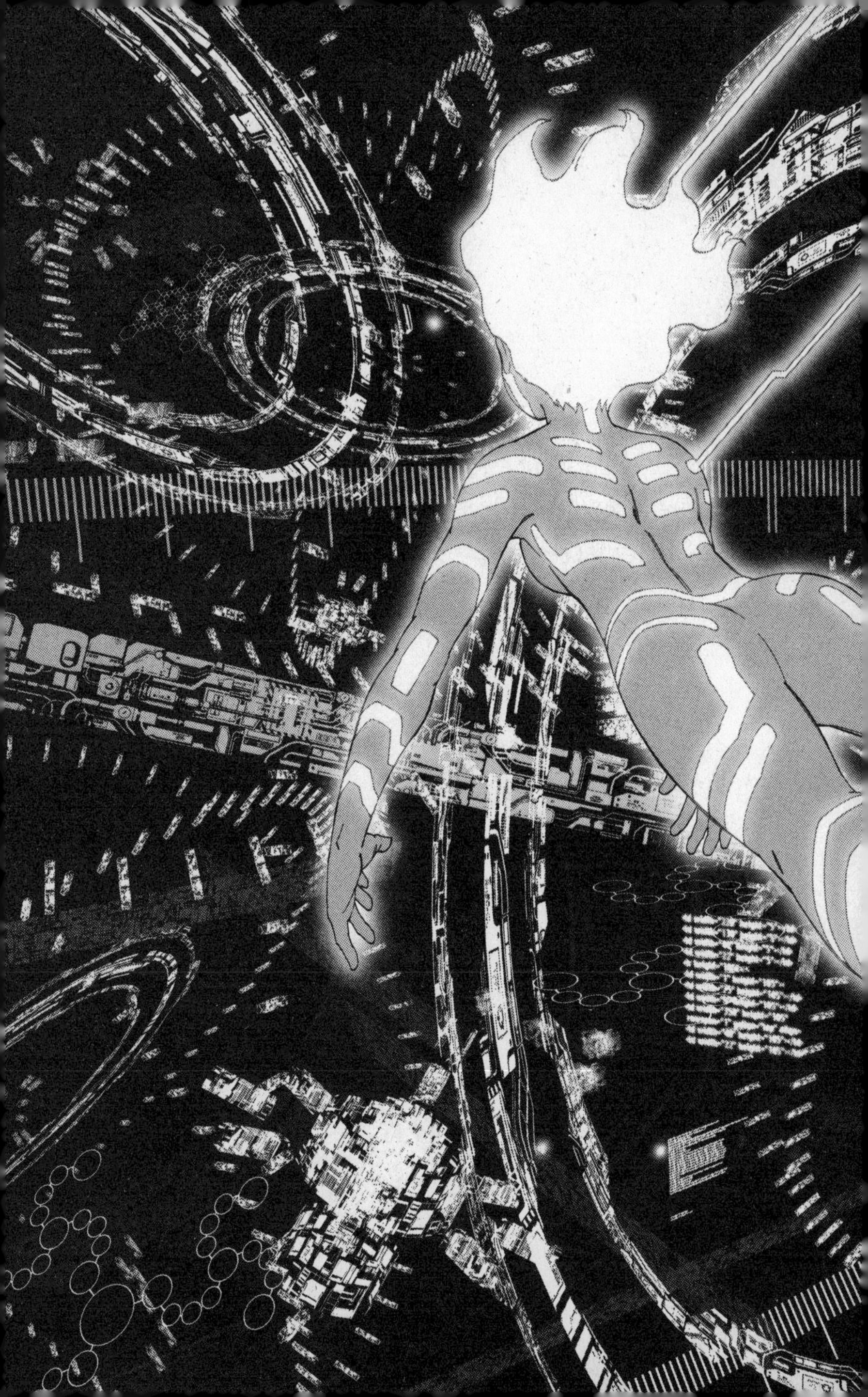

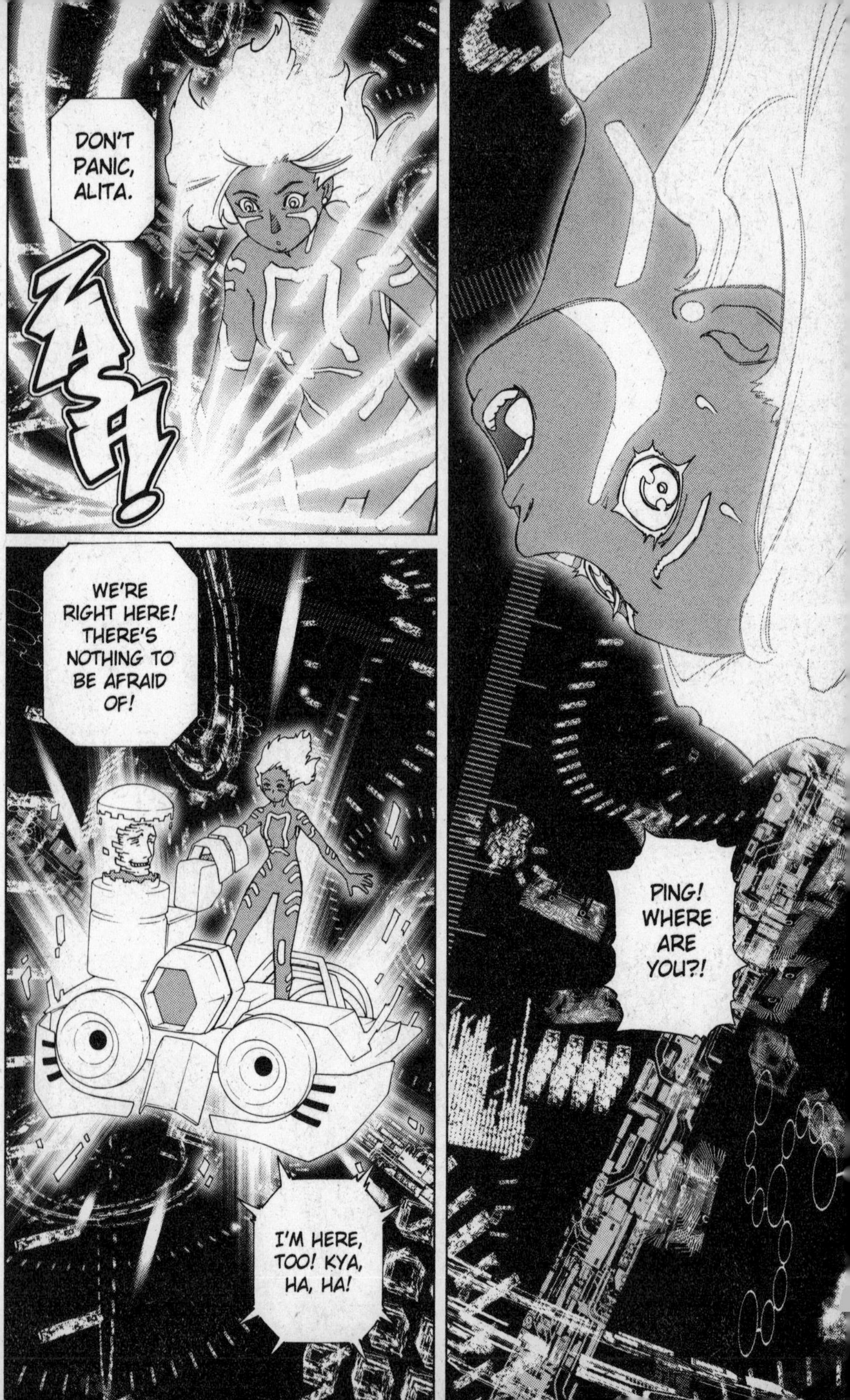
PING! WHERE ARE YOU?!
DON'T PANIC, ALITA.
ZASH!
WE'RE RIGHT HERE! THERE'S NOTHING TO BE AFRAID OF!
I'M HERE, TOO! KYA, HA, HA!

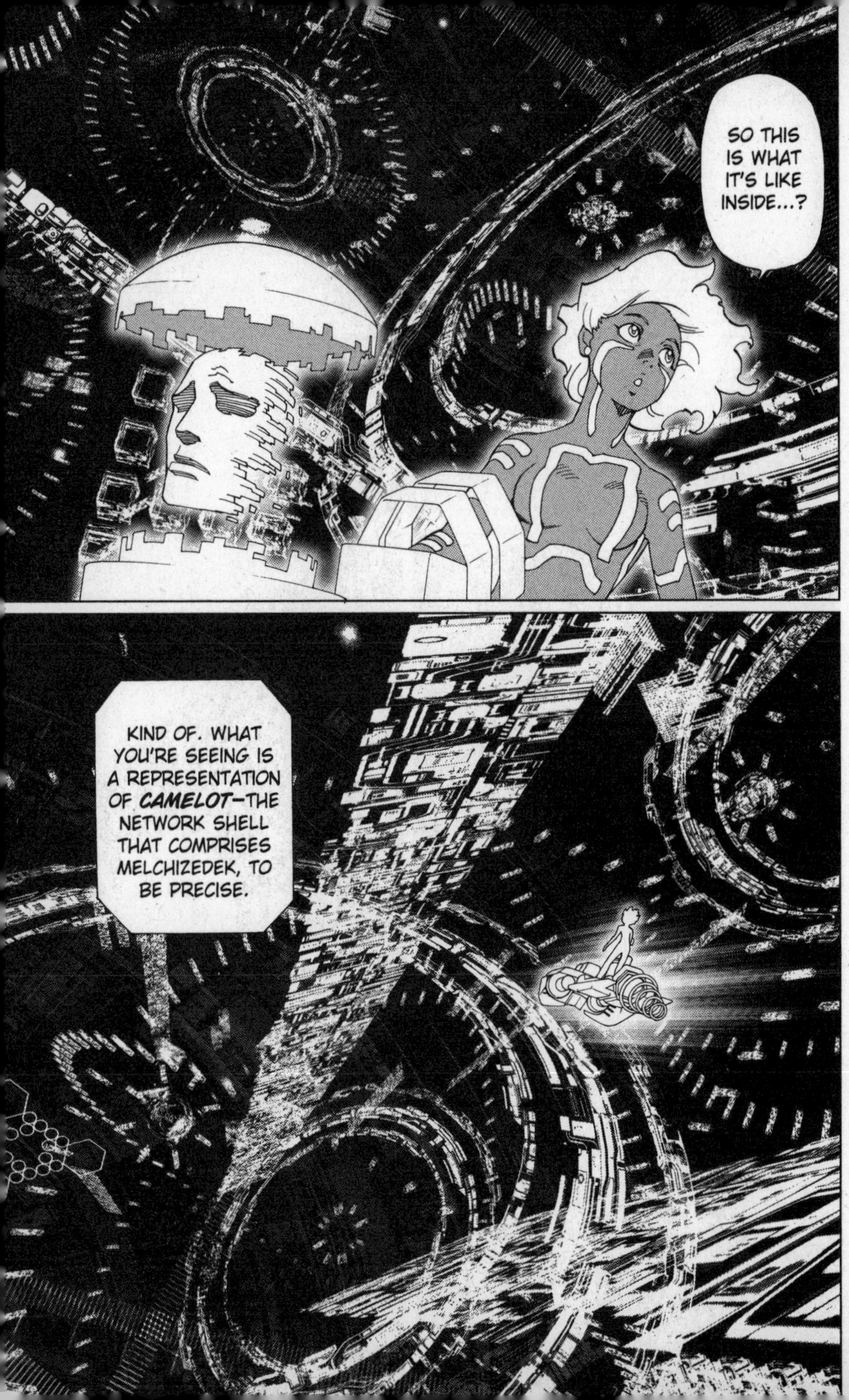
SO THIS IS WHAT IT'S LIKE INSIDE...?
KIND OF. WHAT YOU'RE SEEING IS A REPRESENTATION OF *CAMELOT*—THE NETWORK SHELL THAT COMPRISES MELCHIZEDEK, TO BE PRECISE.

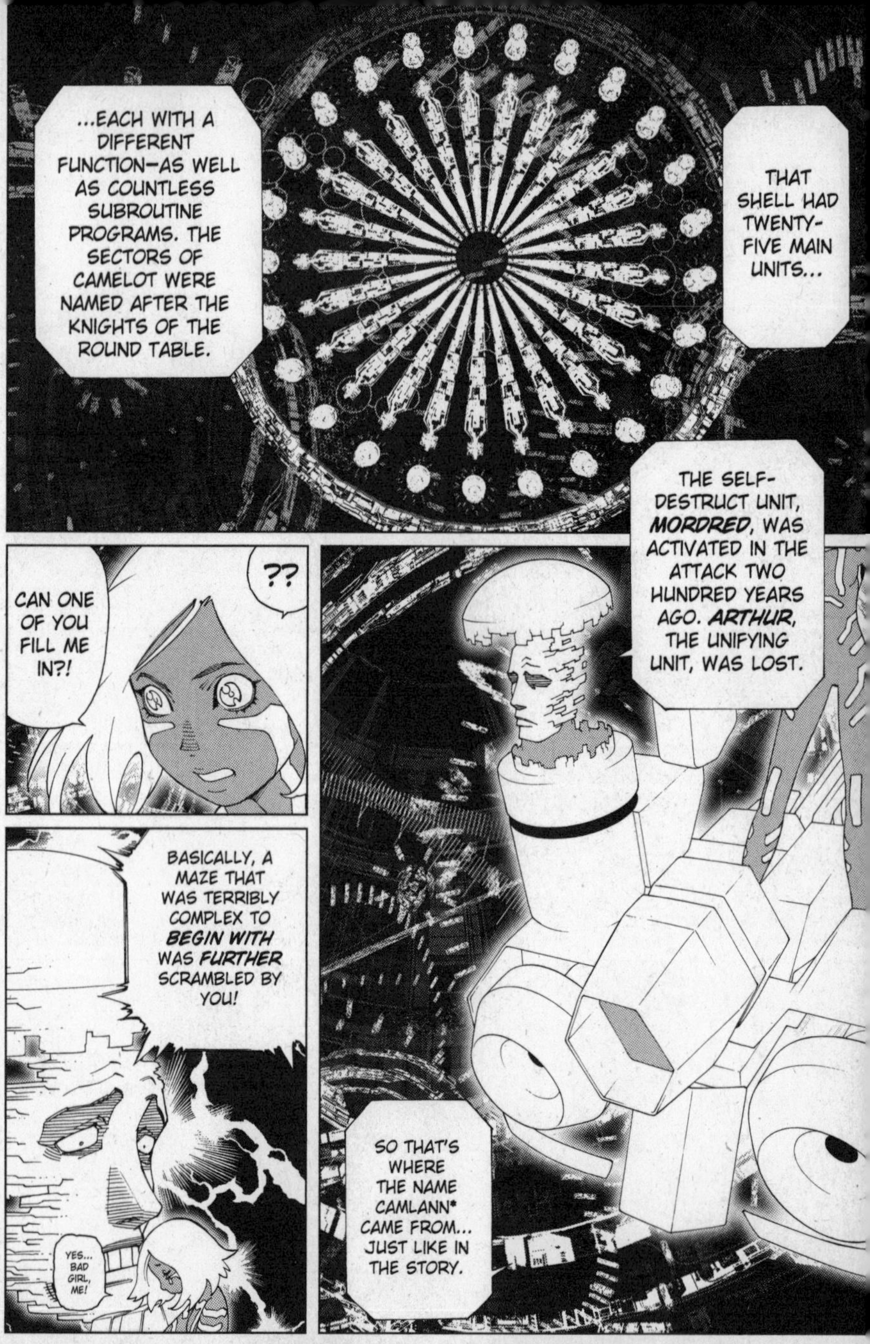
THAT SHELL HAD TWENTY-FIVE MAIN UNITS...
...EACH WITH A DIFFERENT FUNCTION—AS WELL AS COUNTLESS SUBROUTINE PROGRAMS. THE SECTORS OF CAMELOT WERE NAMED AFTER THE KNIGHTS OF THE ROUND TABLE.
THE SELF-DESTRUCT UNIT, ***MORDRED***, WAS ACTIVATED IN THE ATTACK TWO HUNDRED YEARS AGO. ***ARTHUR***, THE UNIFYING UNIT, WAS LOST.
SO THAT'S WHERE THE NAME CAMLANN* CAME FROM... JUST LIKE IN THE STORY.
??
CAN ONE OF YOU FILL ME IN?!
BASICALLY, A MAZE THAT WAS TERRIBLY COMPLEX TO ***BEGIN WITH*** WAS ***FURTHER*** SCRAMBLED BY YOU!
YES... BAD GIRL, ME!

*Camlann: site of King Arthur and Mordred's last battle, a place variously believed to be the Roman fort Camboglanna, Slaughter Bridge over Cornwall's River Camel, and the "Cam (Crooked) Allan" river in Manaan—among others.

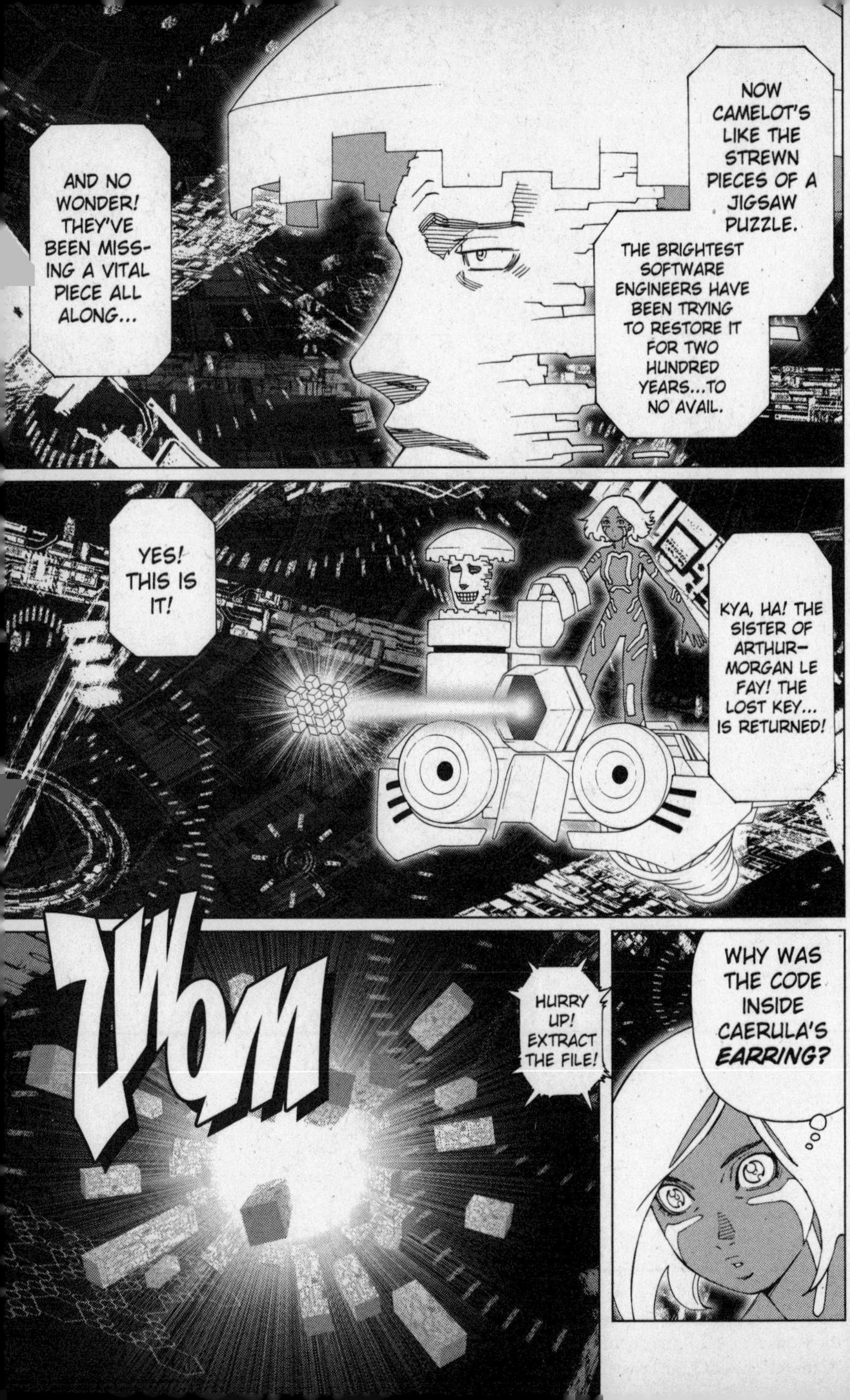
NOW CAMELOT'S LIKE THE STREWN PIECES OF A JIGSAW PUZZLE.
THE BRIGHTEST SOFTWARE ENGINEERS HAVE BEEN TRYING TO RESTORE IT FOR TWO HUNDRED YEARS...TO NO AVAIL.
AND NO WONDER! THEY'VE BEEN MISSING A VITAL PIECE ALL ALONG...
KYA, HA! THE SISTER OF ARTHUR–MORGAN LE FAY! THE LOST KEY... IS RETURNED!
YES! THIS IS IT!
WHY WAS THE CODE INSIDE CAERULA'S *EARRING?*
HURRY UP! EXTRACT THE FILE!
VWOM

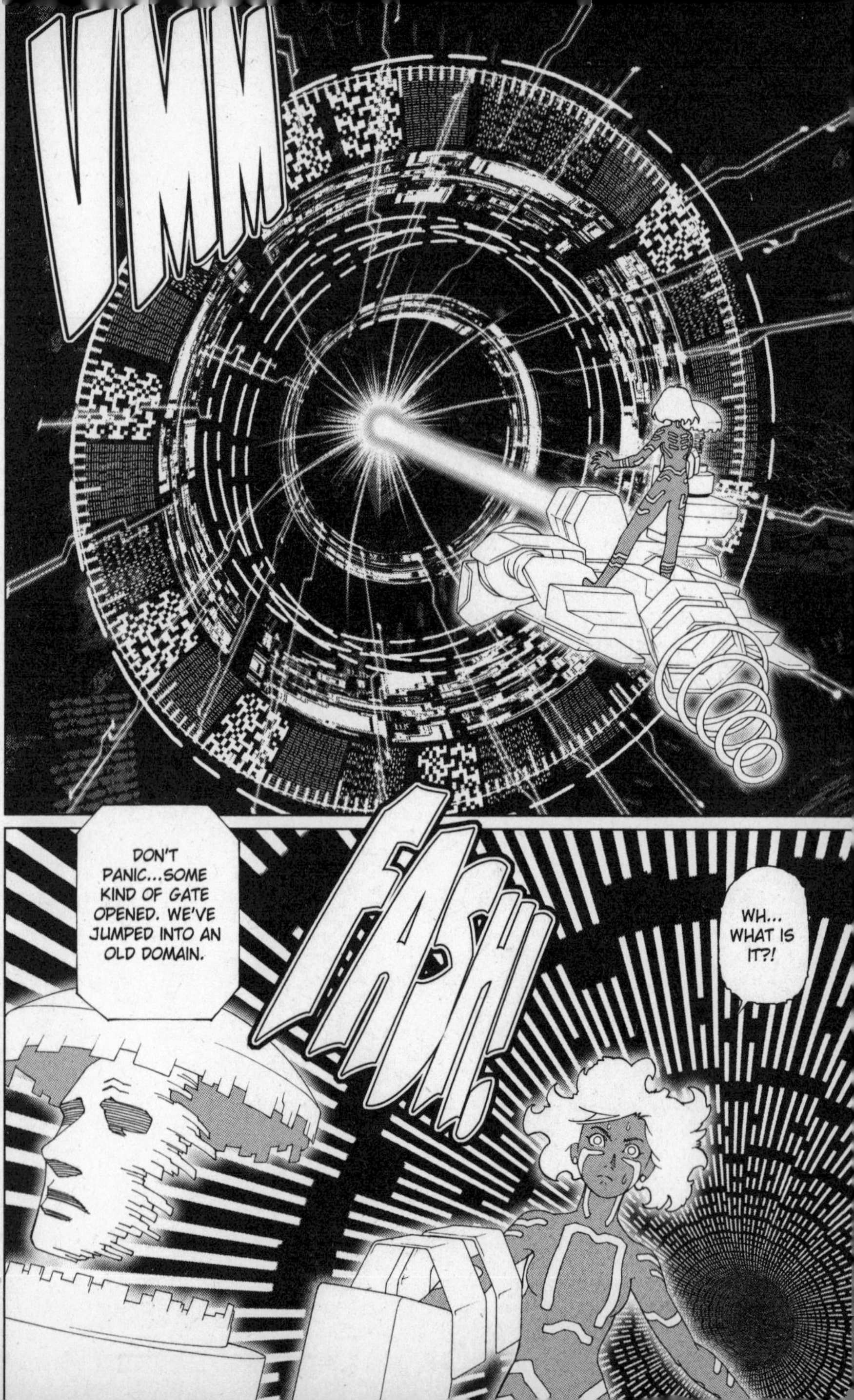
VMM
WH... WHAT IS IT?!
DON'T PANIC...SOME KIND OF GATE OPENED. WE'VE JUMPED INTO AN OLD DOMAIN.

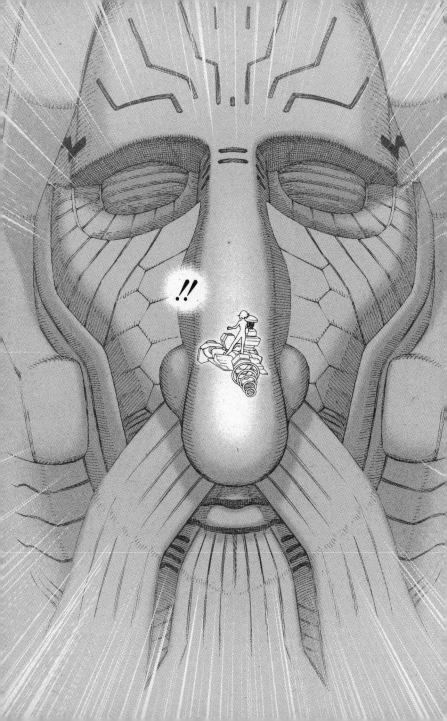

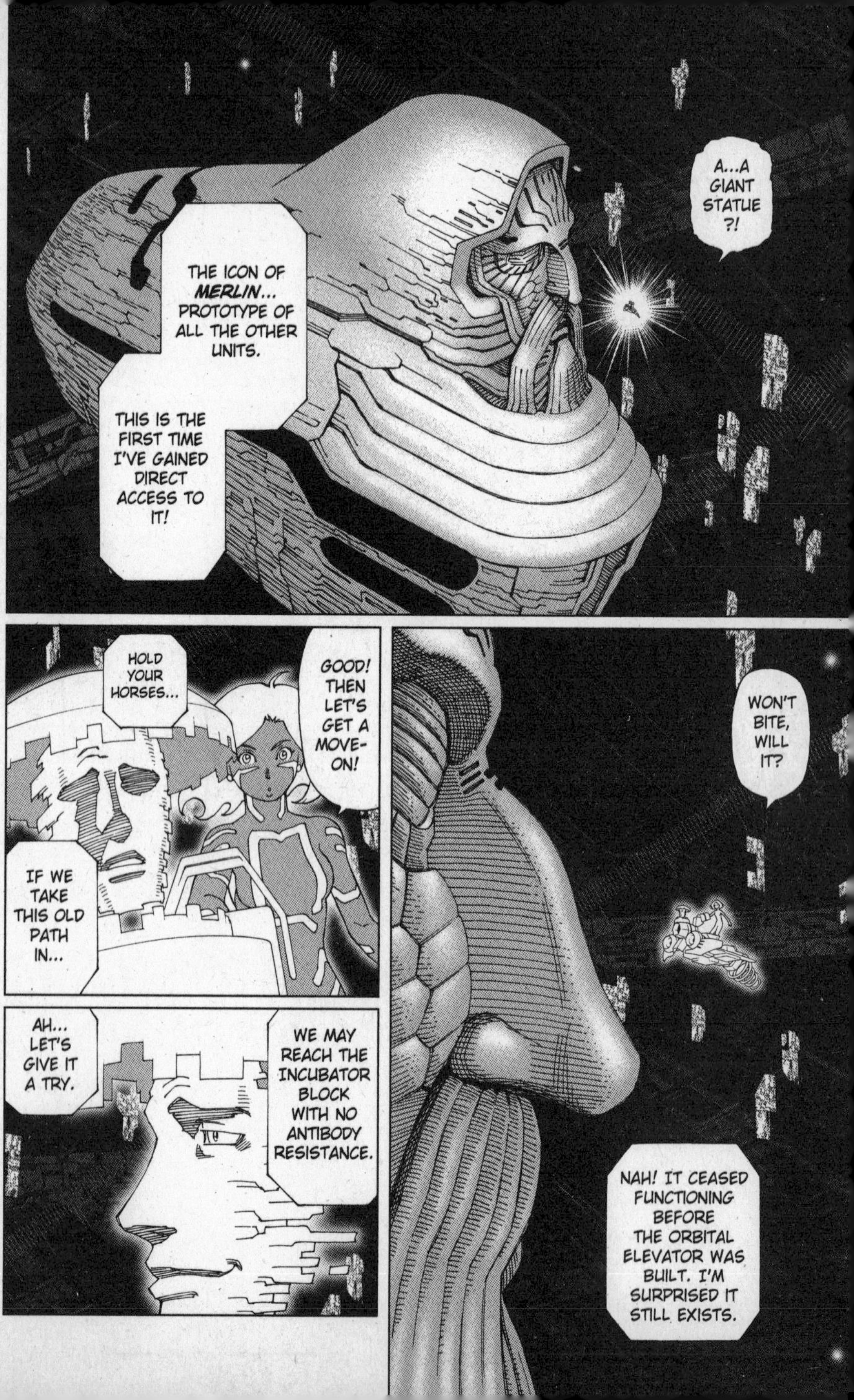
A...A GIANT STATUE ?!
THE ICON OF ***MERLIN***... PROTOTYPE OF ALL THE OTHER UNITS.
THIS IS THE FIRST TIME I'VE GAINED DIRECT ACCESS TO IT!
WON'T BITE, WILL IT?
NAH! IT CEASED FUNCTIONING BEFORE THE ORBITAL ELEVATOR WAS BUILT. I'M SURPRISED IT STILL EXISTS.
GOOD! THEN LET'S GET A MOVE-ON!
HOLD YOUR HORSES...
IF WE TAKE THIS OLD PATH IN...
WE MAY REACH THE INCUBATOR BLOCK WITH NO ANTIBODY RESISTANCE.
AH... LET'S GIVE IT A TRY.

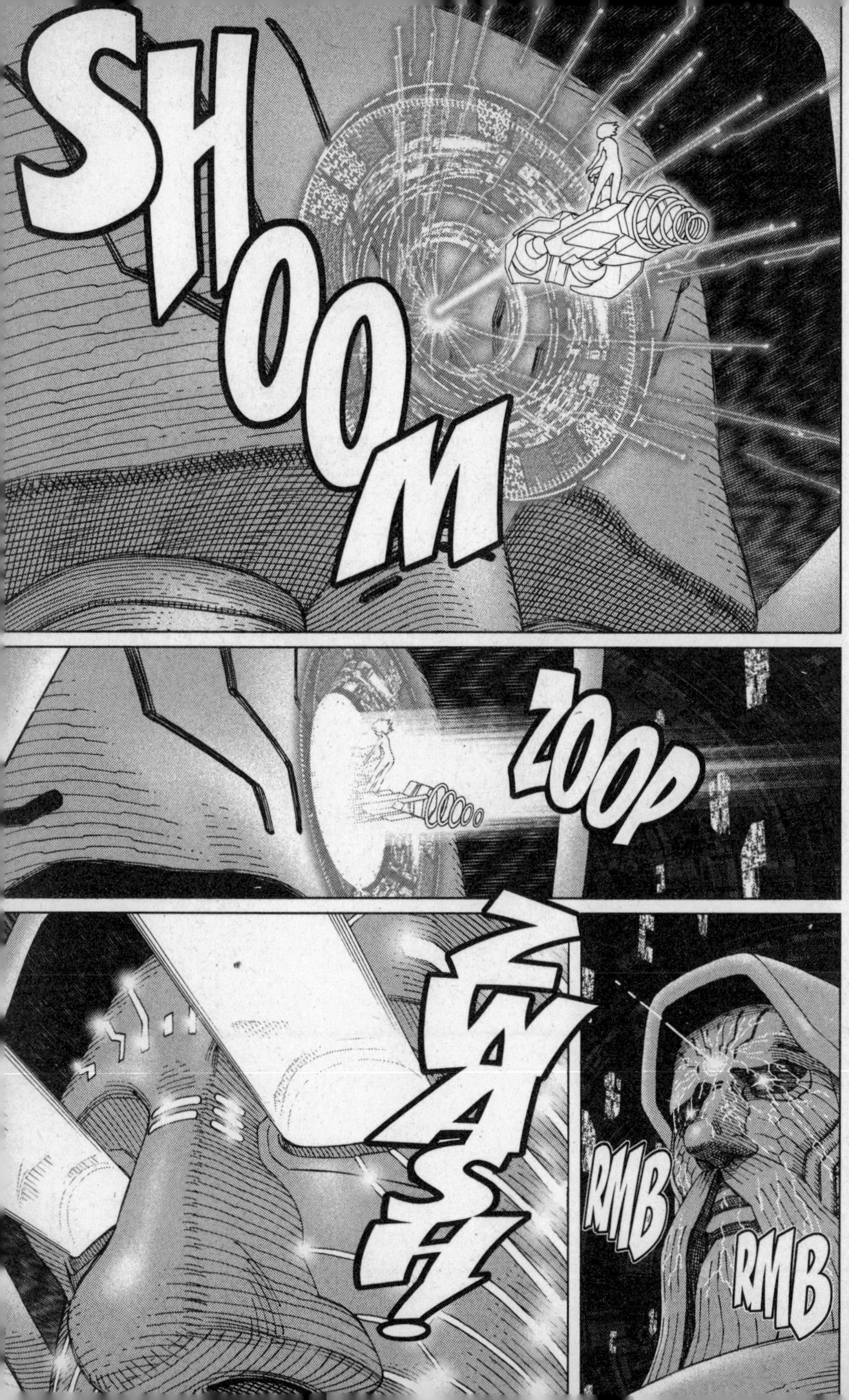
SHOOM
ZOOP
RMB
RMB
ZWASH!

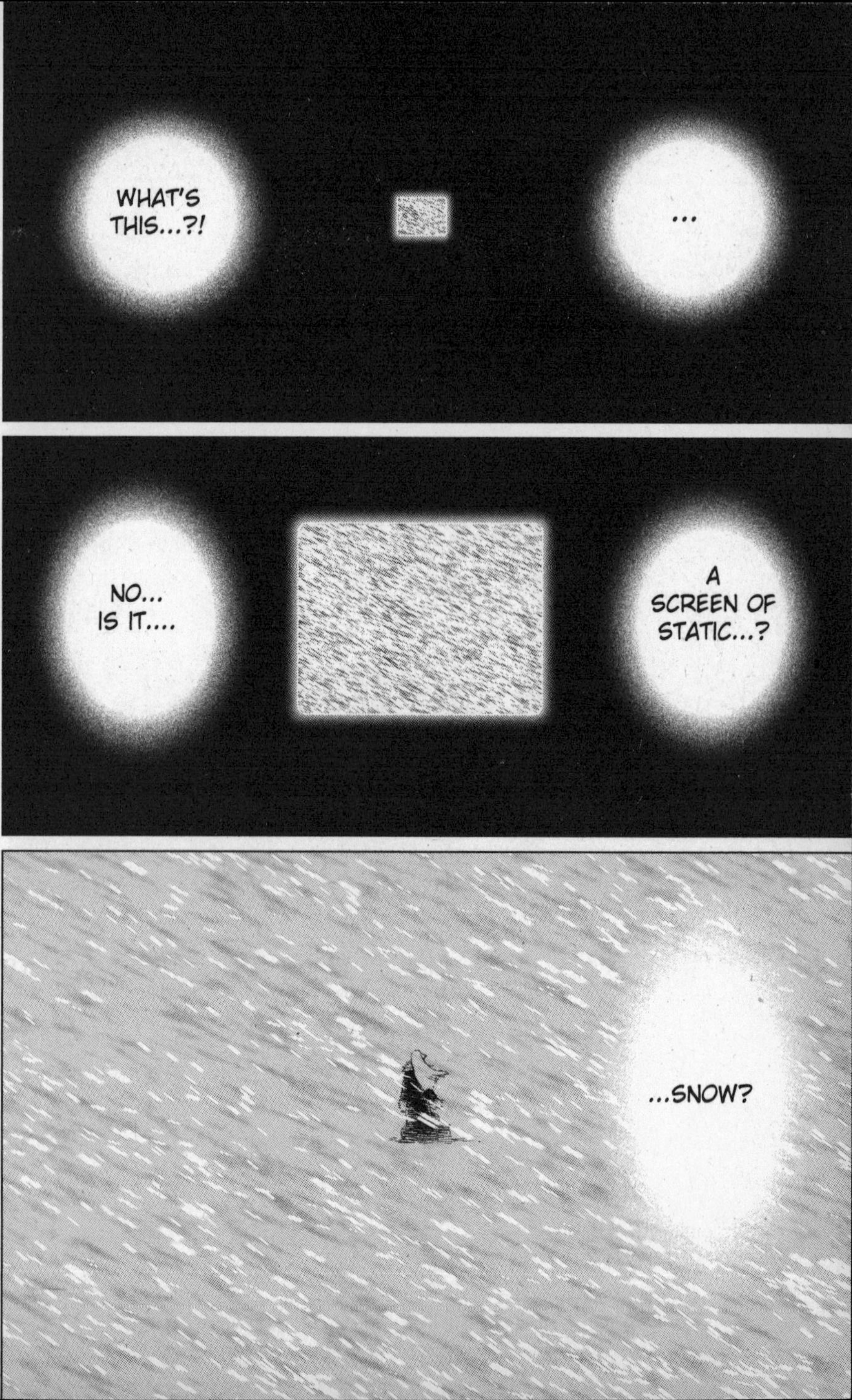
...
WHAT'S THIS...?!
A SCREEN OF STATIC...?
NO... IS IT....
...SNOW?

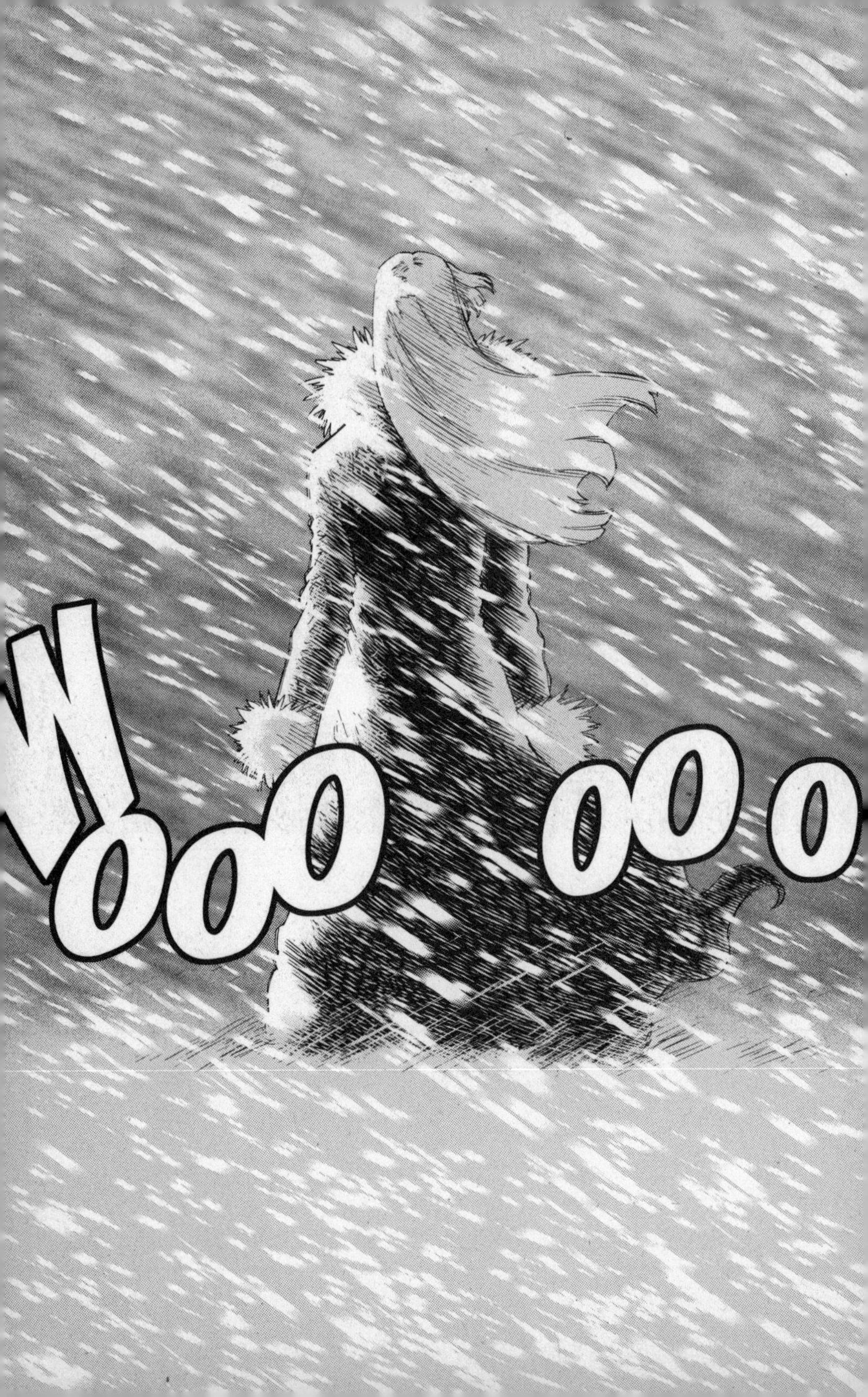
WOOO OOO

ERA SPUTNIK 55

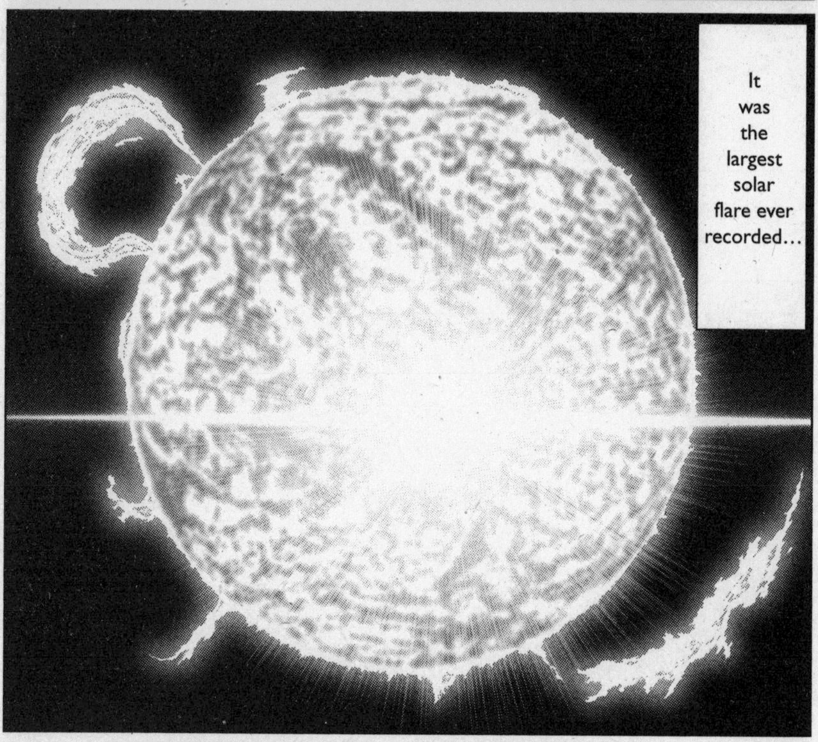
It was the largest solar flare ever recorded...

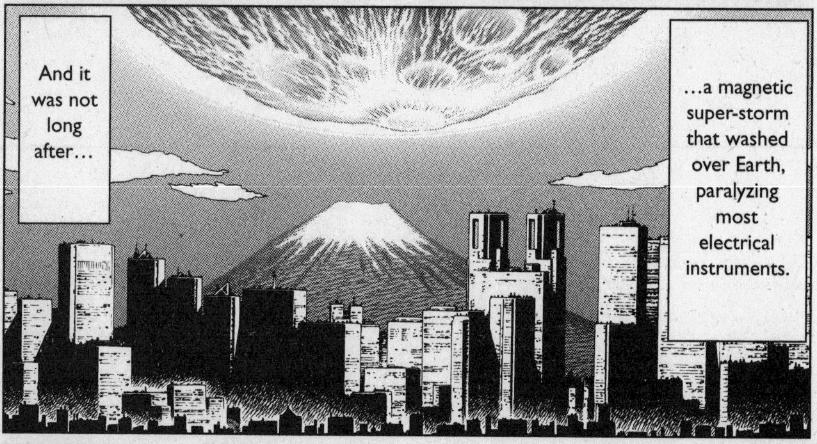
And it was not long after...
...a magnetic super-storm that washed over Earth, paralyzing most electrical instruments.

PHASE 45: Impact Winter

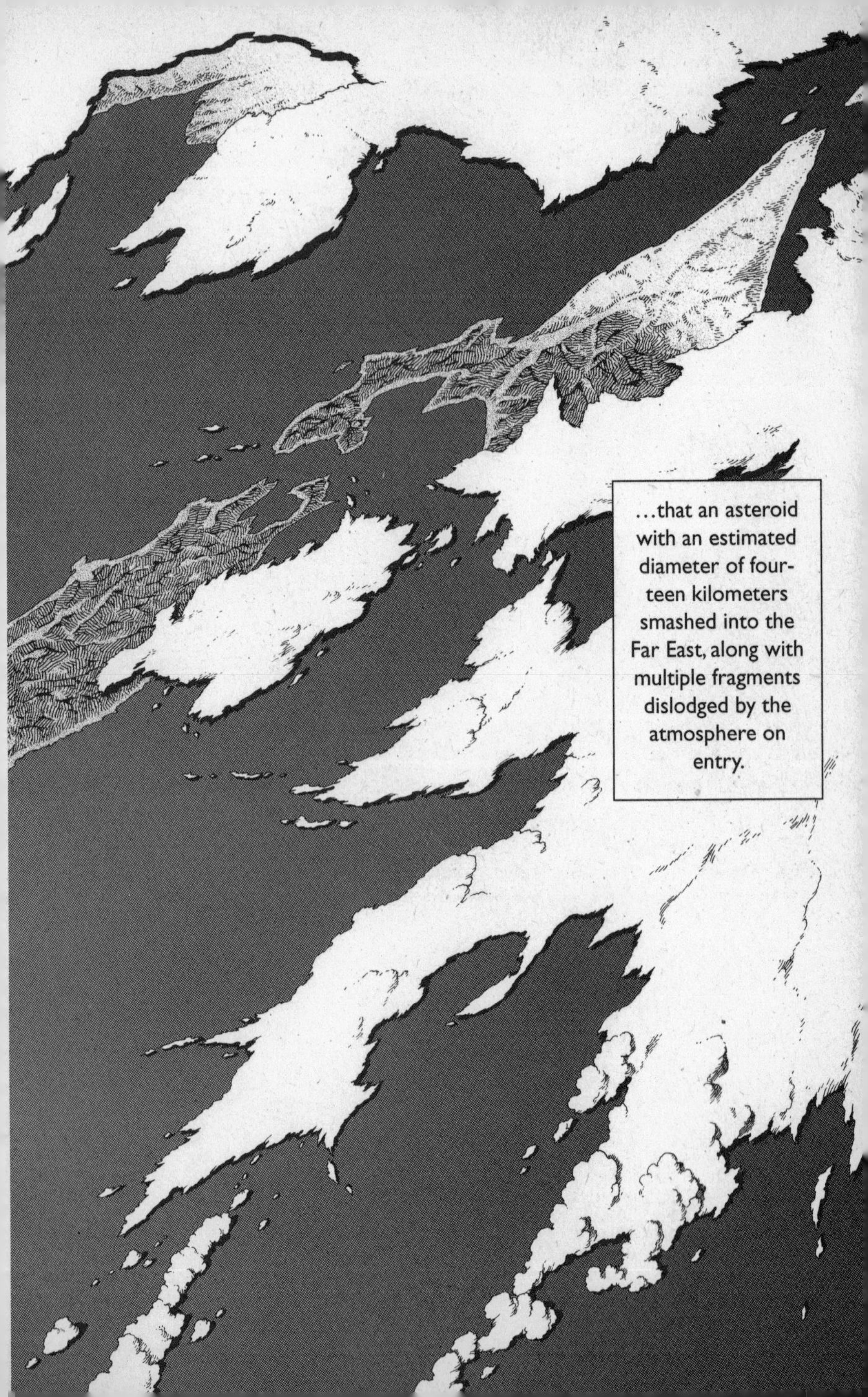
…that an asteroid with an estimated diameter of fourteen kilometers smashed into the Far East, along with multiple fragments dislodged by the atmosphere on entry.

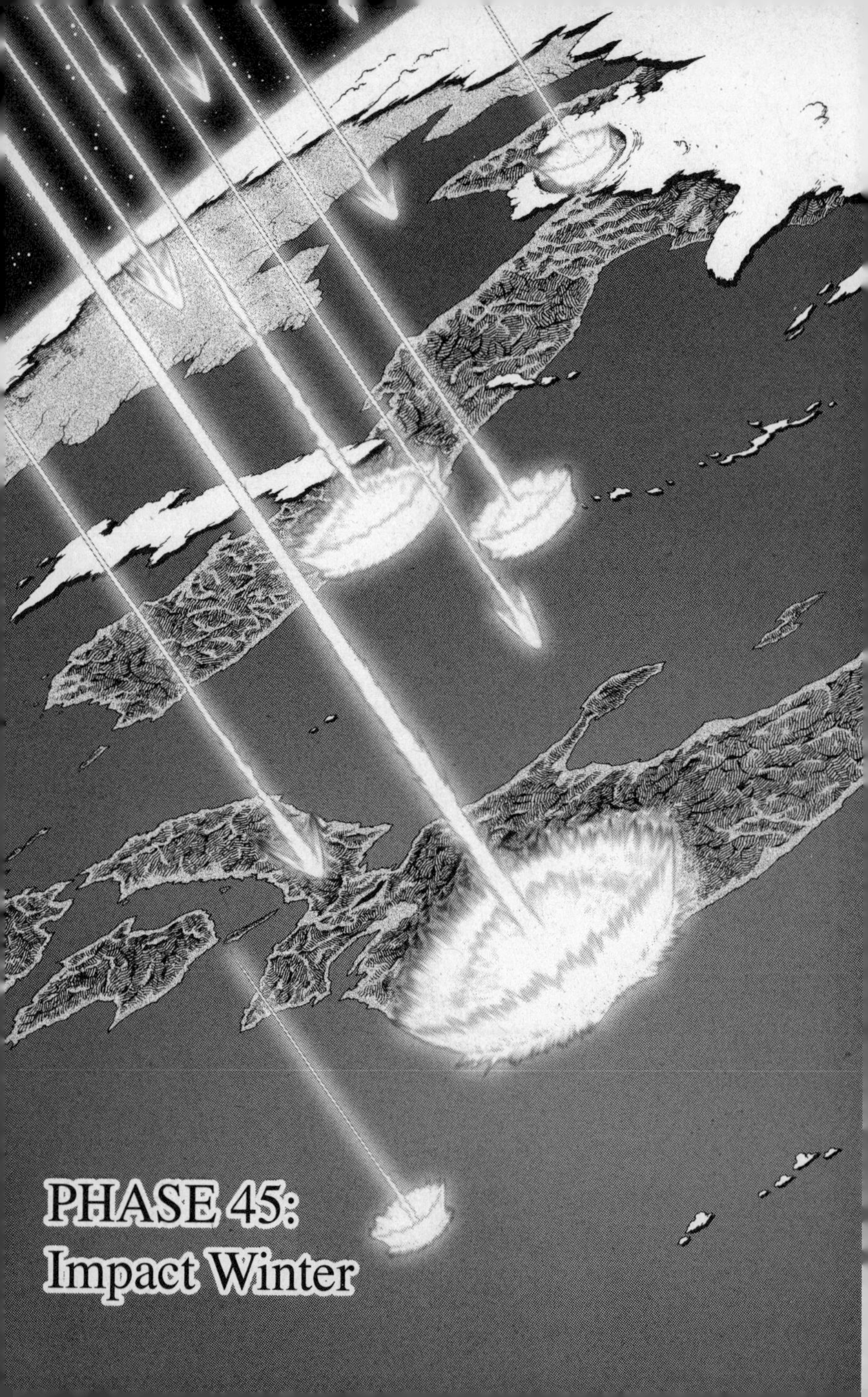
PHASE 45:
Impact Winter

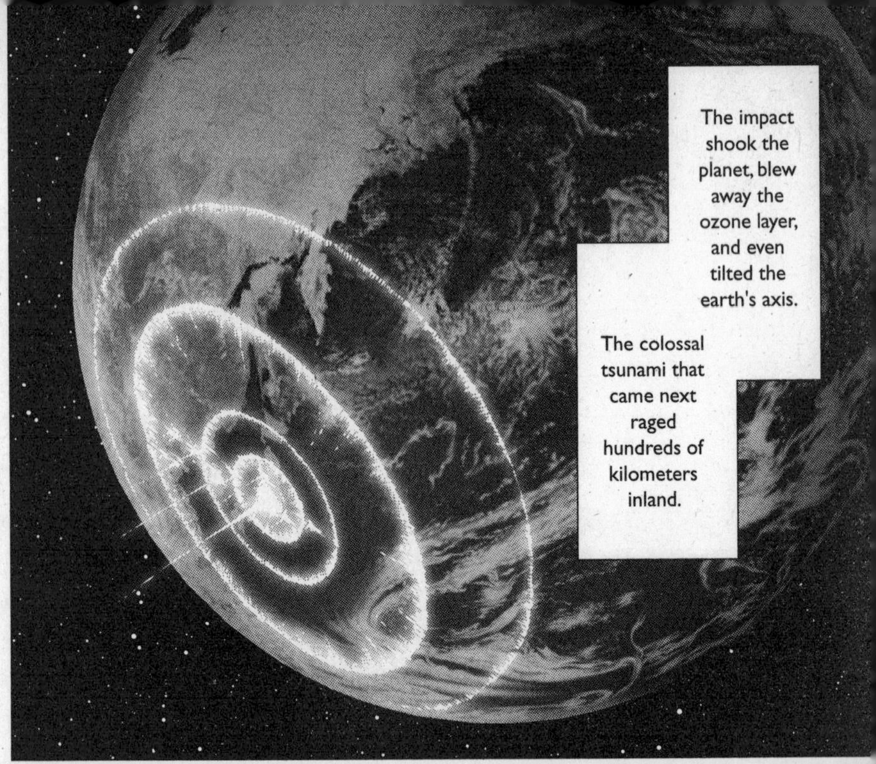
The impact shook the planet, blew away the ozone layer, and even tilted the earth's axis.
The colossal tsunami that came next raged hundreds of kilometers inland.

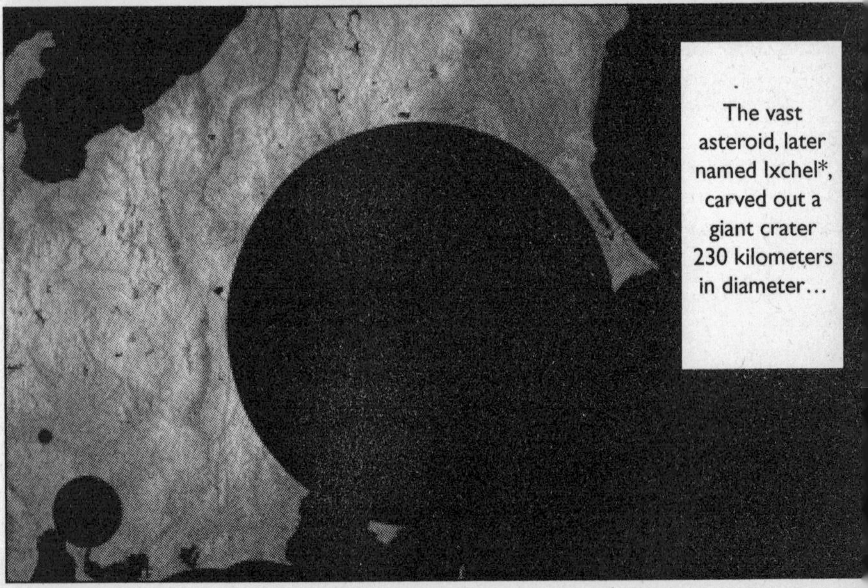
The vast asteroid, later named Ixchel*, carved out a giant crater 230 kilometers in diameter...

*Ixchel: Mayan water and moon goddess, patron of childbirth and consort of Itzamna, lord of the heavens. She is at times depicted as an old woman with sharp claws and called the "Fearsome Crone."

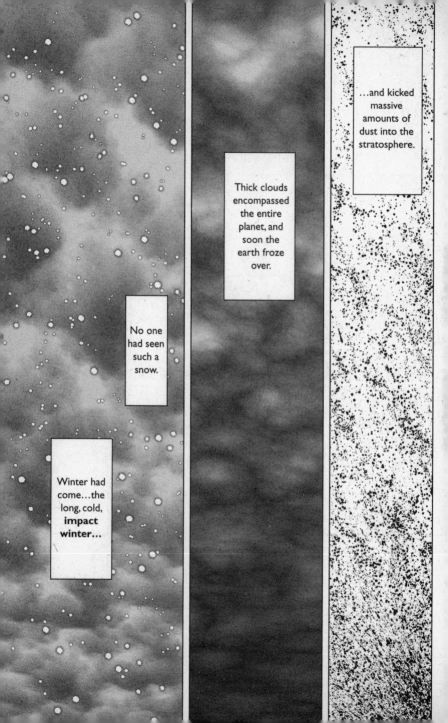

...and kicked massive amounts of dust into the stratosphere.

Thick clouds encompassed the entire planet, and soon the earth froze over.

No one had seen such a snow.

Winter had come...the long, cold, **impact winter...**

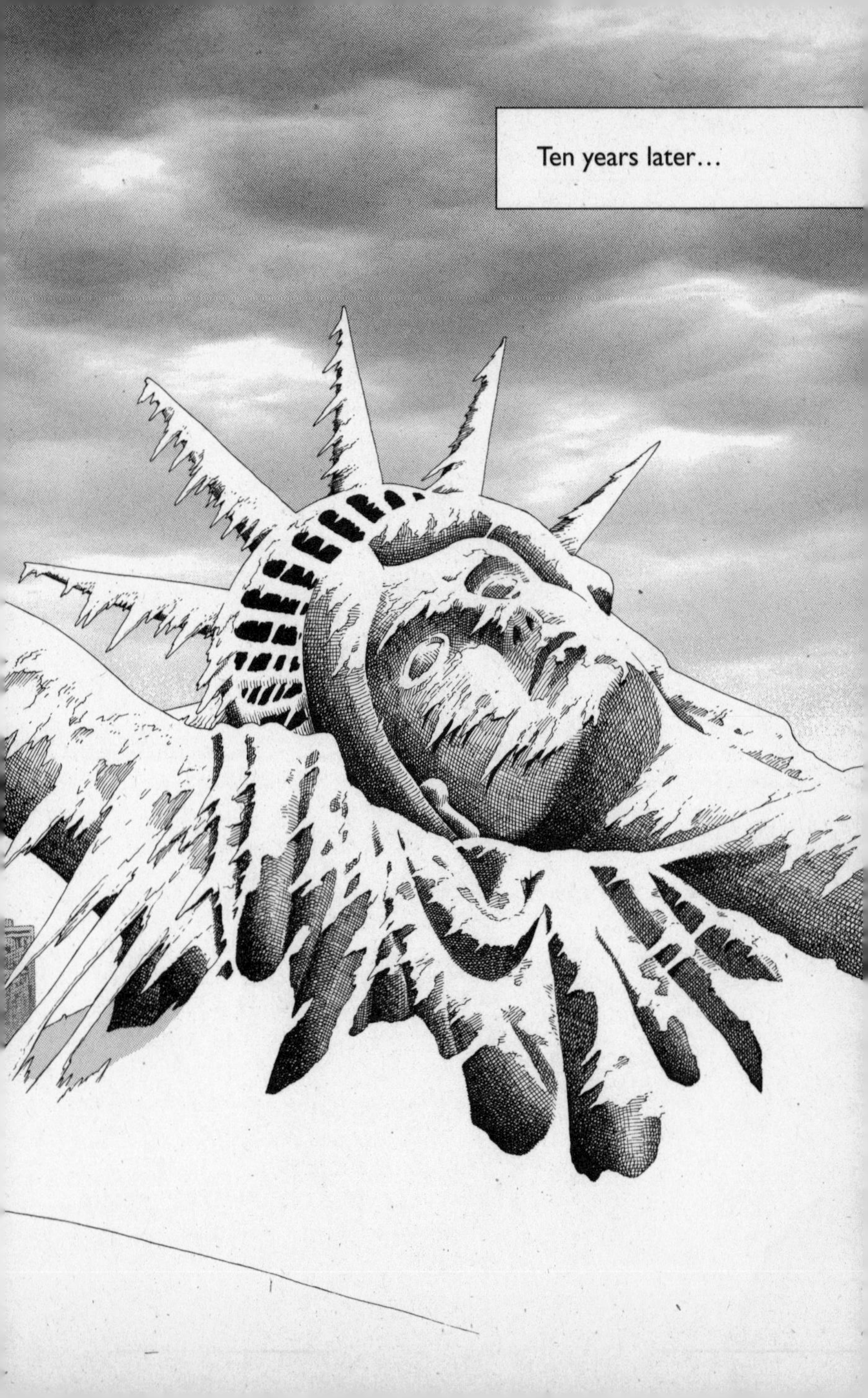
Ten years later...

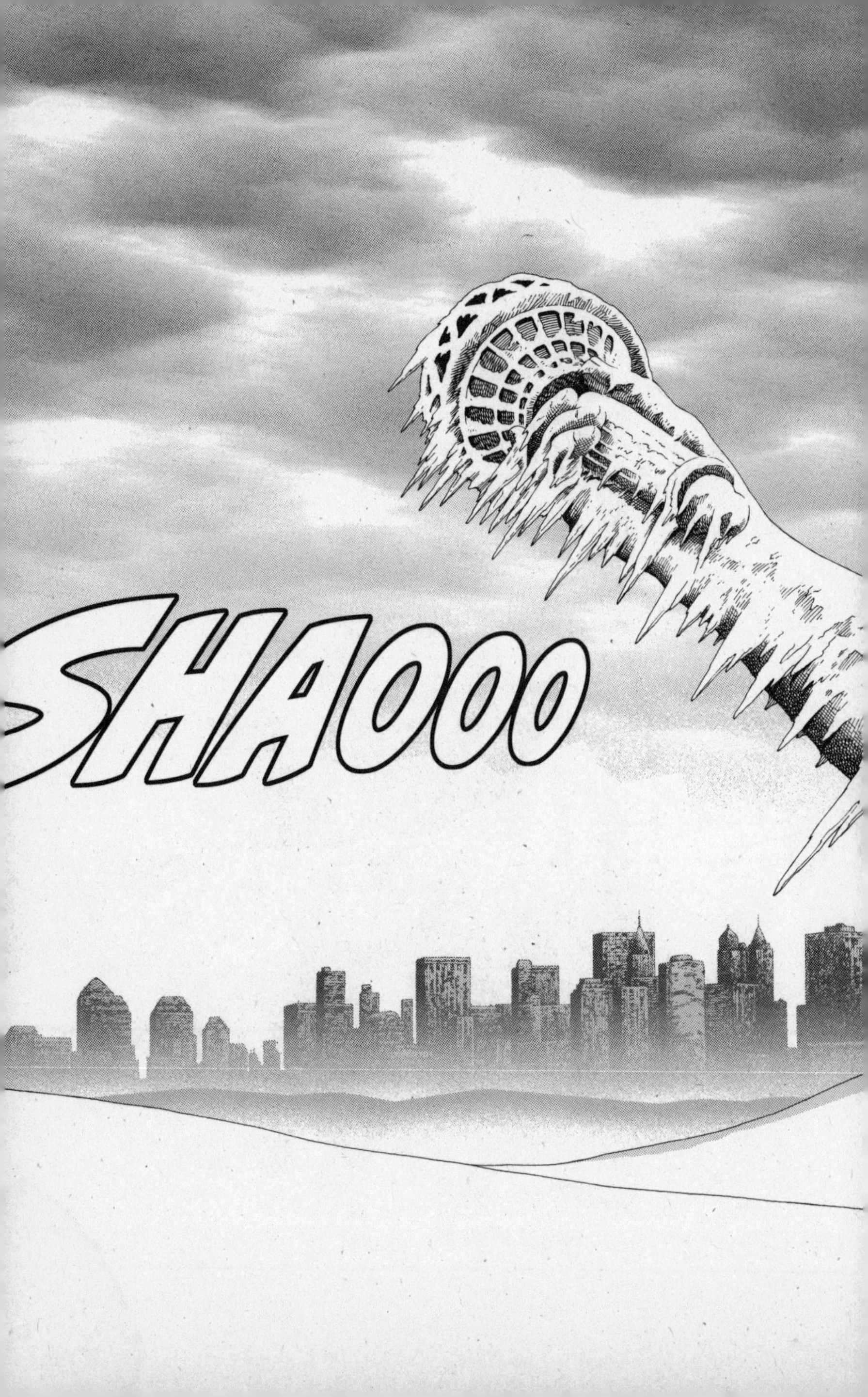
SHAOOO

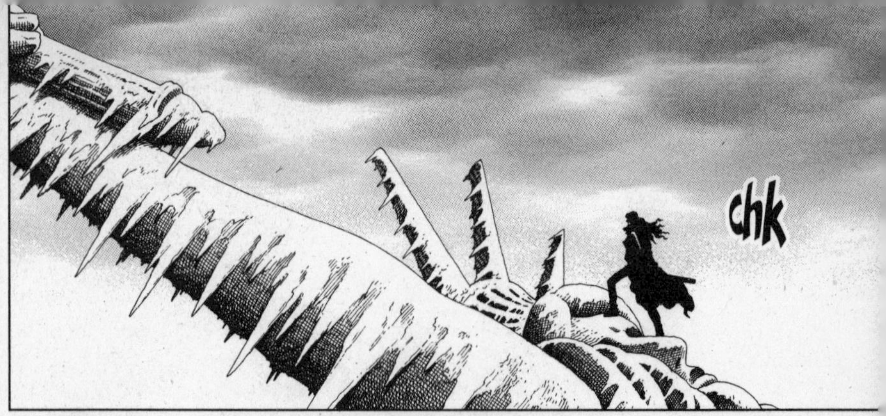
chk
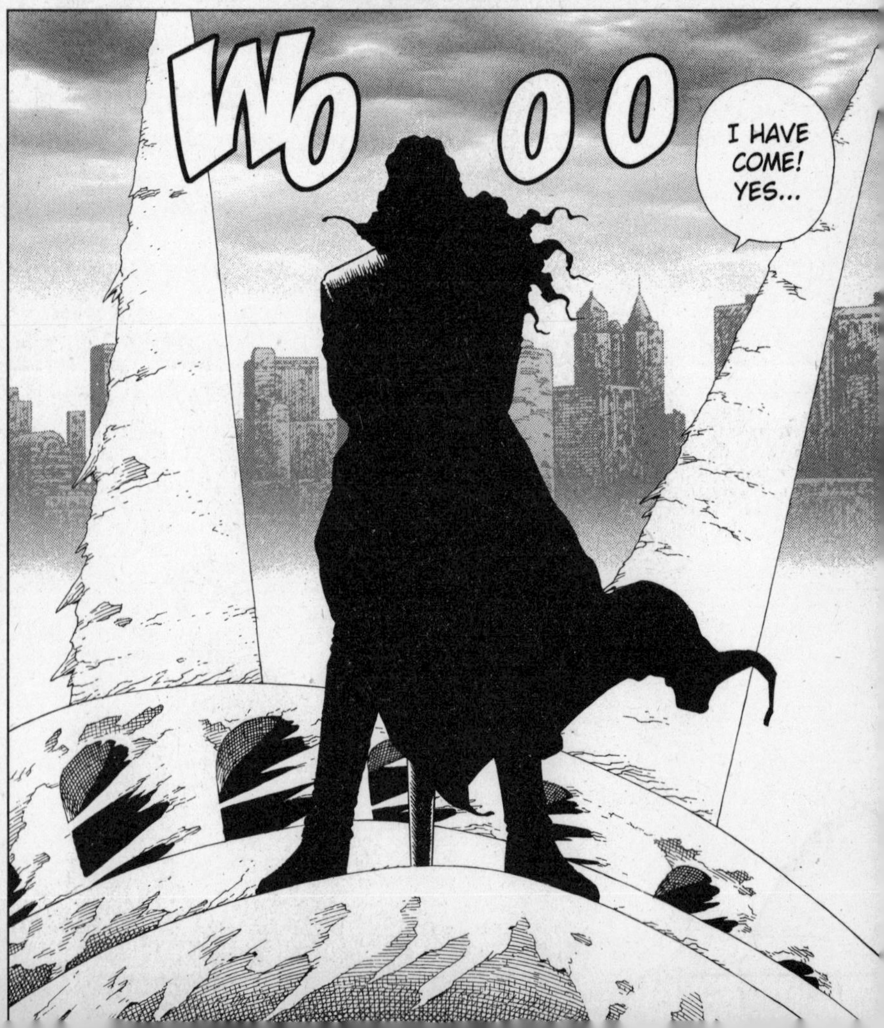
I HAVE
COME!
YES...
WOOO

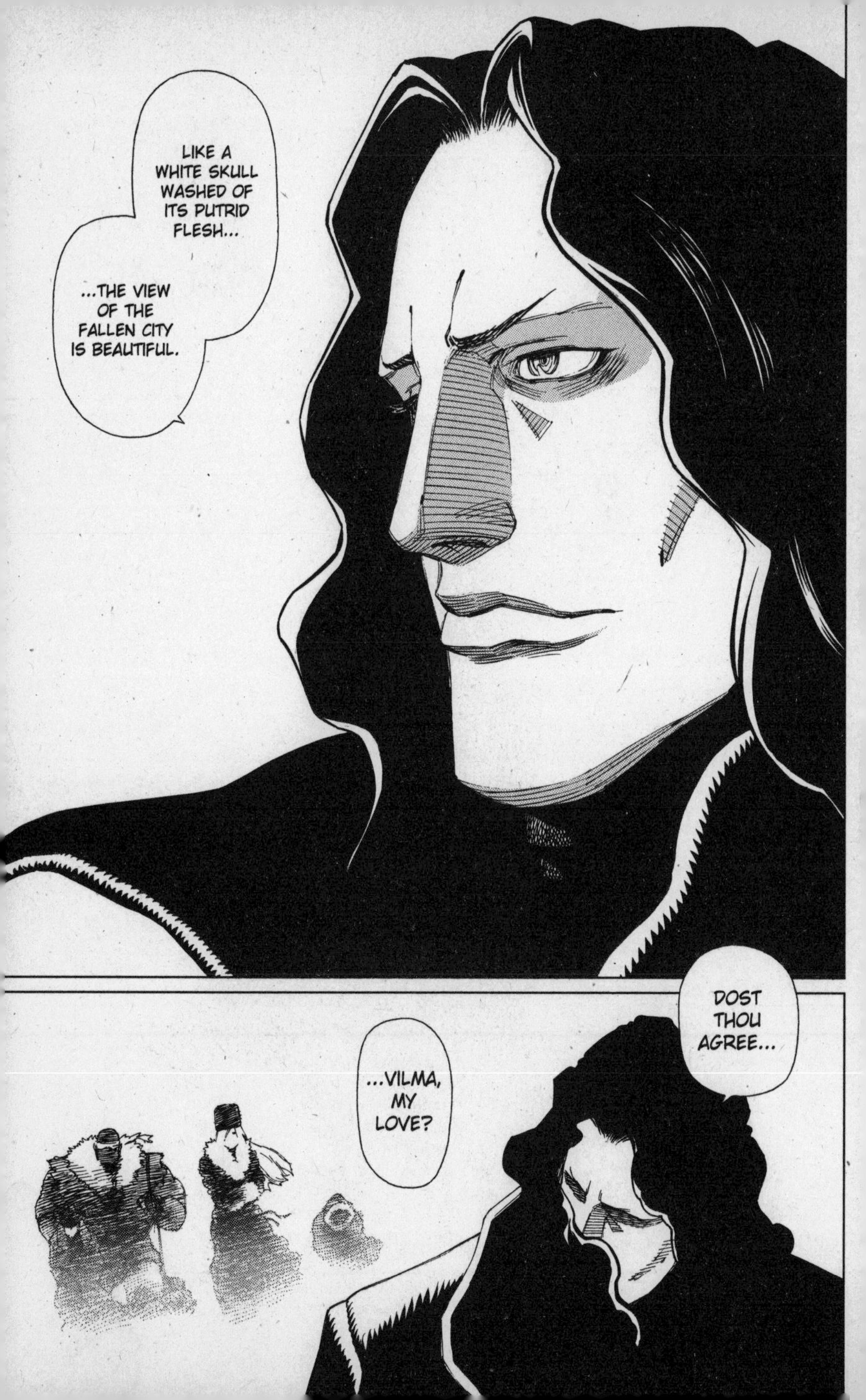
LIKE A WHITE SKULL WASHED OF ITS PUTRID FLESH...
...THE VIEW OF THE FALLEN CITY IS BEAUTIFUL.
DOST THOU AGREE...
...VILMA, MY LOVE?

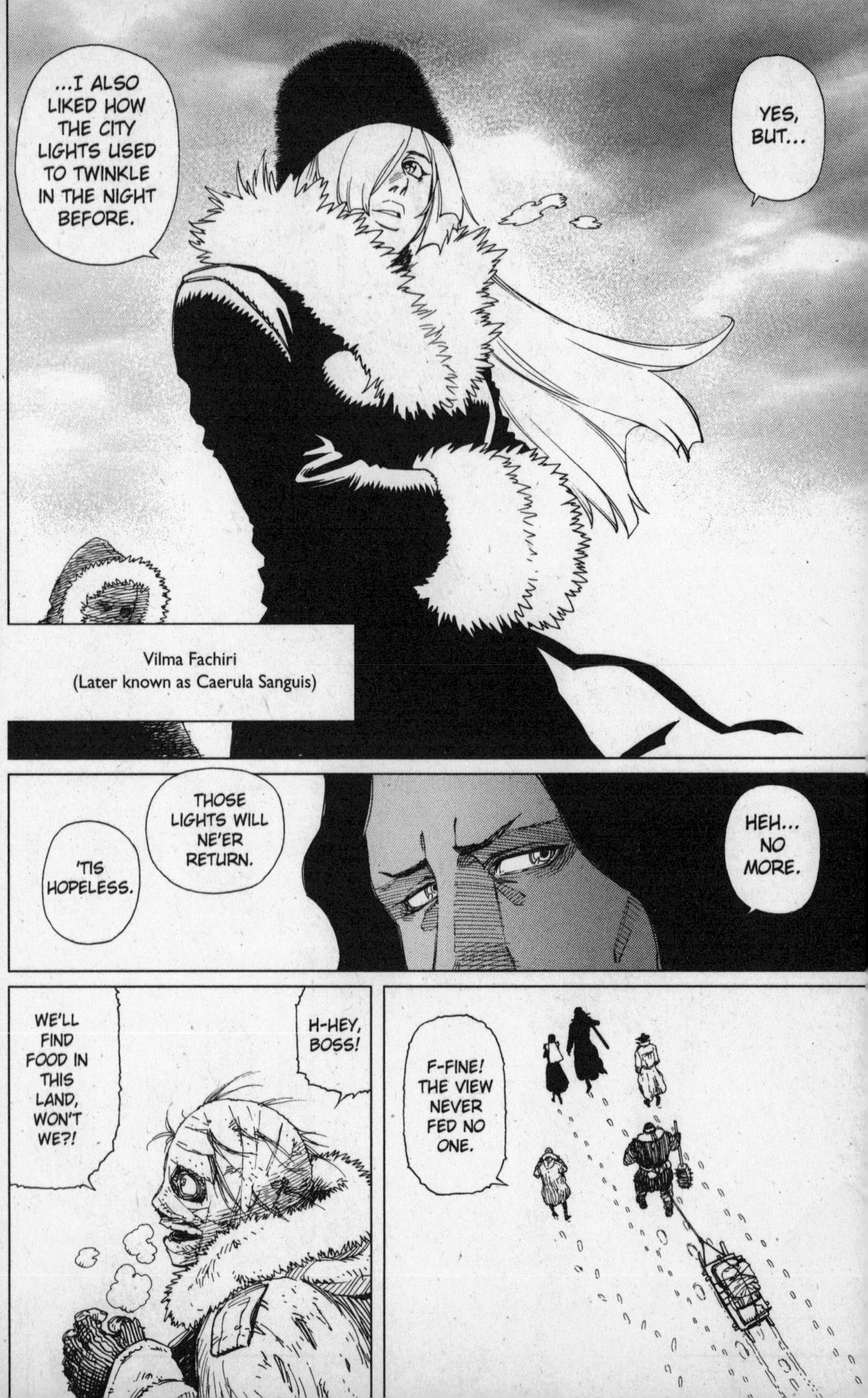
YES, BUT...
...I ALSO LIKED HOW THE CITY LIGHTS USED TO TWINKLE IN THE NIGHT BEFORE.
Vilma Fachiri
(Later known as Caerula Sanguis)
HEH... NO MORE.
THOSE LIGHTS WILL NE'ER RETURN.
'TIS HOPELESS.
F-FINE! THE VIEW NEVER FED NO ONE.
H-HEY, BOSS!
WE'LL FIND FOOD IN THIS LAND, WON'T WE?!

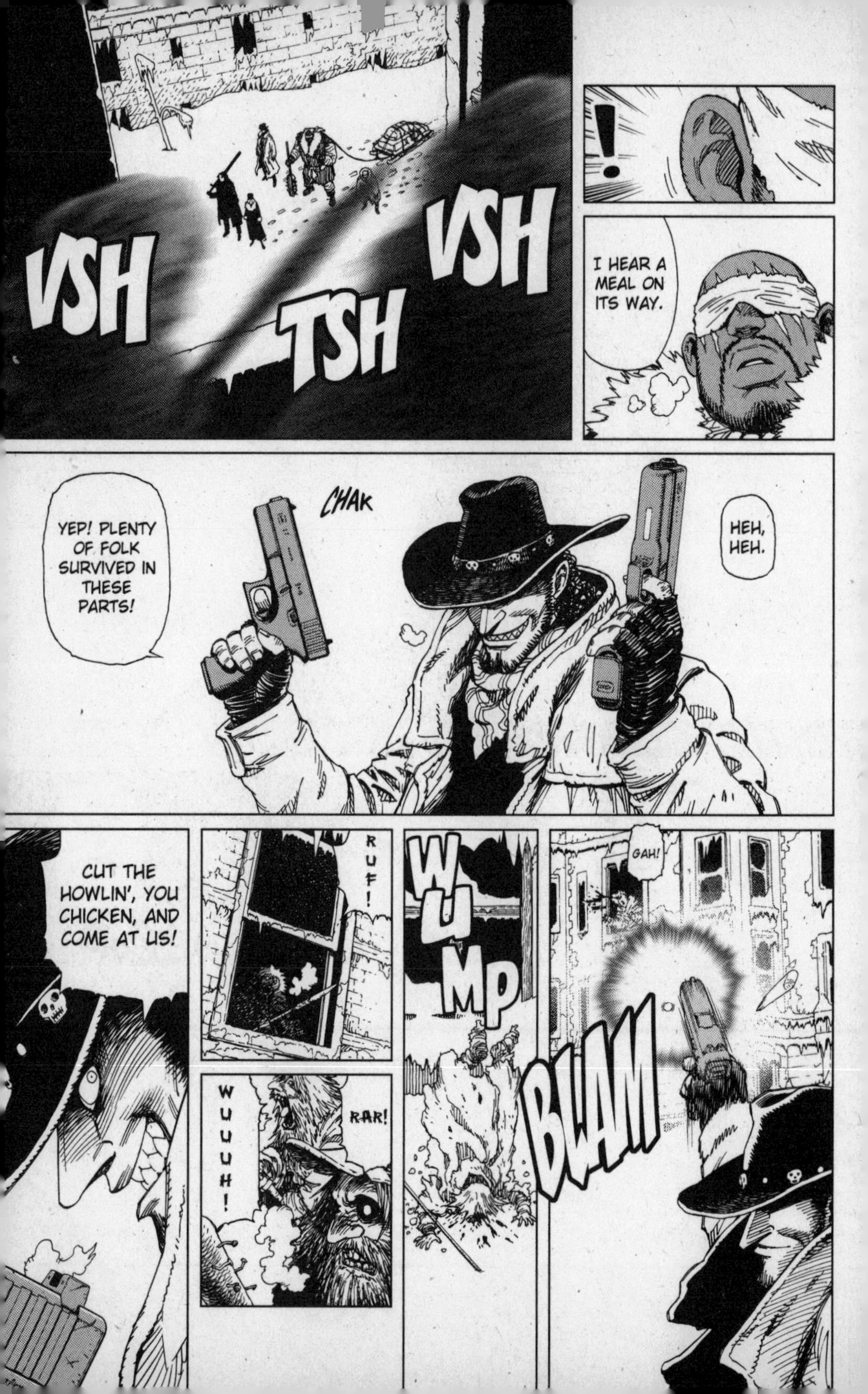
!
I HEAR A MEAL ON ITS WAY.
VSH
VSH
TSH
HEH, HEH.
CHAK
YEP! PLENTY OF FOLK SURVIVED IN THESE PARTS!
GAH!
BLAM
WUMP
RUF!
RAR!
WUUUH!
CUT THE HOWLIN', YOU CHICKEN, AND COME AT US!

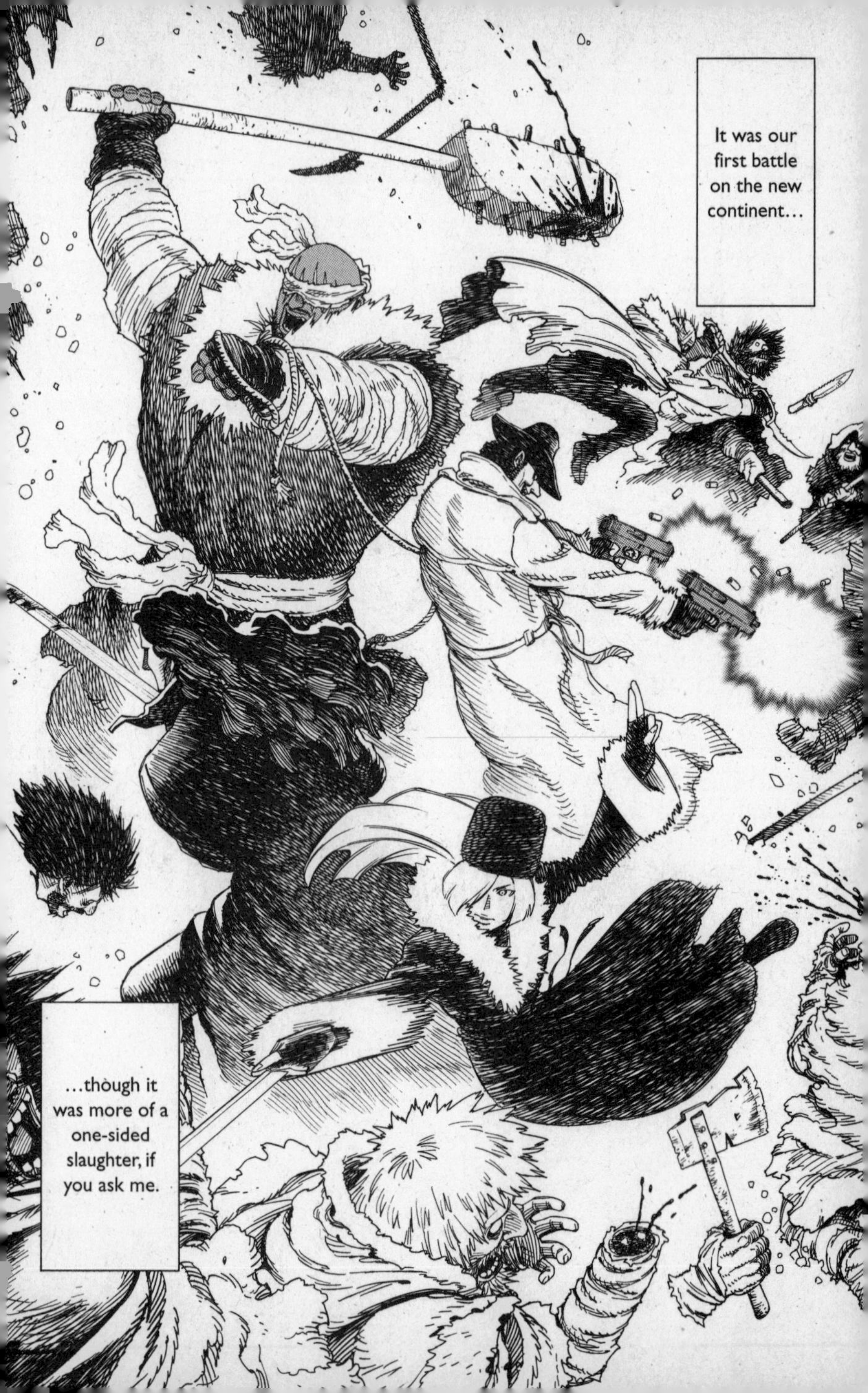
It was our first battle on the new continent…
…though it was more of a one-sided slaughter, if you ask me.

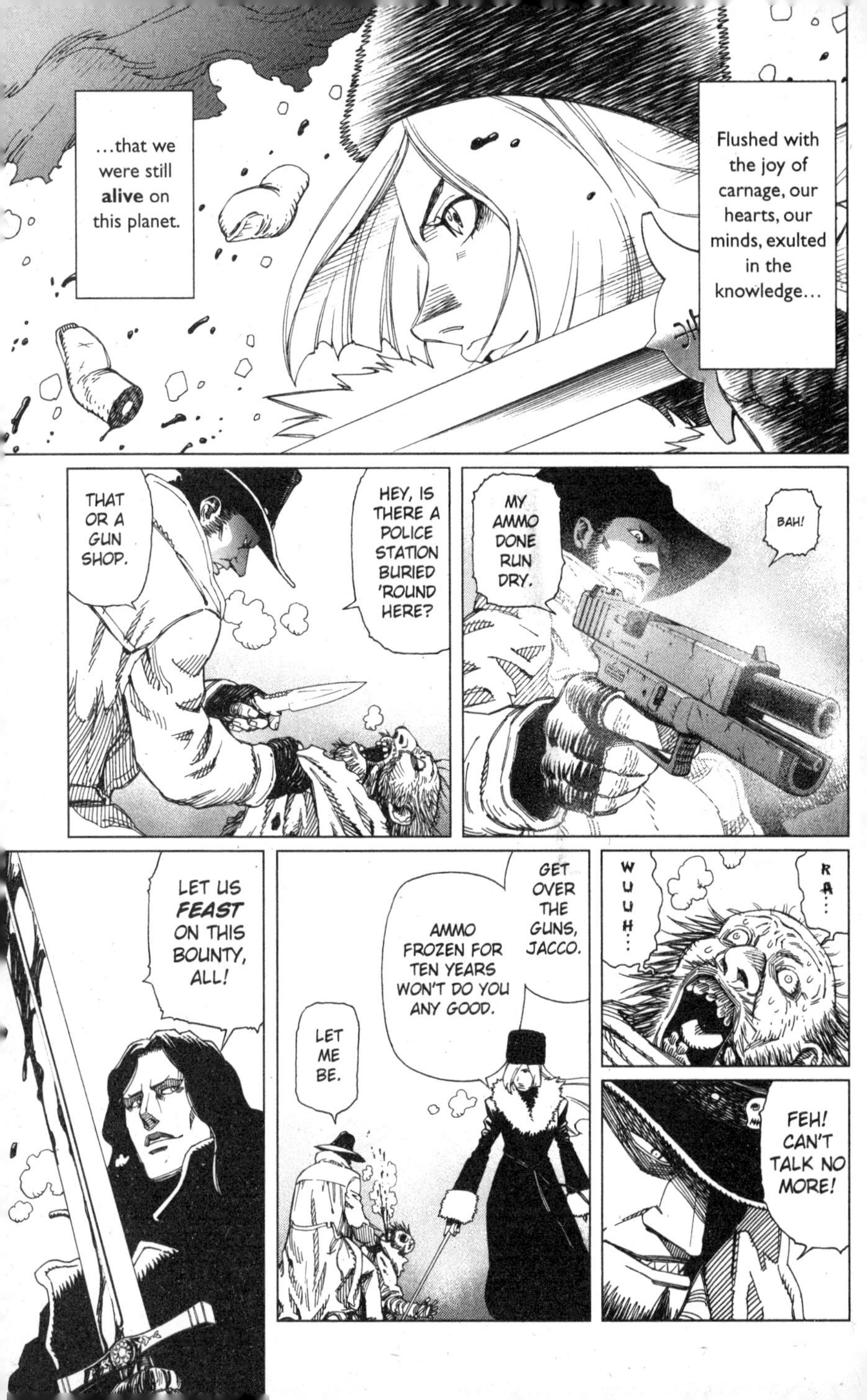
Flushed with the joy of carnage, our hearts, our minds, exulted in the knowledge…
…that we were still **alive** on this planet.
MY AMMO DONE RUN DRY.
BAH!
HEY, IS THERE A POLICE STATION BURIED 'ROUND HERE?
THAT OR A GUN SHOP.
RA…
WUUH…
FEH! CAN'T TALK NO MORE!
GET OVER THE GUNS, JACCO.
AMMO FROZEN FOR TEN YEARS WON'T DO YOU ANY GOOD.
LET ME BE.
LET US *FEAST* ON THIS BOUNTY, ALL!

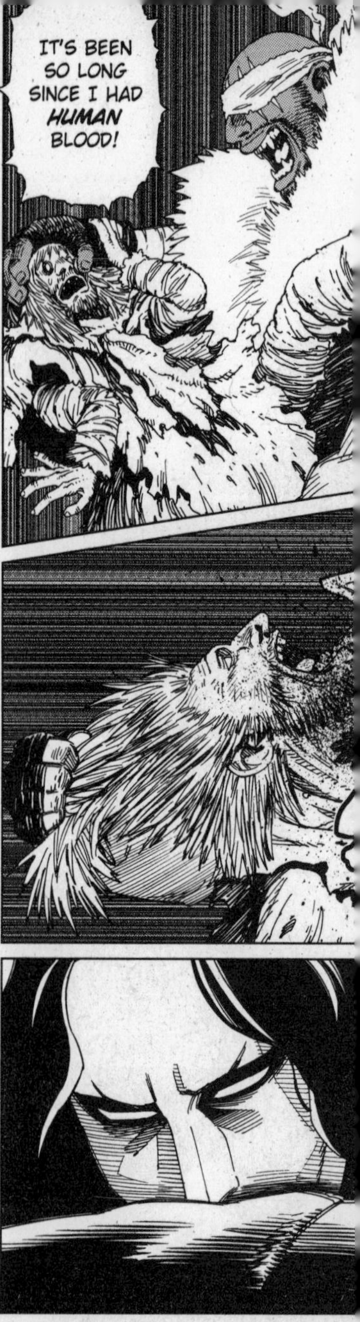
IT'S BEEN SO LONG SINCE I HAD *HUMAN* BLOOD!

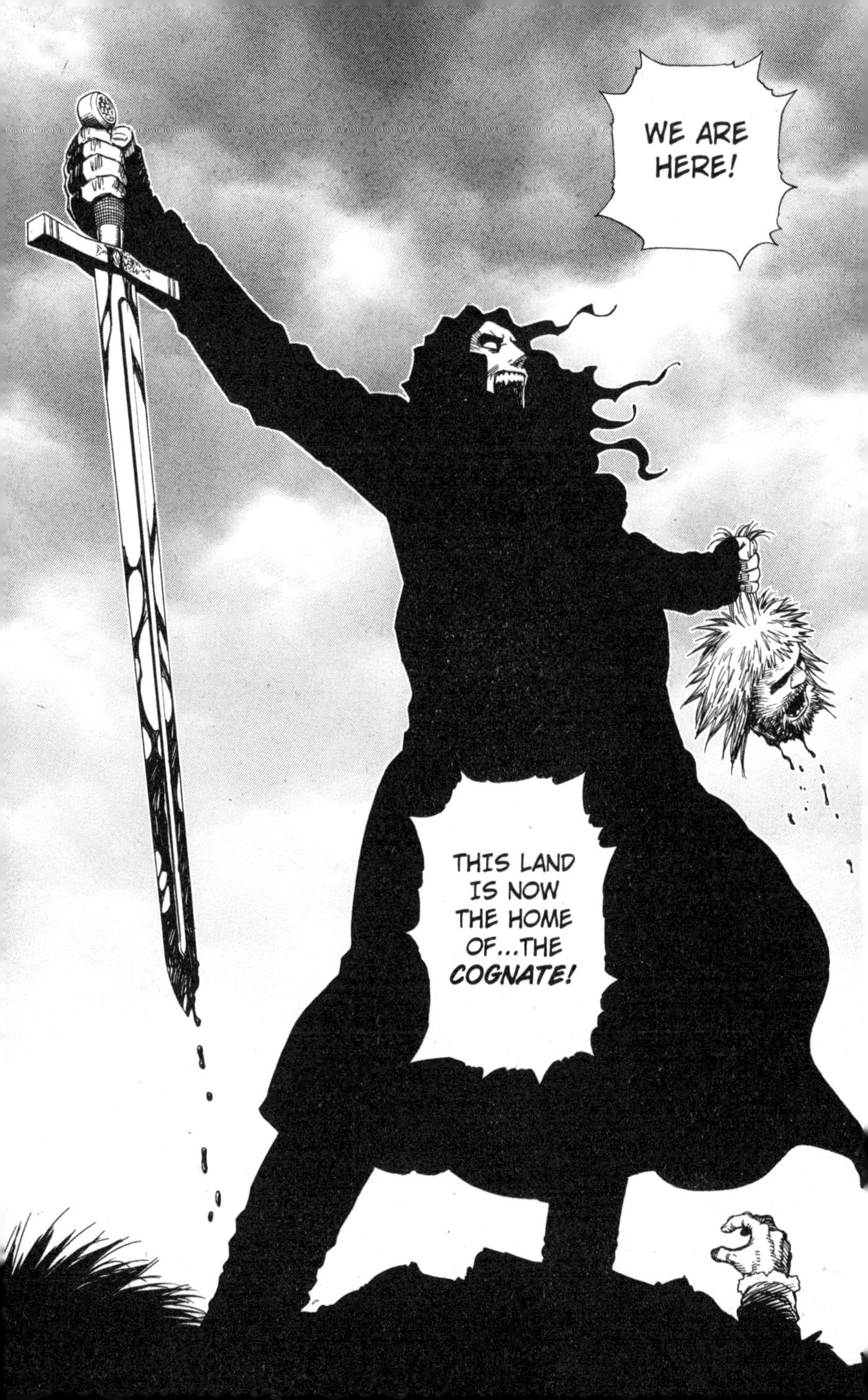
WE ARE HERE!
THIS LAND IS NOW THE HOME OF...THE *COGNATE!*

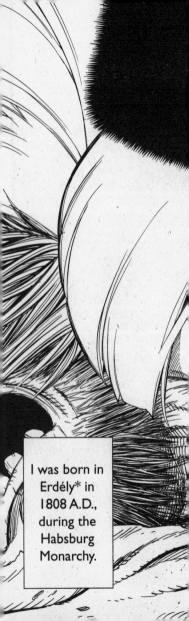

I was born in Erdély* in 1808 A.D., during the Habsburg Monarchy.

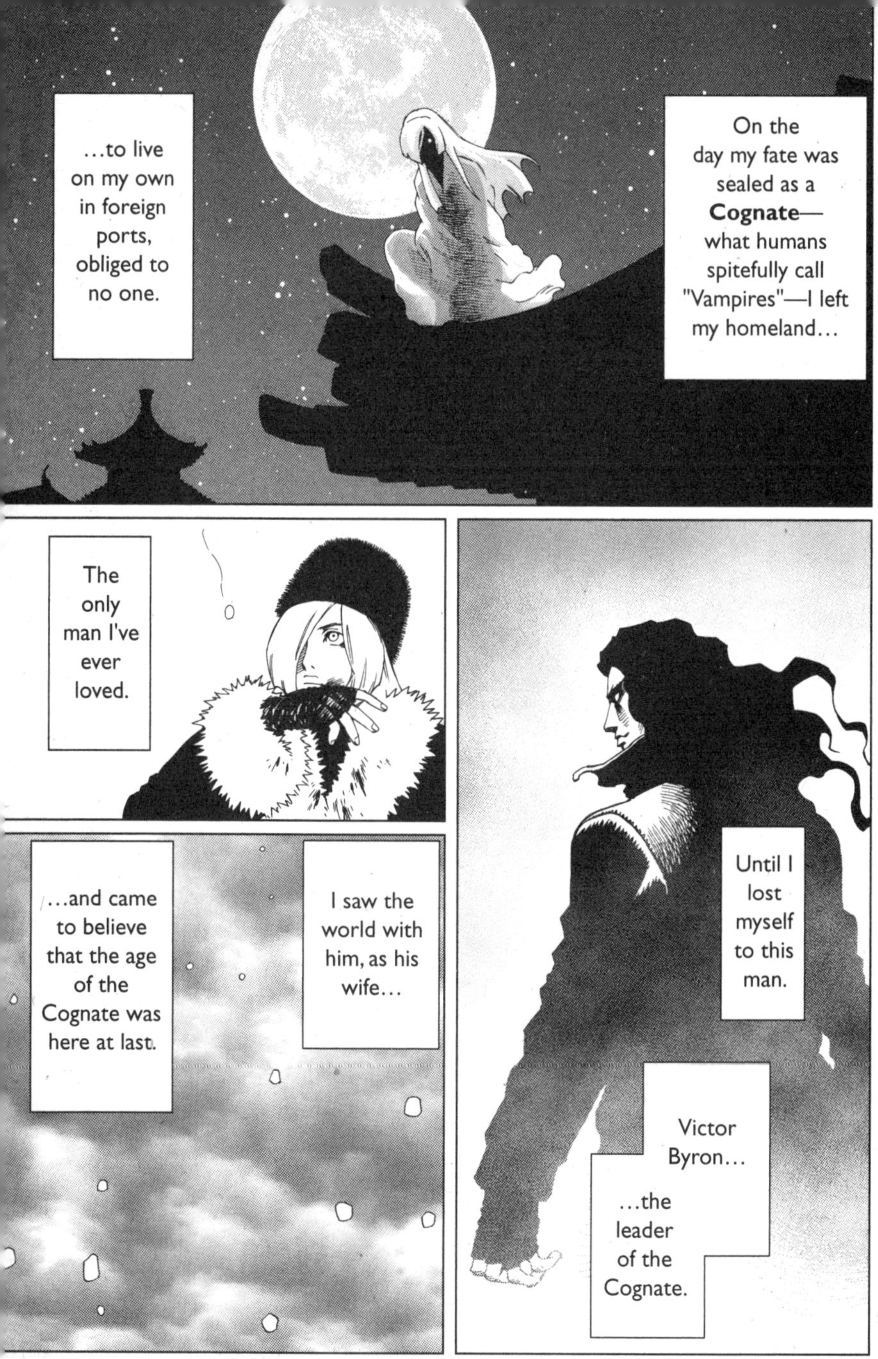
On the day my fate was sealed as a **Cognate**—what humans spitefully call "Vampires"—I left my homeland…
…to live on my own in foreign ports, obliged to no one.
Until I lost myself to this man.
Victor Byron…
…the leader of the Cognate.
The only man I've ever loved.
I saw the world with him, as his wife…
…and came to believe that the age of the Cognate was here at last.

*ERDÉLY: THE HUNGARIAN WORD FOR TRANSYLVANIA.

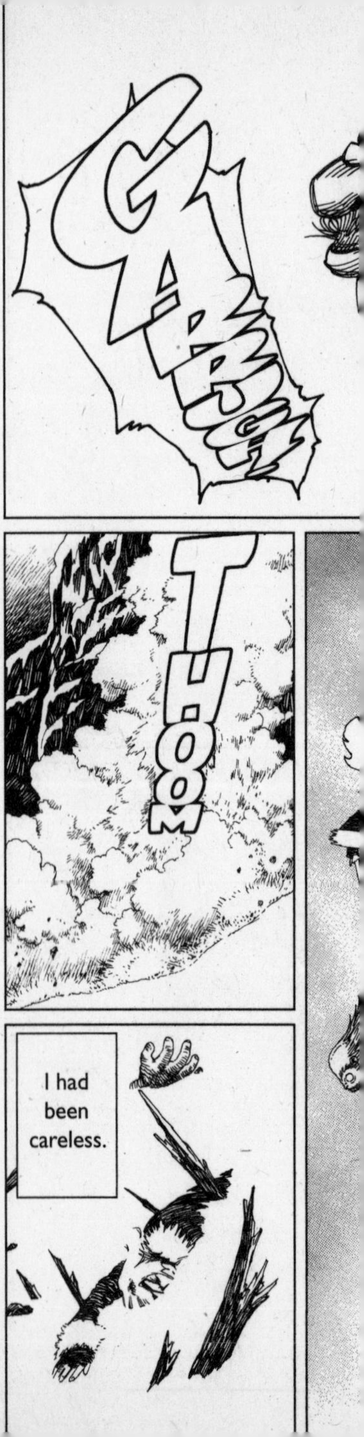
THOOM
I had been careless.

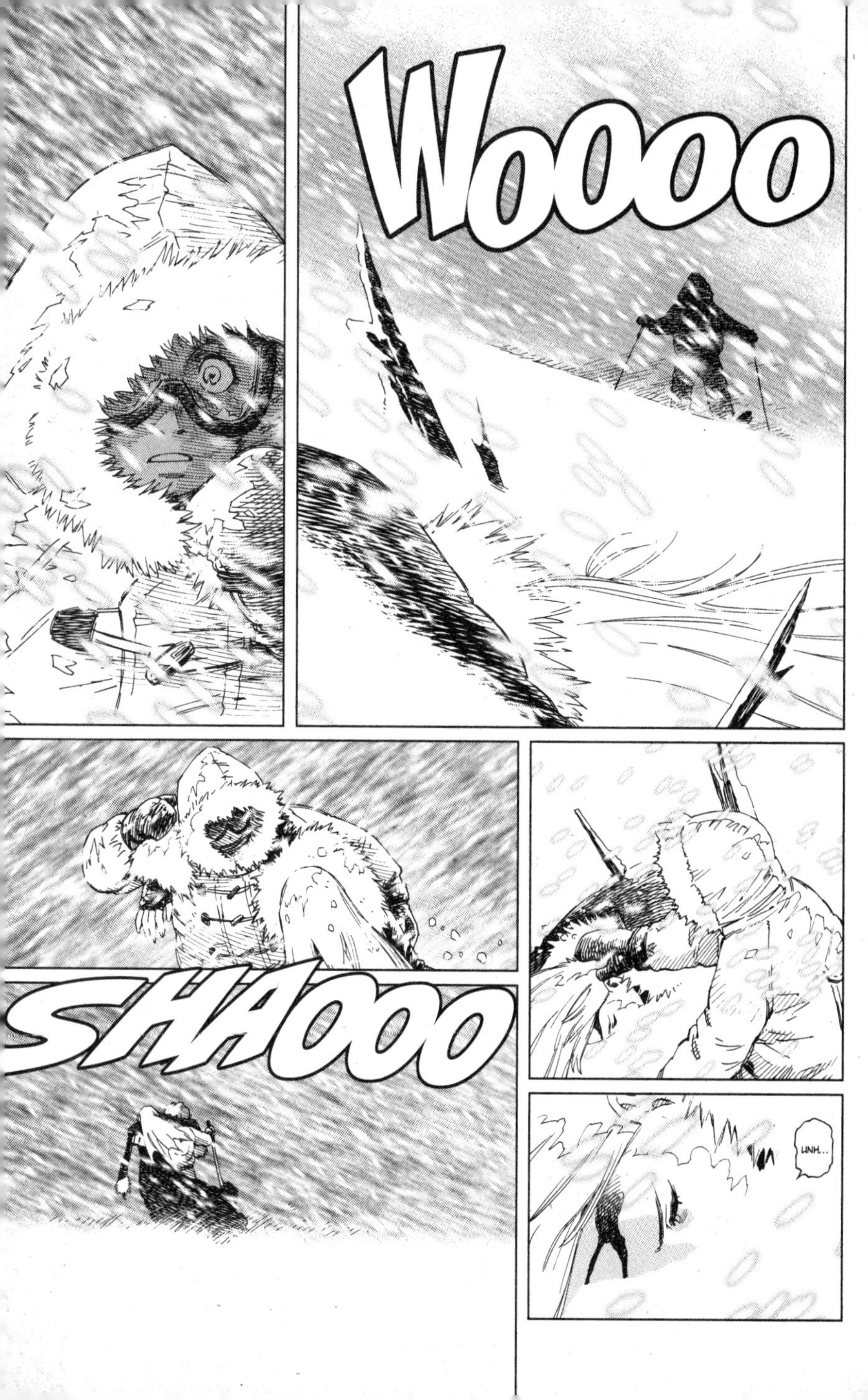
WOOOO
SHAOOO
UNH...

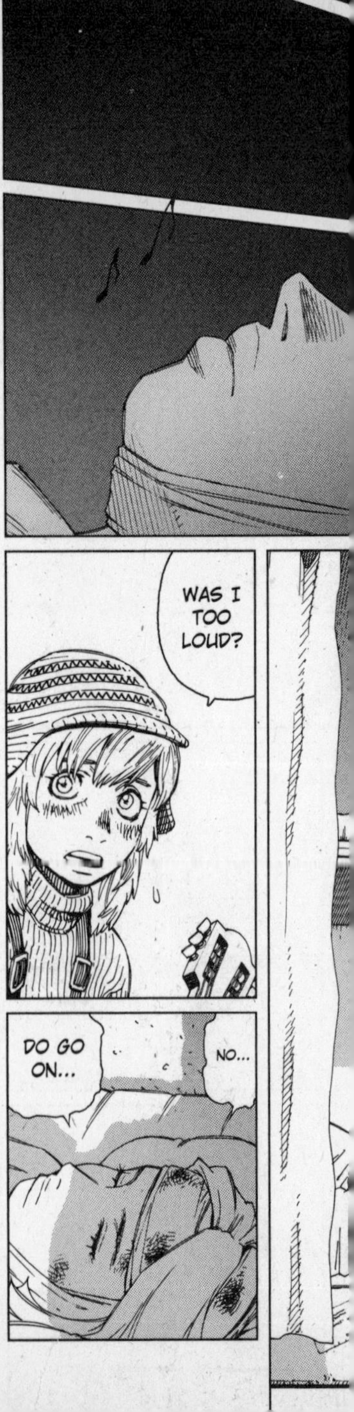
WAS I TOO LOUD?
NO...
DO GO ON...

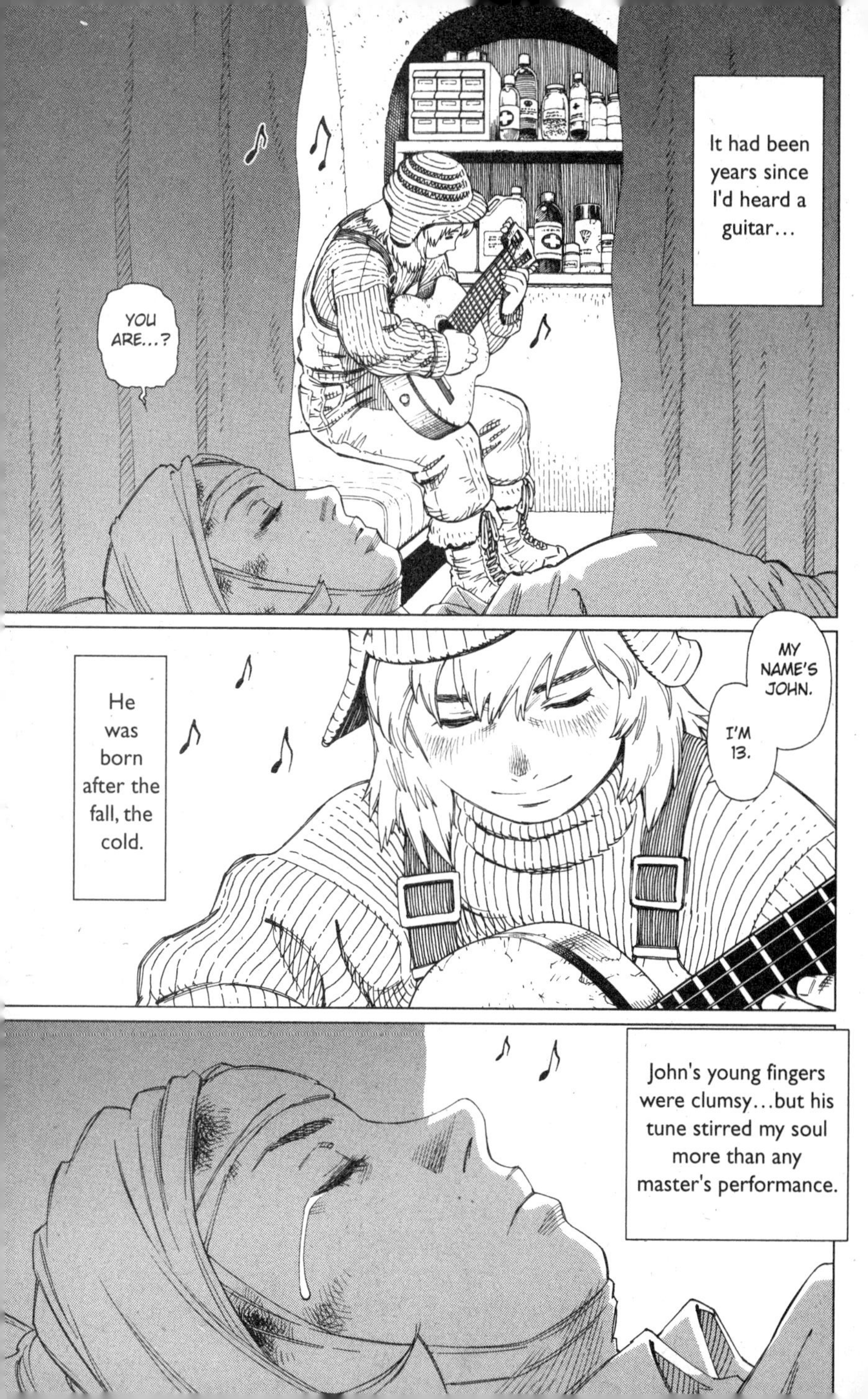
It had been years since I'd heard a guitar…
YOU ARE…?
MY NAME'S JOHN.
I'M 13.
He was born after the fall, the cold.
John's young fingers were clumsy…but his tune stirred my soul more than any master's performance.

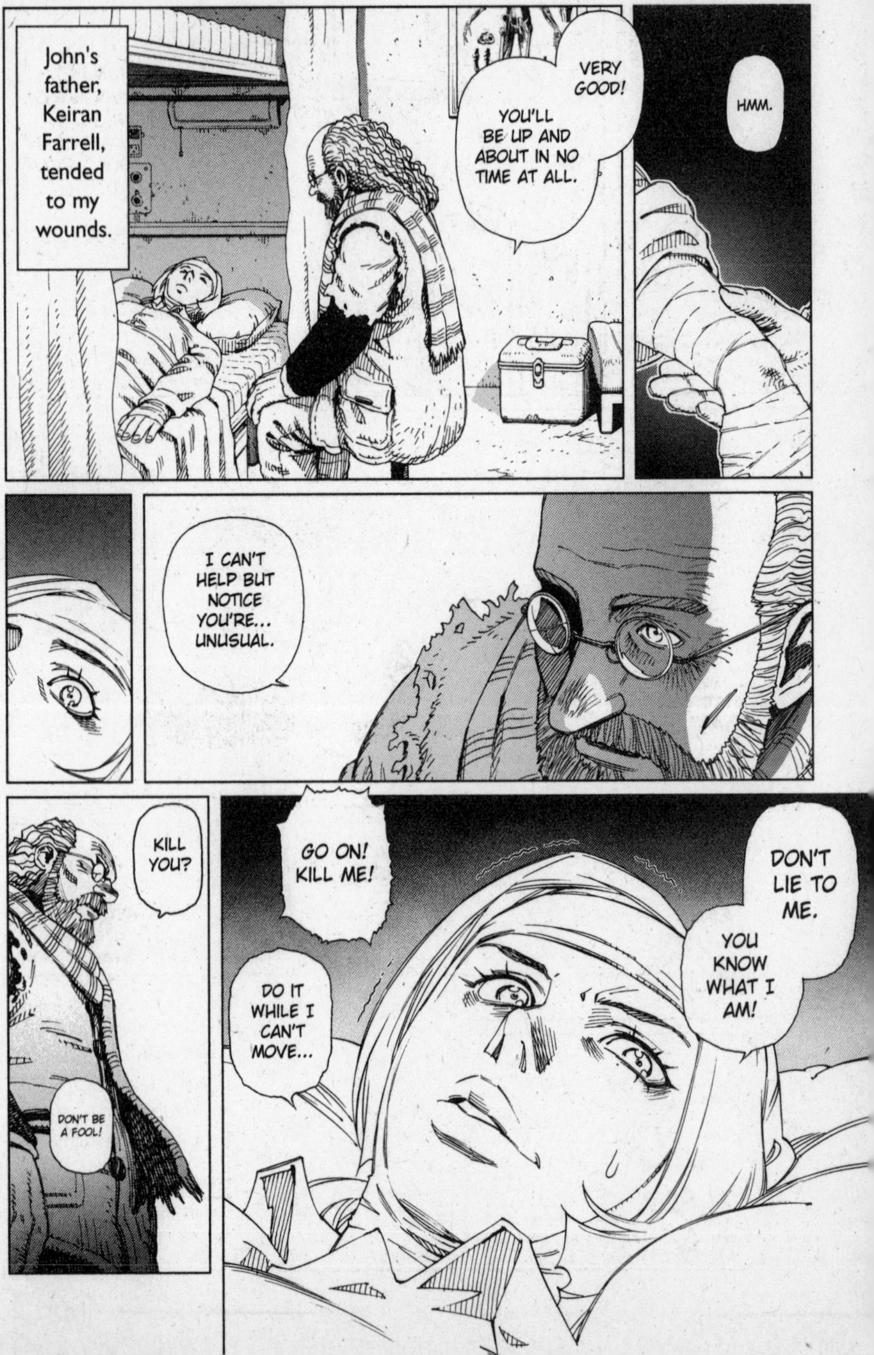
HMM.
VERY GOOD!
YOU'LL BE UP AND ABOUT IN NO TIME AT ALL.
John's father, Keiran Farrell, tended to my wounds.
I CAN'T HELP BUT NOTICE YOU'RE... UNUSUAL.
DON'T LIE TO ME.
YOU KNOW WHAT I AM!
GO ON! KILL ME!
DO IT WHILE I CAN'T MOVE...
KILL YOU?
DON'T BE A FOOL!

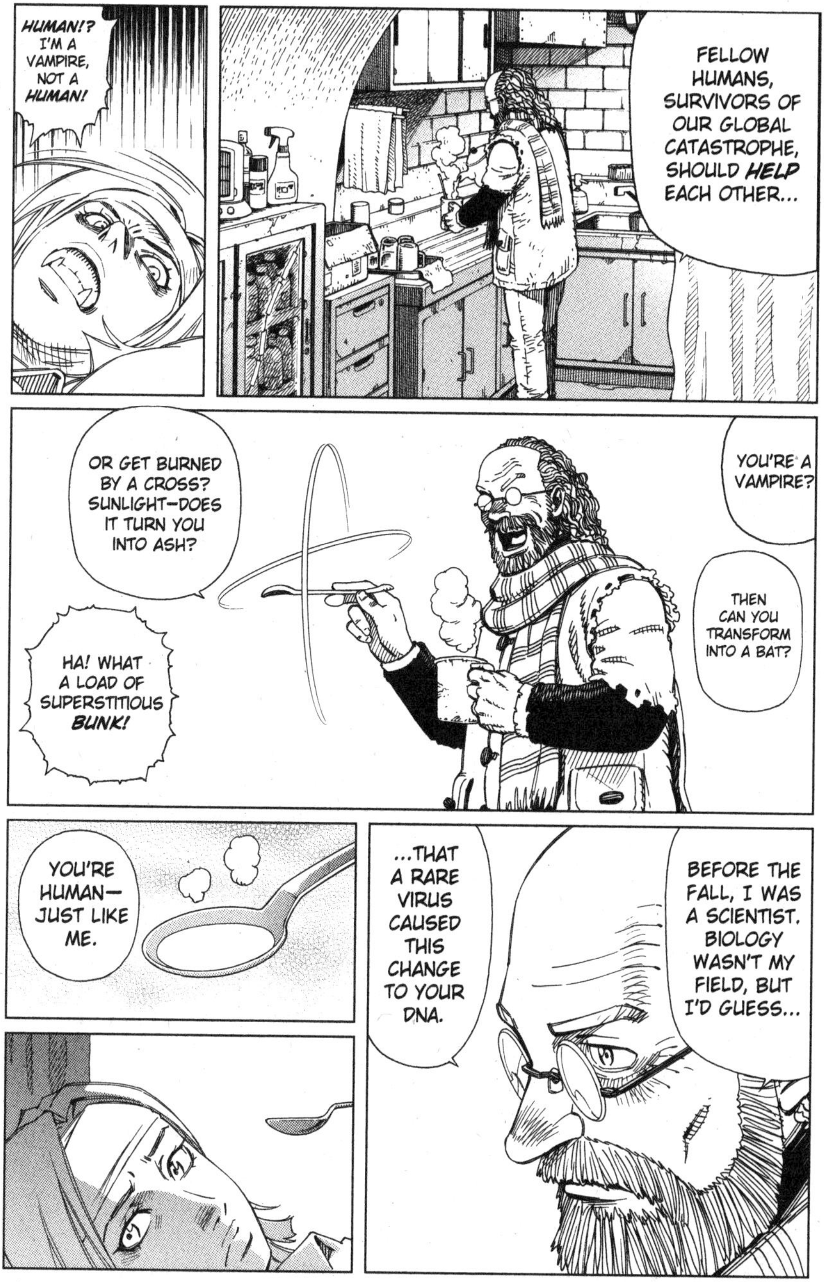
FELLOW HUMANS, SURVIVORS OF OUR GLOBAL CATASTROPHE, SHOULD HELP EACH OTHER...
HUMAN!? I'M A VAMPIRE, NOT A HUMAN!
YOU'RE A VAMPIRE?
THEN CAN YOU TRANSFORM INTO A BAT?
OR GET BURNED BY A CROSS? SUNLIGHT—DOES IT TURN YOU INTO ASH?
HA! WHAT A LOAD OF SUPERSTITIOUS BUNK!
BEFORE THE FALL, I WAS A SCIENTIST. BIOLOGY WASN'T MY FIELD, BUT I'D GUESS...
...THAT A RARE VIRUS CAUSED THIS CHANGE TO YOUR DNA.
YOU'RE HUMAN—JUST LIKE ME.

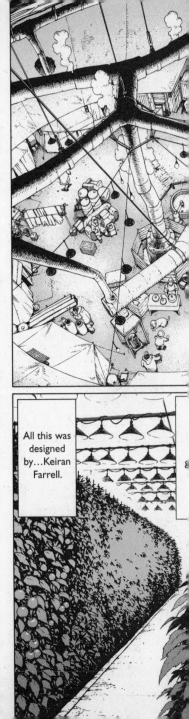

All this was designed by…Keiran Farrell.

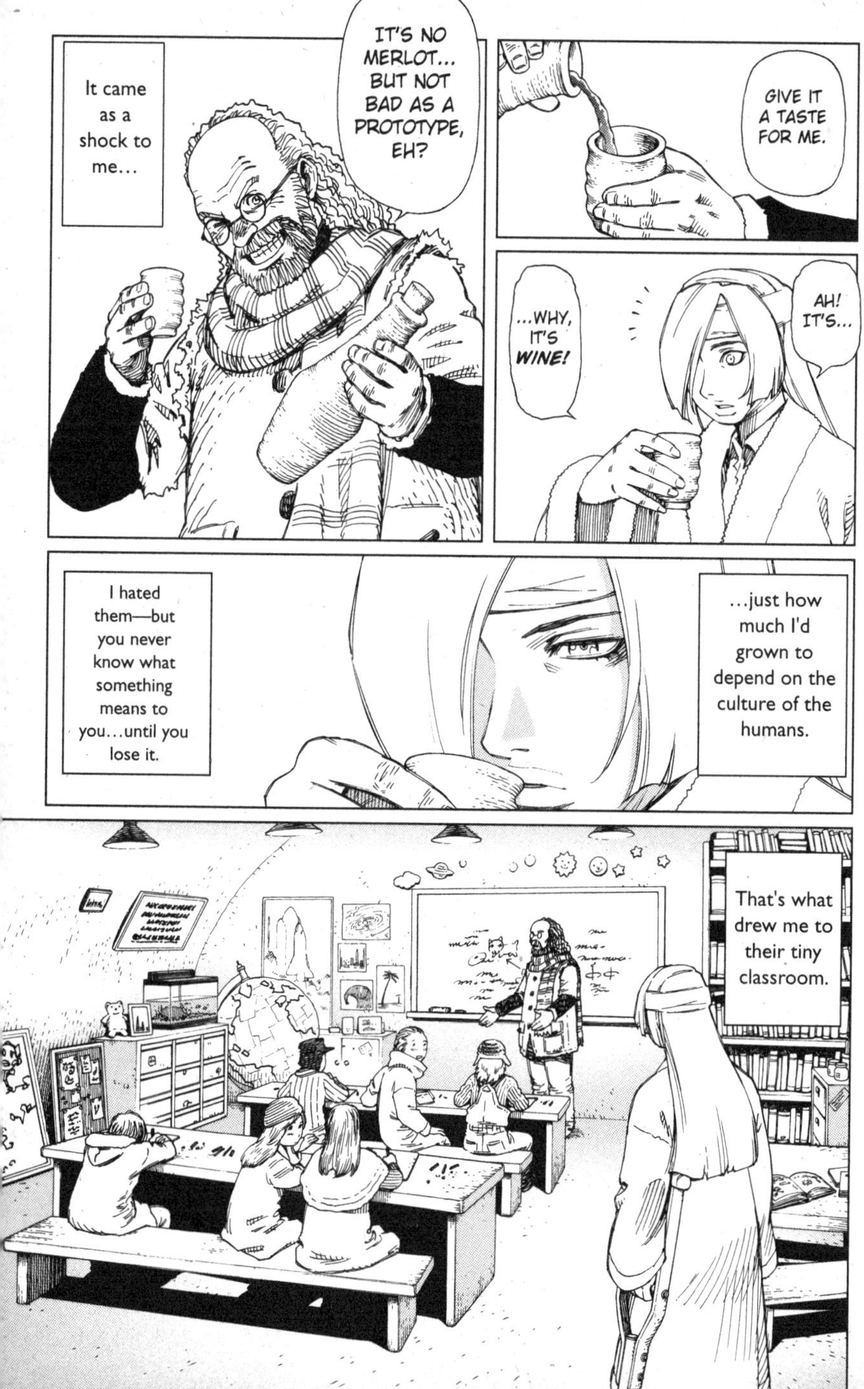
GIVE IT A TASTE FOR ME.
AH! IT'S...
...WHY, IT'S *WINE!*
IT'S NO MERLOT... BUT NOT BAD AS A PROTOTYPE, EH?
It came as a shock to me...
...just how much I'd grown to depend on the culture of the humans.
I hated them—but you never know what something means to you...until you lose it.
That's what drew me to their tiny classroom.

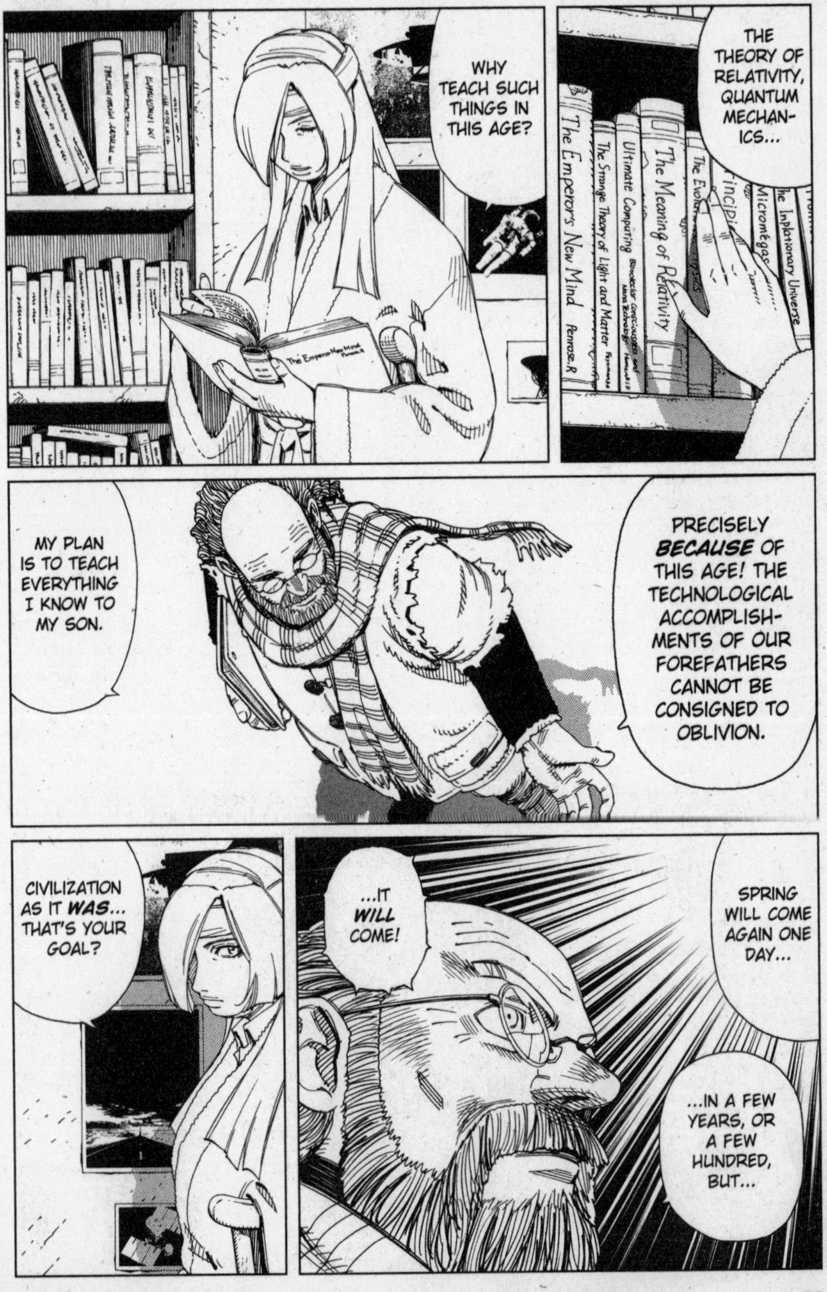
THE THEORY OF RELATIVITY, QUANTUM MECHAN-ICS...
The Emperor's New Mind
Penrose.R
The Strange Theory of Light and Matter
Ultimate Computing
The Meaning of Relativity
Micromégas
WHY TEACH SUCH THINGS IN THIS AGE?
PRECISELY **BECAUSE** OF THIS AGE! THE TECHNOLOGICAL ACCOMPLISH-MENTS OF OUR FOREFATHERS CANNOT BE CONSIGNED TO OBLIVION.
MY PLAN IS TO TEACH EVERYTHING I KNOW TO MY SON.
SPRING WILL COME AGAIN ONE DAY...
...IN A FEW YEARS, OR A FEW HUNDRED, BUT...
...IT **WILL** COME!
CIVILIZATION AS IT **WAS**... THAT'S YOUR GOAL?

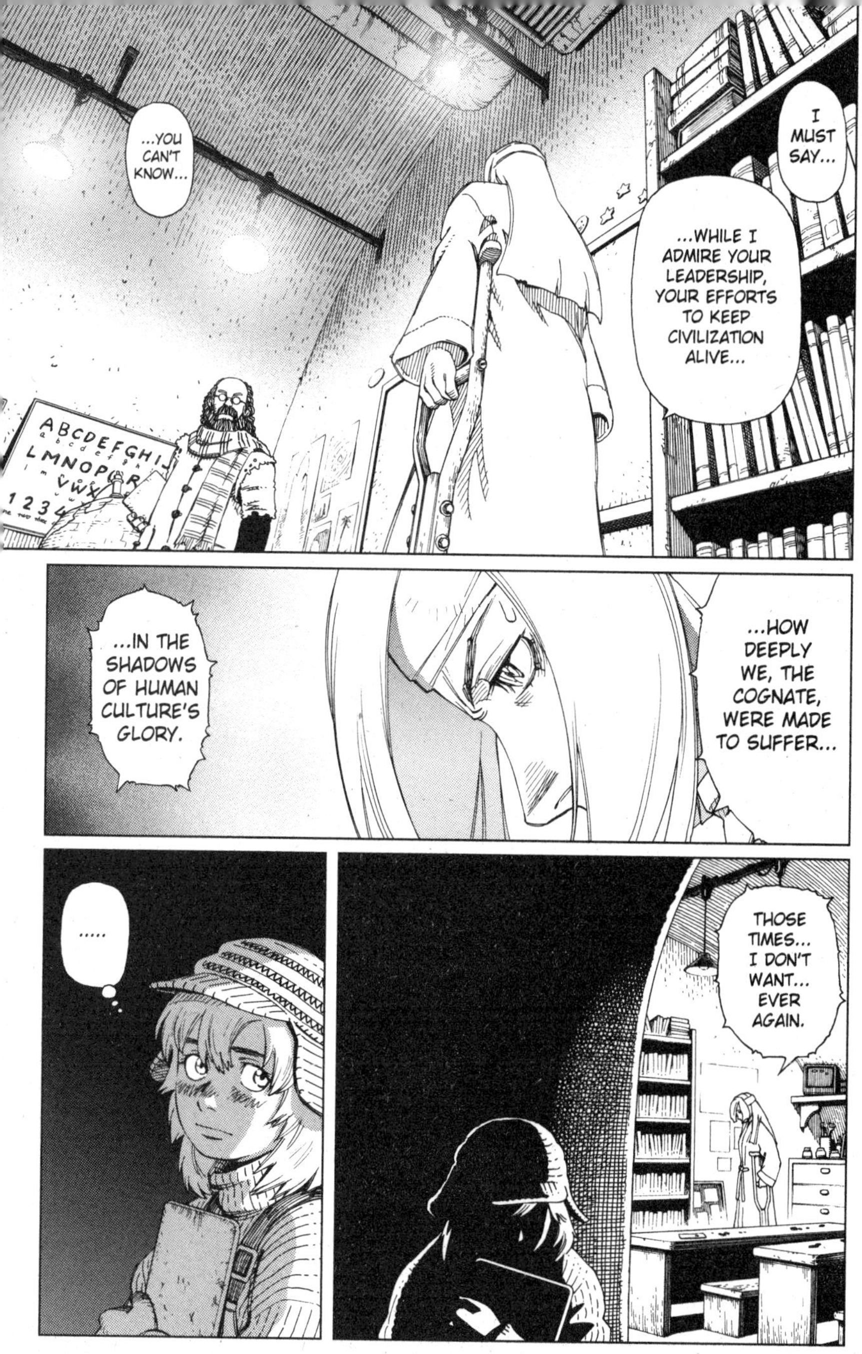
I MUST SAY...
...WHILE I ADMIRE YOUR LEADERSHIP, YOUR EFFORTS TO KEEP CIVILIZATION ALIVE...
...YOU CAN'T KNOW...
...HOW DEEPLY WE, THE COGNATE, WERE MADE TO SUFFER...
...IN THE SHADOWS OF HUMAN CULTURE'S GLORY.
THOSE TIMES... I DON'T WANT... EVER AGAIN.
.....

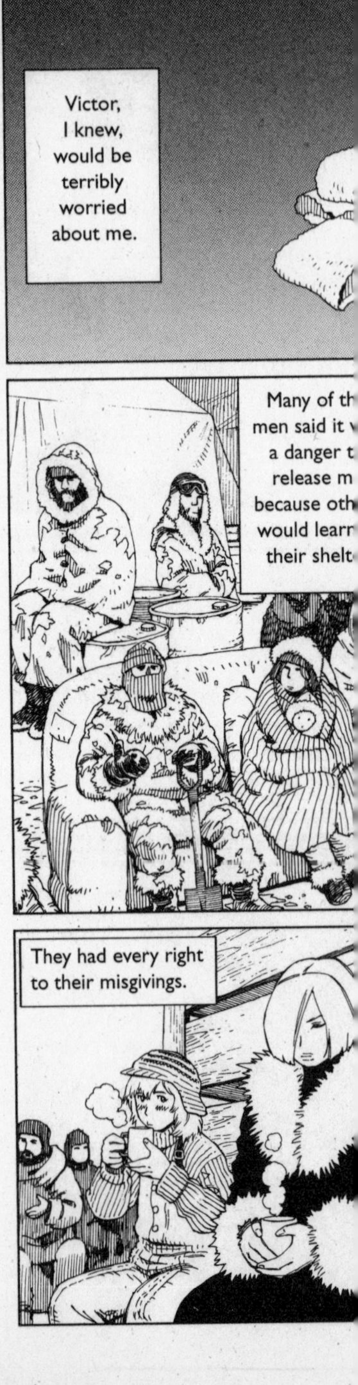
Victor, I knew, would be terribly worried about me.
Many of th men said it a danger t release m because oth would learn their shelt
They had every right to their misgivings.

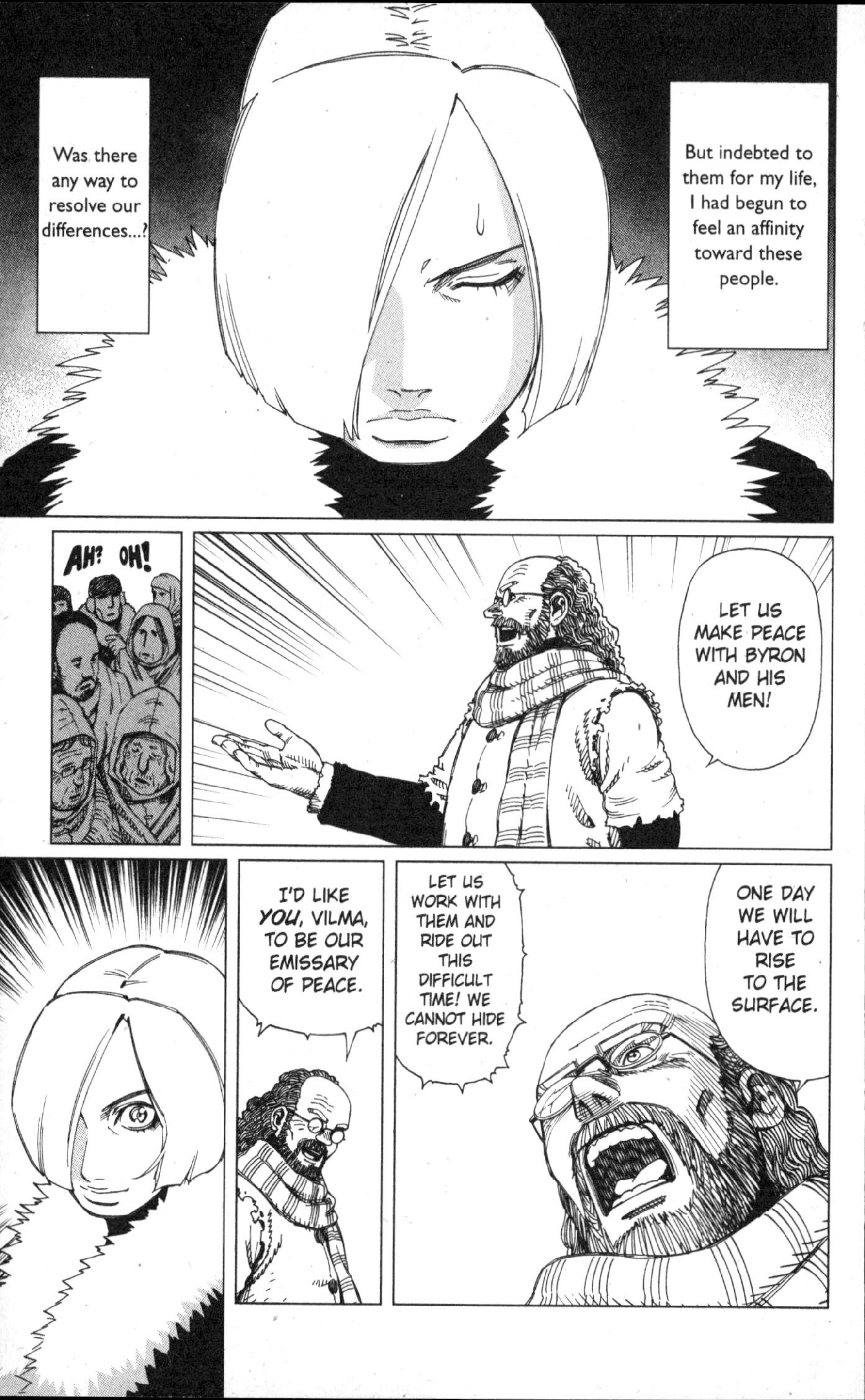
But indebted to them for my life, I had begun to feel an affinity toward these people.
Was there any way to resolve our differences...?
LET US MAKE PEACE WITH BYRON AND HIS MEN!
AH? OH!
ONE DAY WE WILL HAVE TO RISE TO THE SURFACE.
LET US WORK WITH THEM AND RIDE OUT THIS DIFFICULT TIME! WE CANNOT HIDE FOREVER.
I'D LIKE *YOU*, VILMA, TO BE OUR EMISSARY OF PEACE.

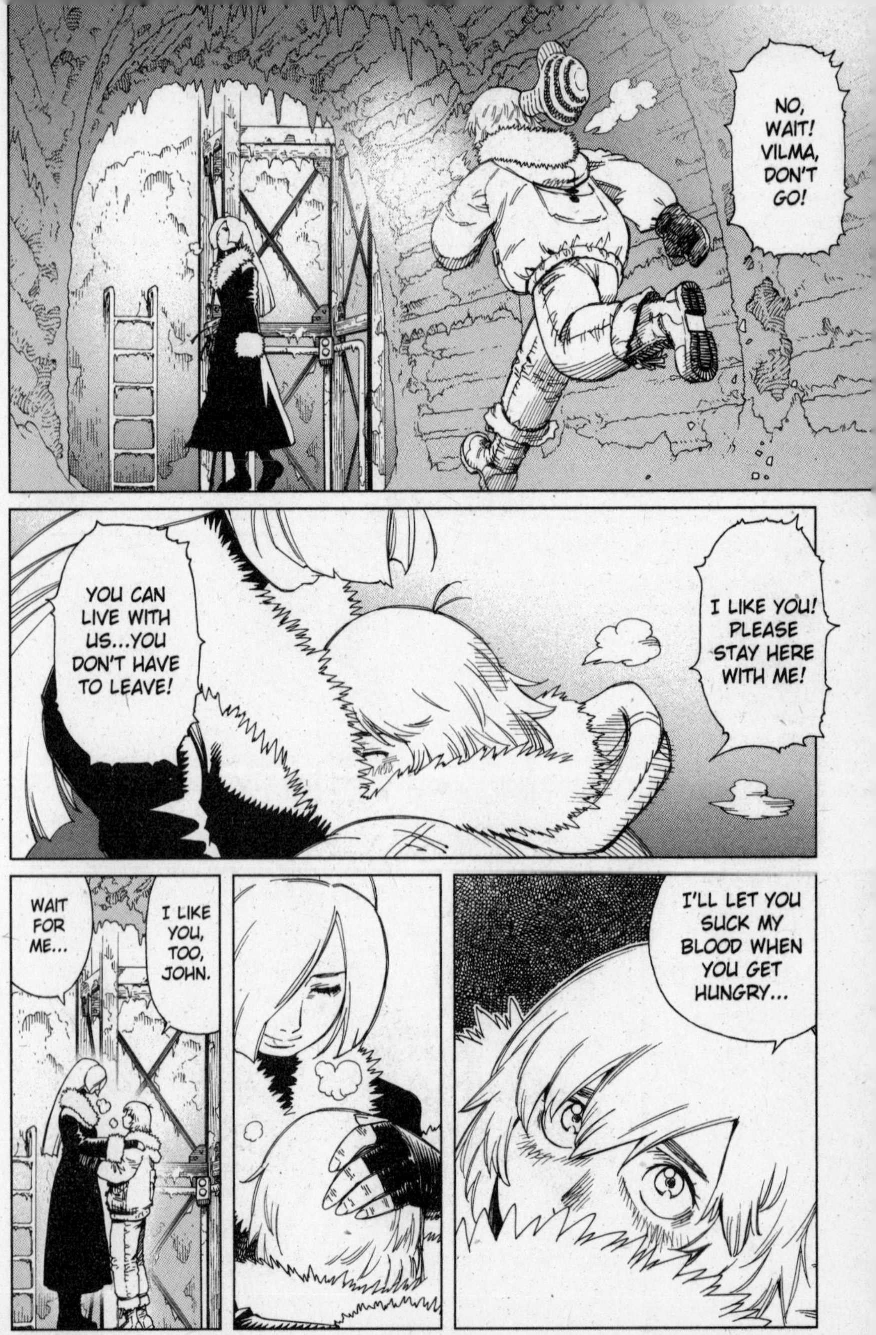
NO, WAIT! VILMA, DON'T GO!
I LIKE YOU! PLEASE STAY HERE WITH ME!
YOU CAN LIVE WITH US...YOU DON'T HAVE TO LEAVE!
I'LL LET YOU SUCK MY BLOOD WHEN YOU GET HUNGRY...
I LIKE YOU, TOO, JOHN.
WAIT FOR ME...

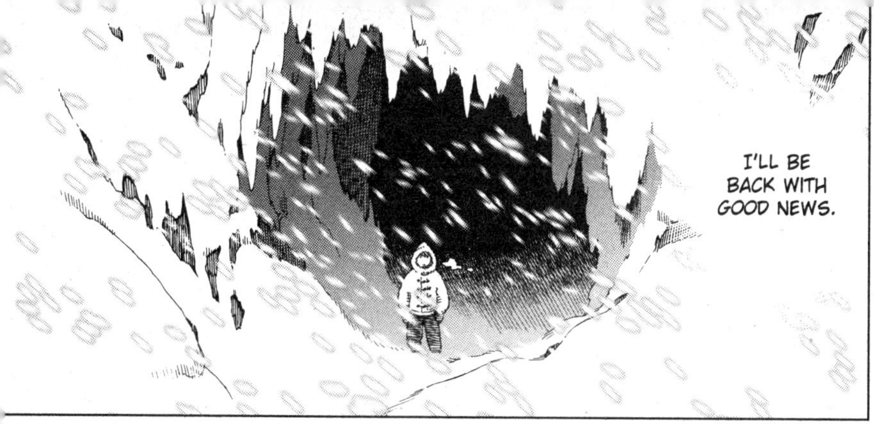
I'LL BE BACK WITH GOOD NEWS.
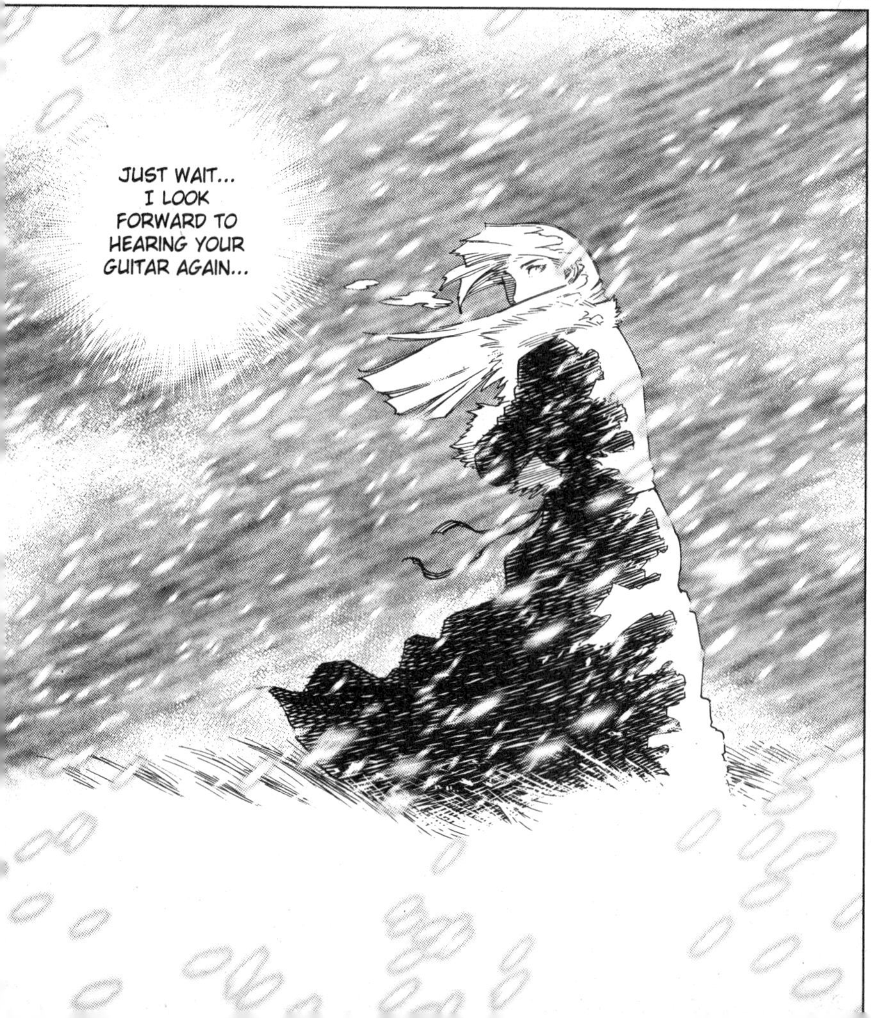
JUST WAIT... I LOOK FORWARD TO HEARING YOUR GUITAR AGAIN...

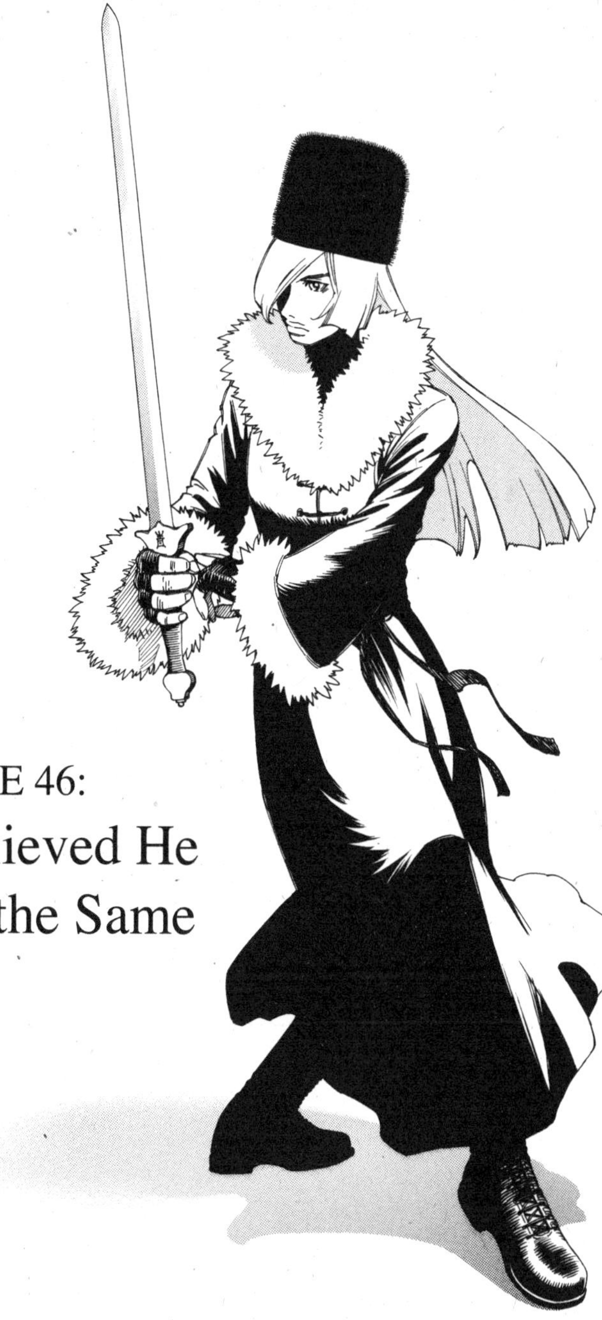

PHASE 46:
I Believed He Felt the Same

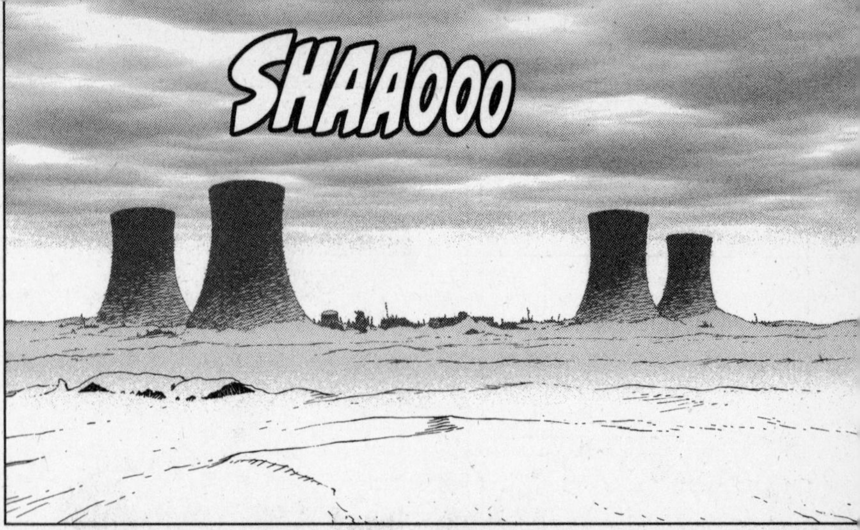
SHAAOOO
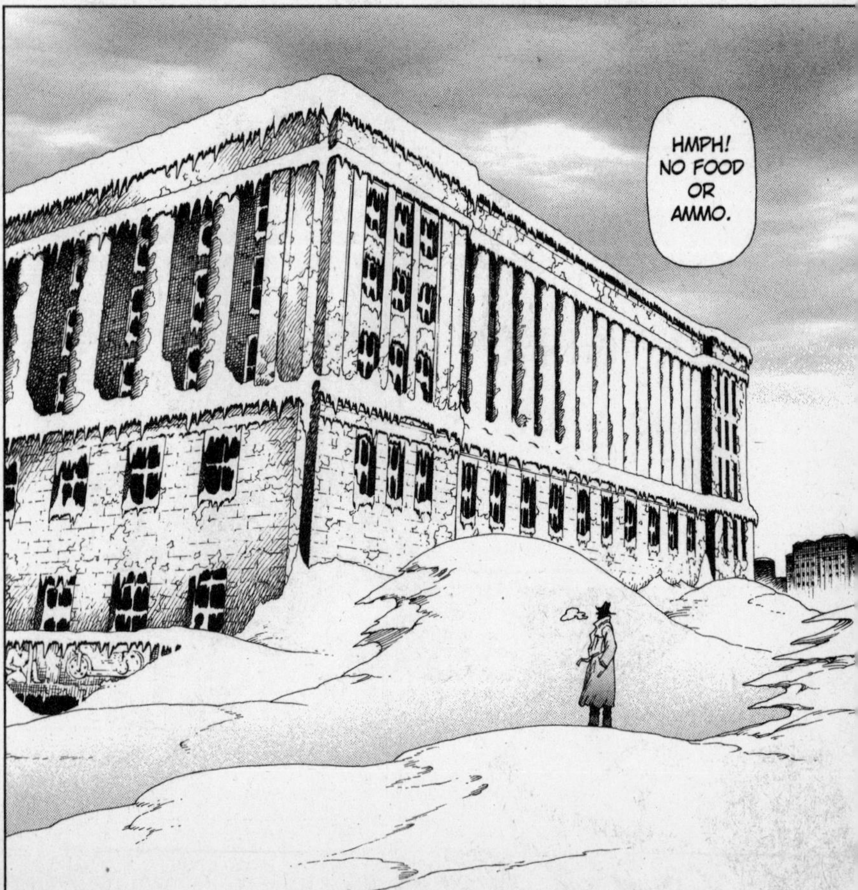
HMPH! NO FOOD OR AMMO.

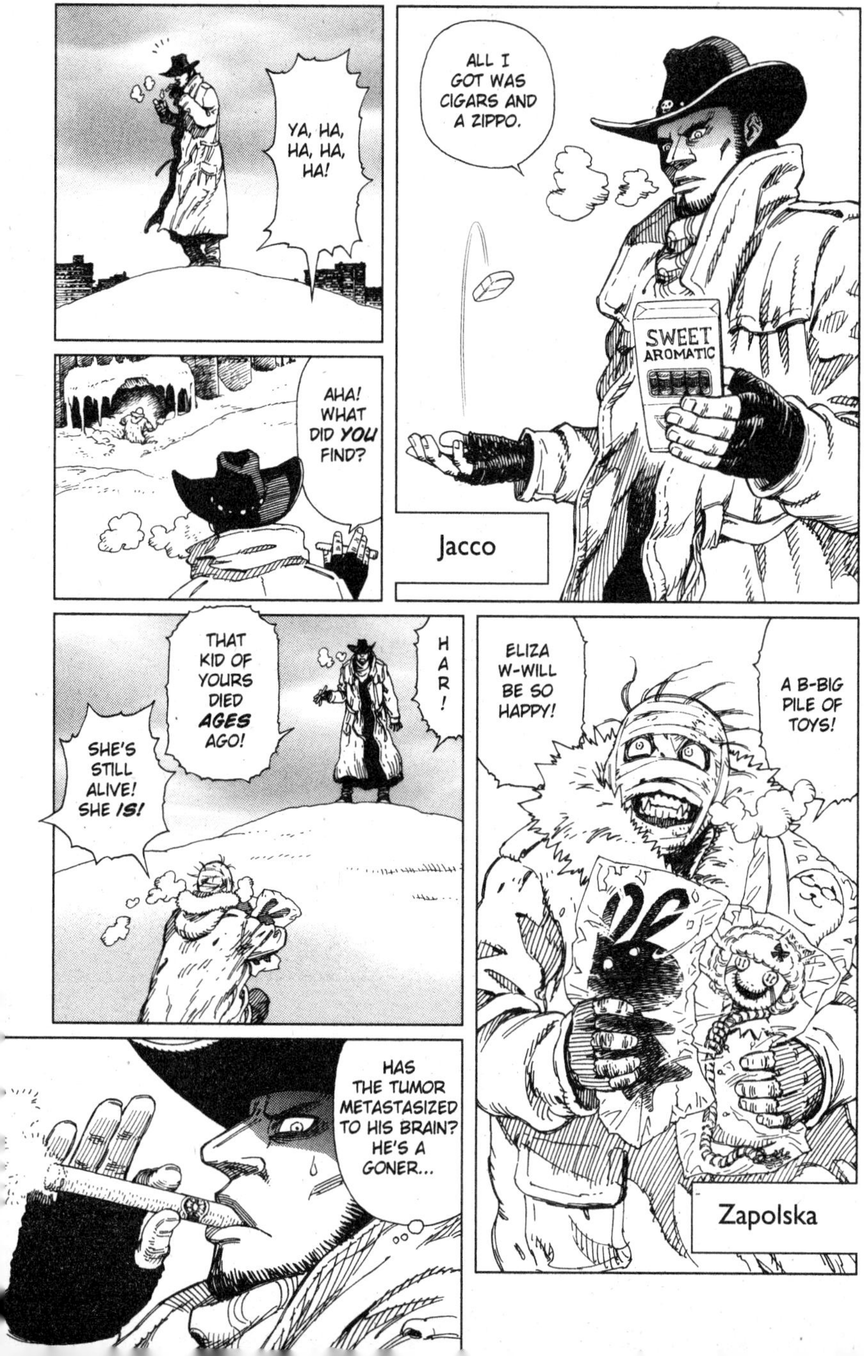
ALL I GOT WAS CIGARS AND A ZIPPO.
SWEET AROMATIC
Jacco
YA, HA, HA, HA, HA!
AHA! WHAT DID **YOU** FIND?
A B-BIG PILE OF TOYS!
ELIZA W-WILL BE SO HAPPY!
Zapolska
HAR!
THAT KID OF YOURS DIED **AGES** AGO!
SHE'S STILL ALIVE! SHE **IS!**
HAS THE TUMOR METASTASIZED TO HIS BRAIN? HE'S A GONER...

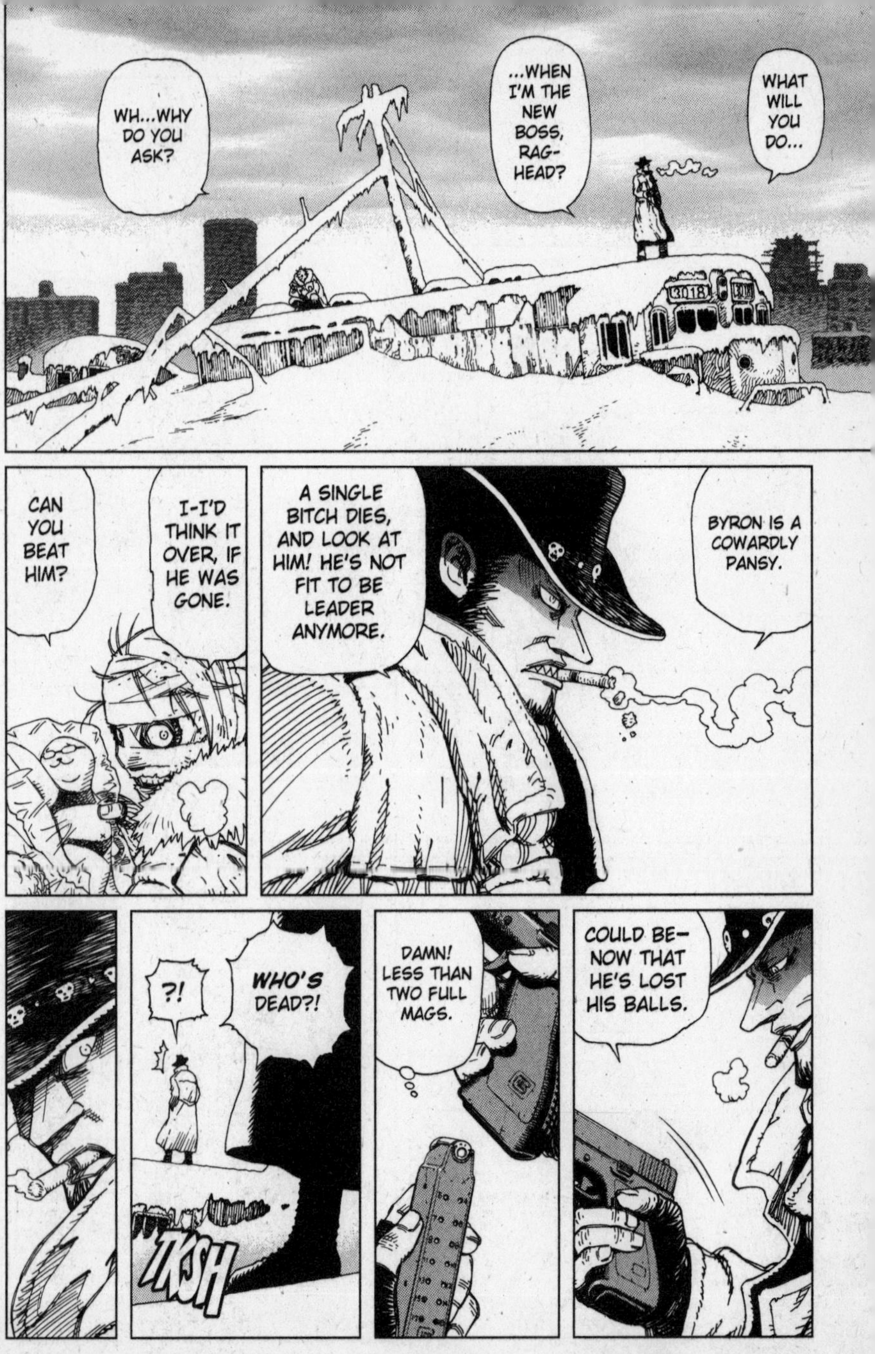
WHAT WILL YOU DO...
...WHEN I'M THE NEW BOSS, RAG-HEAD?
WH...WHY DO YOU ASK?
BYRON IS A COWARDLY PANSY.
A SINGLE BITCH DIES, AND LOOK AT HIM! HE'S NOT FIT TO BE LEADER ANYMORE.
I-I'D THINK IT OVER, IF HE WAS GONE.
CAN YOU BEAT HIM?
COULD BE— NOW THAT HE'S LOST HIS BALLS.
DAMN! LESS THAN TWO FULL MAGS.
WHO'S DEAD?!
?!
TKSH

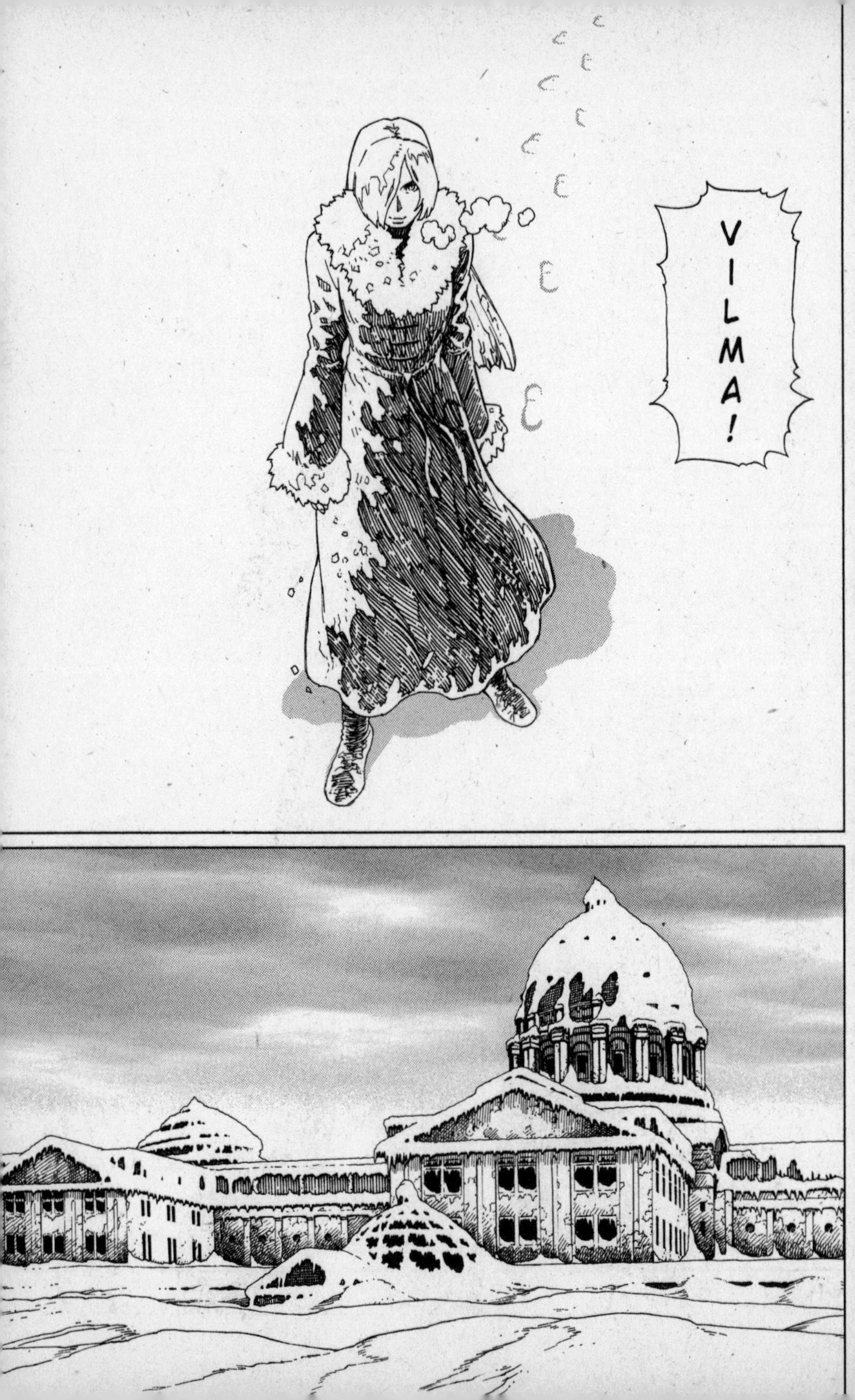
VILMA!

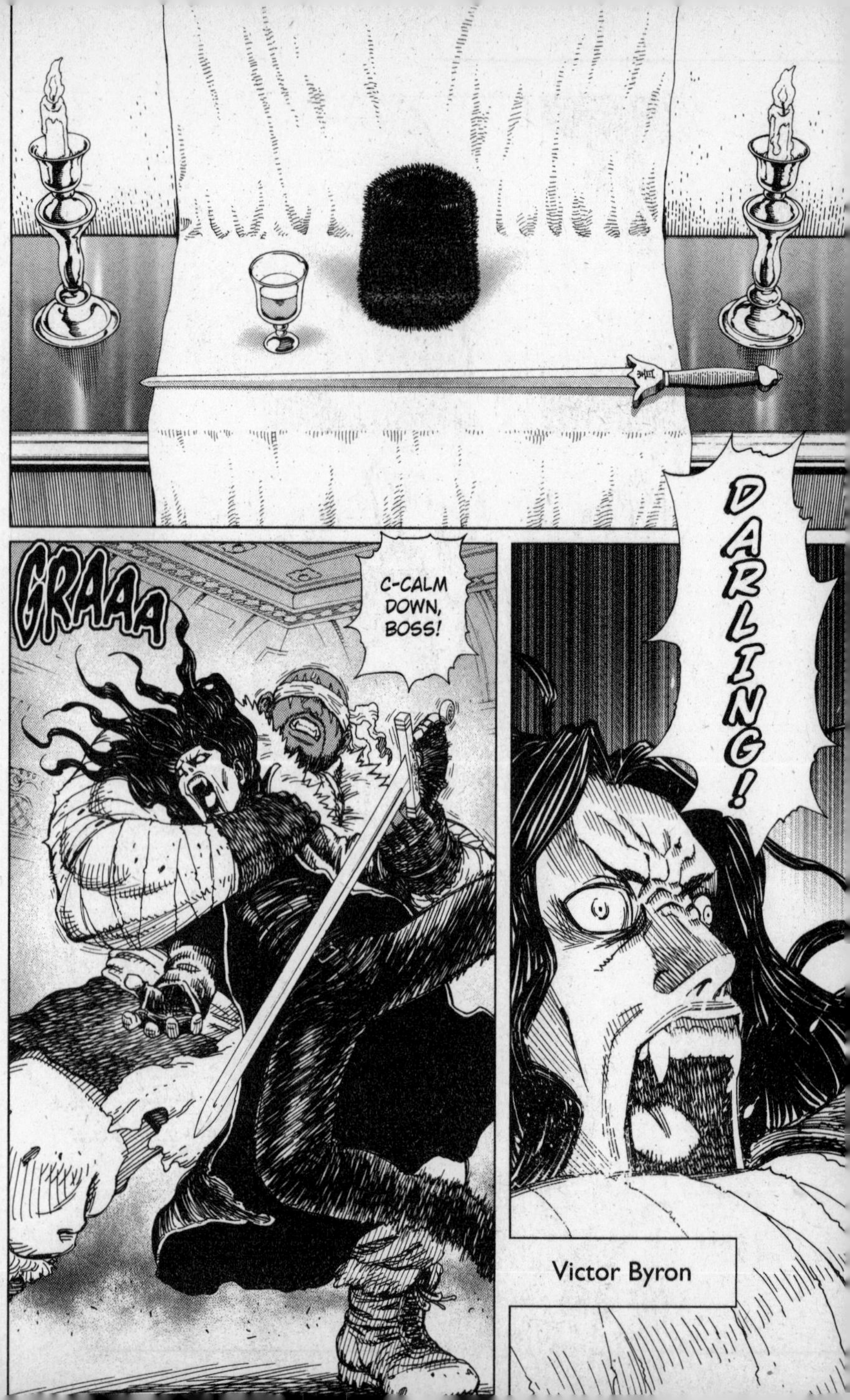
DARLING!
Victor Byron
GRAAA
C-CALM DOWN, BOSS!

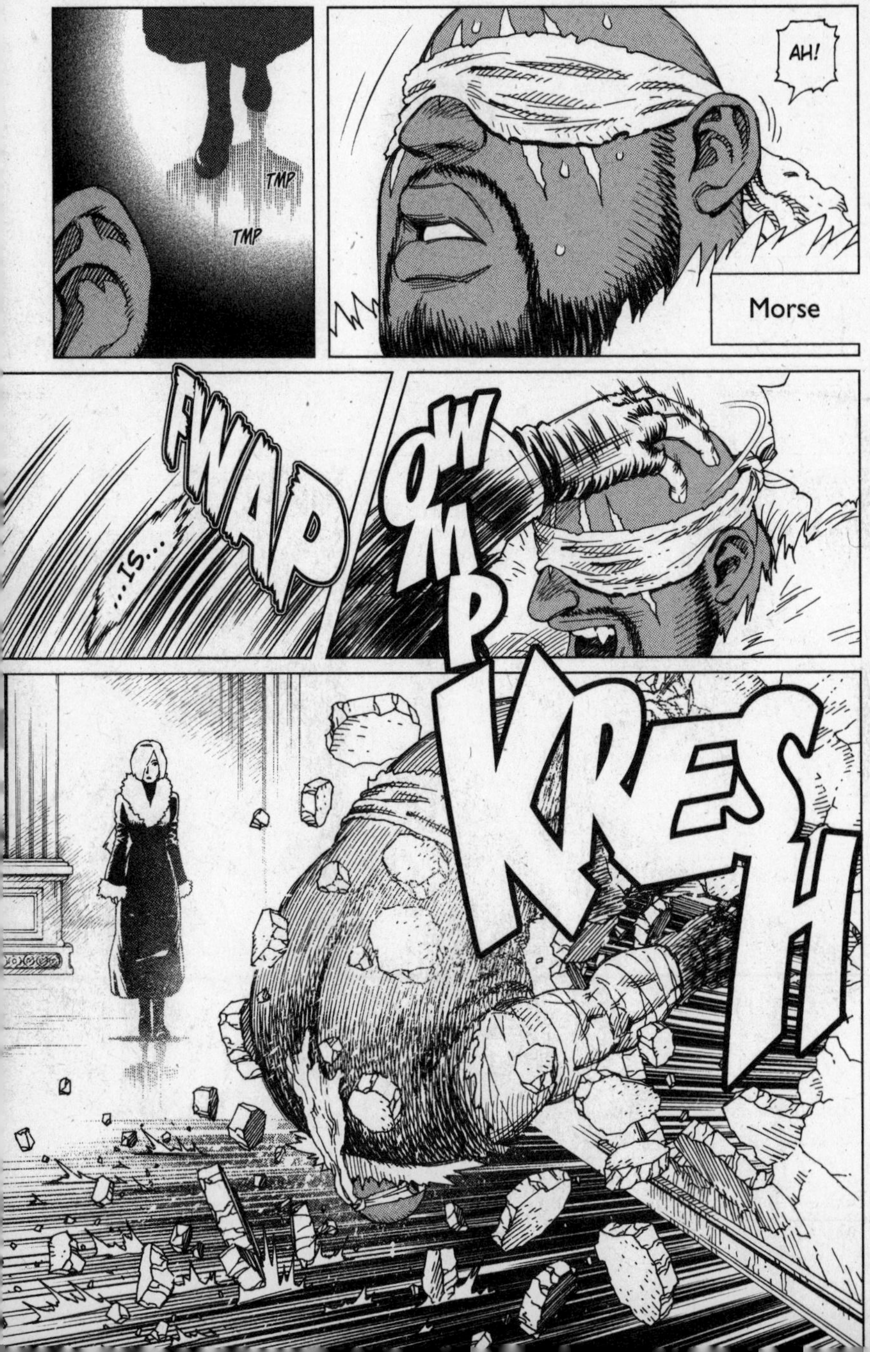
AH!
Morse
TMP
TMP
OWMP
FWAP
...IS...
KRESH

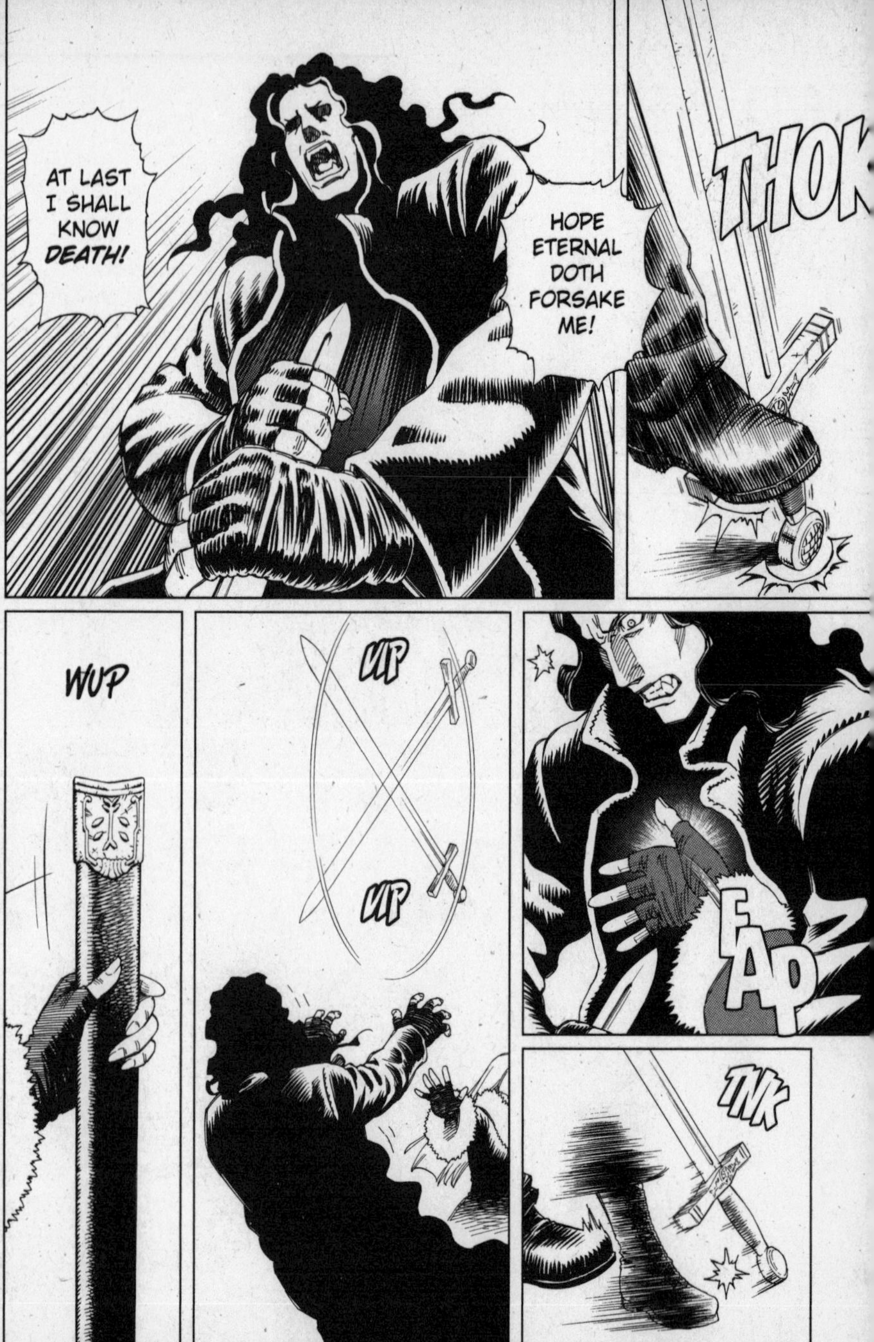
THOK
HOPE ETERNAL DOTH FORSAKE ME!
AT LAST I SHALL KNOW DEATH!
FAP
TNK
VIP
VIP
WUP

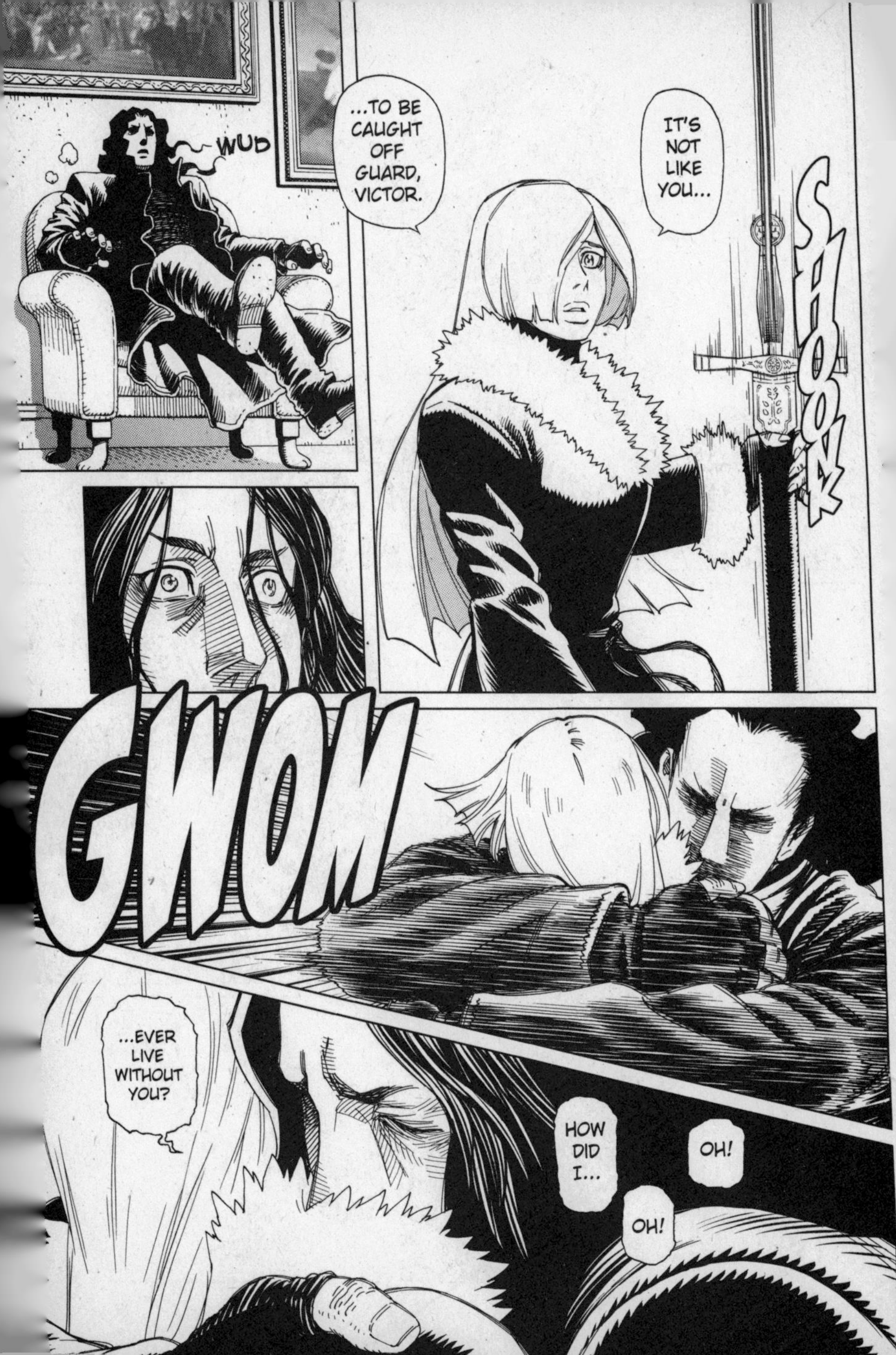
SHOONK
IT'S NOT LIKE YOU...
...TO BE CAUGHT OFF GUARD, VICTOR.
WUD
GWOM
OH!
HOW DID I...
OH!
...EVER LIVE WITHOUT YOU?

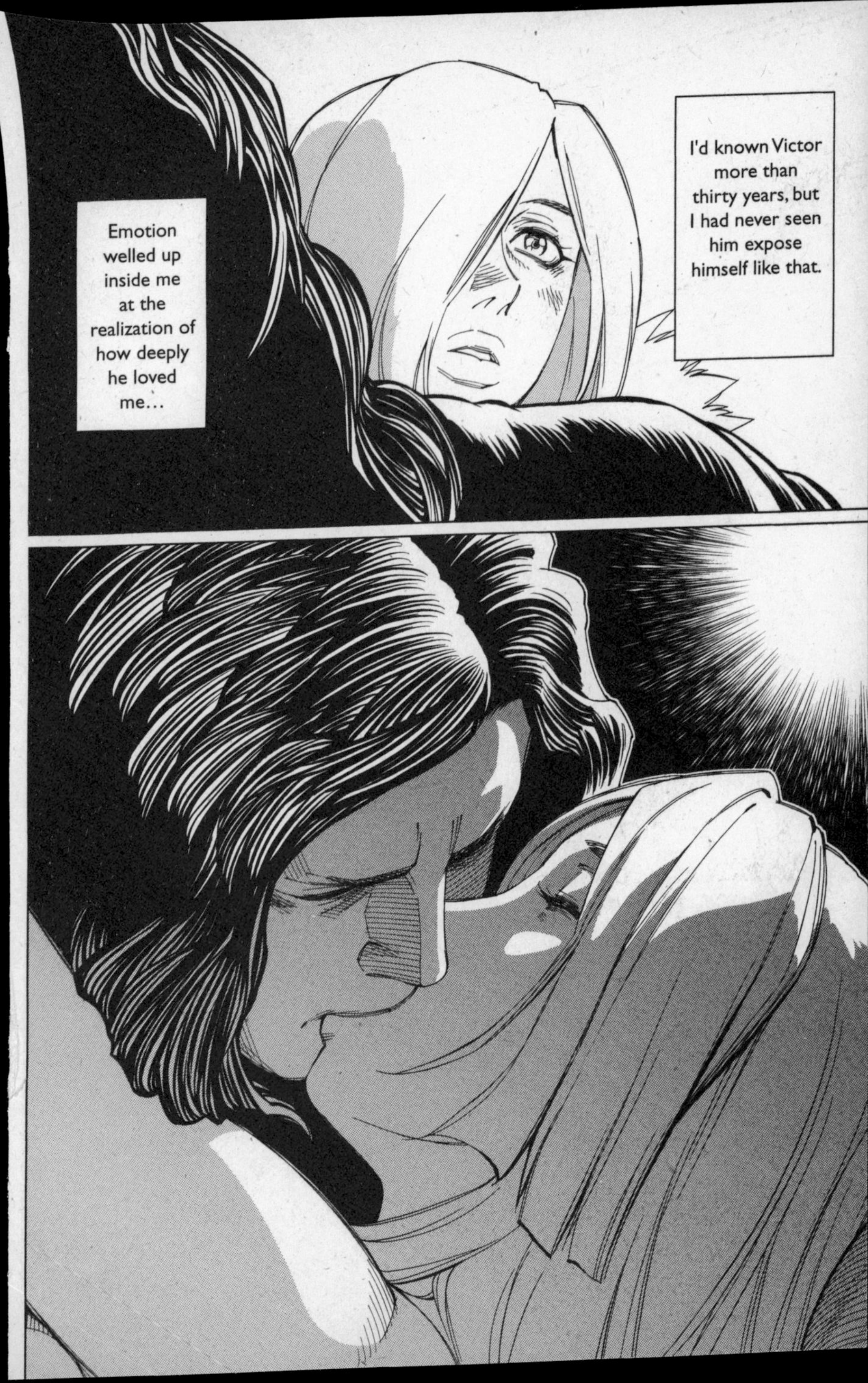
I'd known Victor more than thirty years, but I had never seen him expose himself like that.
Emotion welled up inside me at the realization of how deeply he loved me...

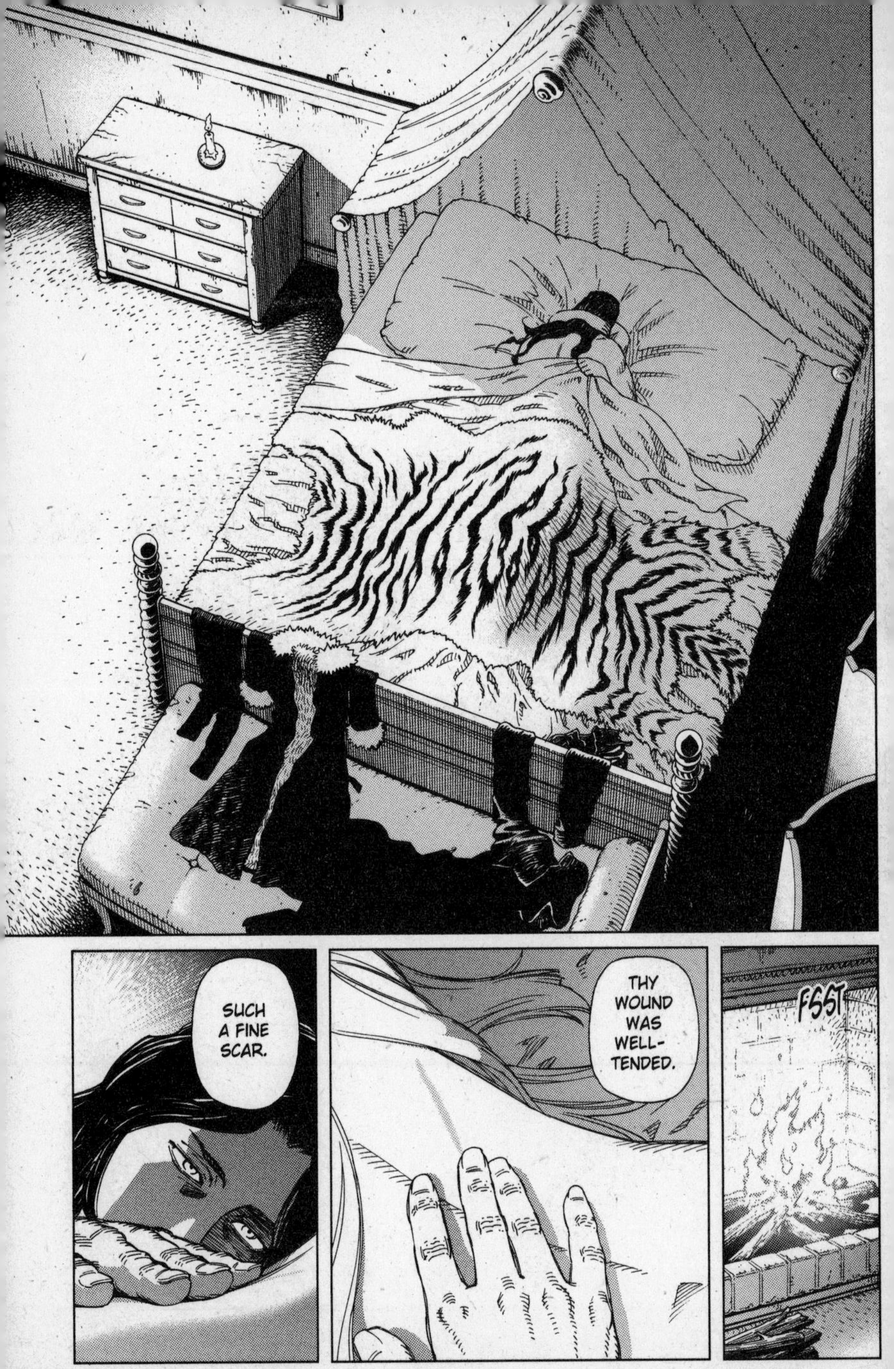
FSST
THY WOUND WAS WELL-TENDED.
SUCH A FINE SCAR.

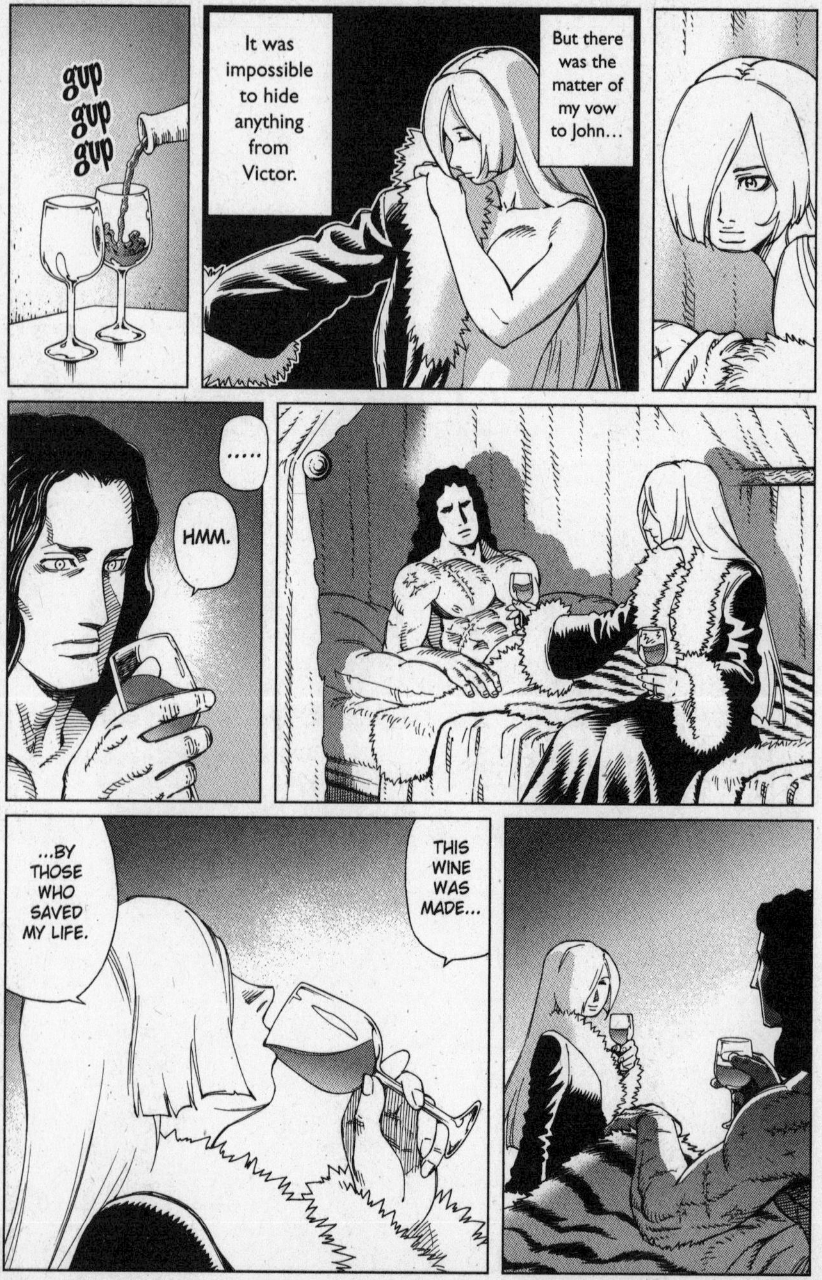
It was impossible to hide anything from Victor.
But there was the matter of my vow to John...
gup gup gup
......
HMM.
THIS WINE WAS MADE...
...BY THOSE WHO SAVED MY LIFE.

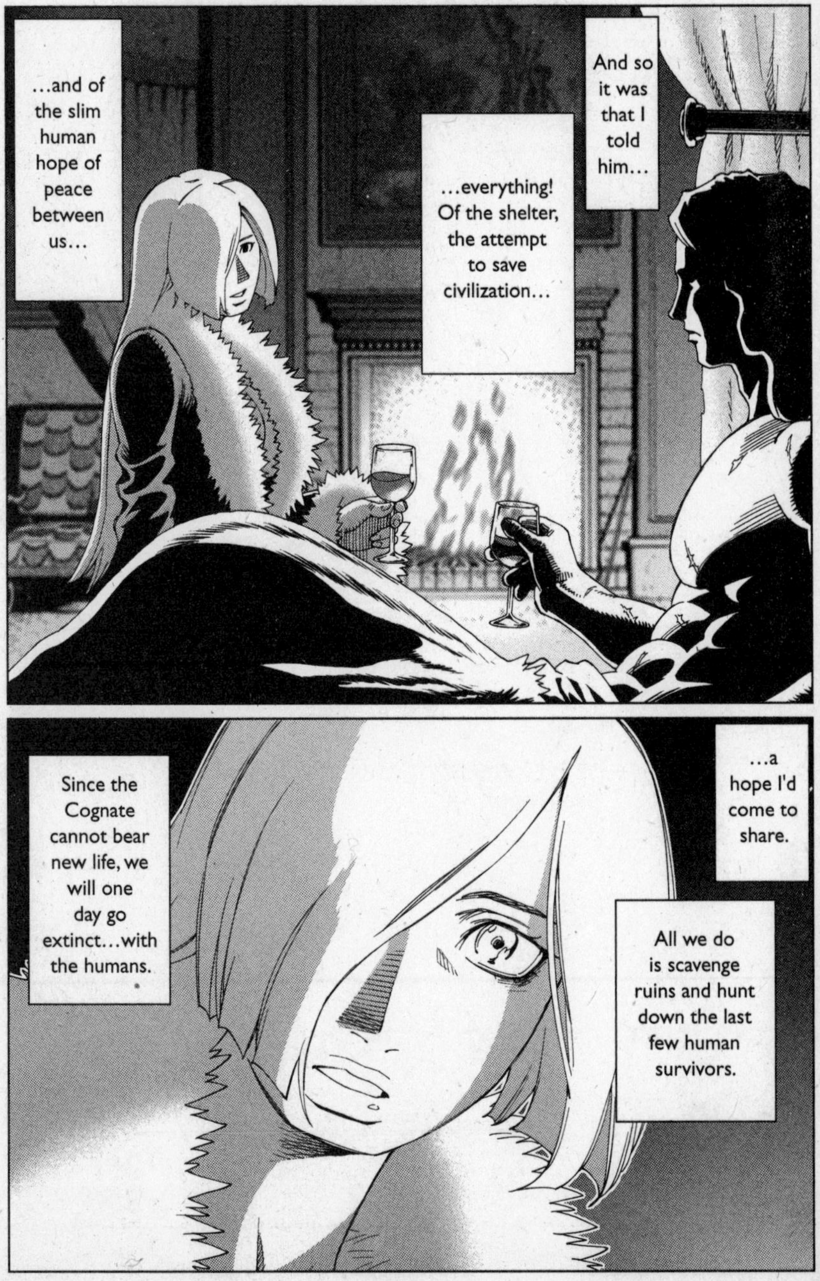
And so it was that I told him...
...everything! Of the shelter, the attempt to save civilization...
...and of the slim human hope of peace between us...
...a hope I'd come to share.
All we do is scavenge ruins and hunt down the last few human survivors.
Since the Cognate cannot bear new life, we will one day go extinct...with the humans.

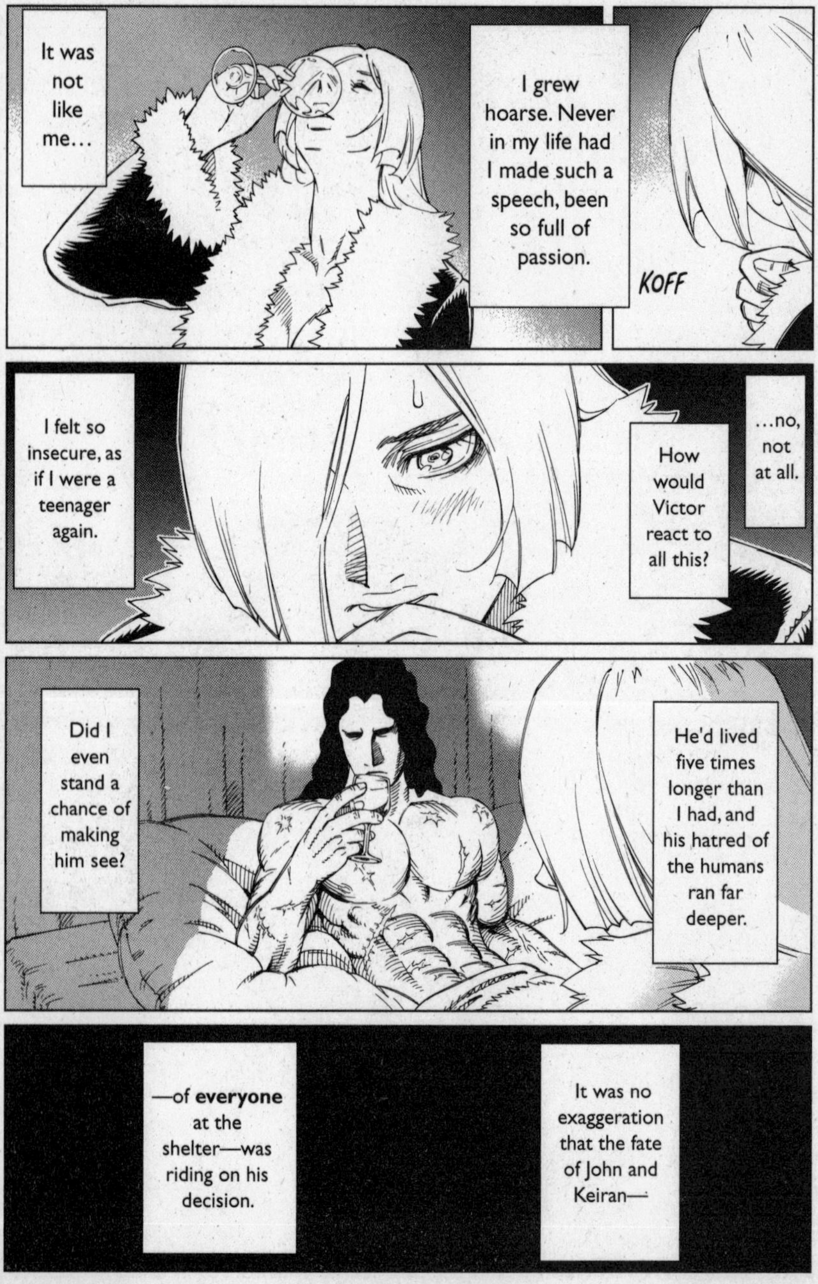
KOFF
I grew hoarse. Never in my life had I made such a speech, been so full of passion.
It was not like me...
...no, not at all.
How would Victor react to all this?
I felt so insecure, as if I were a teenager again.
He'd lived five times longer than I had, and his hatred of the humans ran far deeper.
Did I even stand a chance of making him see?
It was no exaggeration that the fate of John and Keiran—
—of **everyone** at the shelter—was riding on his decision.

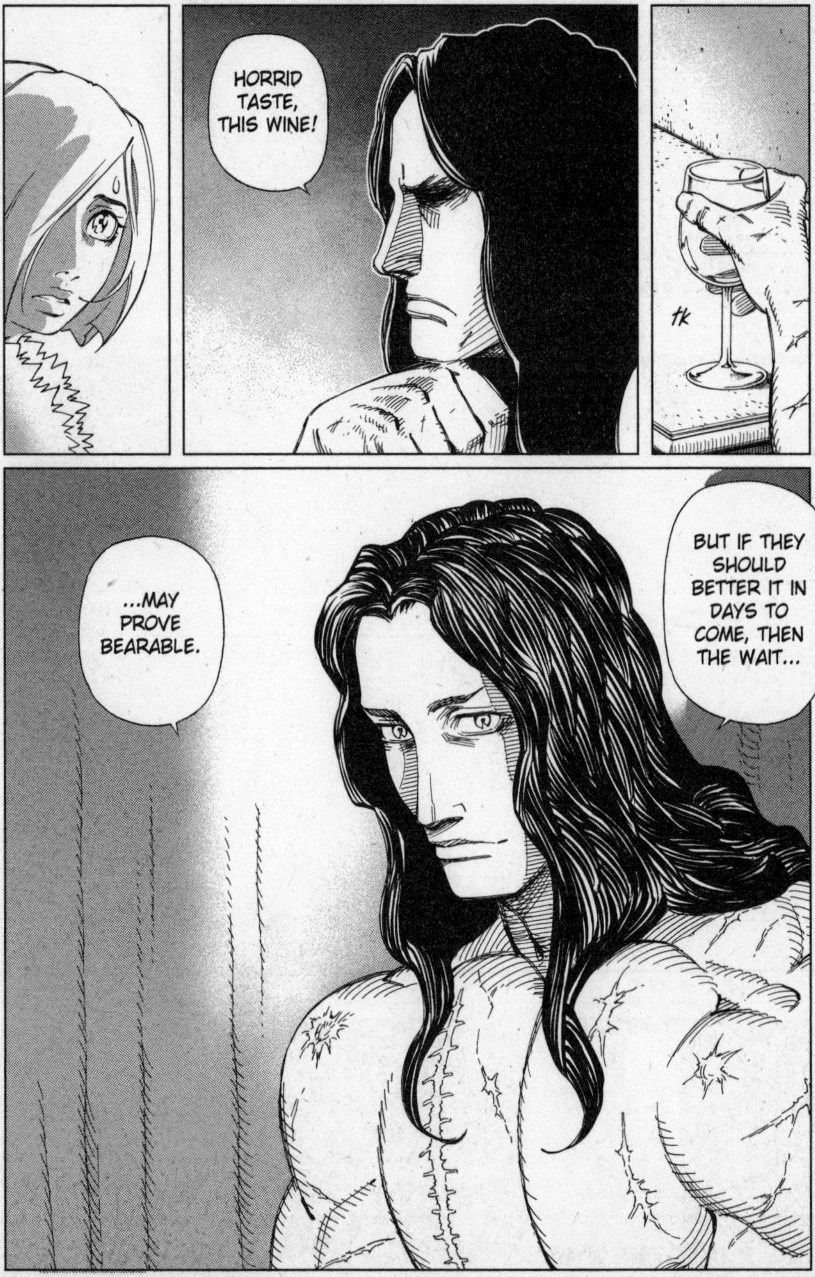
tk
HORRID TASTE, THIS WINE!
BUT IF THEY SHOULD BETTER IT IN DAYS TO COME, THEN THE WAIT...
...MAY PROVE BEARABLE.

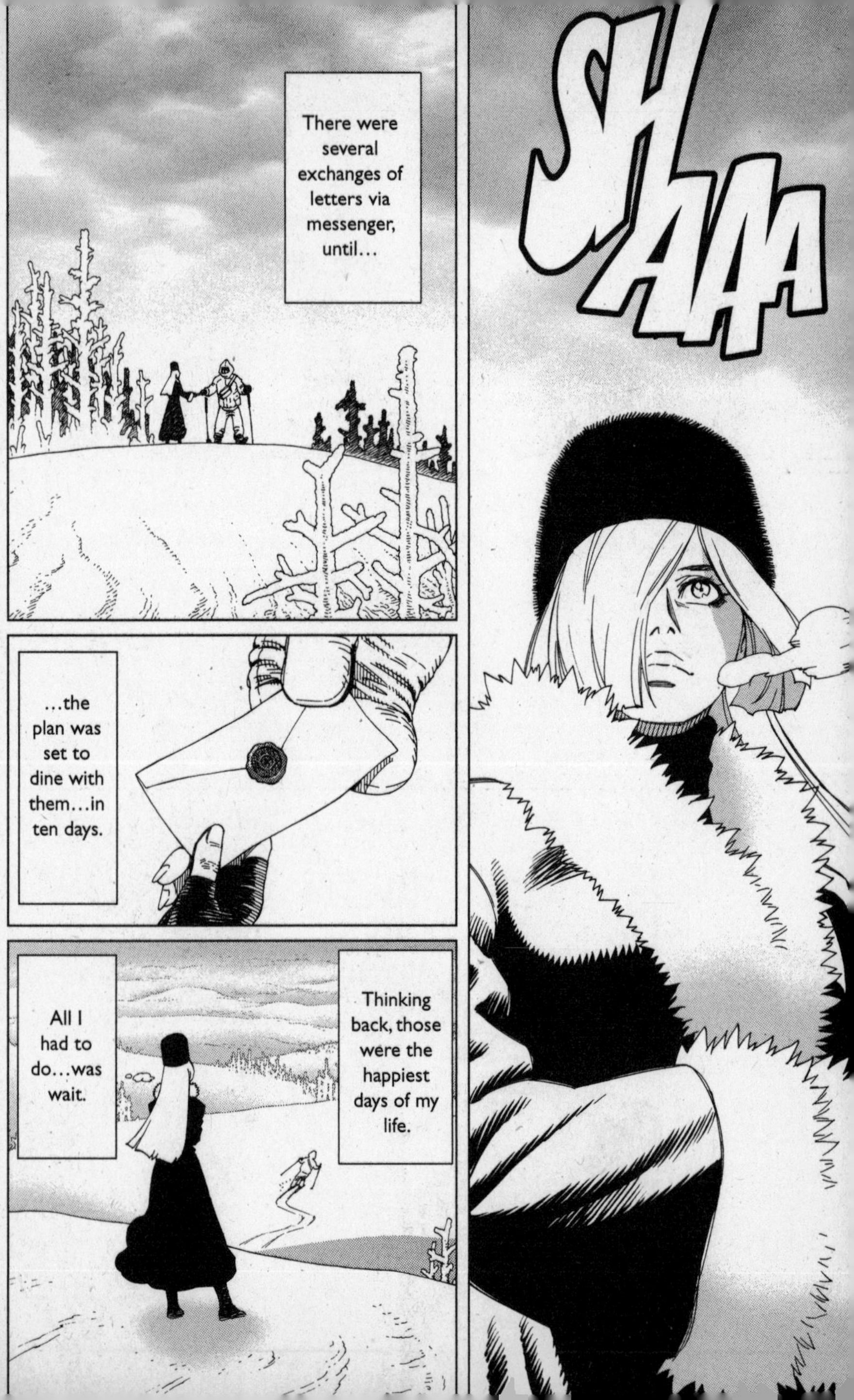
SHAAA
There were several exchanges of letters via messenger, until…
…the plan was set to dine with them…in ten days.
Thinking back, those were the happiest days of my life.
All I had to do…was wait.

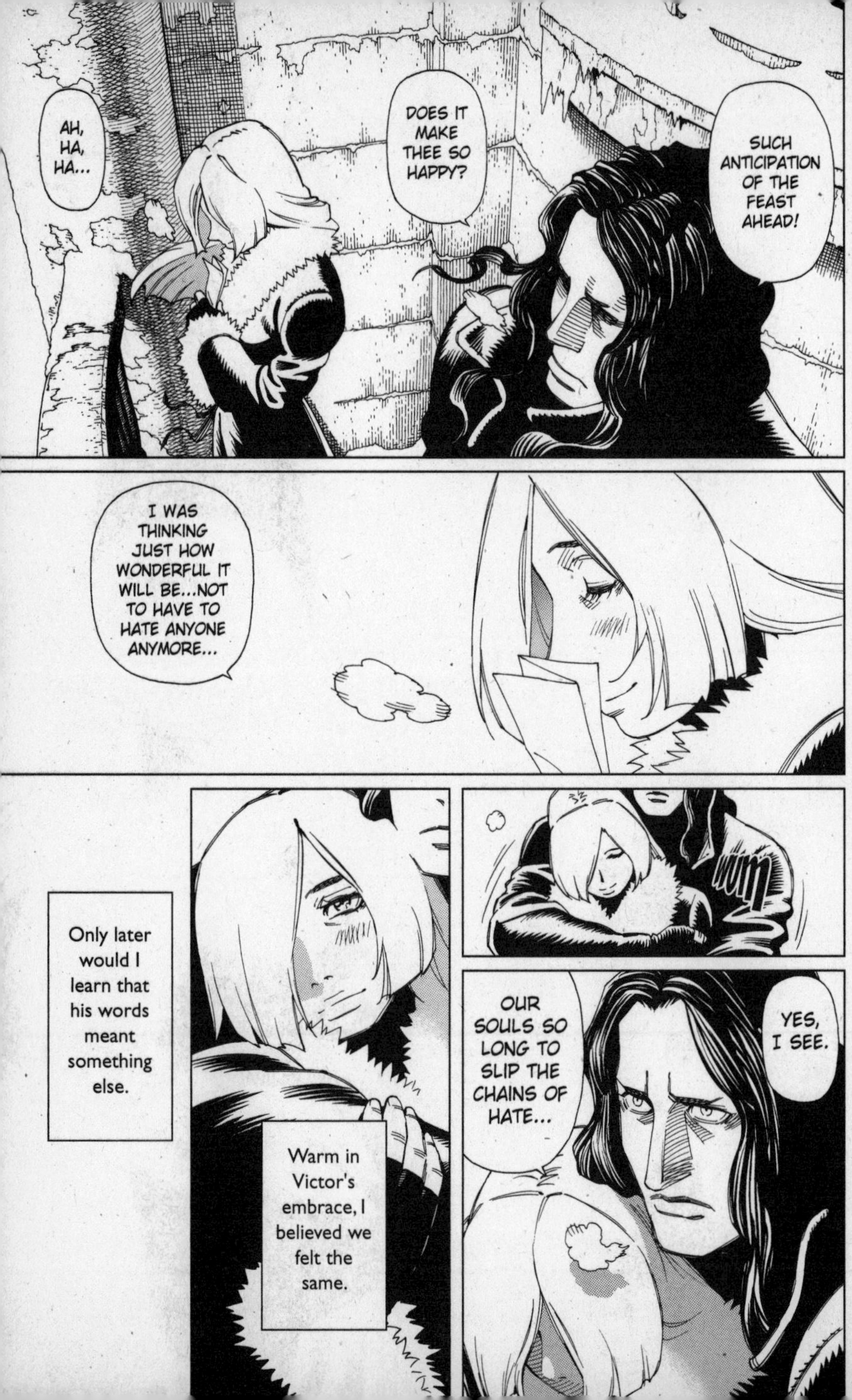
SUCH ANTICIPATION OF THE FEAST AHEAD!
DOES IT MAKE THEE SO HAPPY?
AH, HA, HA...
I WAS THINKING JUST HOW WONDERFUL IT WILL BE...NOT TO HAVE TO HATE ANYONE ANYMORE...
YES, I SEE.
OUR SOULS SO LONG TO SLIP THE CHAINS OF HATE...
Warm in Victor's embrace, I believed we felt the same.
Only later would I learn that his words meant something else.

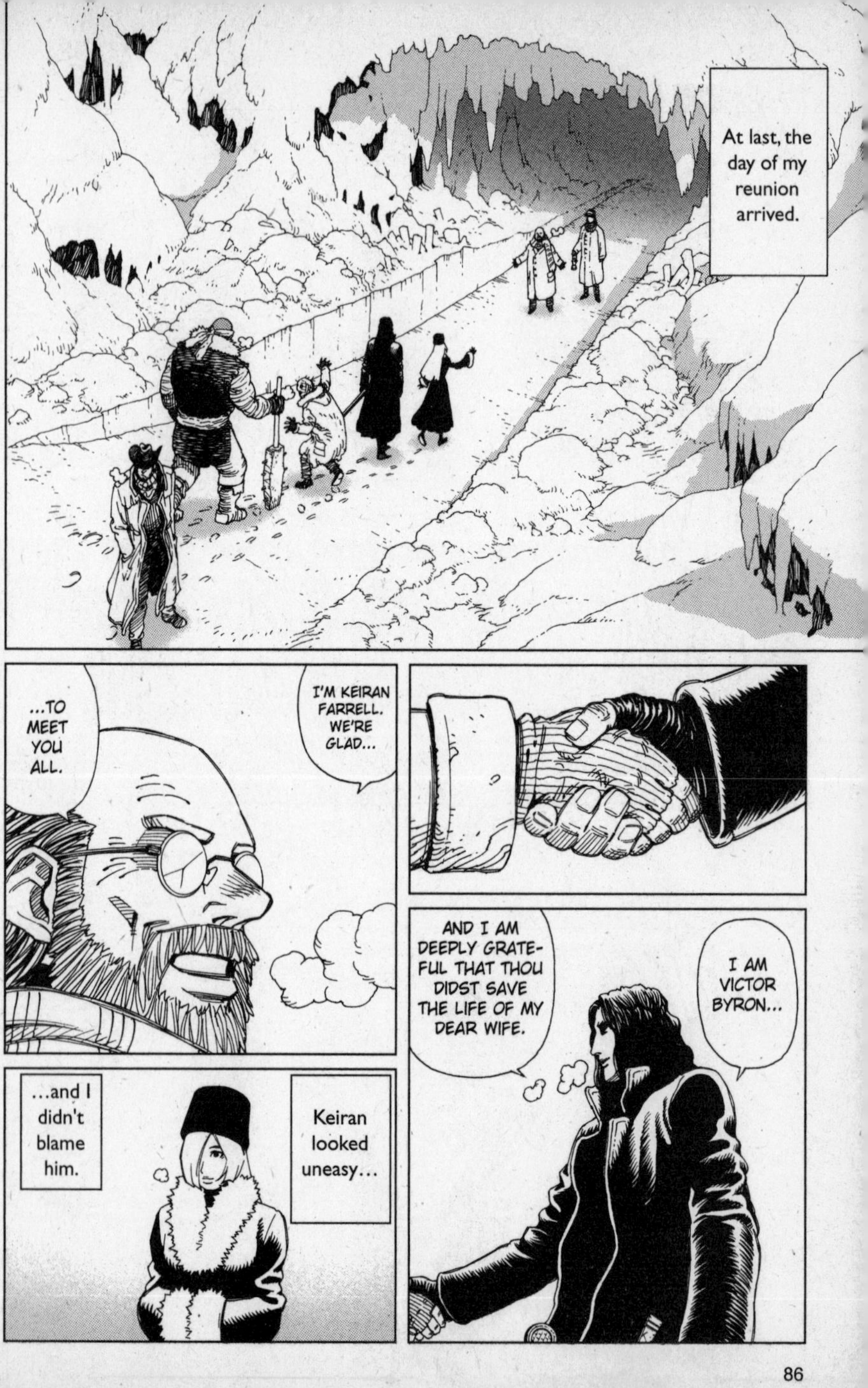
At last, the day of my reunion arrived.
I'M KEIRAN FARRELL. WE'RE GLAD...
...TO MEET YOU ALL.
I AM VICTOR BYRON...
AND I AM DEEPLY GRATEFUL THAT THOU DIDST SAVE THE LIFE OF MY DEAR WIFE.
Keiran looked uneasy...
...and I didn't blame him.

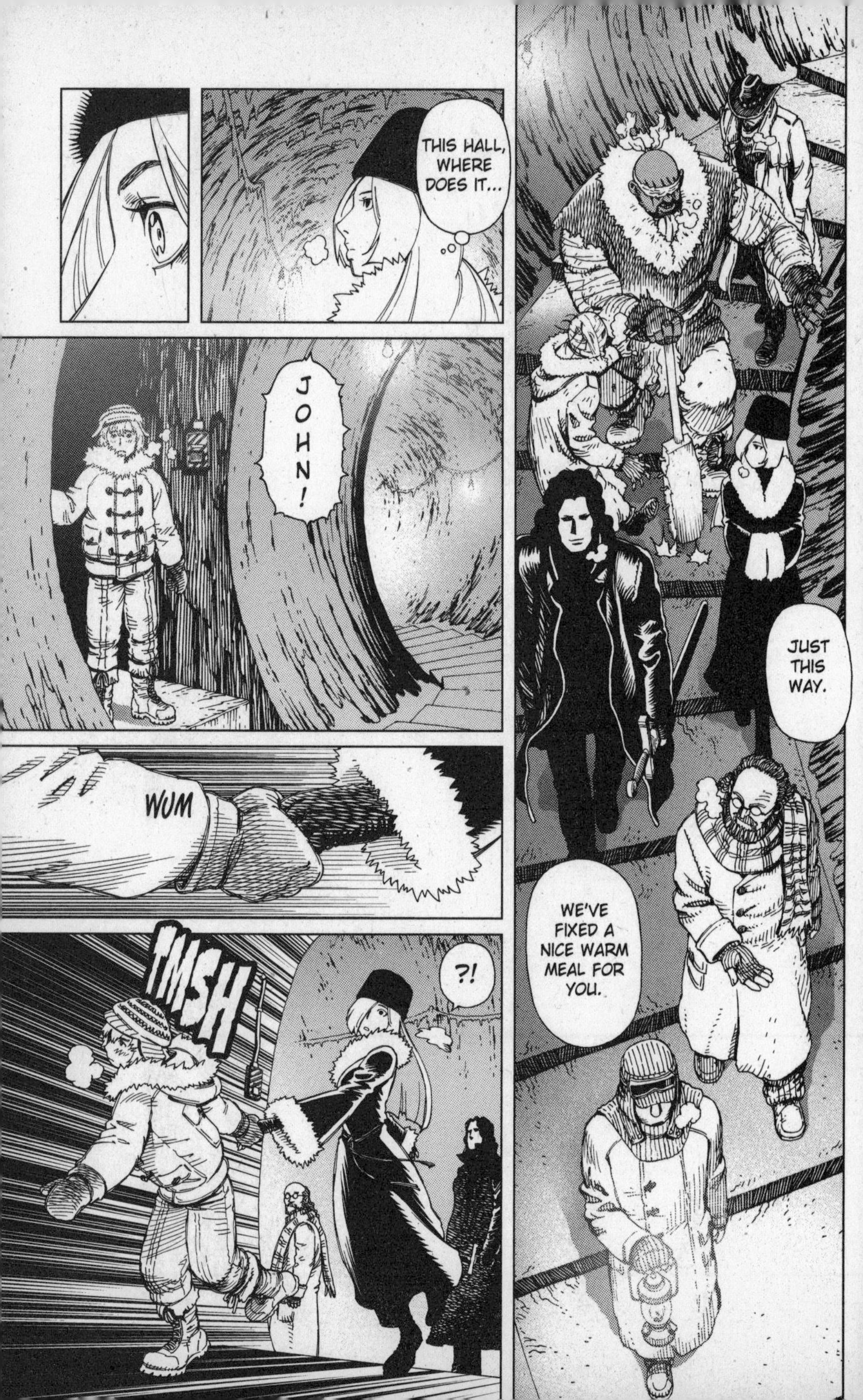
JUST THIS WAY.
WE'VE FIXED A NICE WARM MEAL FOR YOU.
THIS HALL, WHERE DOES IT...
JOHN!
WUM
TMSH
?!

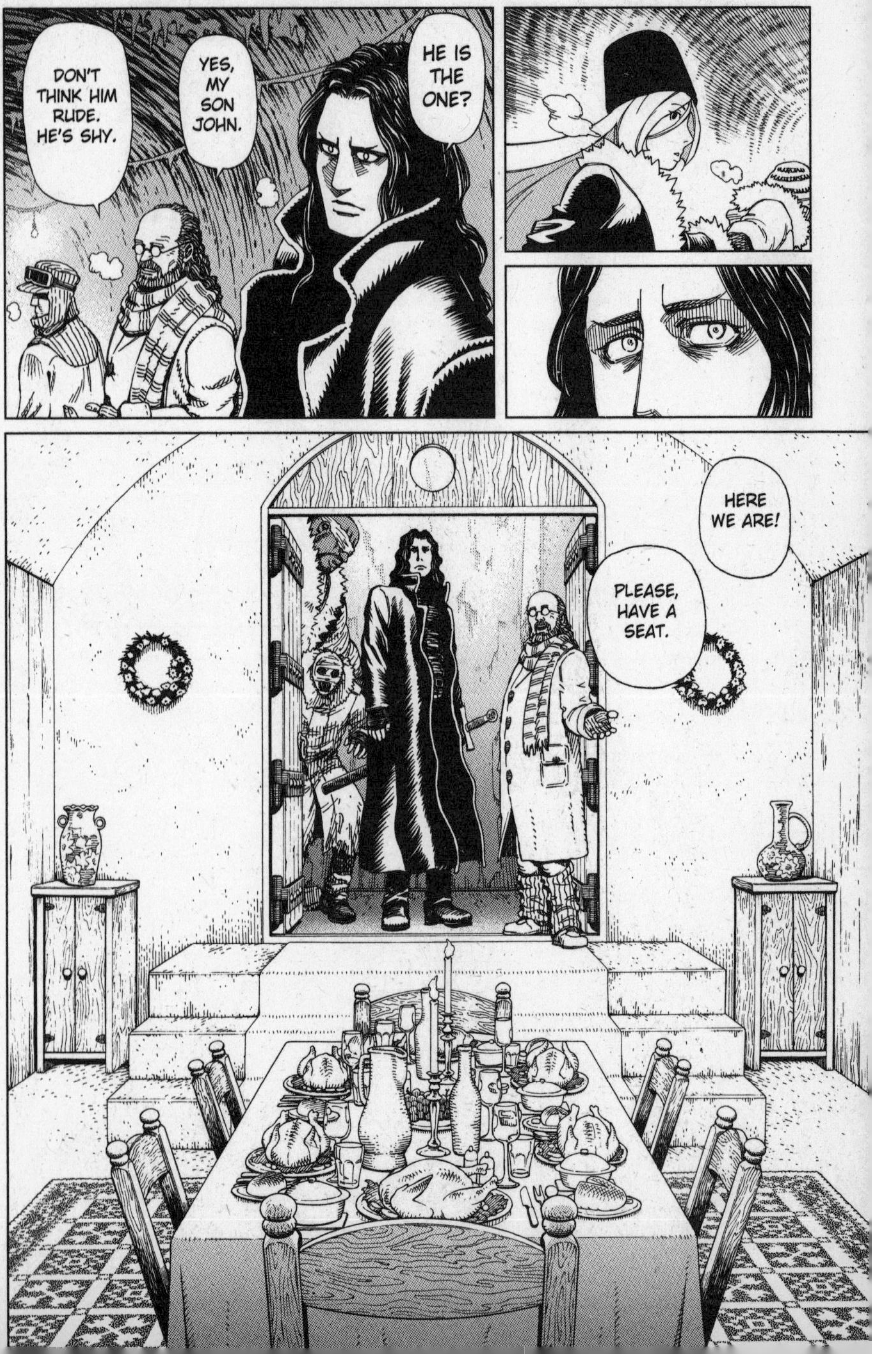
HE IS THE ONE?
YES, MY SON JOHN.
DON'T THINK HIM RUDE. HE'S SHY.
HERE WE ARE!
PLEASE, HAVE A SEAT.

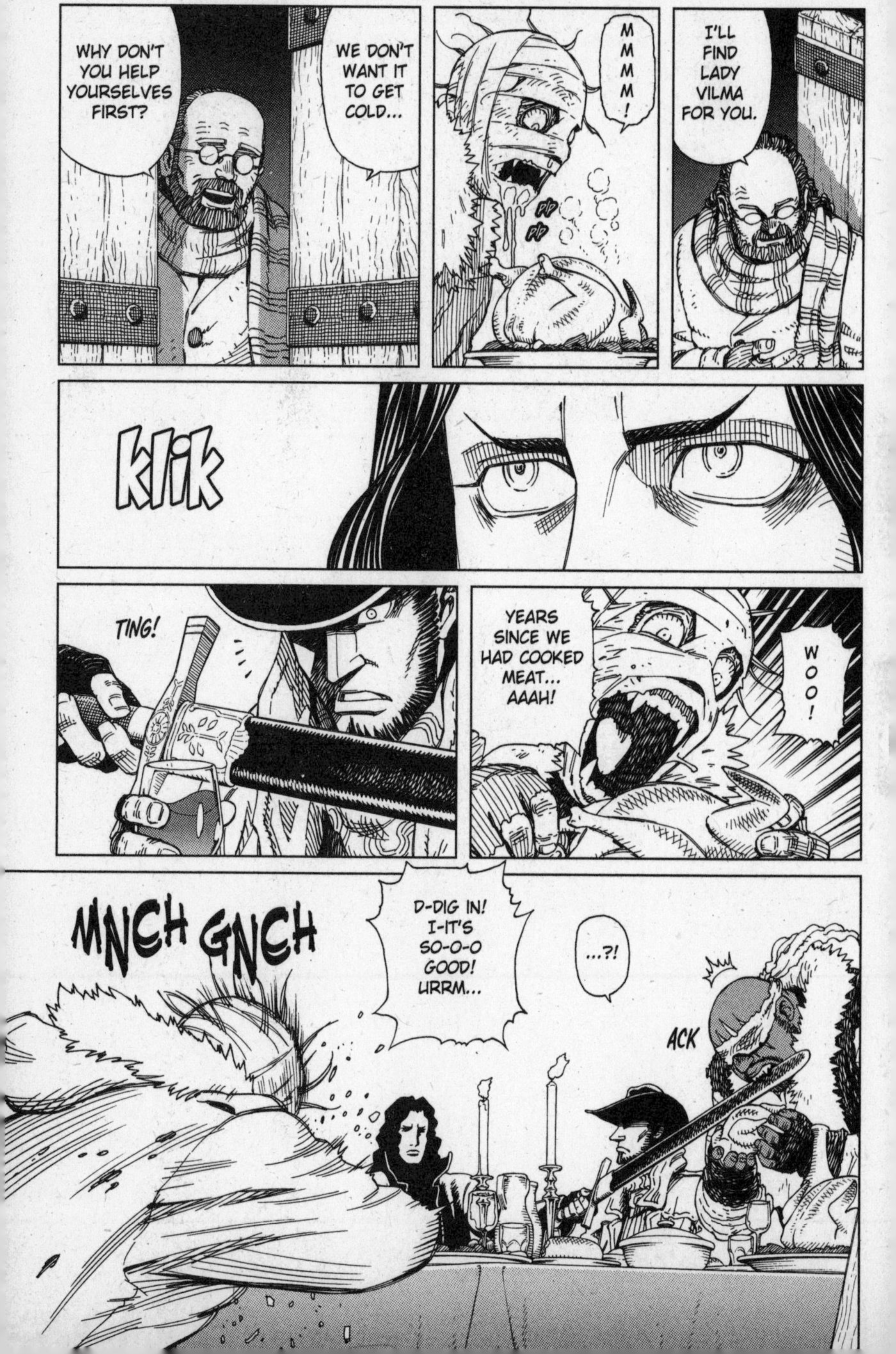
I'LL FIND LADY VILMA FOR YOU.
MMMM!
WE DON'T WANT IT TO GET COLD...
WHY DON'T YOU HELP YOURSELVES FIRST?
klik
WOOO!
YEARS SINCE WE HAD COOKED MEAT... AAAH!
TING!
...?!
ACK
D-DIG IN! I-IT'S SO-O-O GOOD! URRM...
MNCH GNCH

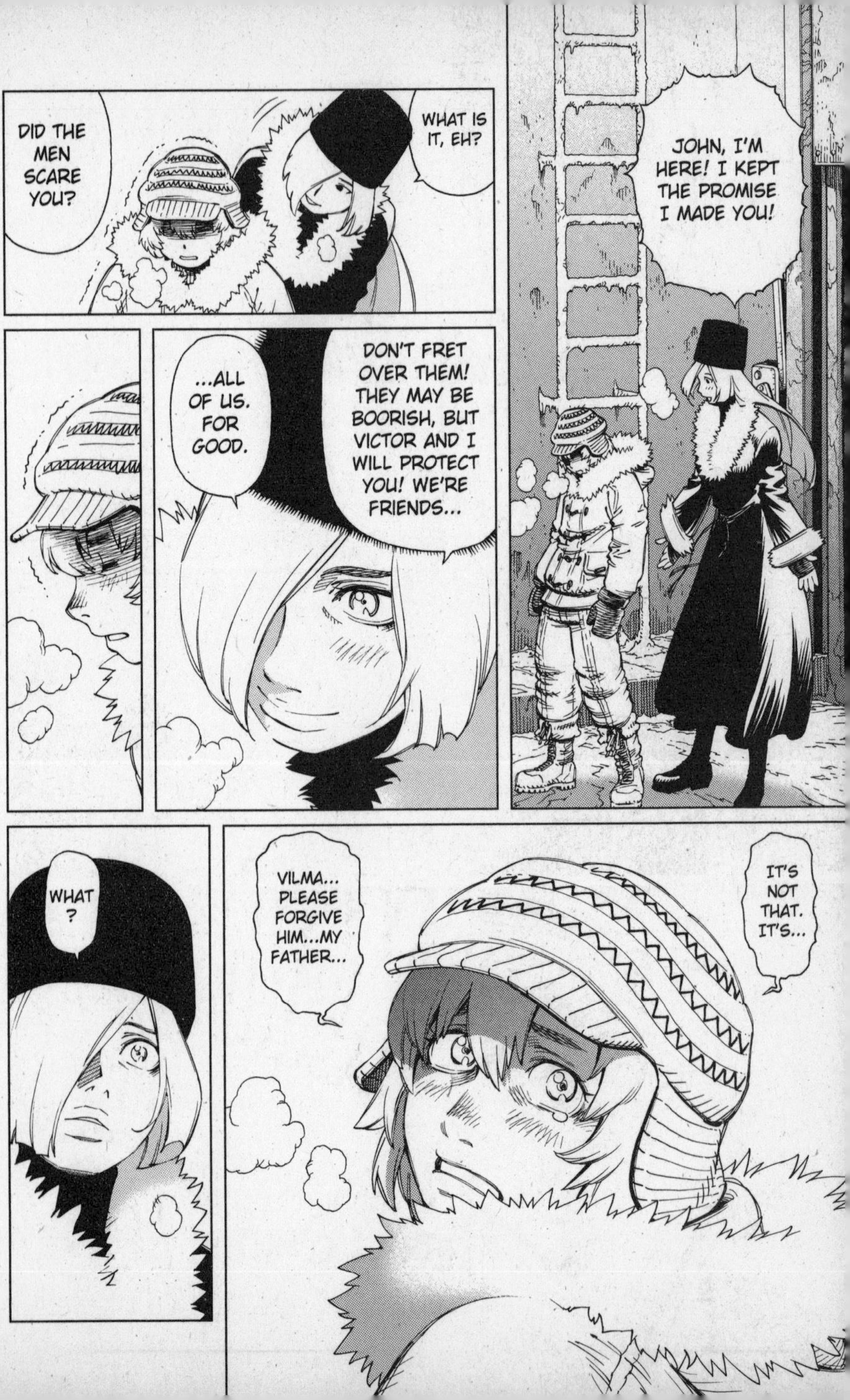
JOHN, I'M HERE! I KEPT THE PROMISE I MADE YOU!
WHAT IS IT, EH?
DID THE MEN SCARE YOU?
DON'T FRET OVER THEM! THEY MAY BE BOORISH, BUT VICTOR AND I WILL PROTECT YOU! WE'RE FRIENDS...
...ALL OF US. FOR GOOD.
IT'S NOT THAT. IT'S...
VILMA... PLEASE FORGIVE HIM...MY FATHER...
WHAT?

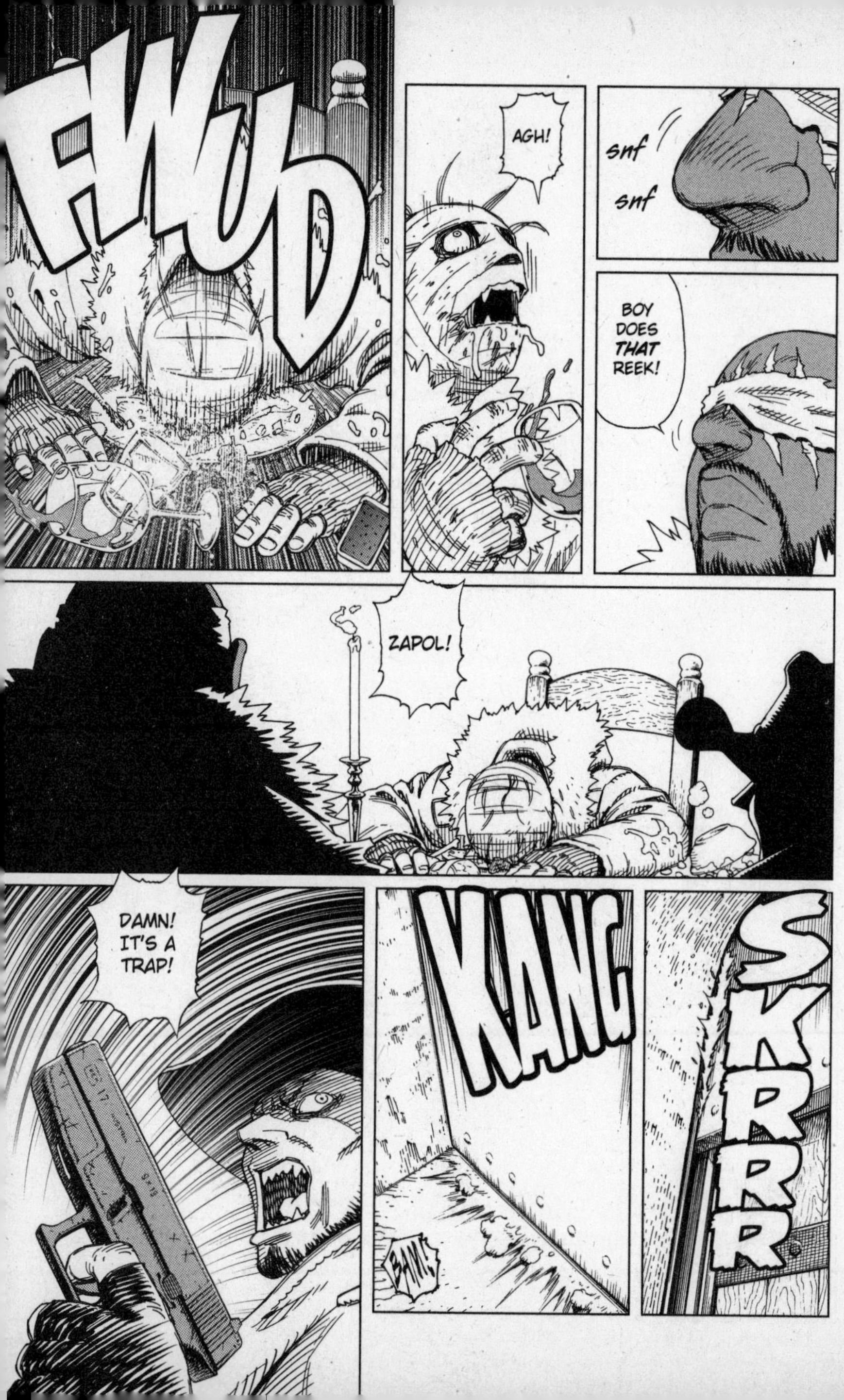
snf
snf
BOY DOES THAT REEK!
AGH!
FWUD
ZAPOL!
SKRRR
KANG
BAM!
DAMN! IT'S A TRAP!

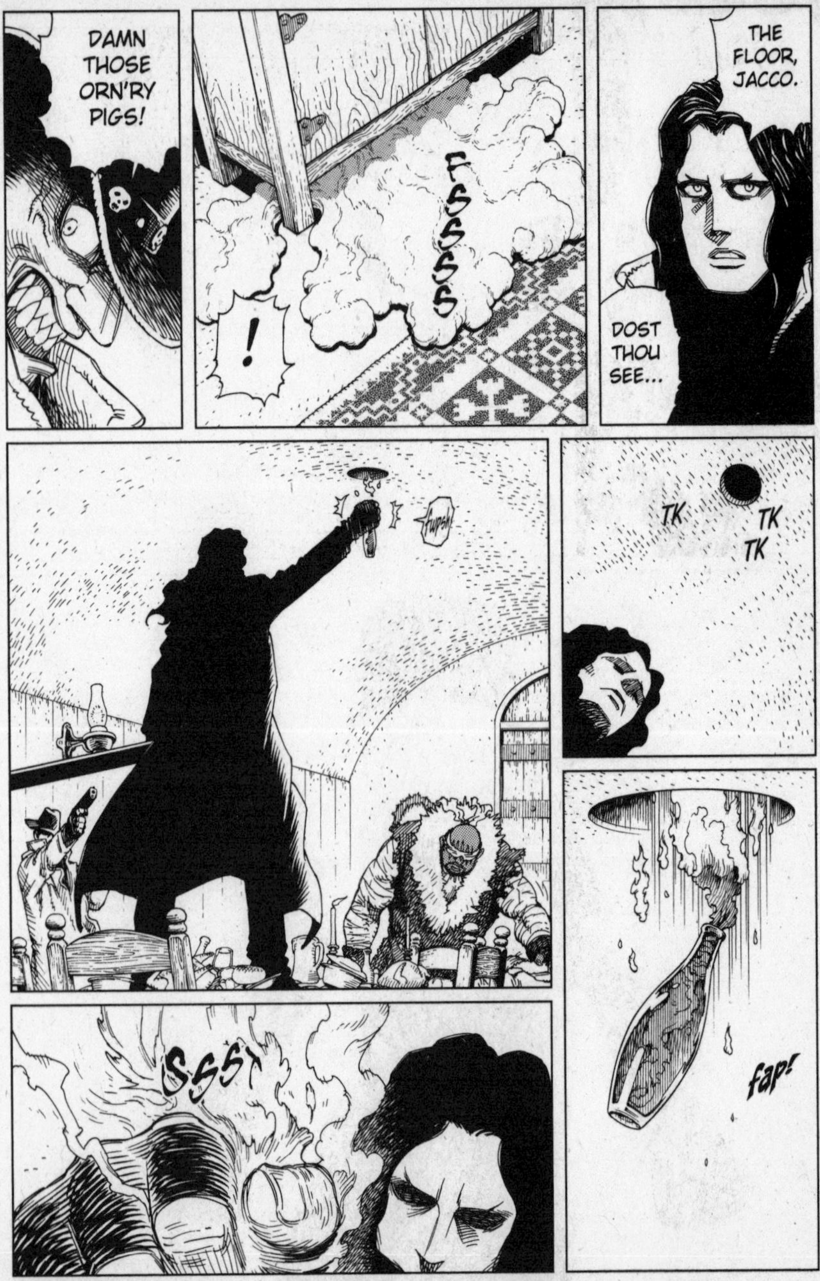
THE FLOOR, JACCO.
DOST THOU SEE...
FSSSS
!
DAMN THOSE ORN'RY PIGS!
TK
TK
TK
fap!
fupsh!
SSS

*Carbon disulfide: A compound of carbon and sulfur, in its pure state CS_2 is a sweet-smelling, colorless liquid, though impurities can give it an unpleasant smell. CS_2 is volatile; its vapor is heavier than air, poisonous, and extremely flammable.

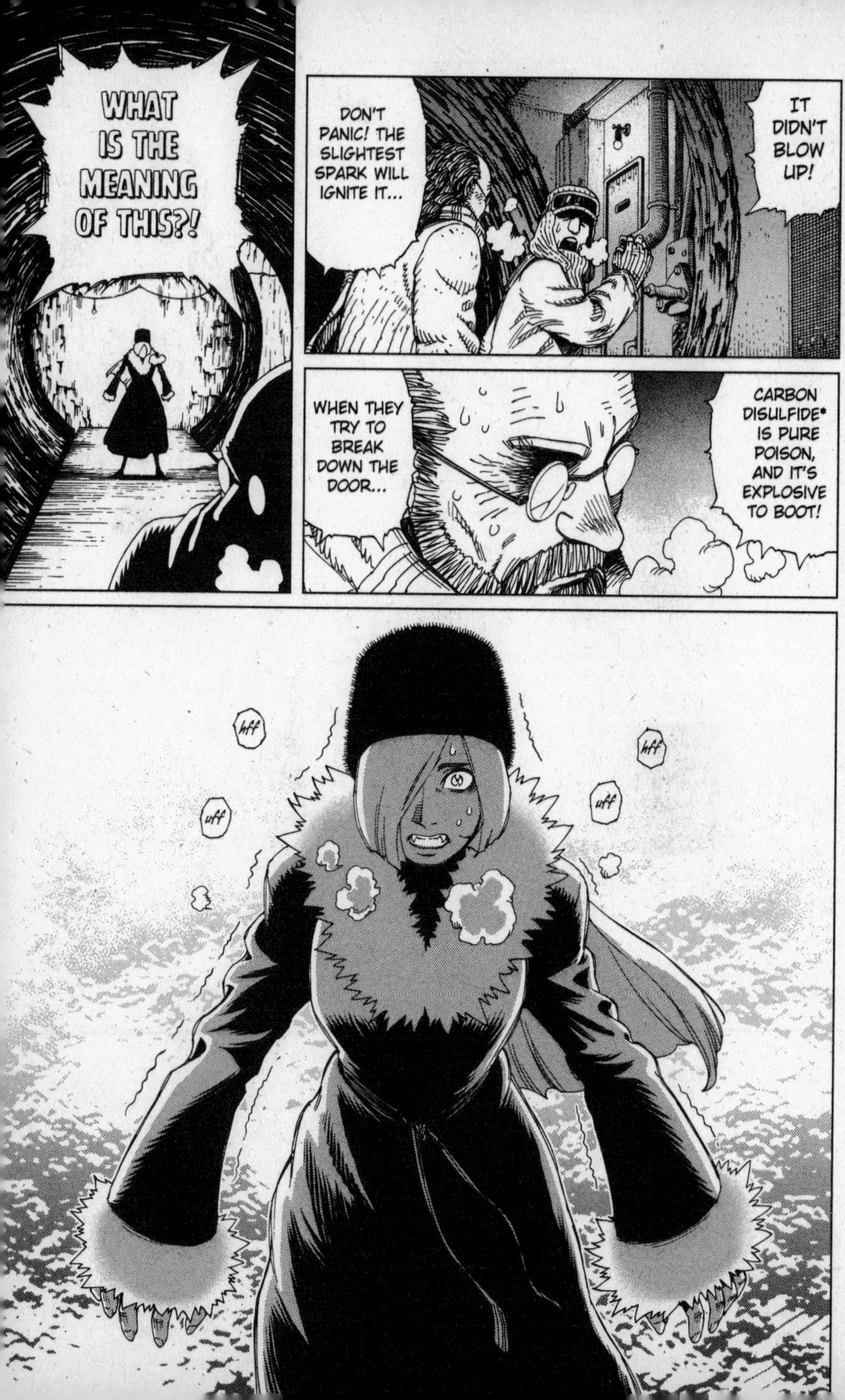
IT DIDN'T BLOW UP!
DON'T PANIC! THE SLIGHTEST SPARK WILL IGNITE IT...
CARBON DISULFIDE* IS PURE POISON, AND IT'S EXPLOSIVE TO BOOT!
WHEN THEY TRY TO BREAK DOWN THE DOOR...
WHAT IS THE MEANING OF THIS?!
hff
hff
uff
uff

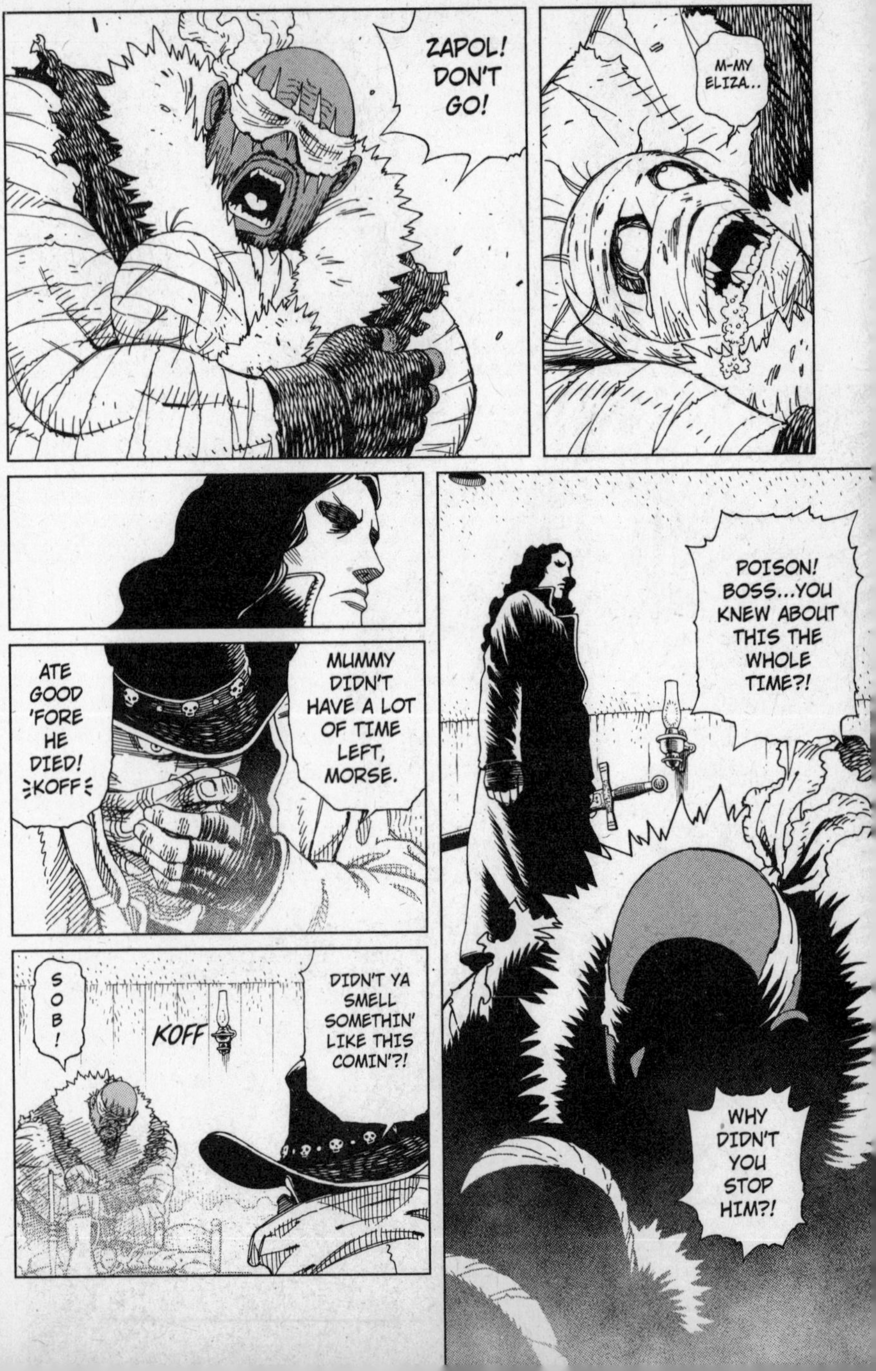
M-MY ELIZA...
ZAPOL! DON'T GO!
POISON! BOSS...YOU KNEW ABOUT THIS THE WHOLE TIME?!
WHY DIDN'T YOU STOP HIM?!
MUMMY DIDN'T HAVE A LOT OF TIME LEFT, MORSE.
ATE GOOD 'FORE HE DIED! KOFF
DIDN'T YA SMELL SOMETHIN' LIKE THIS COMIN'?!
KOFF
SOB!

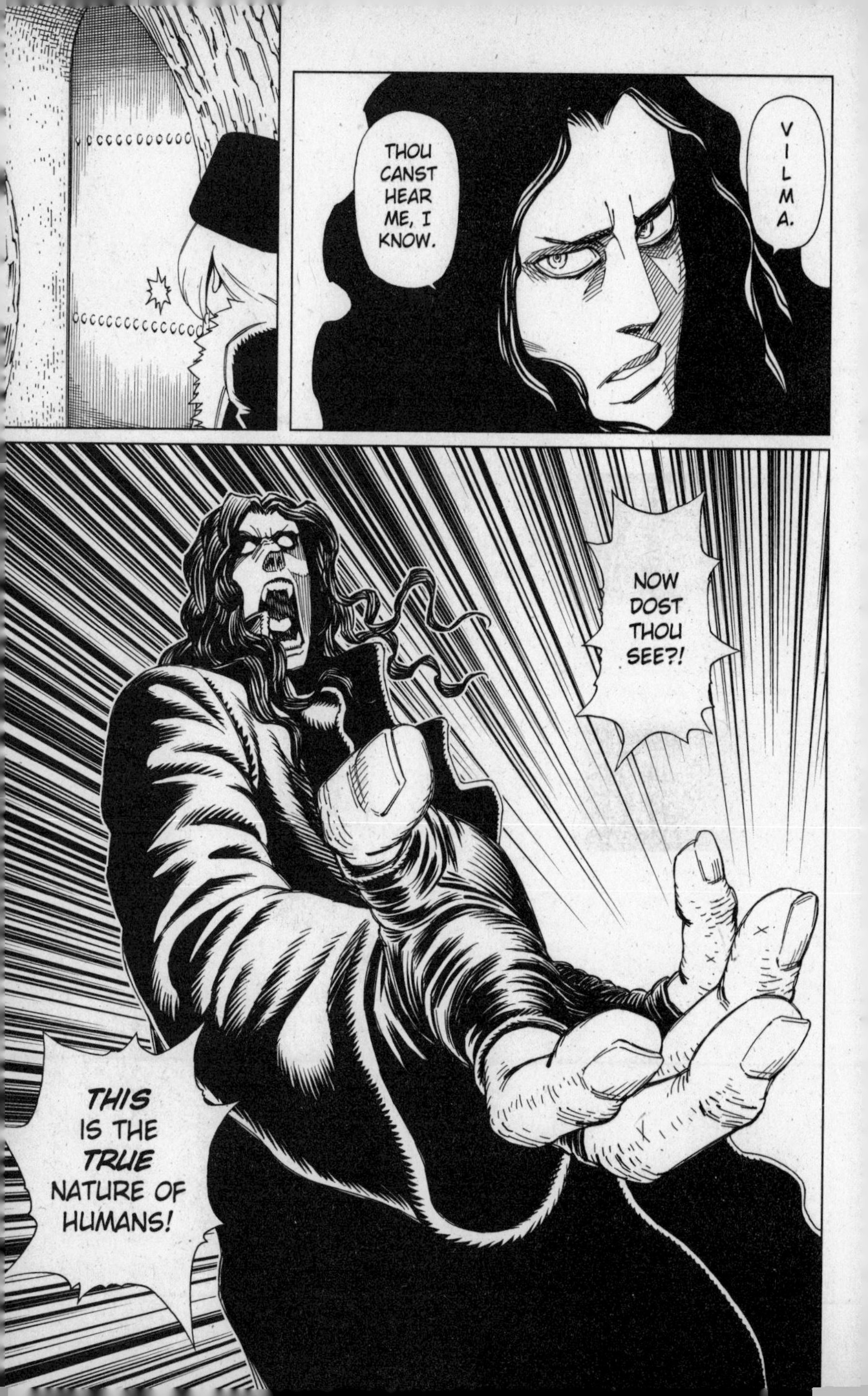
VILMA.
THOU CANST HEAR ME, I KNOW.
NOW DOST THOU SEE?!
THIS IS THE *TRUE* NATURE OF HUMANS!

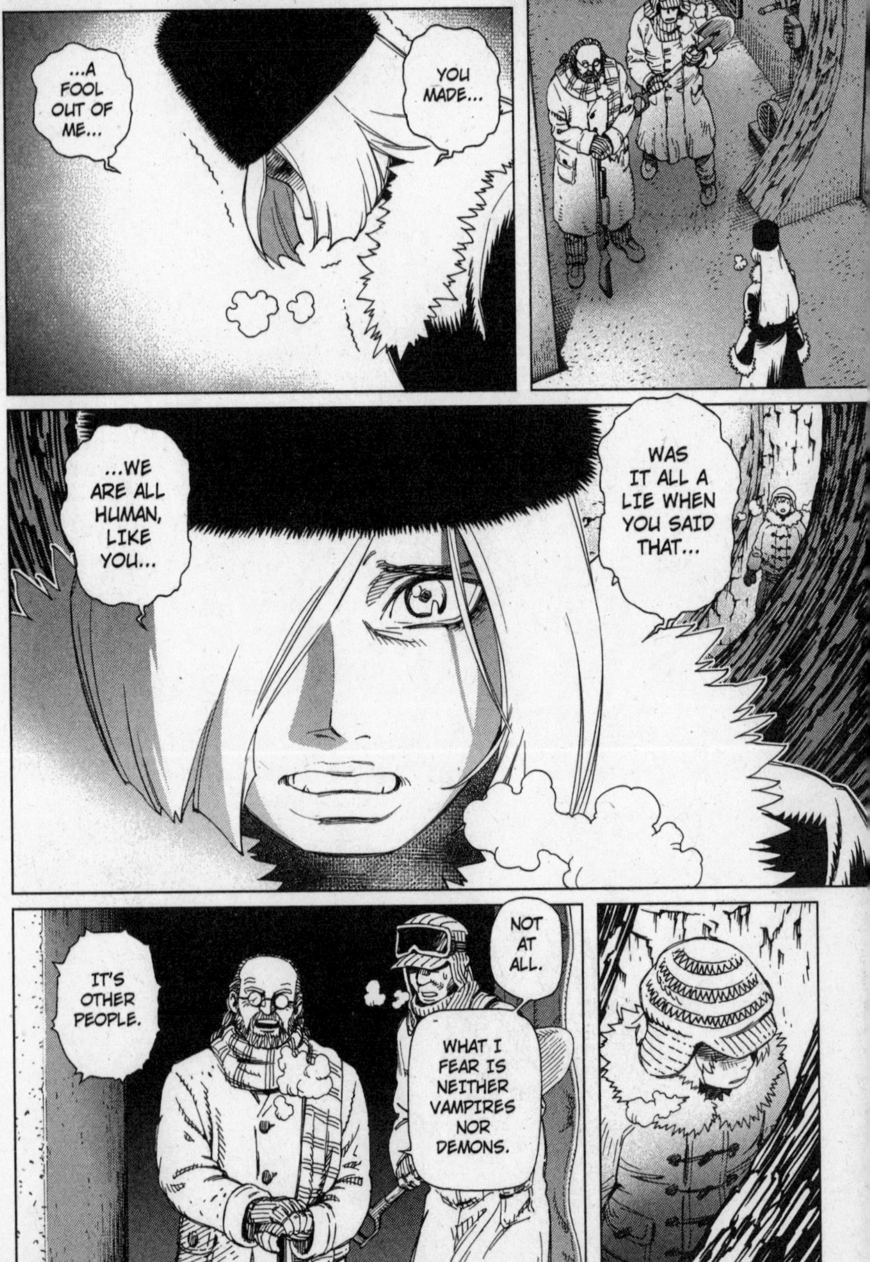
YOU MADE...
...A FOOL OUT OF ME...
WAS IT ALL A LIE WHEN YOU SAID THAT...
...WE ARE ALL HUMAN, LIKE YOU...
NOT AT ALL.
WHAT I FEAR IS NEITHER VAMPIRES NOR DEMONS.
IT'S OTHER PEOPLE.

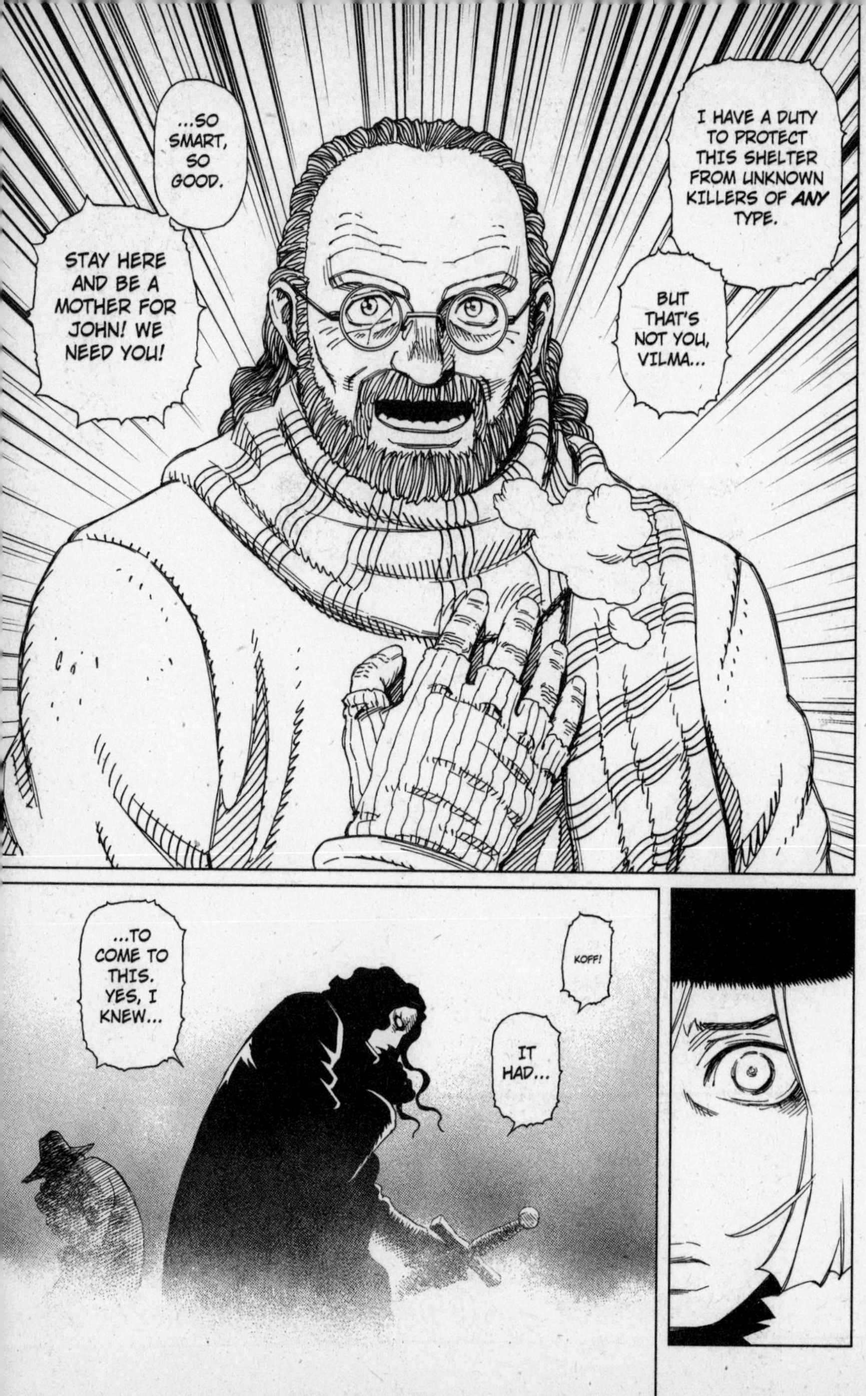
I HAVE A DUTY TO PROTECT THIS SHELTER FROM UNKNOWN KILLERS OF *ANY* TYPE.
BUT THAT'S NOT YOU, VILMA...
...SO SMART, SO GOOD.
STAY HERE AND BE A MOTHER FOR JOHN! WE NEED YOU!
KOFF!
IT HAD...
...TO COME TO THIS. YES, I KNEW...

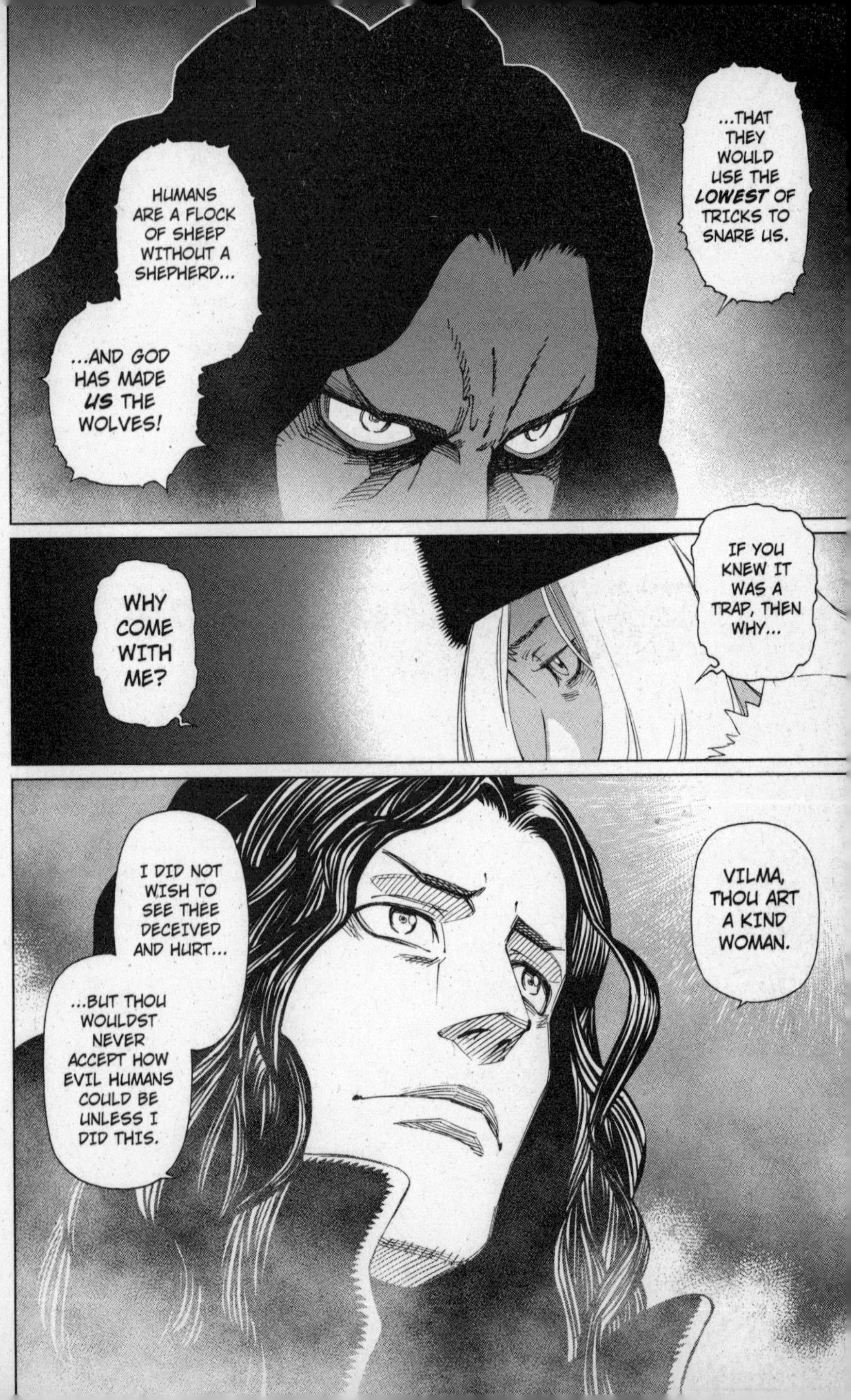
...THAT THEY WOULD USE THE LOWEST OF TRICKS TO SNARE US.
HUMANS ARE A FLOCK OF SHEEP WITHOUT A SHEPHERD...
...AND GOD HAS MADE US THE WOLVES!
IF YOU KNEW IT WAS A TRAP, THEN WHY...
WHY COME WITH ME?
VILMA, THOU ART A KIND WOMAN.
I DID NOT WISH TO SEE THEE DECEIVED AND HURT...
...BUT THOU WOULDST NEVER ACCEPT HOW EVIL HUMANS COULD BE UNLESS I DID THIS.

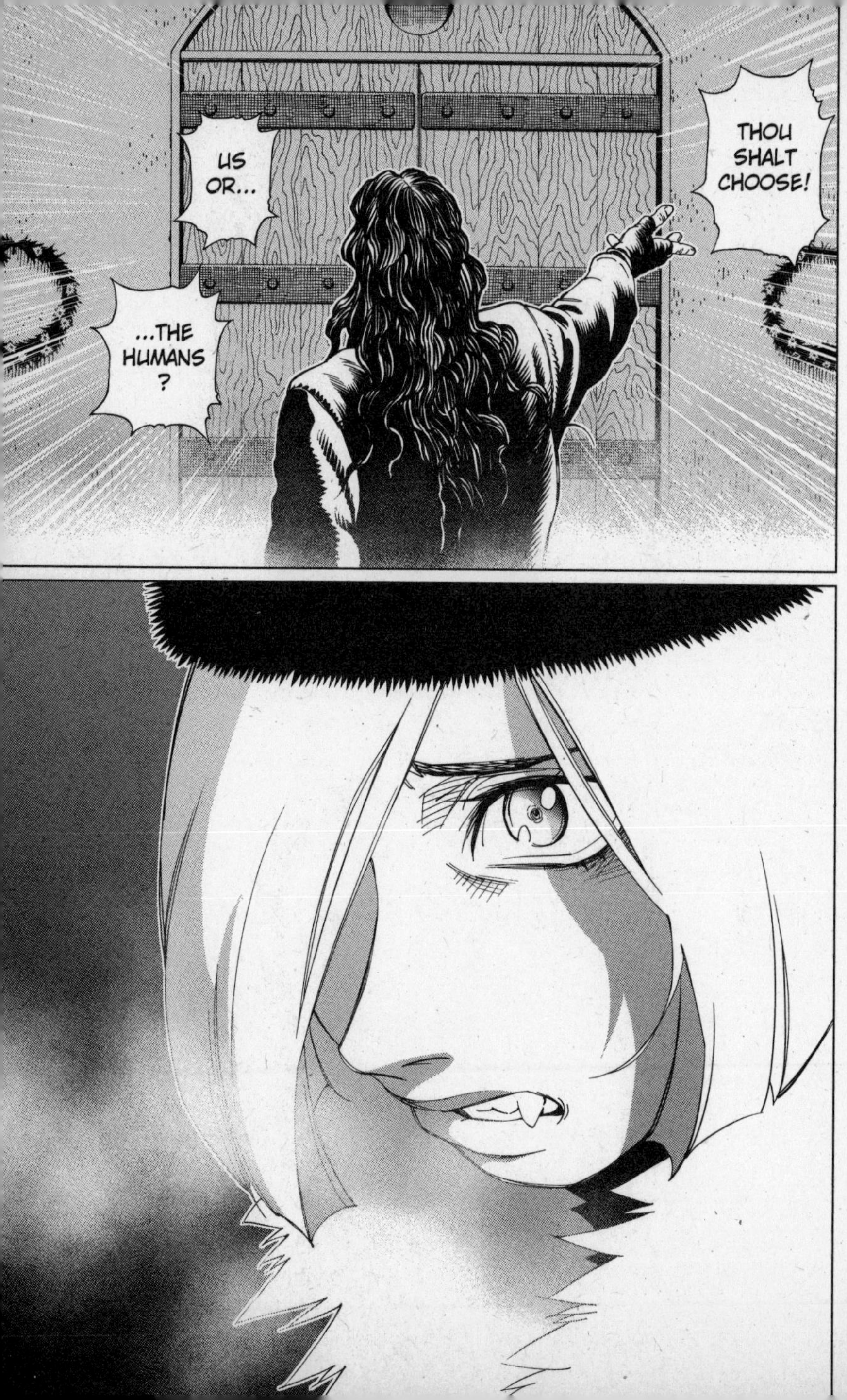
THOU SHALT CHOOSE!
US OR...
...THE HUMANS?

PHASE 47: WHOMEVER IT MAY BE

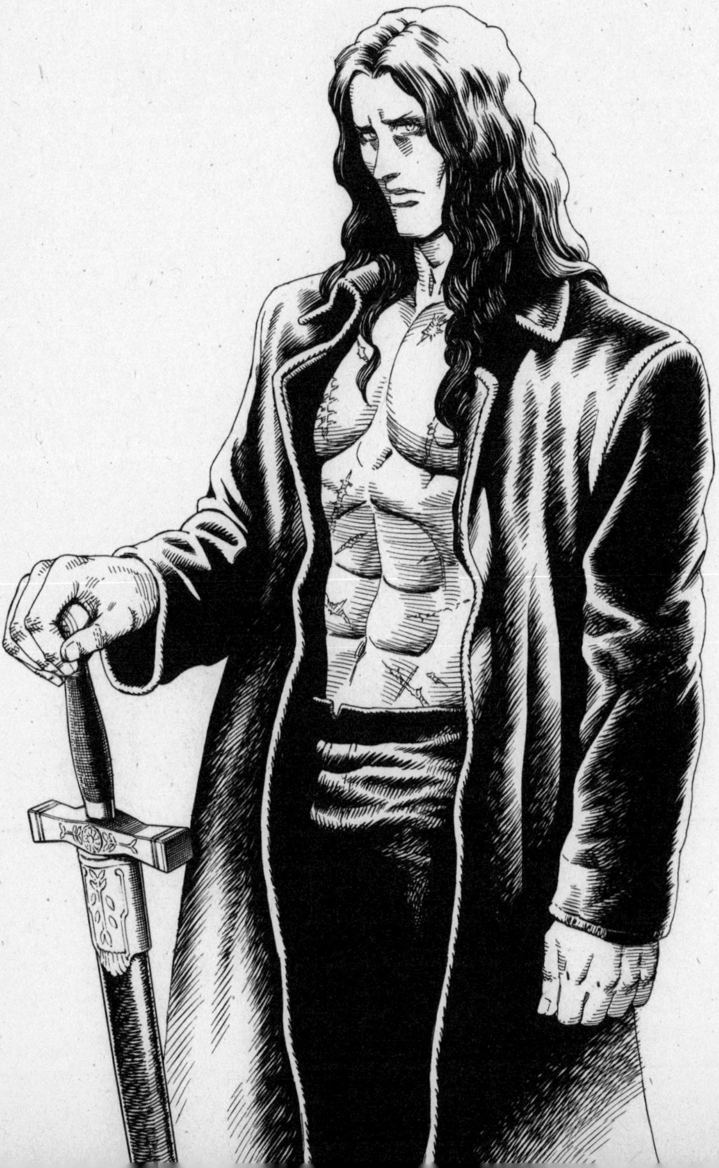

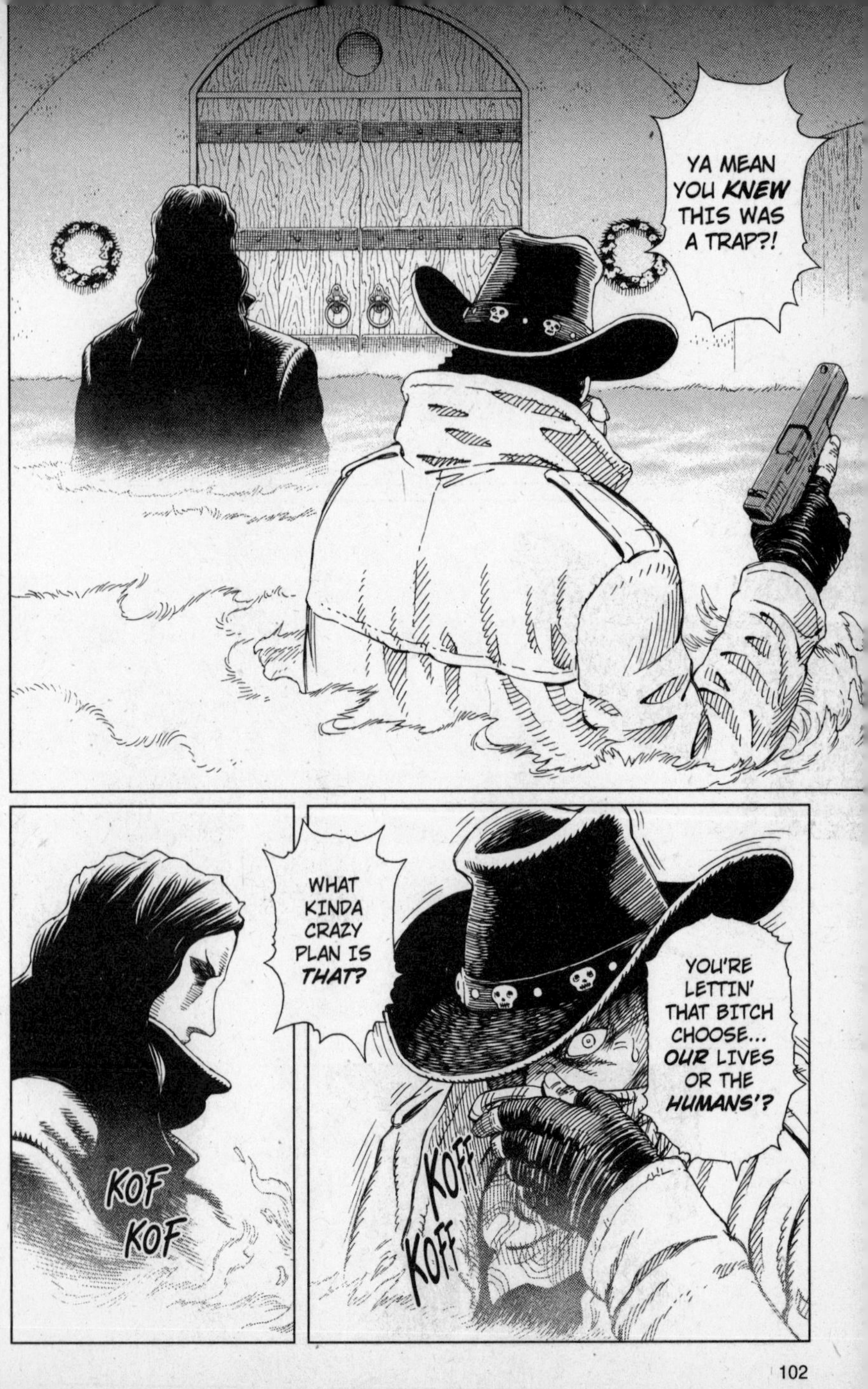
YA MEAN YOU ***KNEW*** THIS WAS A TRAP?!
WHAT KINDA CRAZY PLAN IS ***THAT?***
YOU'RE LETTIN' THAT BITCH CHOOSE... ***OUR*** LIVES OR THE ***HUMANS'?***
KOFF KOFF
KOF KOF

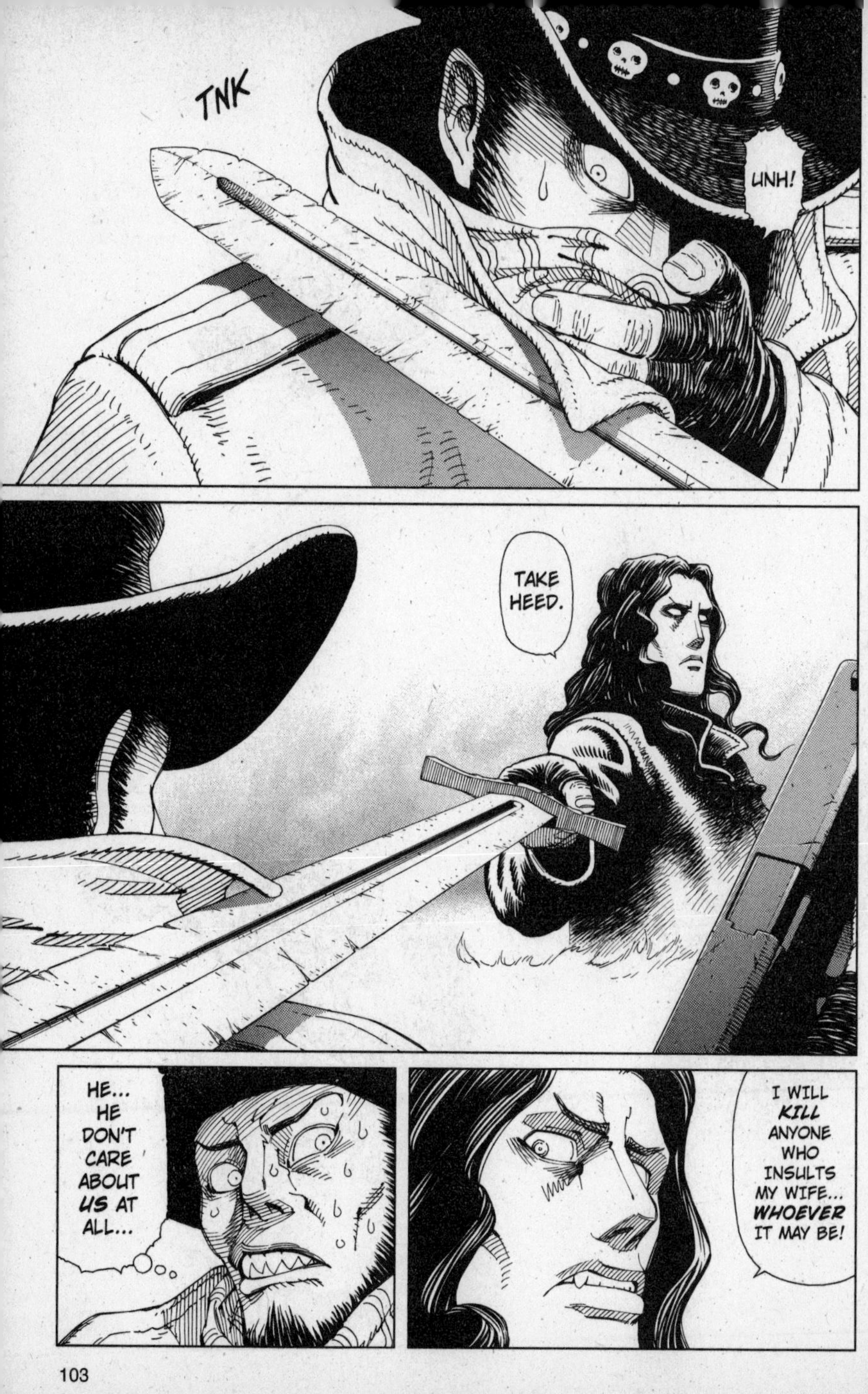
TNK
UNH!
TAKE HEED.
I WILL **KILL** ANYONE WHO INSULTS MY WIFE... **WHOEVER** IT MAY BE!
HE... HE DON'T CARE ABOUT **US** AT ALL...

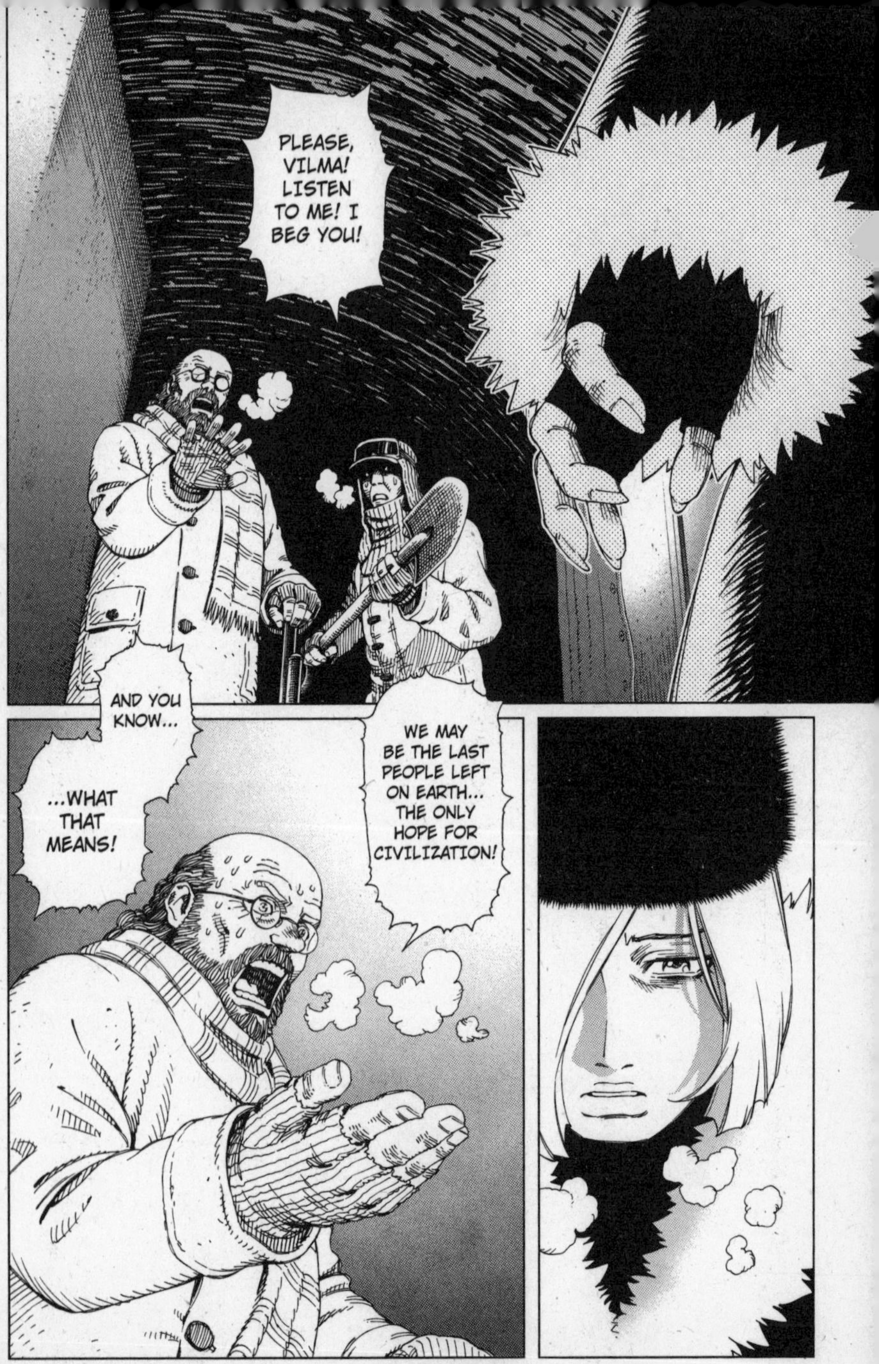
PLEASE, VILMA! LISTEN TO ME! I BEG YOU!
WE MAY BE THE LAST PEOPLE LEFT ON EARTH... THE ONLY HOPE FOR CIVILIZATION!
AND YOU KNOW...
...WHAT THAT MEANS!

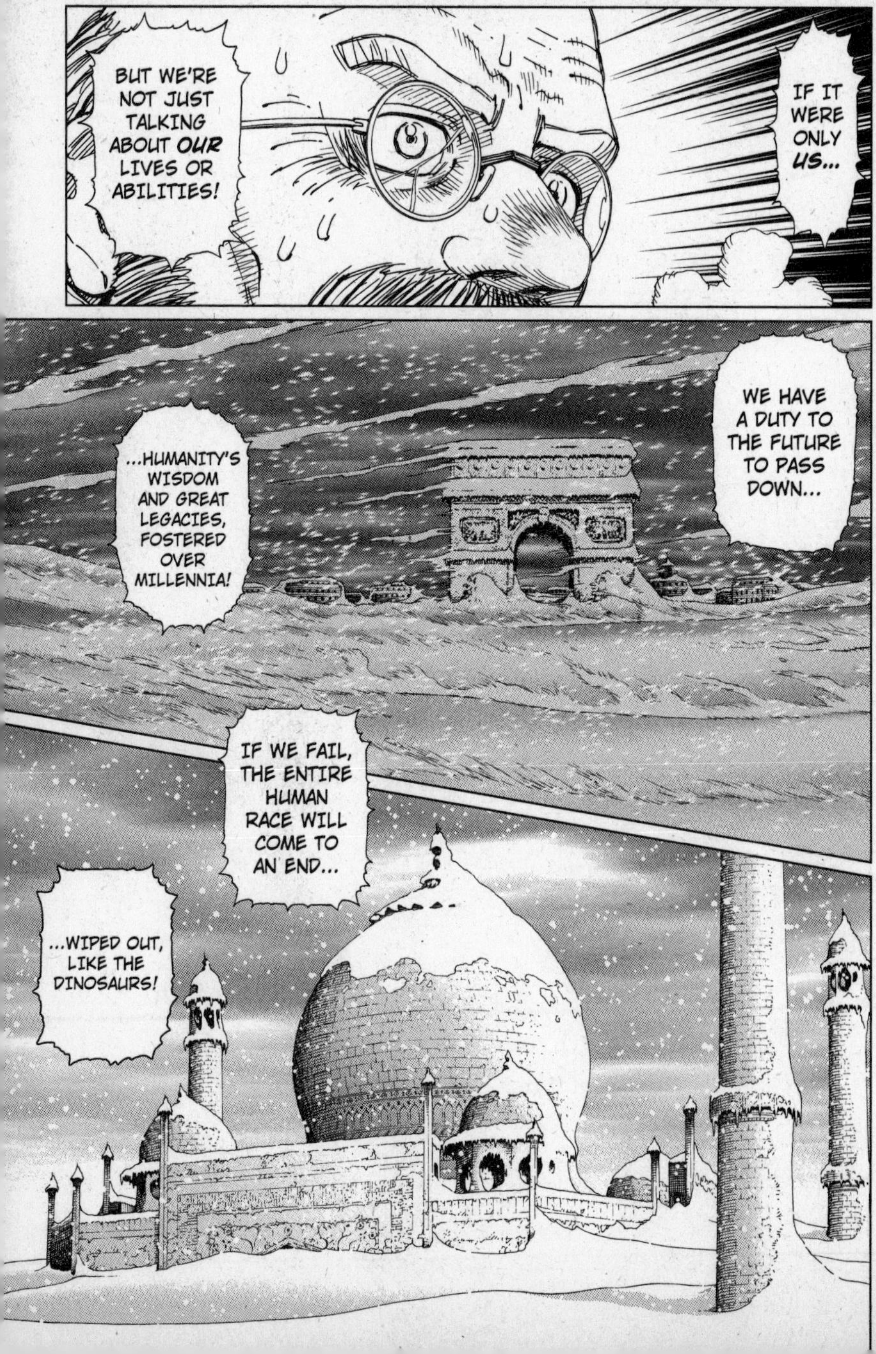
IF IT WERE ONLY US...
BUT WE'RE NOT JUST TALKING ABOUT OUR LIVES OR ABILITIES!
WE HAVE A DUTY TO THE FUTURE TO PASS DOWN...
...HUMANITY'S WISDOM AND GREAT LEGACIES, FOSTERED OVER MILLENNIA!
IF WE FAIL, THE ENTIRE HUMAN RACE WILL COME TO AN END...
...WIPED OUT, LIKE THE DINOSAURS!

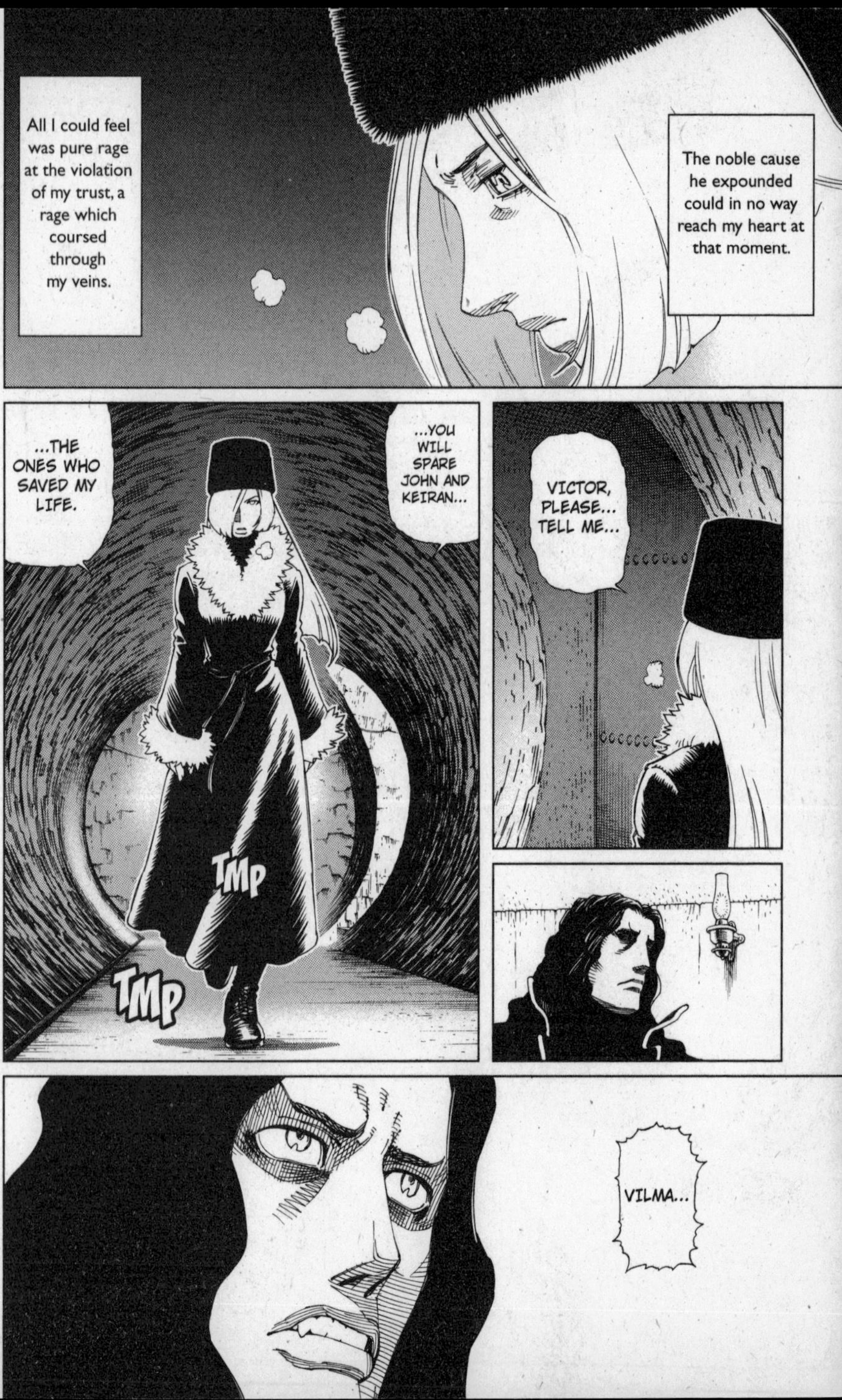
The noble cause he expounded could in no way reach my heart at that moment.
All I could feel was pure rage at the violation of my trust, a rage which coursed through my veins.
VICTOR, PLEASE... TELL ME...
...YOU WILL SPARE JOHN AND KEIRAN...
...THE ONES WHO SAVED MY LIFE.
TMP
TMP
VILMA...

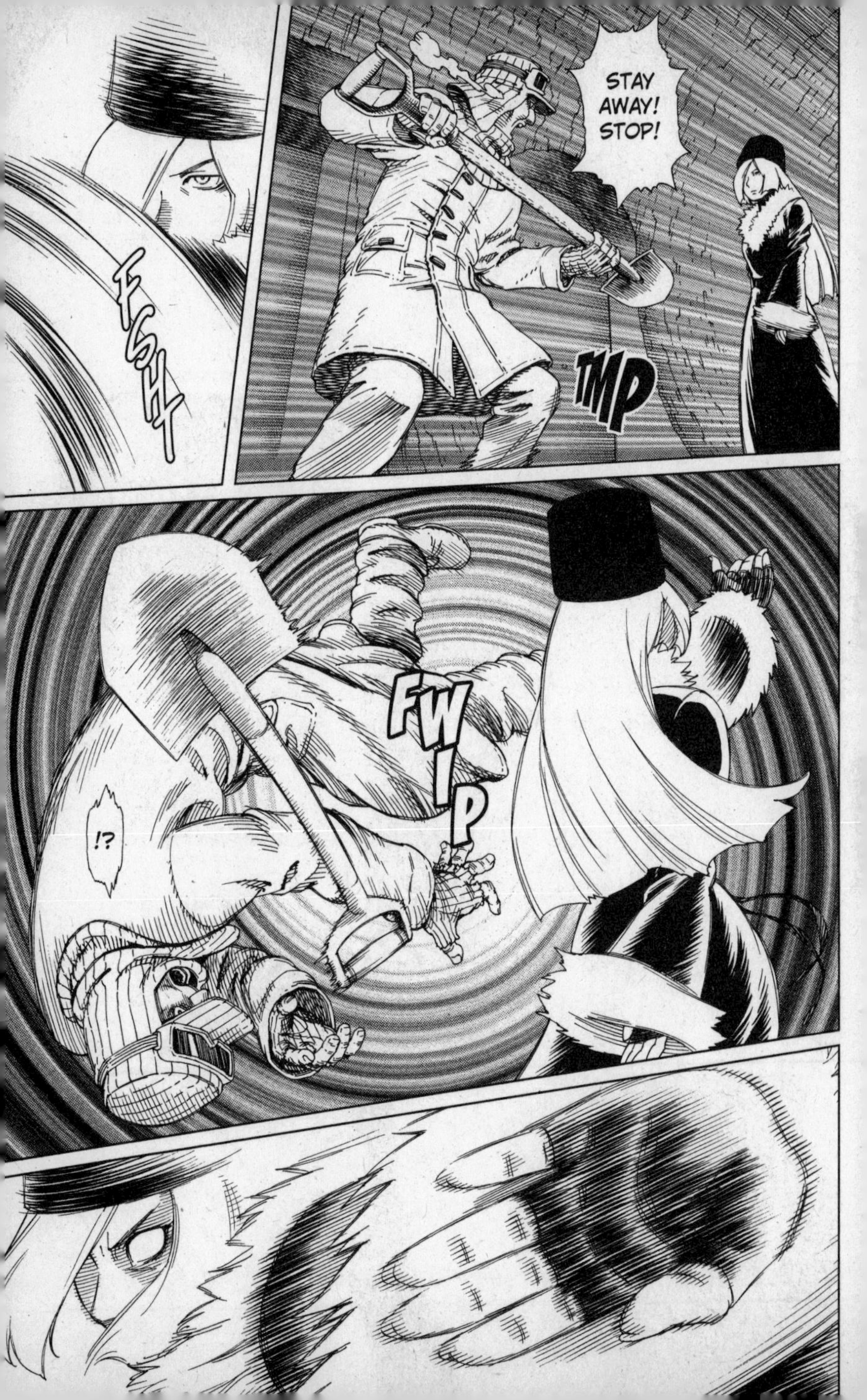
STAY AWAY! STOP!
TMP
FSHH
FWIP
!?

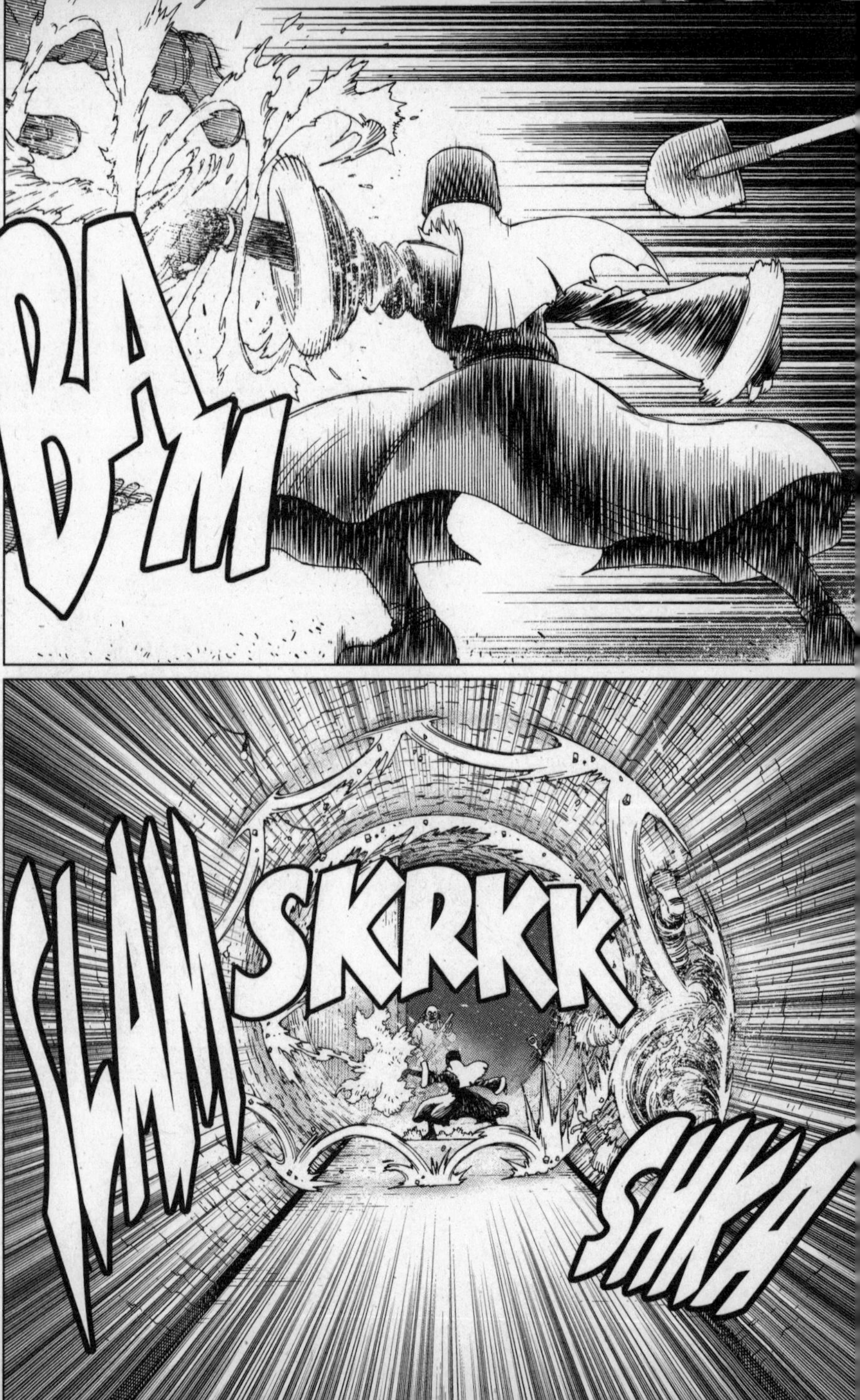
BAM
SKRKK
SHKA
SLAM

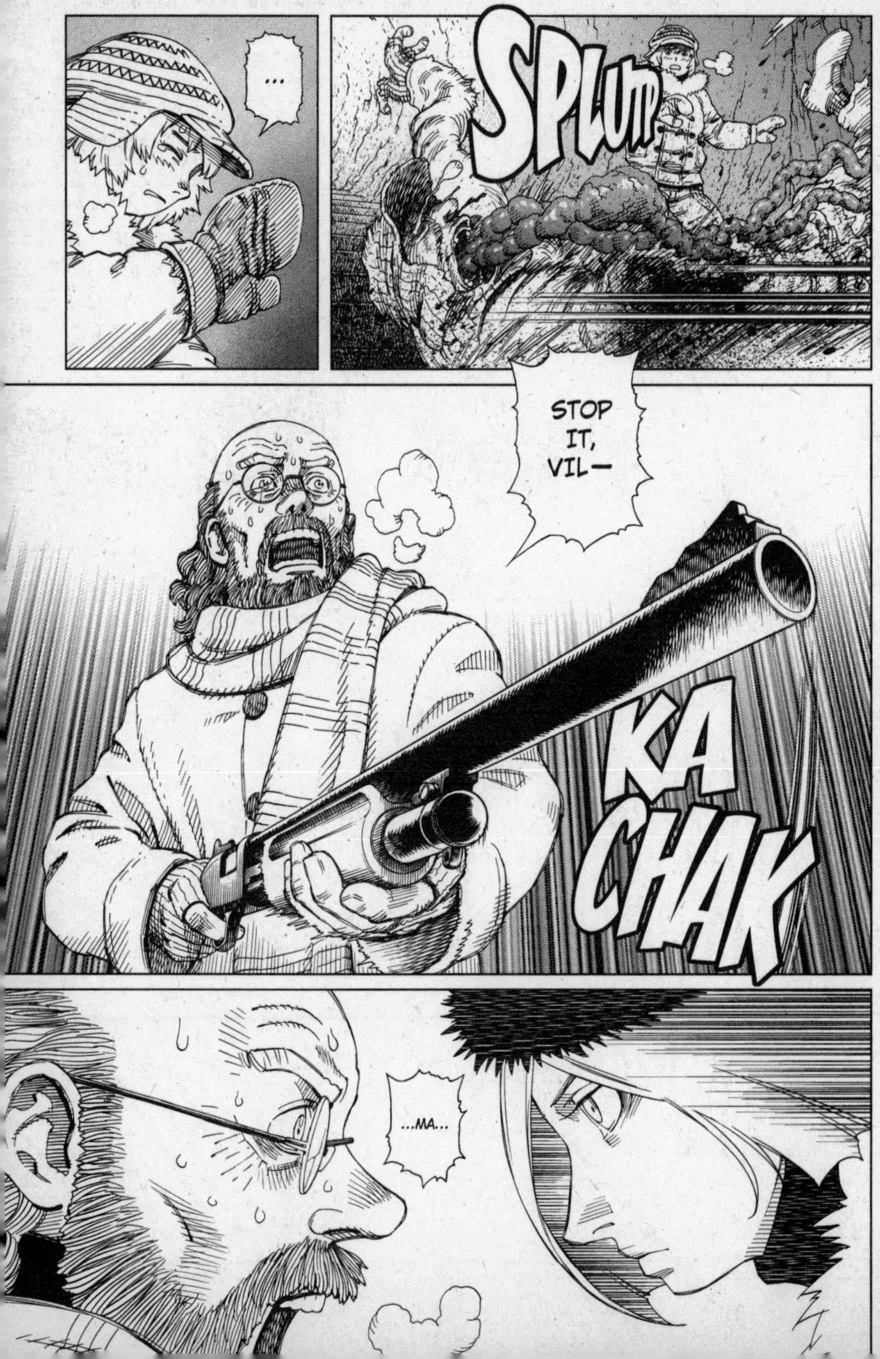
SPLUMP
...
STOP IT, VIL—
KA CHAK
...MA...

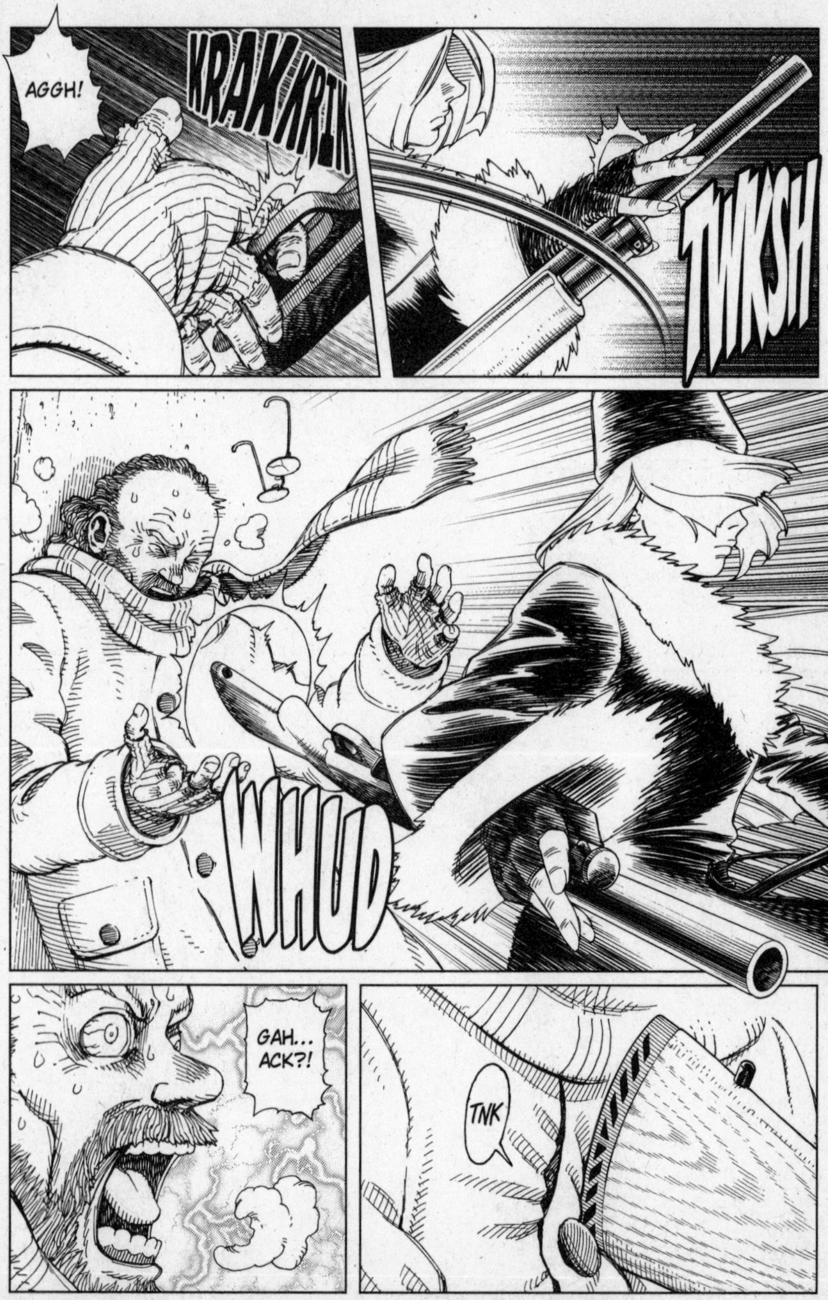
TWKSH
KRAKKRIK
AGGH!
WHUD
TNK
GAH... ACK?!

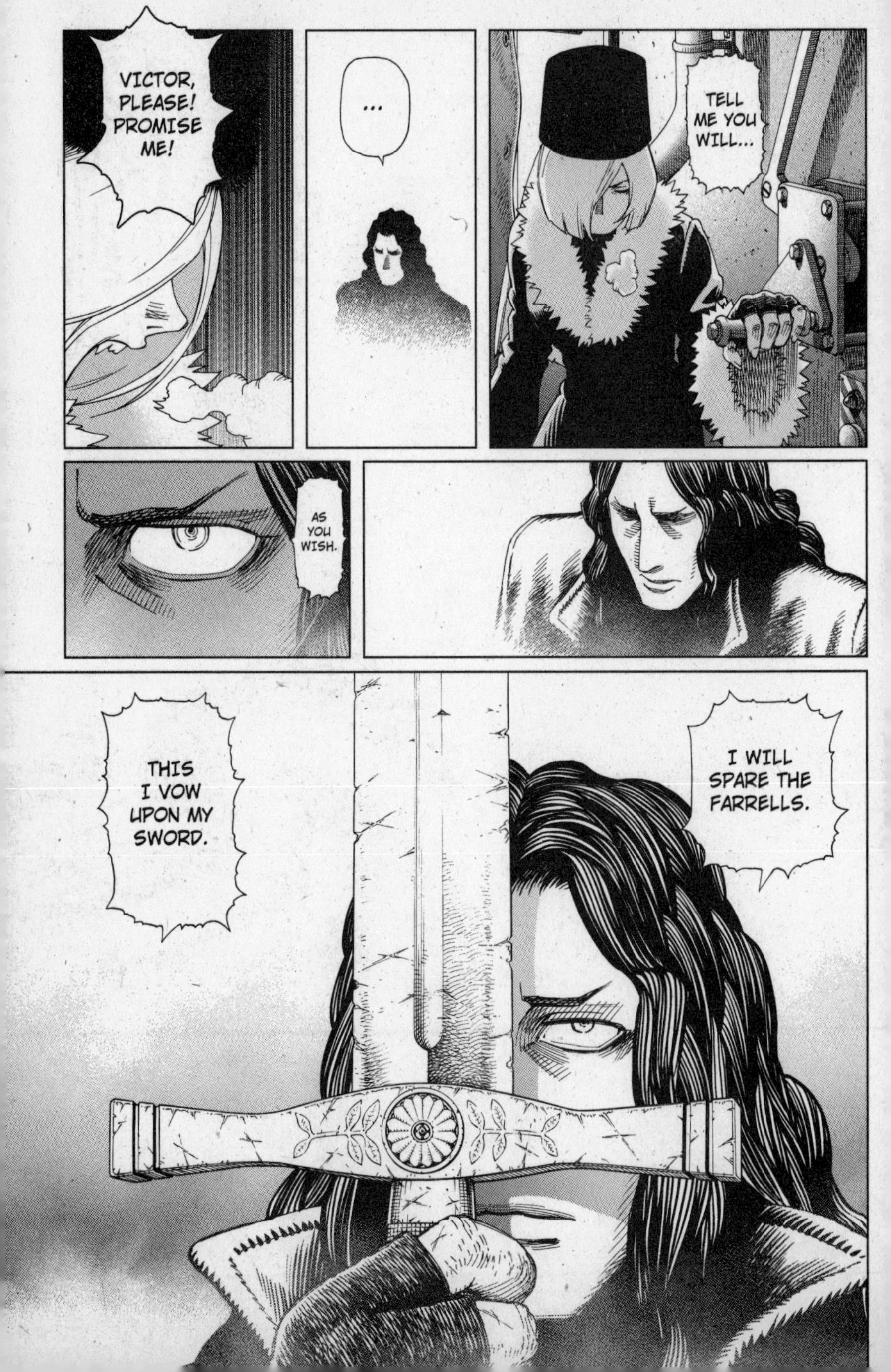
TELL ME YOU WILL...
...
VICTOR, PLEASE! PROMISE ME!
AS YOU WISH.
I WILL SPARE THE FARRELLS.
THIS I VOW UPON MY SWORD.

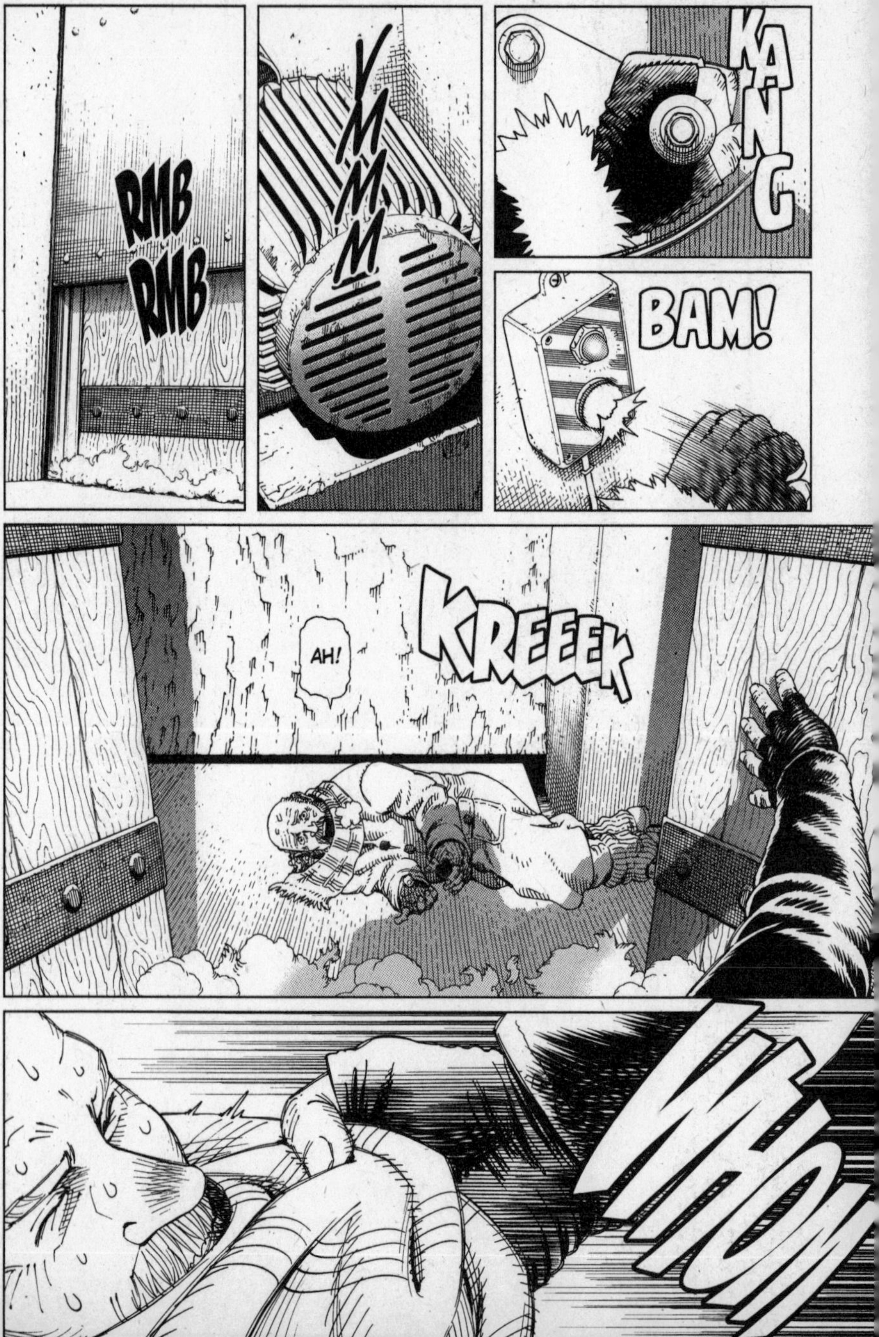
KANG
BAM!
VMMM
RMB RMB
KREEEK
AH!
WHOM

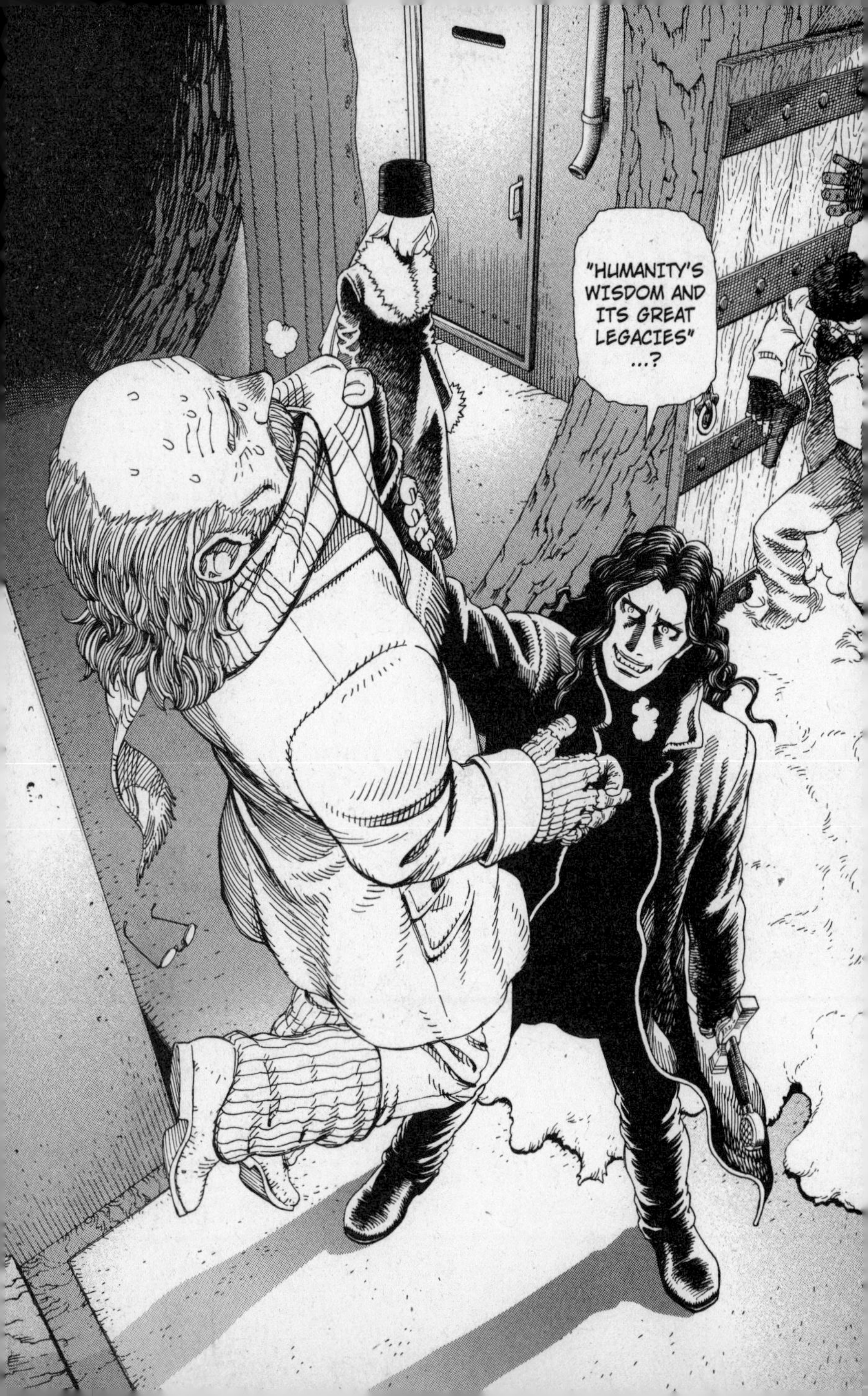
"HUMANITY'S WISDOM AND ITS GREAT LEGACIES" ...?

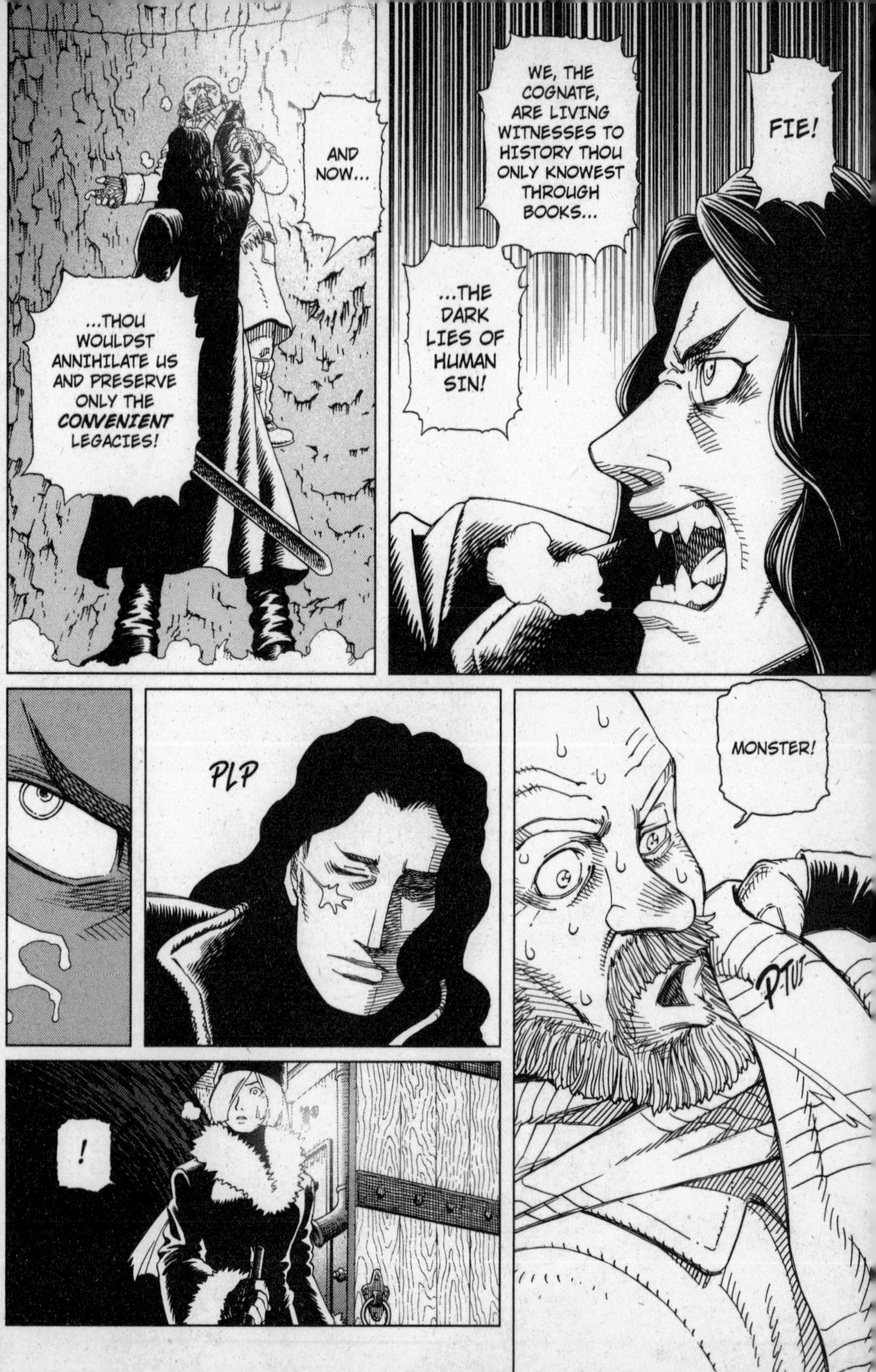
FIE!
WE, THE COGNATE, ARE LIVING WITNESSES TO HISTORY THOU ONLY KNOWEST THROUGH BOOKS...
...THE DARK LIES OF HUMAN SIN!
AND NOW...
...THOU WOULDST ANNIHILATE US AND PRESERVE ONLY THE CONVENIENT LEGACIES!
MONSTER!
P-TUI
PLP
!

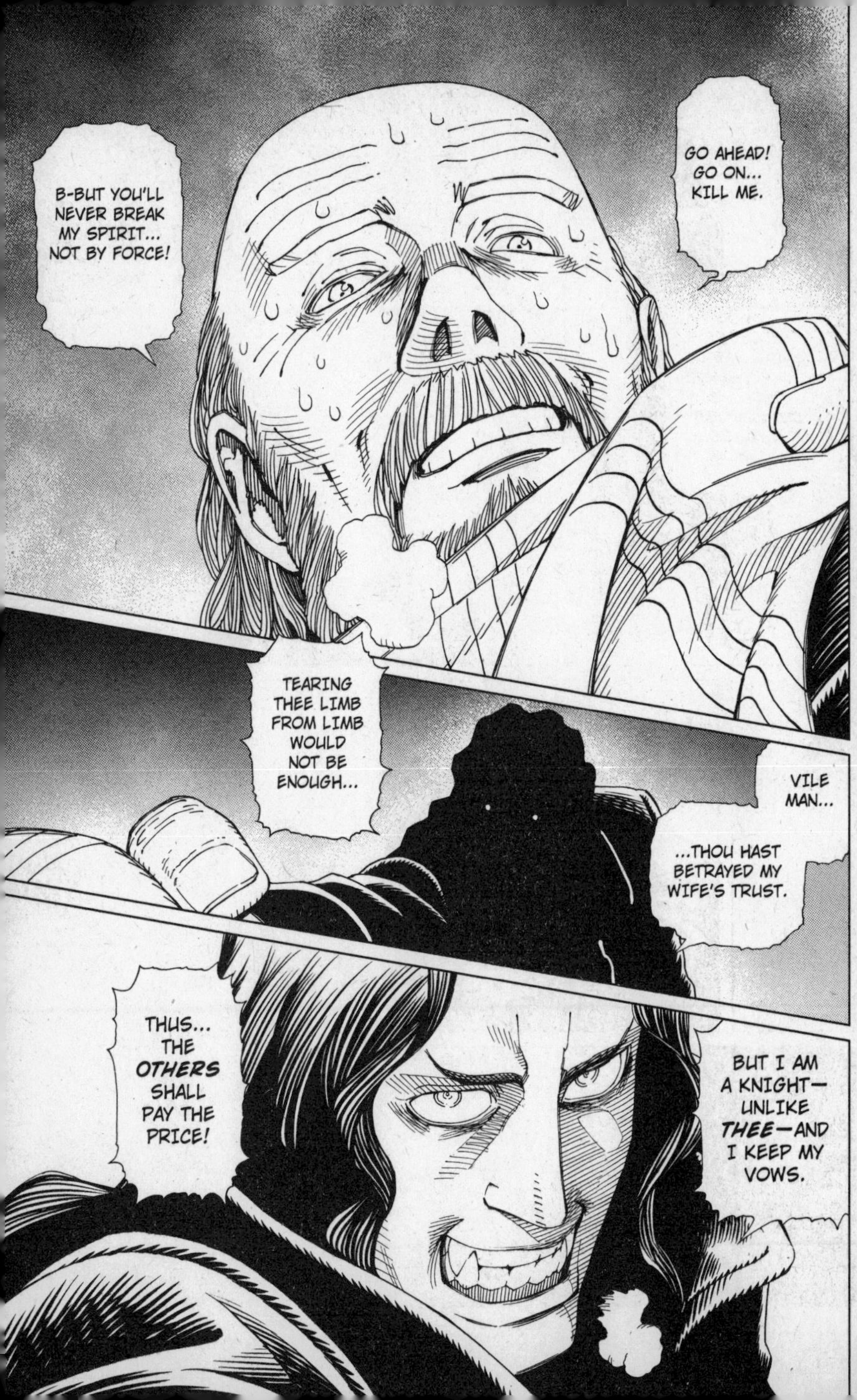
GO AHEAD! GO ON... KILL ME.
B-BUT YOU'LL NEVER BREAK MY SPIRIT... NOT BY FORCE!
VILE MAN...
...THOU HAST BETRAYED MY WIFE'S TRUST.
TEARING THEE LIMB FROM LIMB WOULD NOT BE ENOUGH...
BUT I AM A KNIGHT—UNLIKE THEE—AND I KEEP MY VOWS.
THUS... THE OTHERS SHALL PAY THE PRICE!

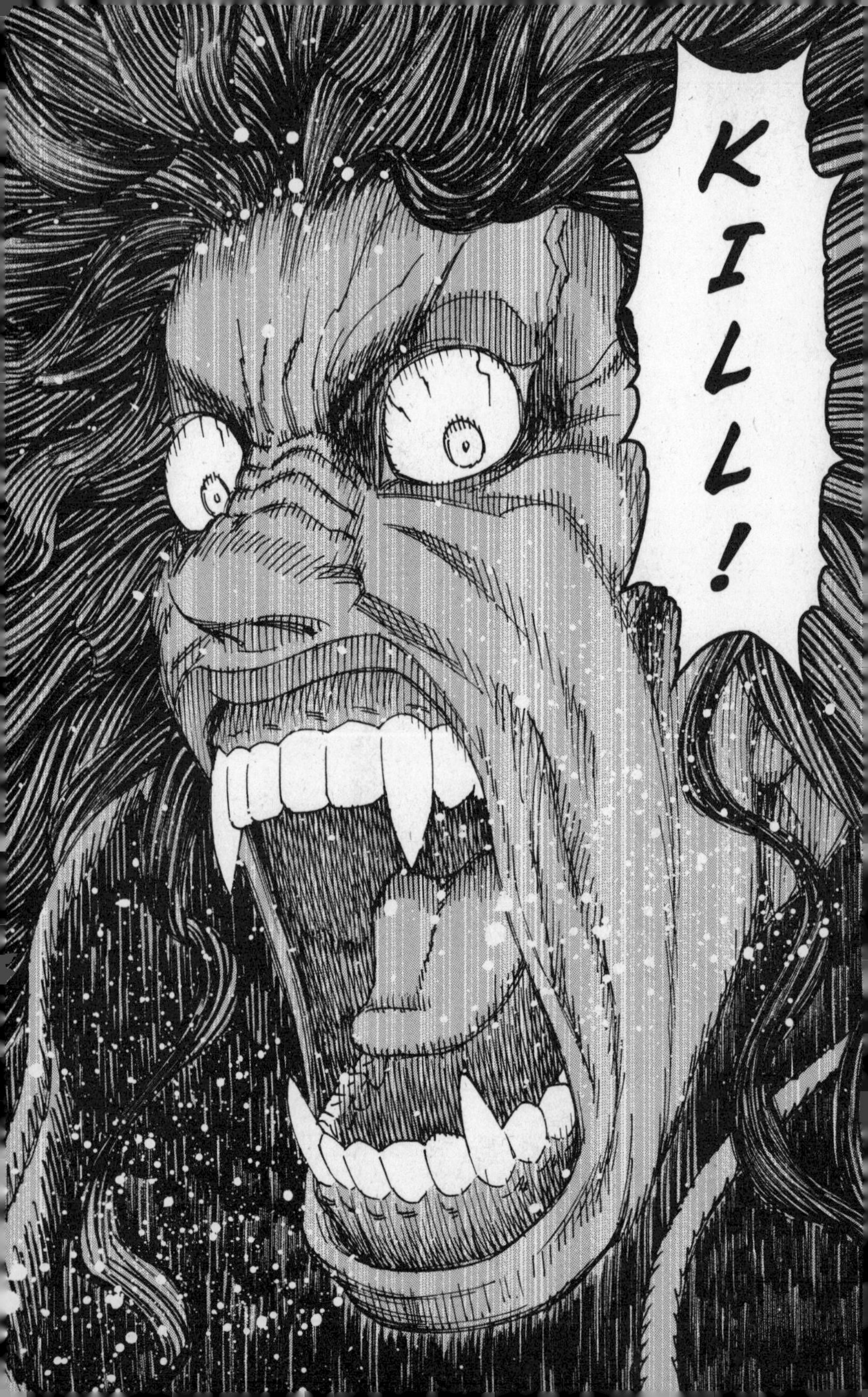
KILL!

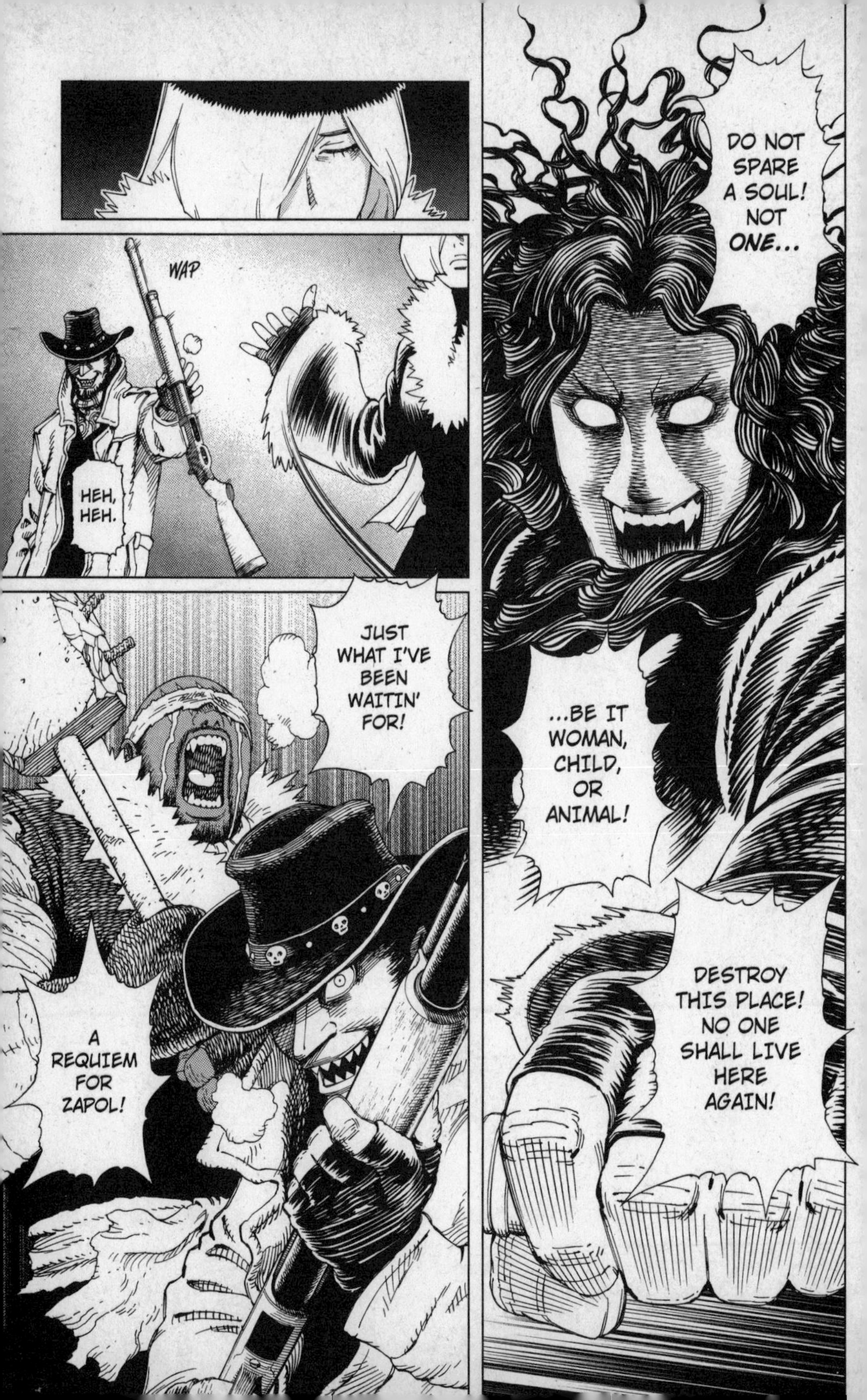
DO NOT SPARE A SOUL! NOT ONE...
...BE IT WOMAN, CHILD, OR ANIMAL!
DESTROY THIS PLACE! NO ONE SHALL LIVE HERE AGAIN!
WAP
HEH, HEH.
JUST WHAT I'VE BEEN WAITIN' FOR!
A REQUIEM FOR ZAPOL!

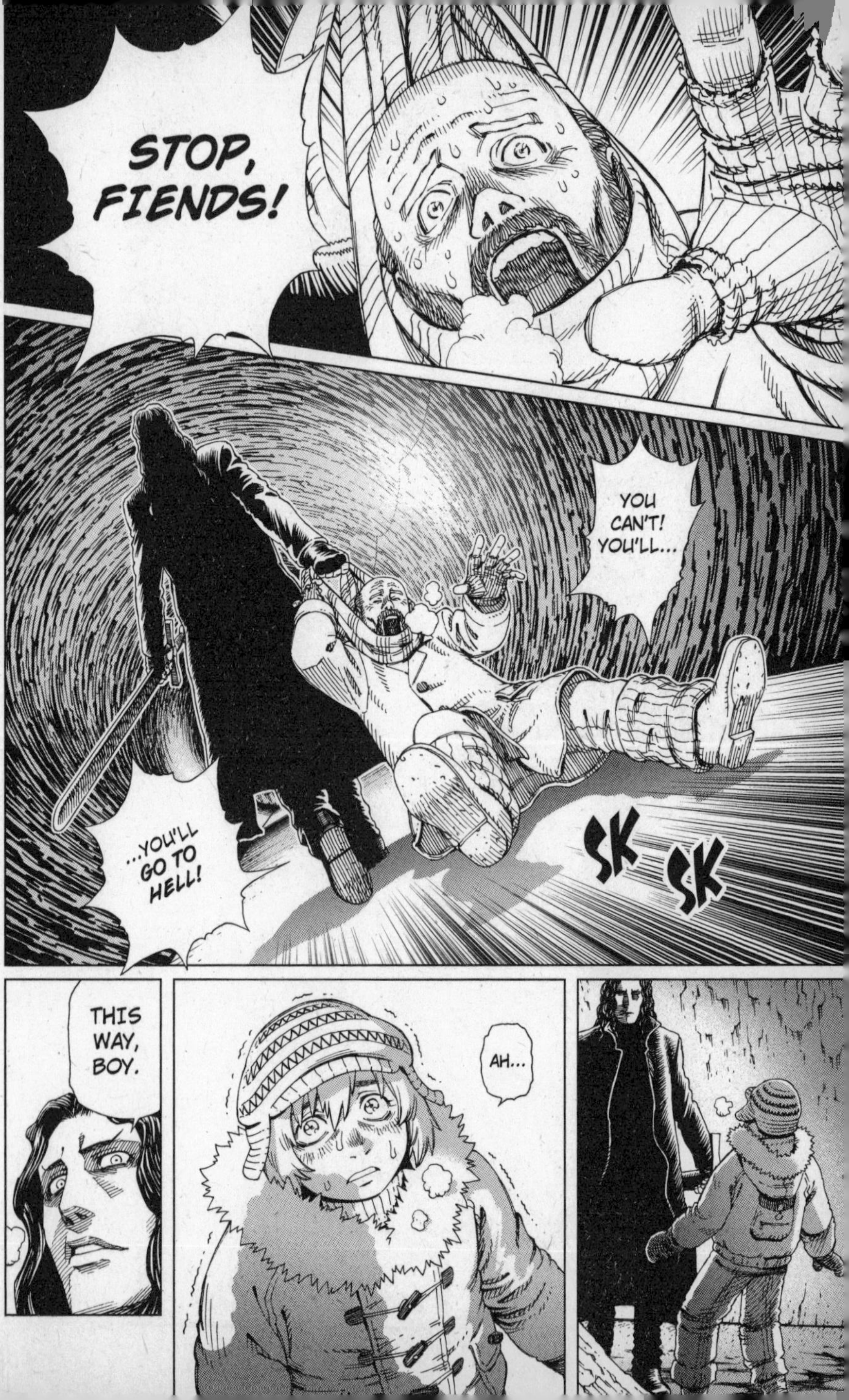
STOP, FIENDS!
YOU CAN'T! YOU'LL...
...YOU'LL GO TO HELL!
SK SK
AH...
THIS WAY, BOY.

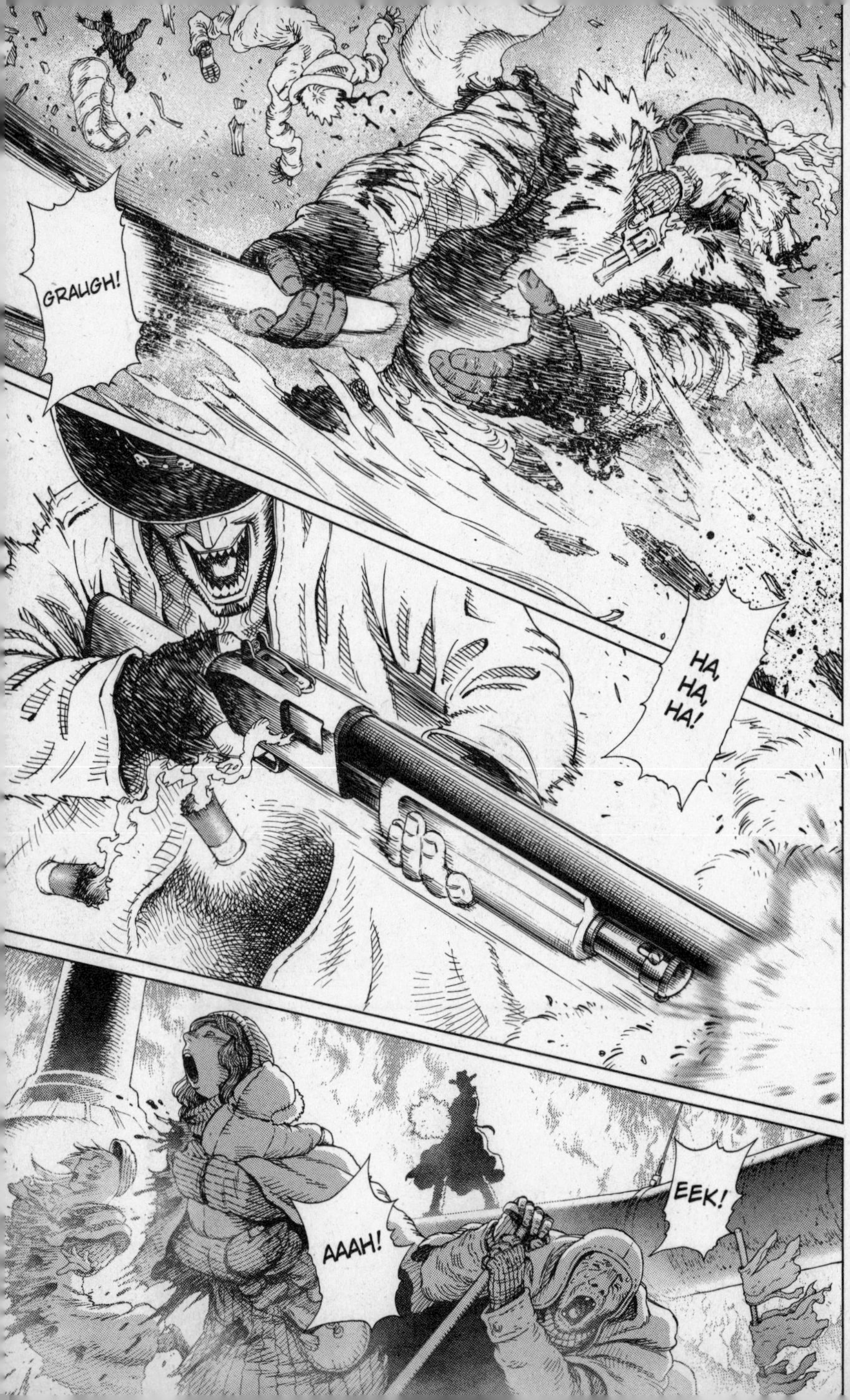
GRAUGH!
HA, HA, HA!
EEK!
AAAH!

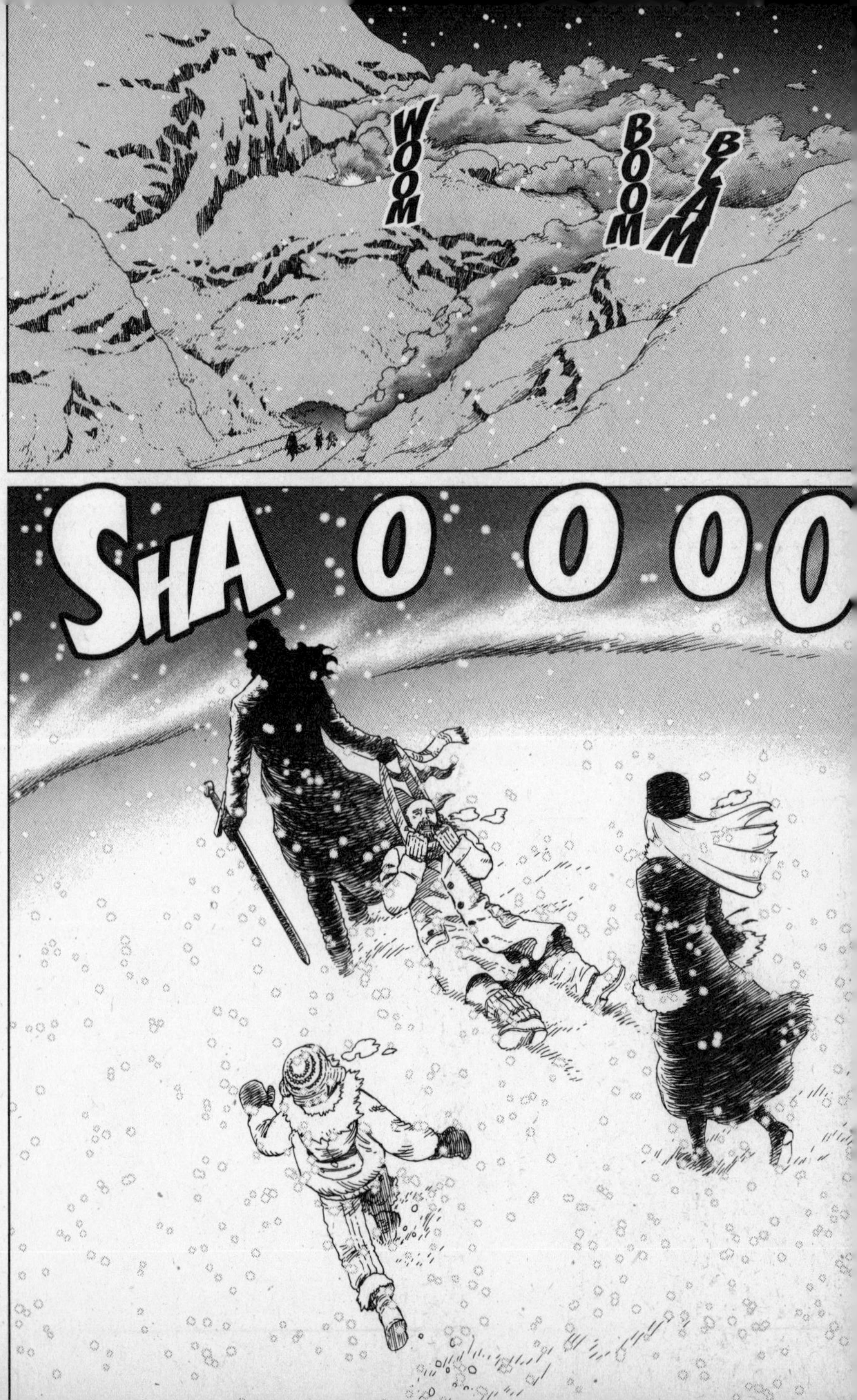
BLAM
BOOM
WOOM
SHA O O OO

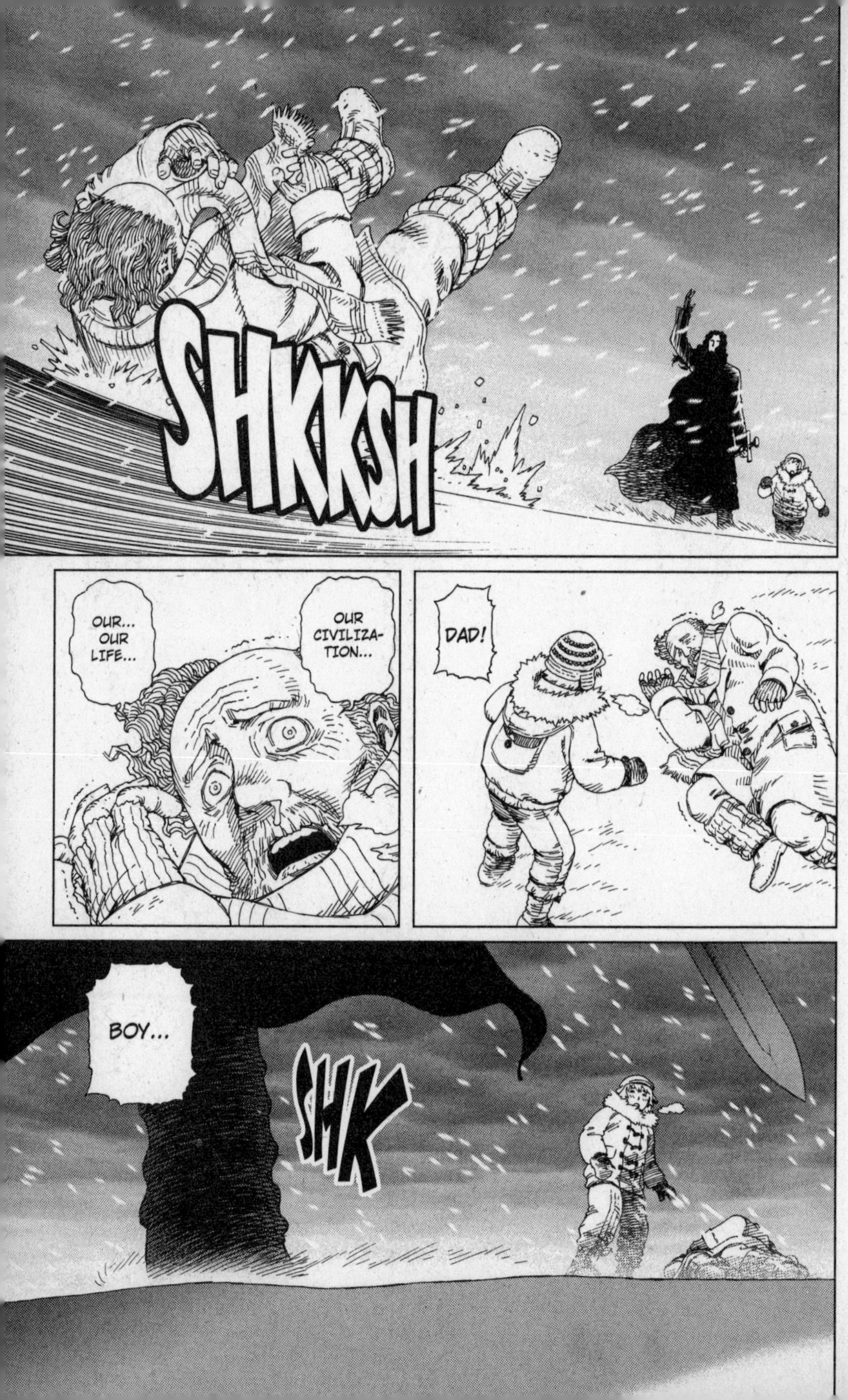
SHKKSH
DAD!
OUR CIVILIZATION...
OUR... OUR LIFE...
SHK
BOY...

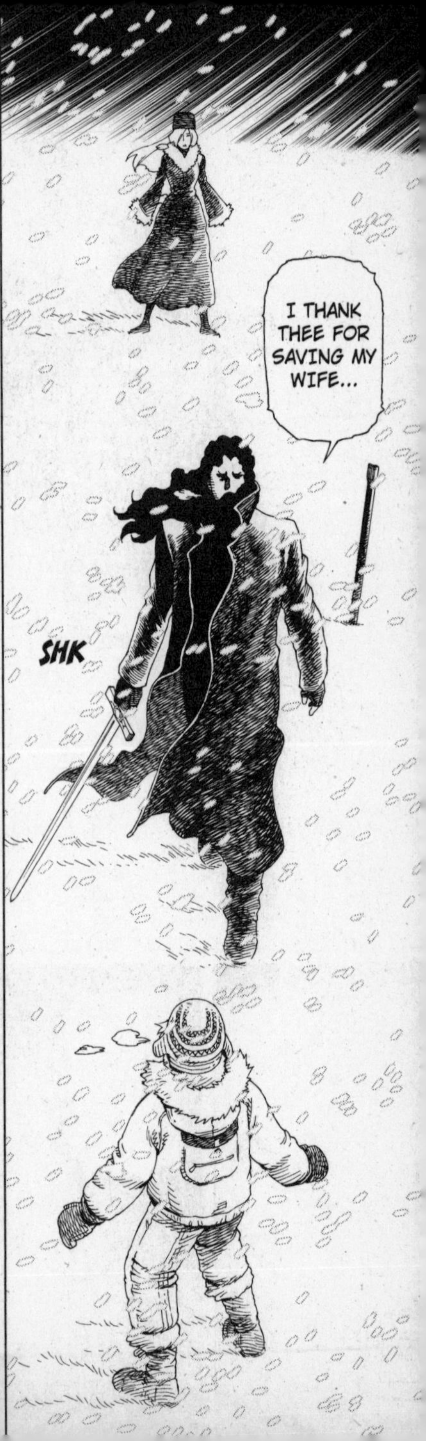
I THANK THEE FOR SAVING MY WIFE...
SHK

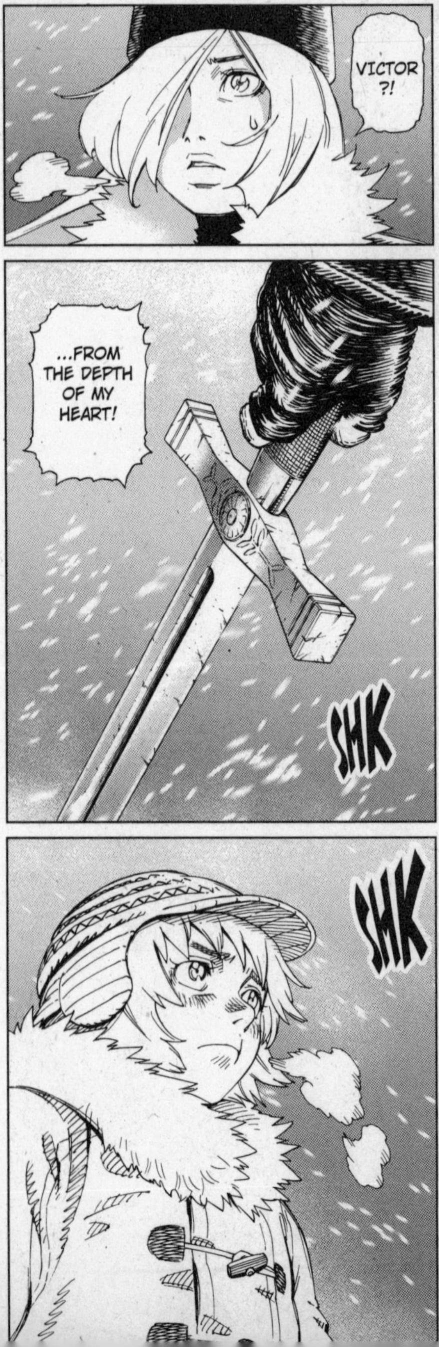
VICTOR ?!
...FROM THE DEPTH OF MY HEART!
SHK
SHK

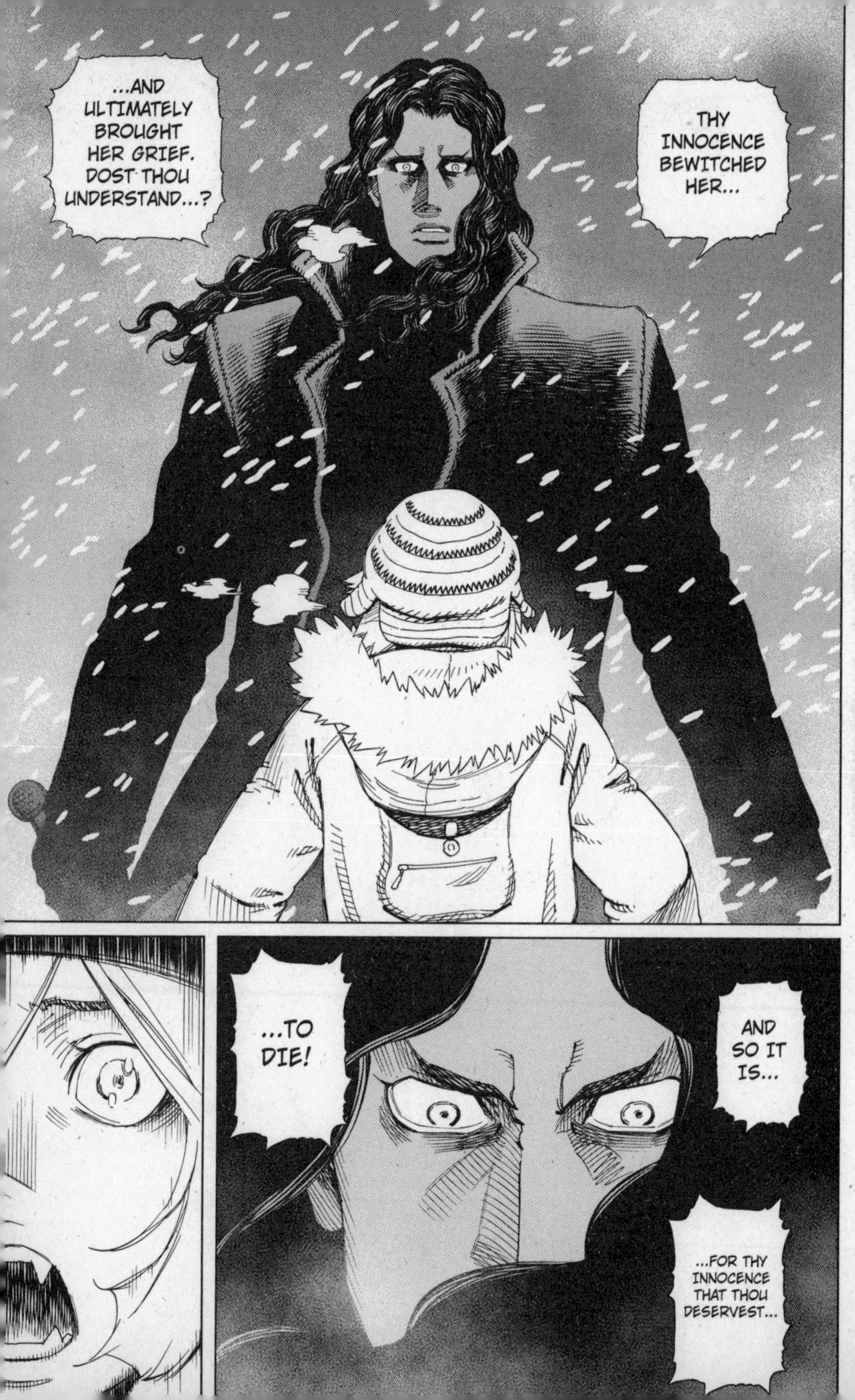
THY INNOCENCE BEWITCHED HER...
...AND ULTIMATELY BROUGHT HER GRIEF. DOST THOU UNDERSTAND...?
AND SO IT IS...
...FOR THY INNOCENCE THAT THOU DESERVEST...
...TO DIE!

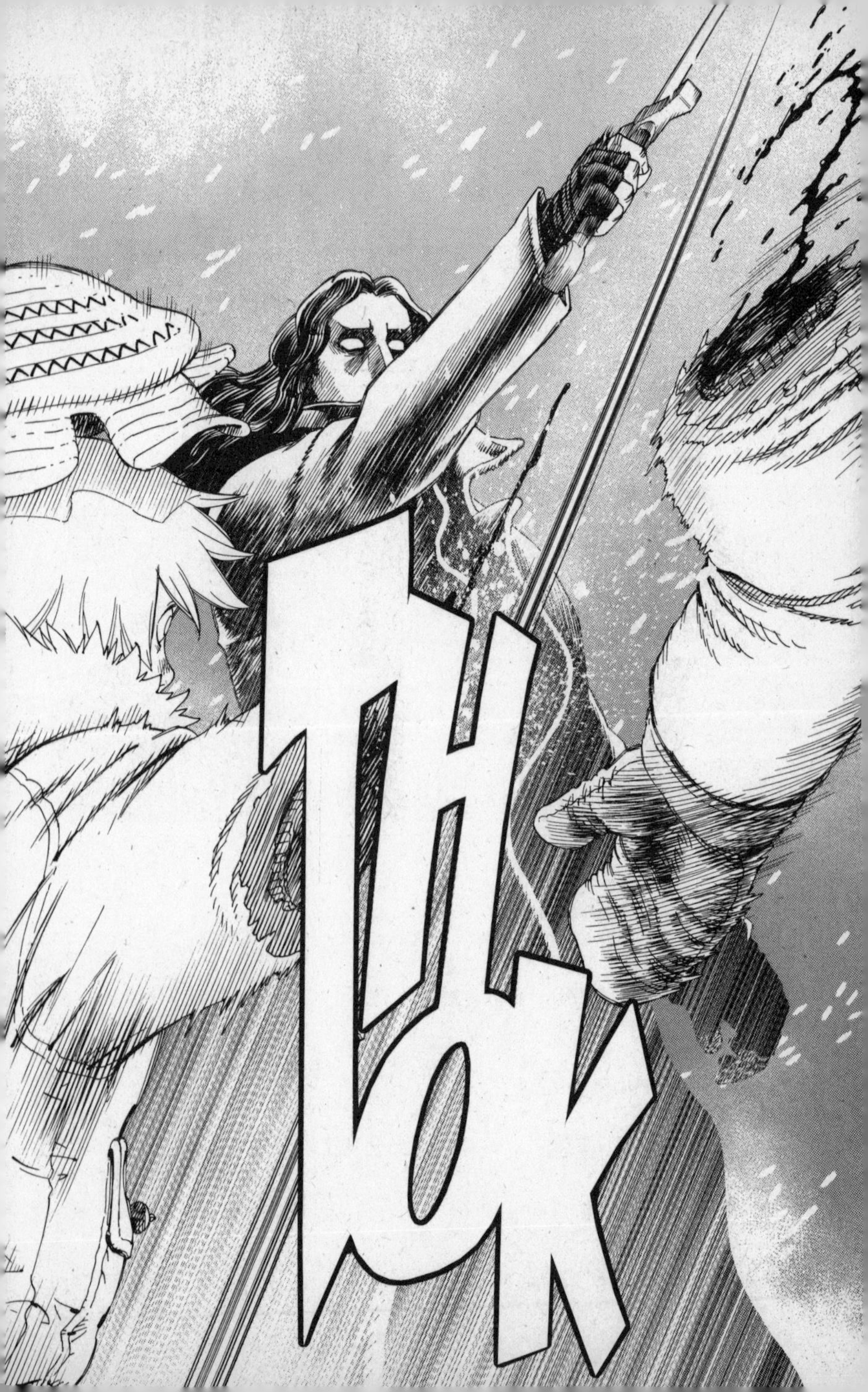
THOK

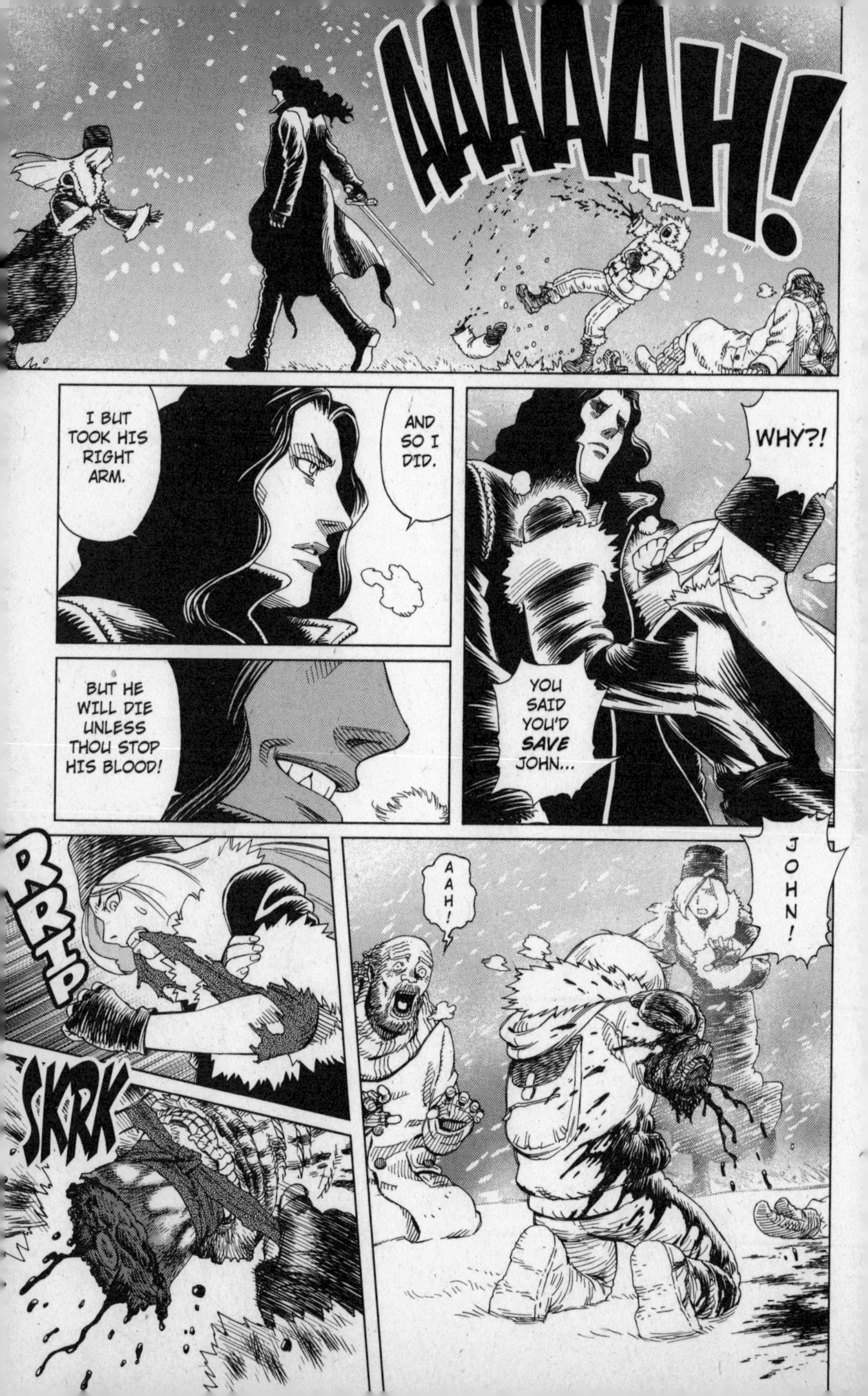
AAAAAH!
WHY?!
YOU SAID YOU'D **SAVE** JOHN...
AND SO I DID.
I BUT TOOK HIS RIGHT ARM.
BUT HE WILL DIE UNLESS THOU STOP HIS BLOOD!
JOHN!
AAH!
RRIP
SKRK

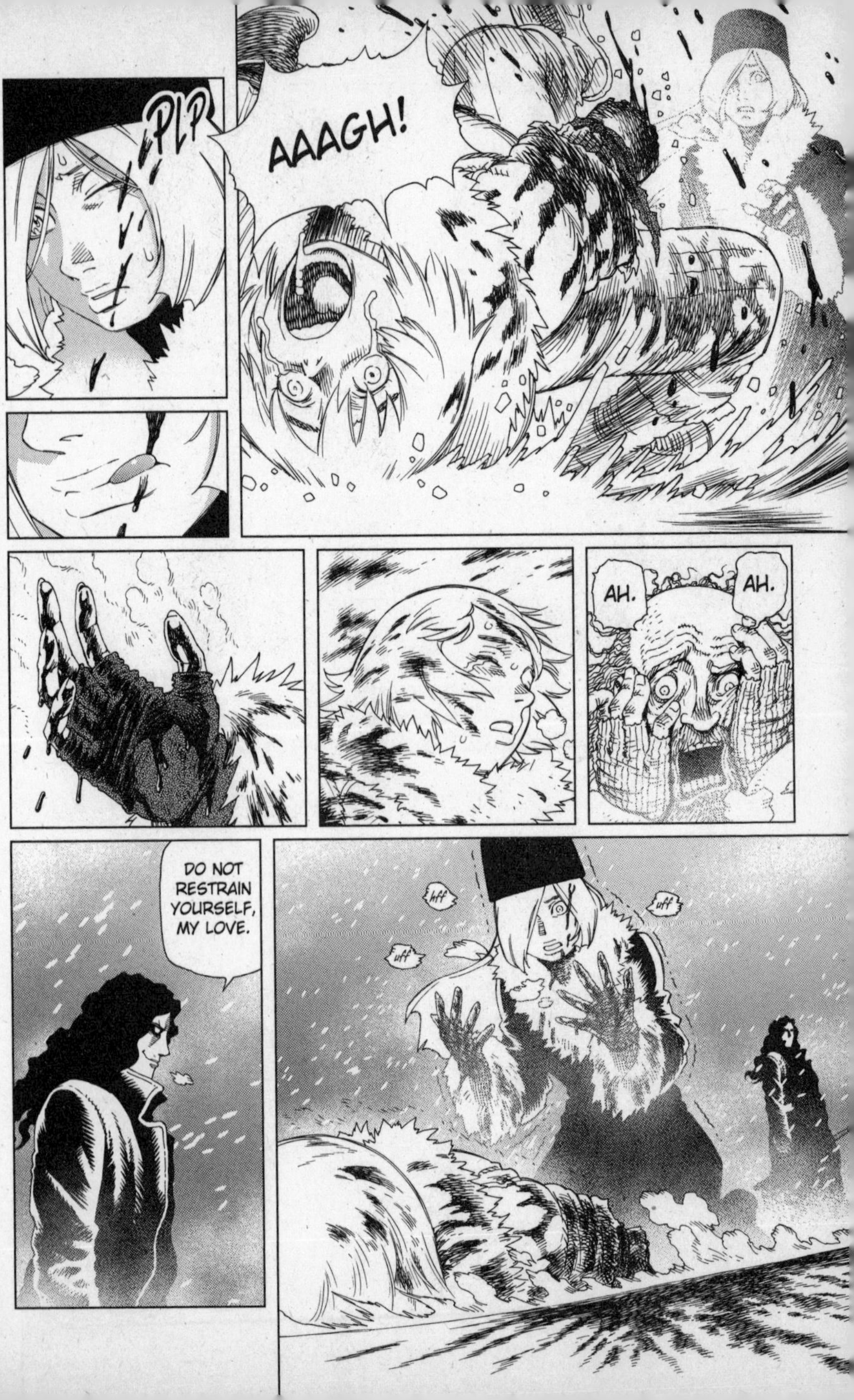
AAAGH!
PLP
AH.
AH.
hff
uff
uff
DO NOT RESTRAIN YOURSELF, MY LOVE.

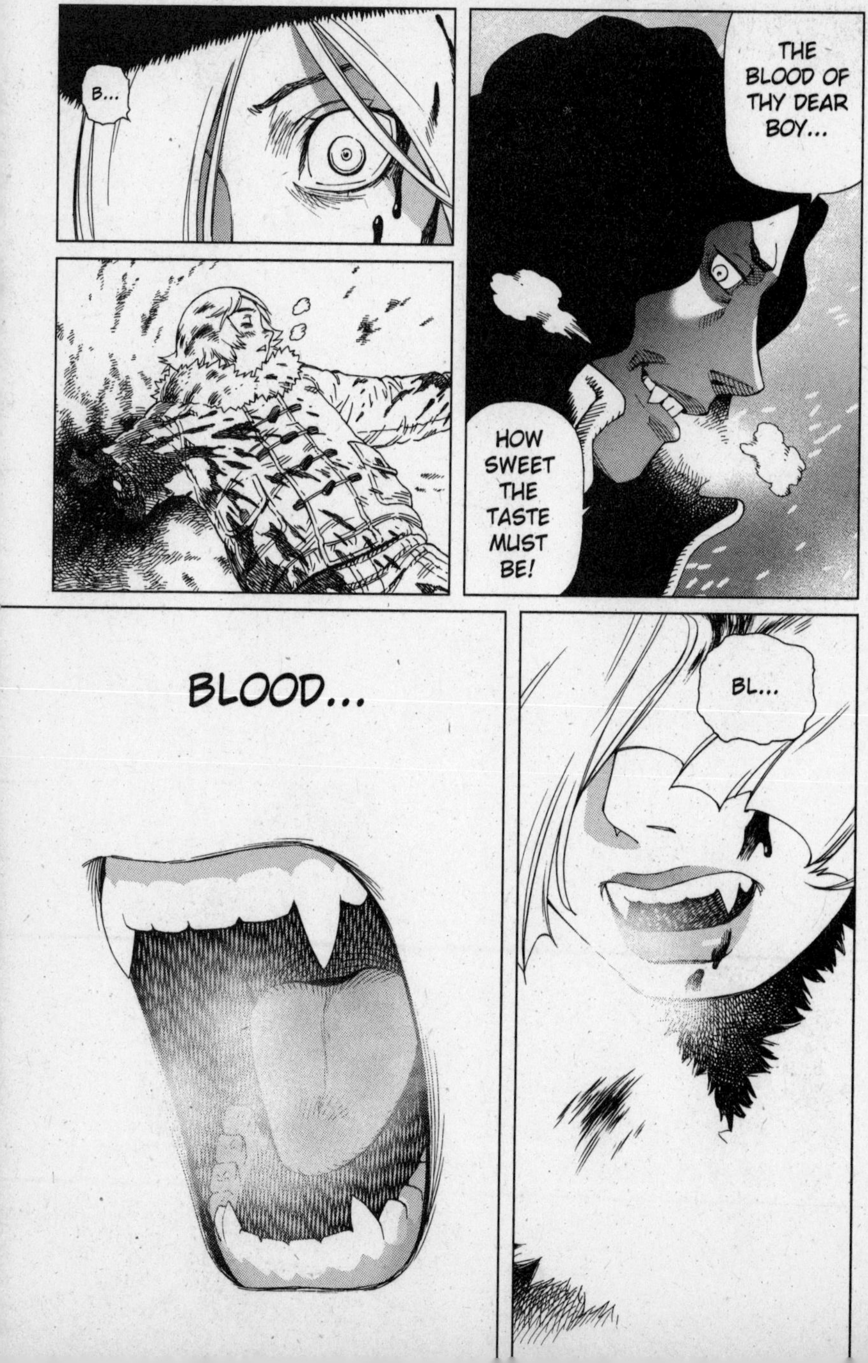
THE BLOOD OF THY DEAR BOY...
HOW SWEET THE TASTE MUST BE!
B...
BL...
BLOOD...

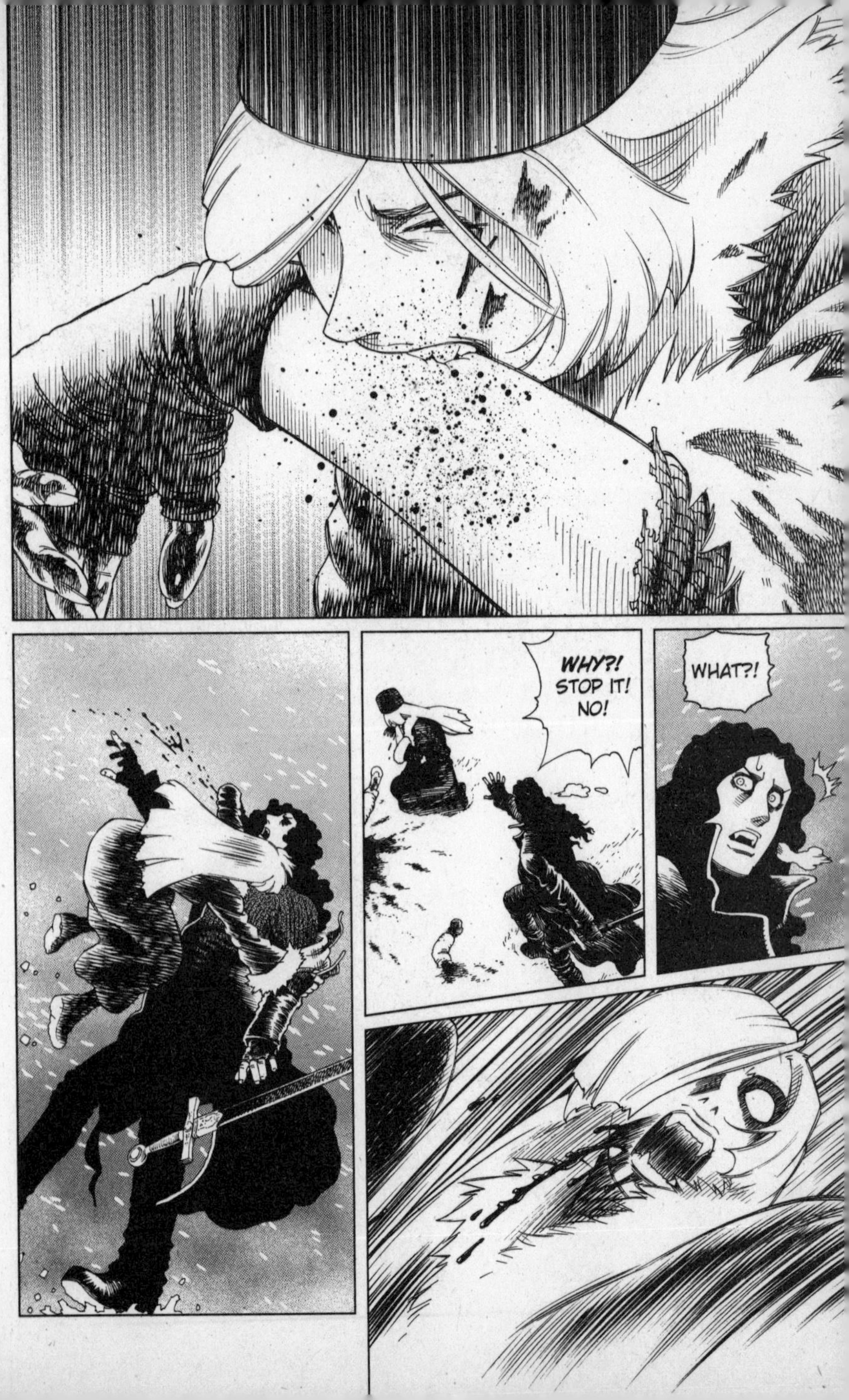
WHAT?!
WHY?! STOP IT! NO!

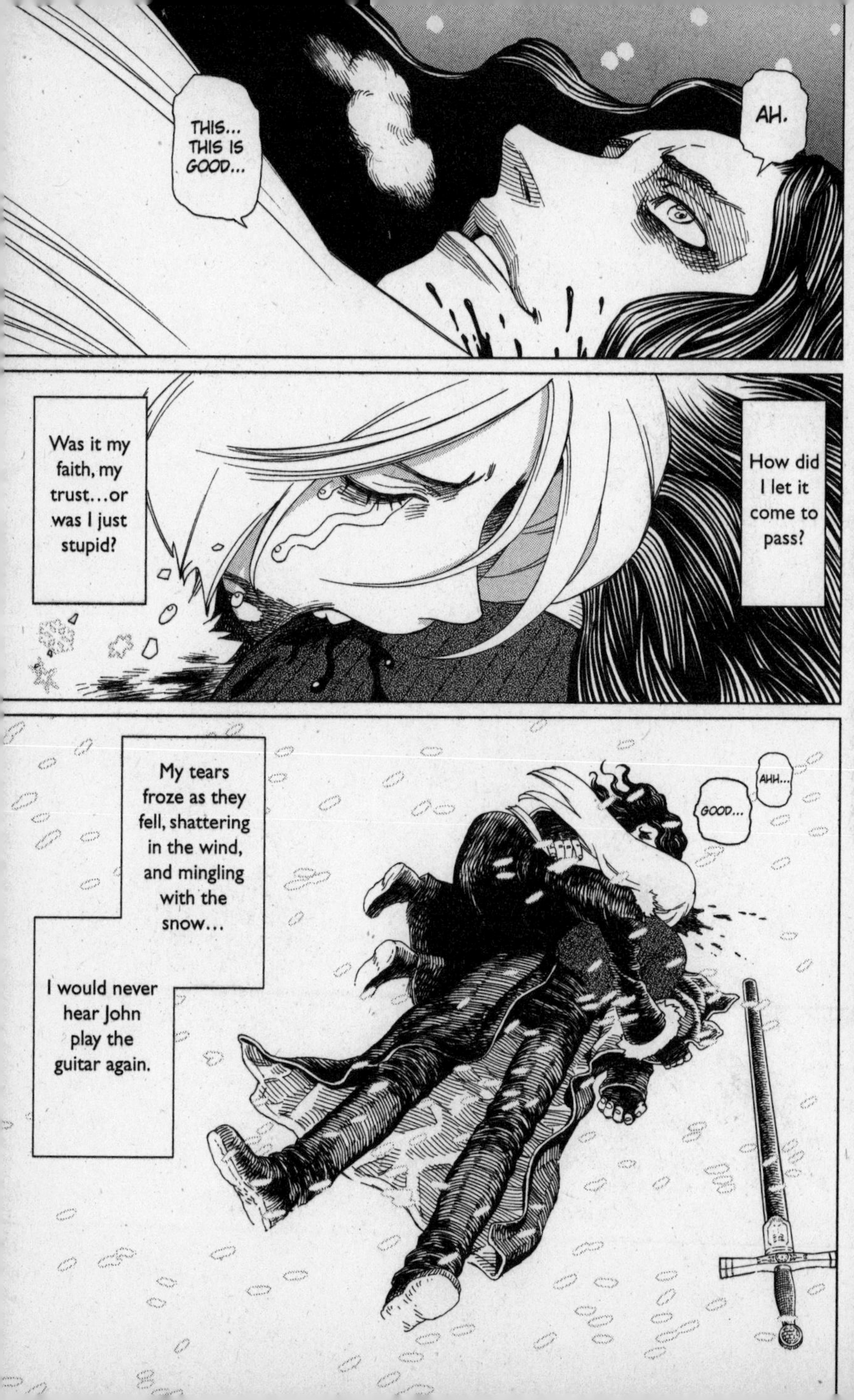
AH.
THIS... THIS IS GOOD...
How did I let it come to pass?
Was it my faith, my trust...or was I just stupid?
AHH...
GOOD...
My tears froze as they fell, shattering in the wind, and mingling with the snow...
I would never hear John play the guitar again.

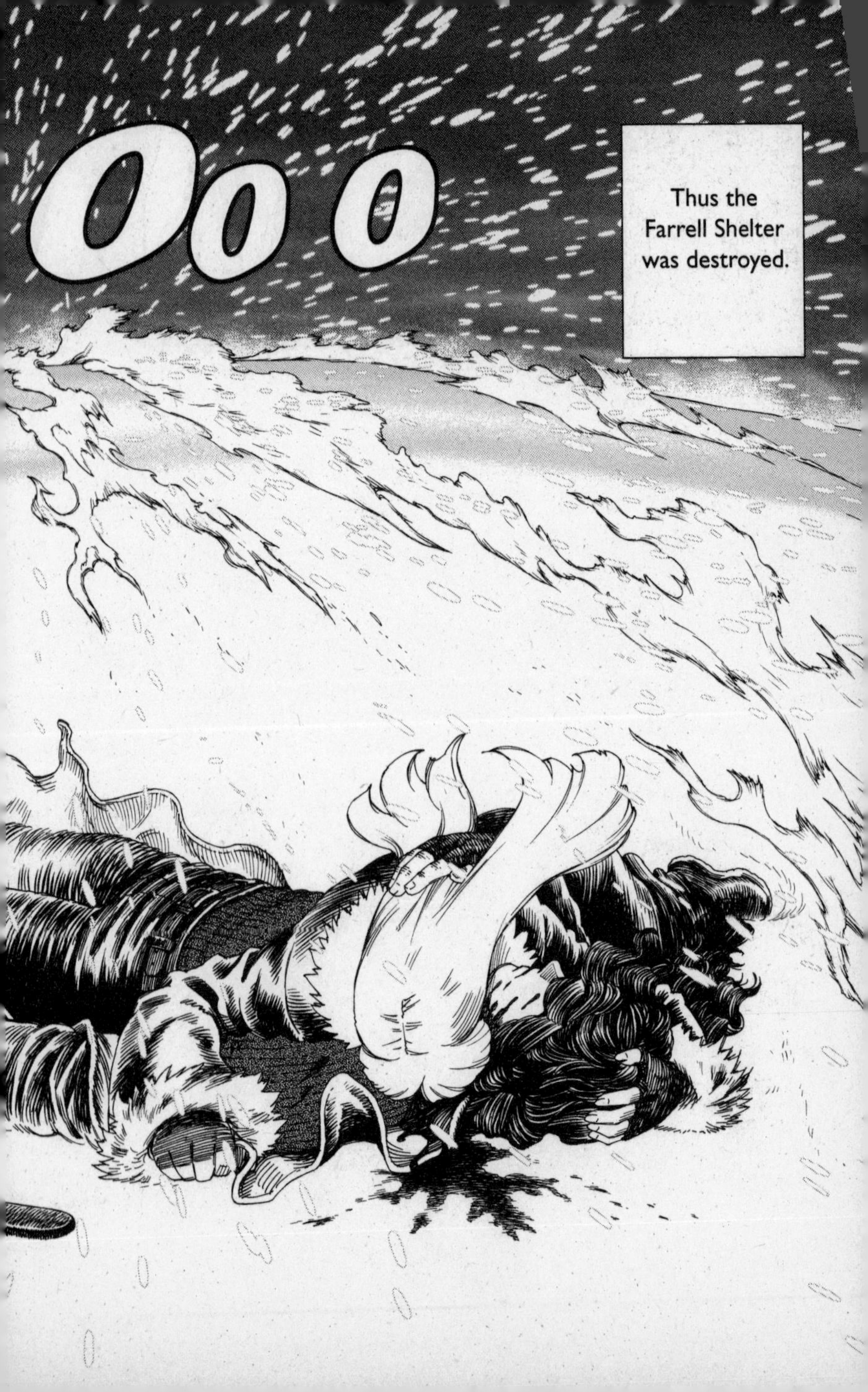
Thus the Farrell Shelter was destroyed.
OOO

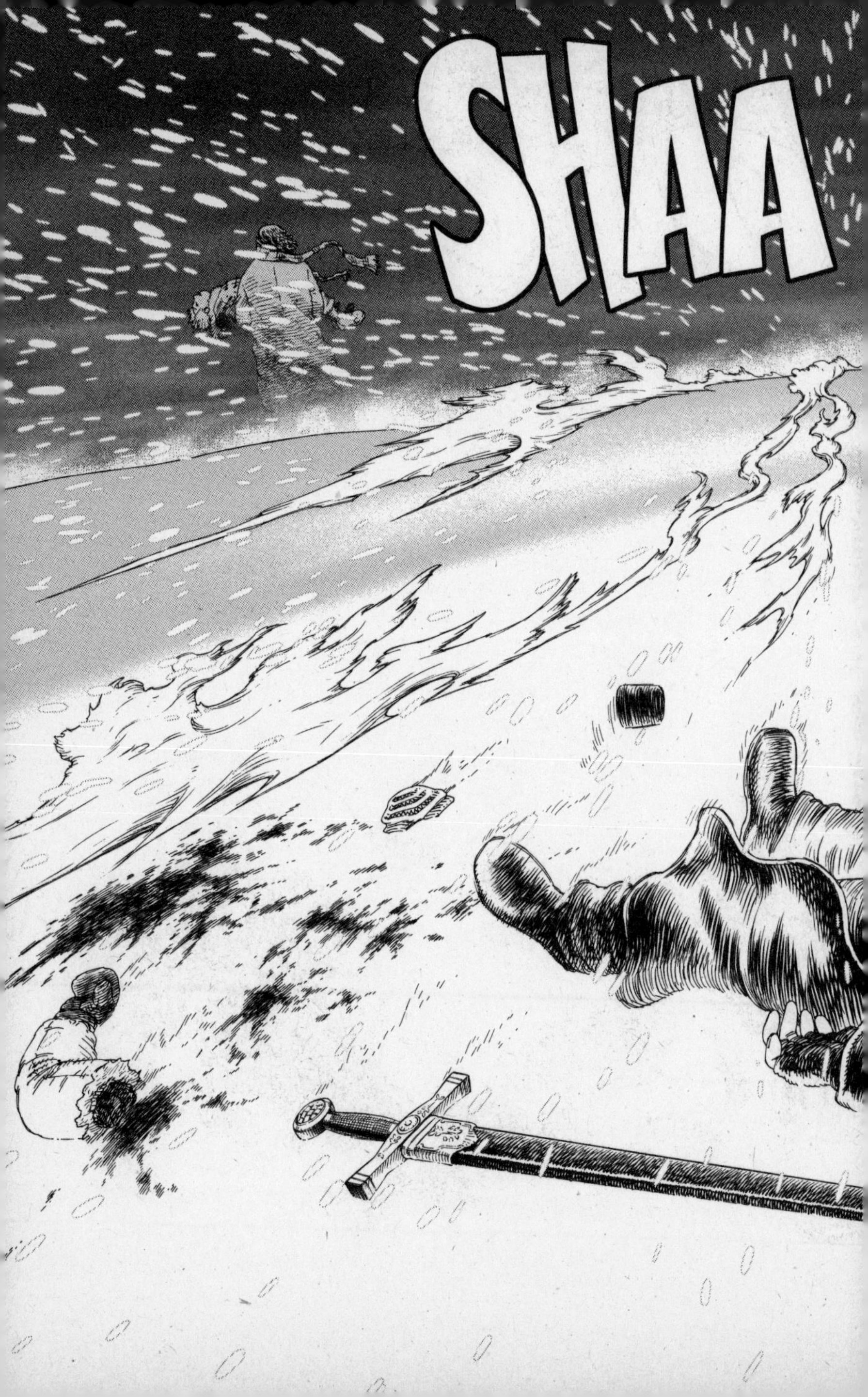
SHAA

PHASE 48: Dream of an Icy Sleep

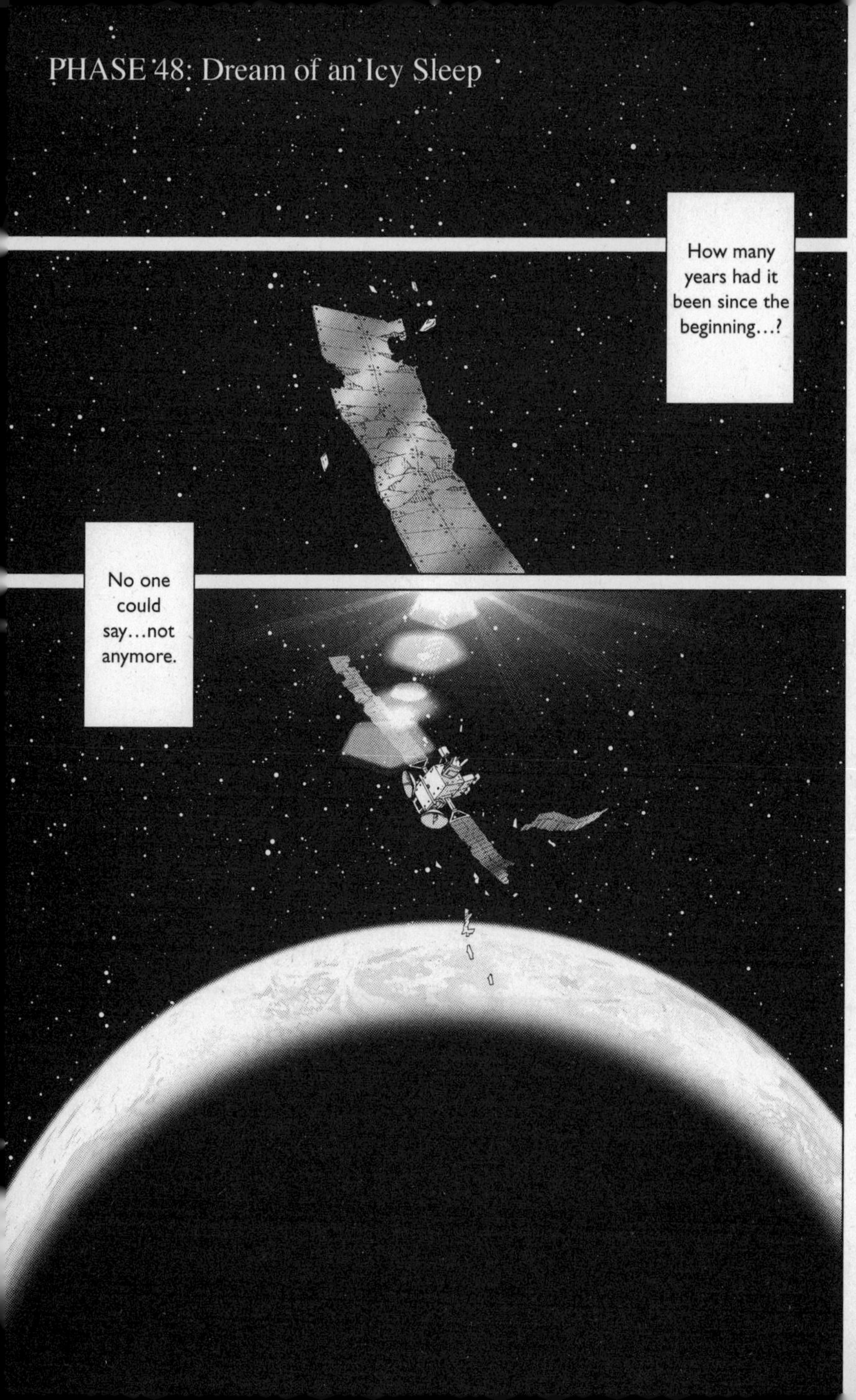
How many years had it been since the beginning...?
No one could say...not anymore.

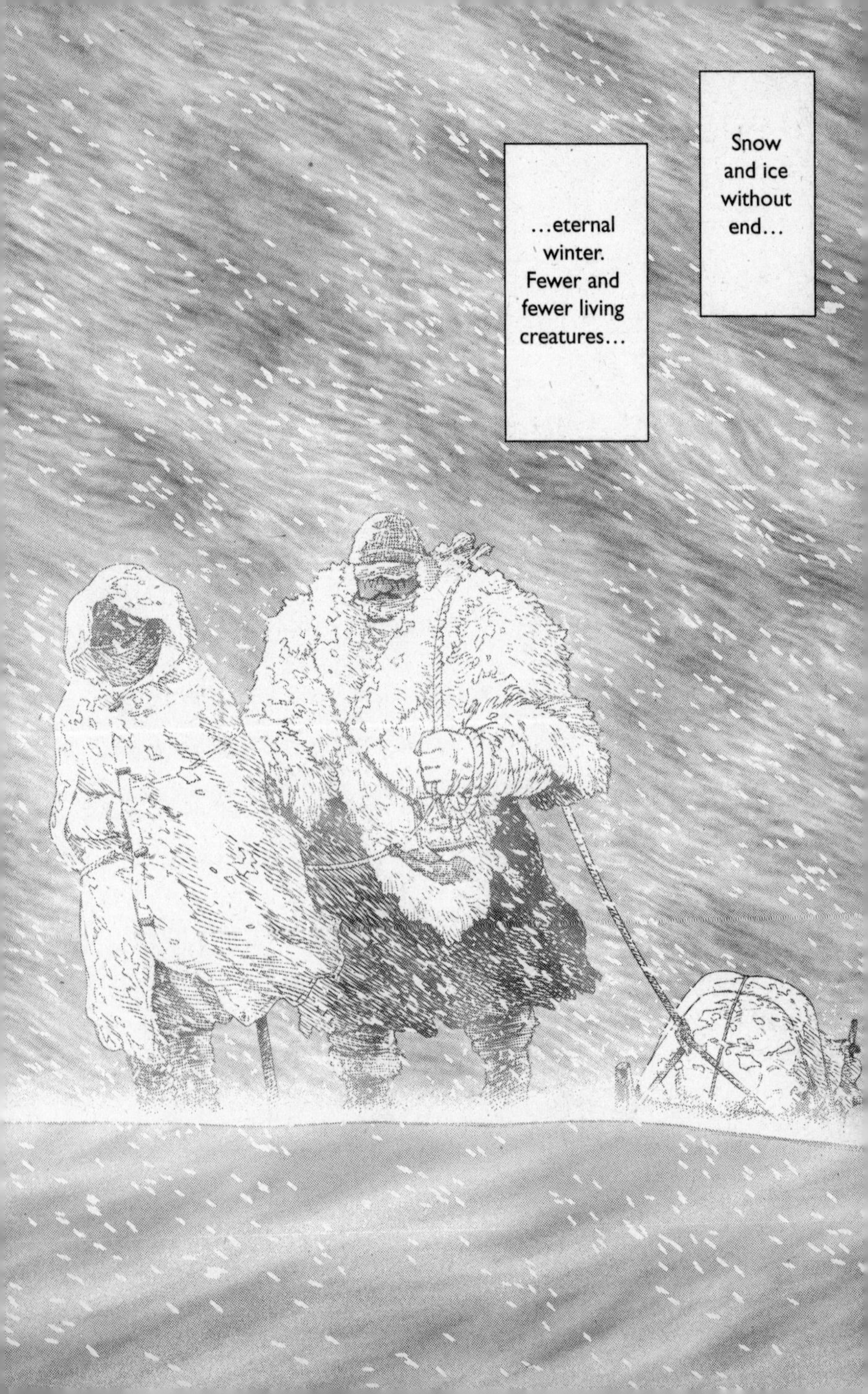
Snow and ice without end…
…eternal winter. Fewer and fewer living creatures…

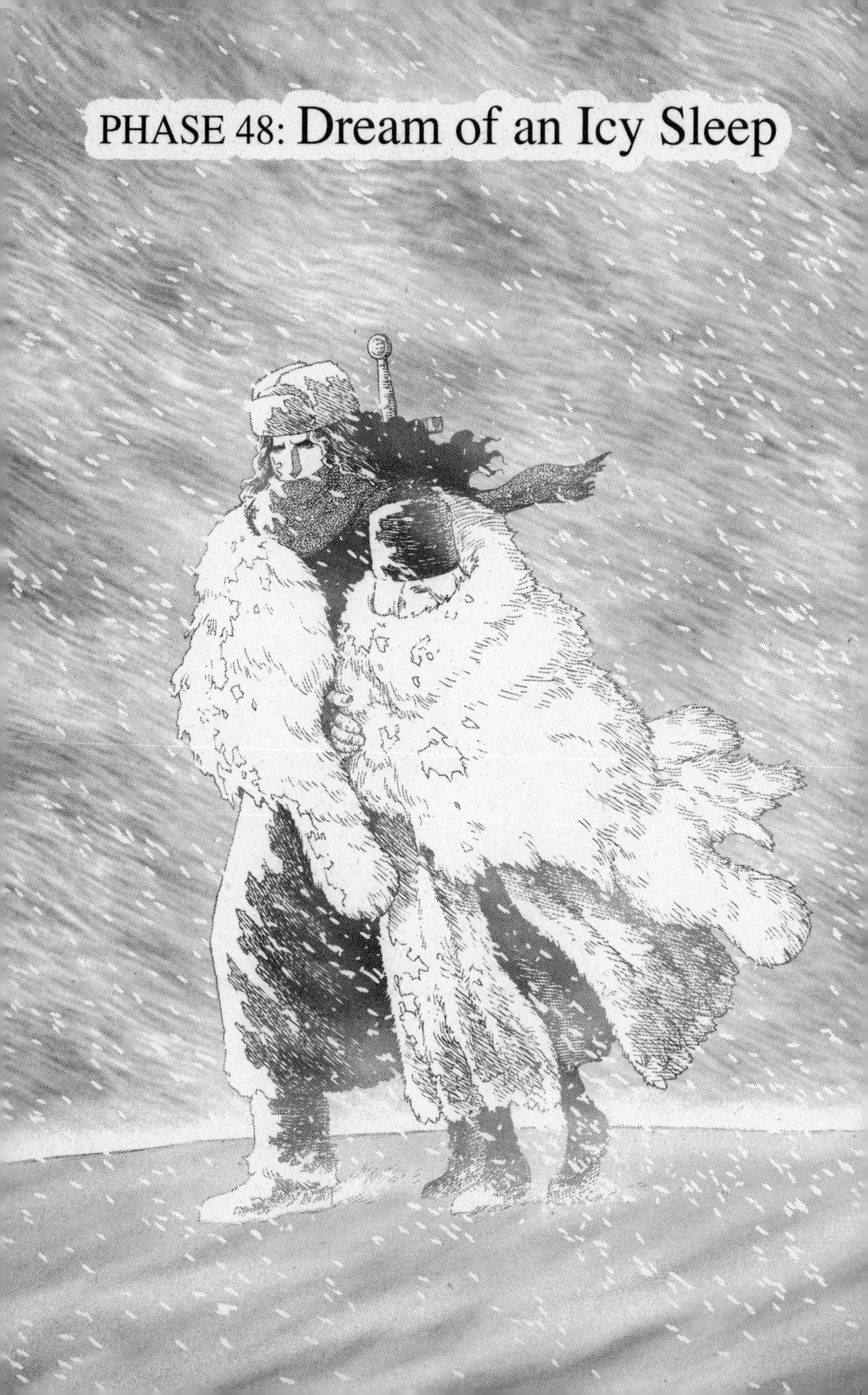
PHASE 48: Dream of an Icy Sleep

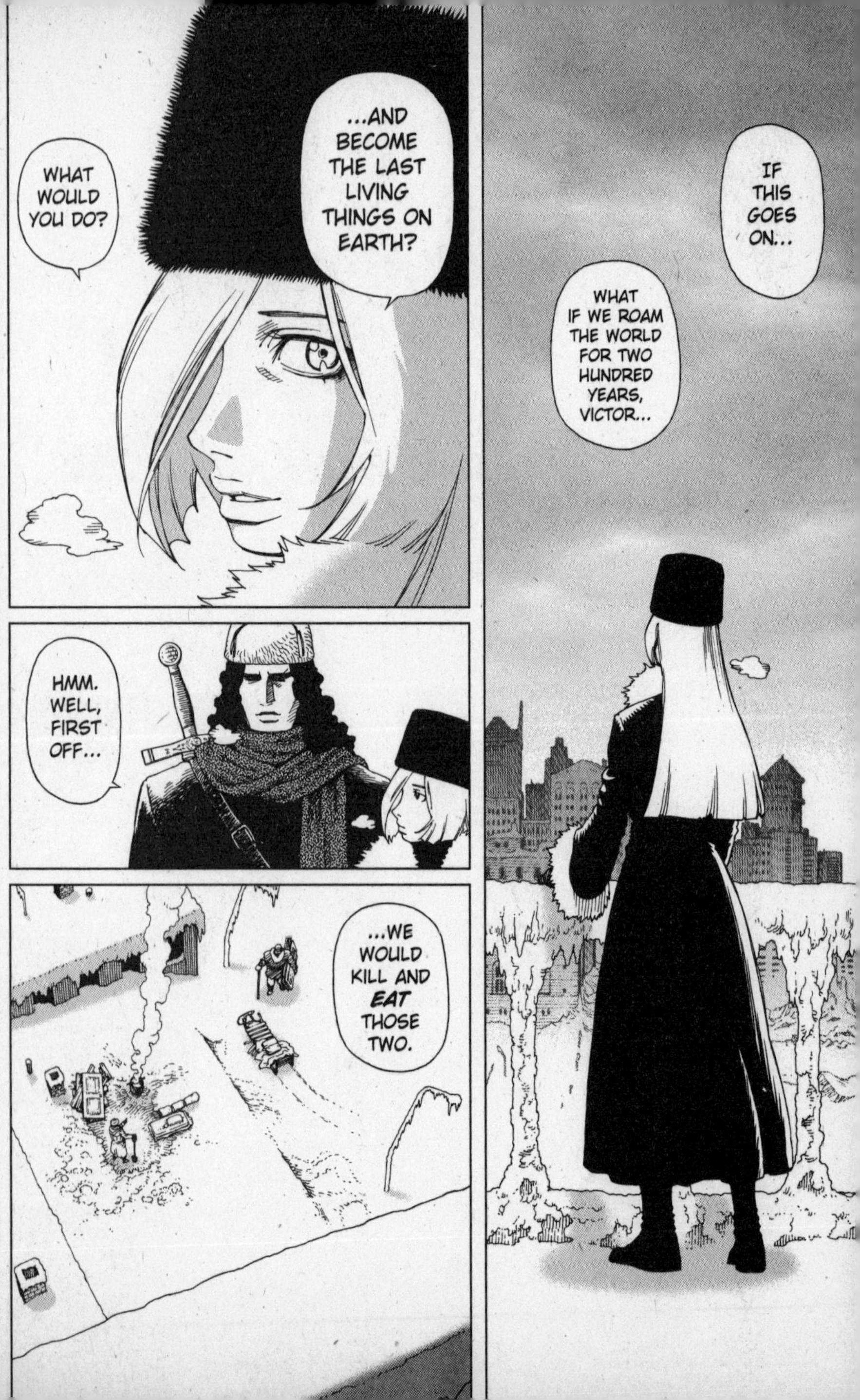
IF THIS GOES ON...
WHAT IF WE ROAM THE WORLD FOR TWO HUNDRED YEARS, VICTOR...
...AND BECOME THE LAST LIVING THINGS ON EARTH?
WHAT WOULD YOU DO?
HMM. WELL, FIRST OFF...
...WE WOULD KILL AND *EAT* THOSE TWO.

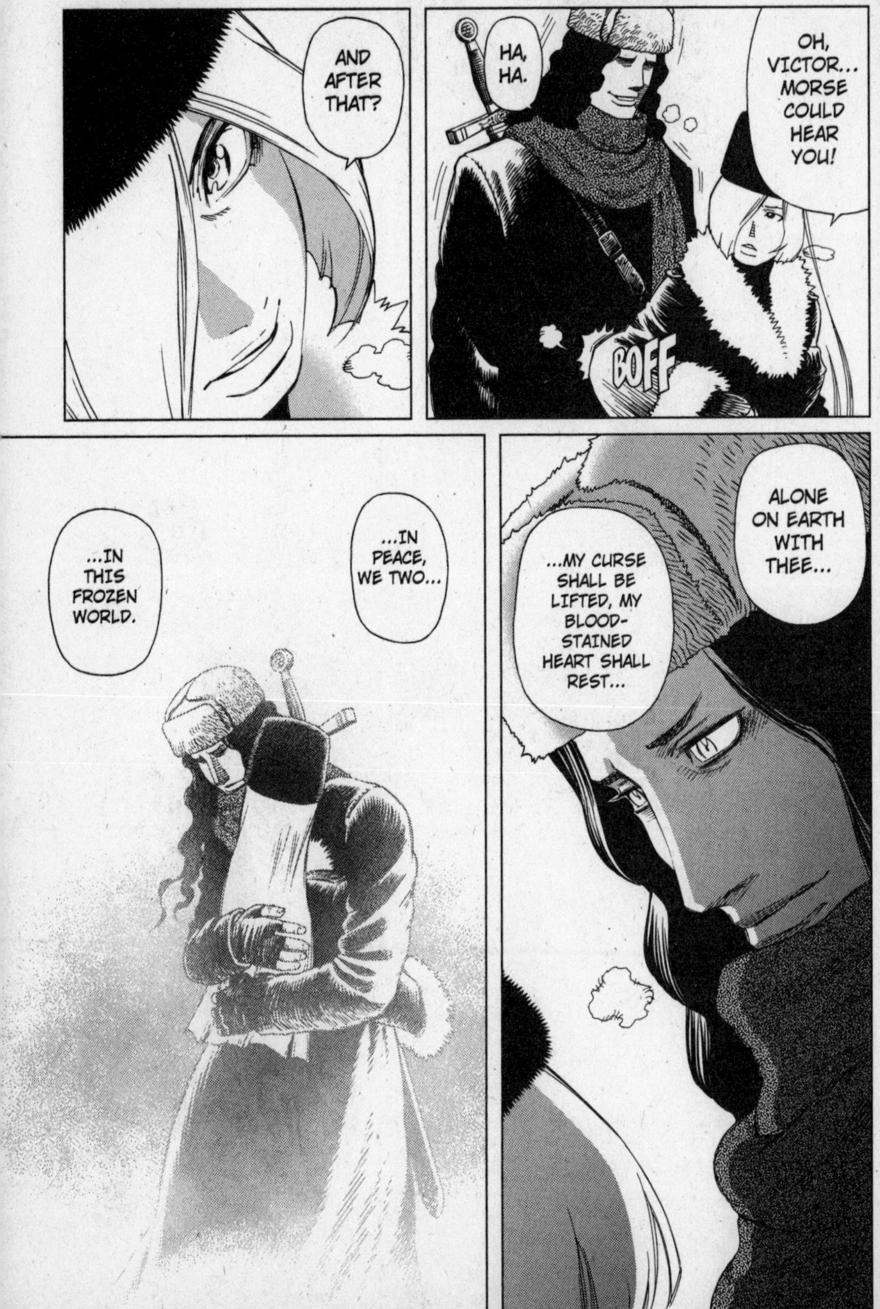
OH, VICTOR... MORSE COULD HEAR YOU!
HA, HA.
BOFF
AND AFTER THAT?
ALONE ON EARTH WITH THEE...
...MY CURSE SHALL BE LIFTED, MY BLOOD-STAINED HEART SHALL REST...
...IN PEACE, WE TWO...
...IN THIS FROZEN WORLD.

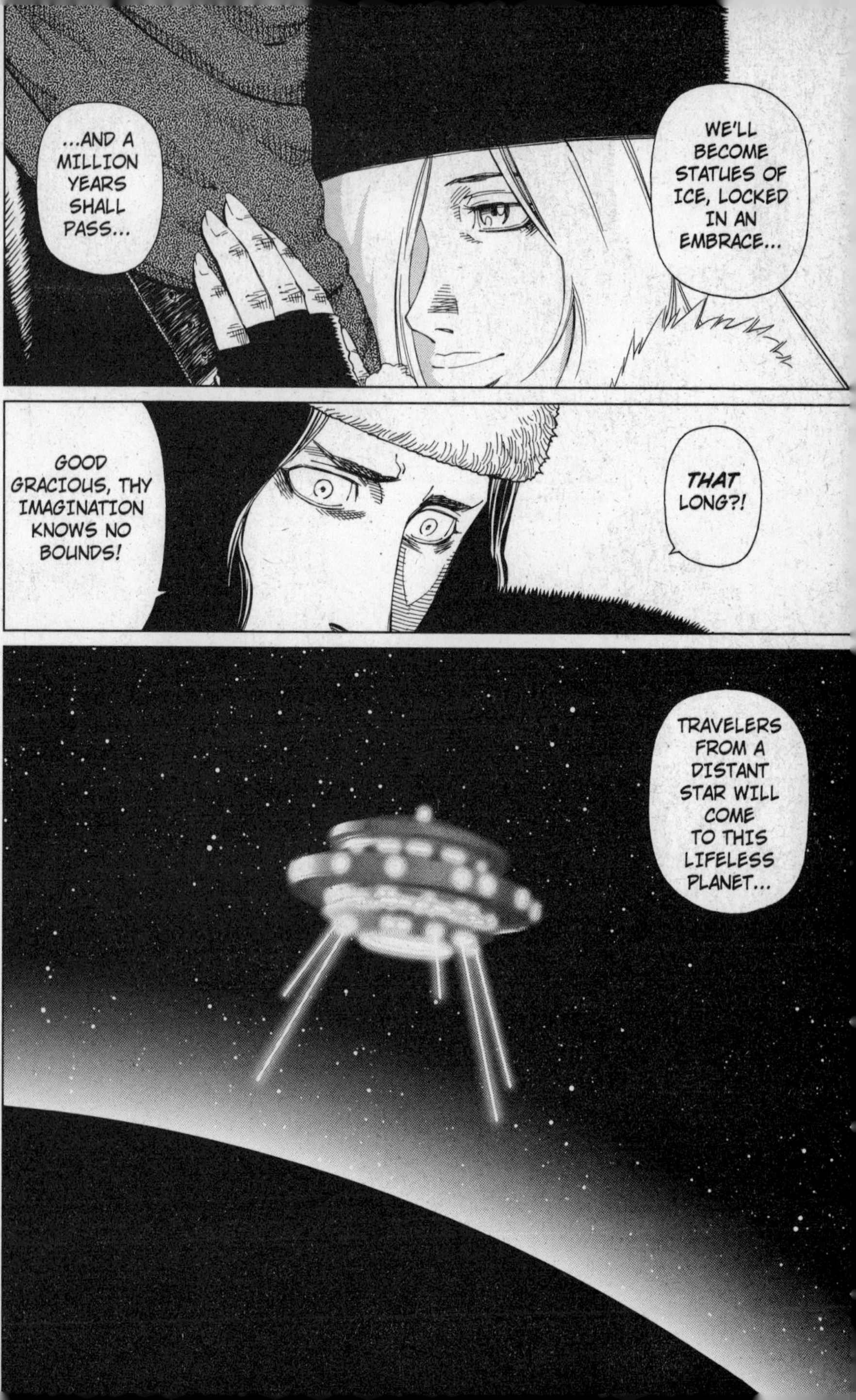
WE'LL BECOME STATUES OF ICE, LOCKED IN AN EMBRACE...
...AND A MILLION YEARS SHALL PASS...
THAT LONG?!
GOOD GRACIOUS, THY IMAGINATION KNOWS NO BOUNDS!
TRAVELERS FROM A DISTANT STAR WILL COME TO THIS LIFELESS PLANET...

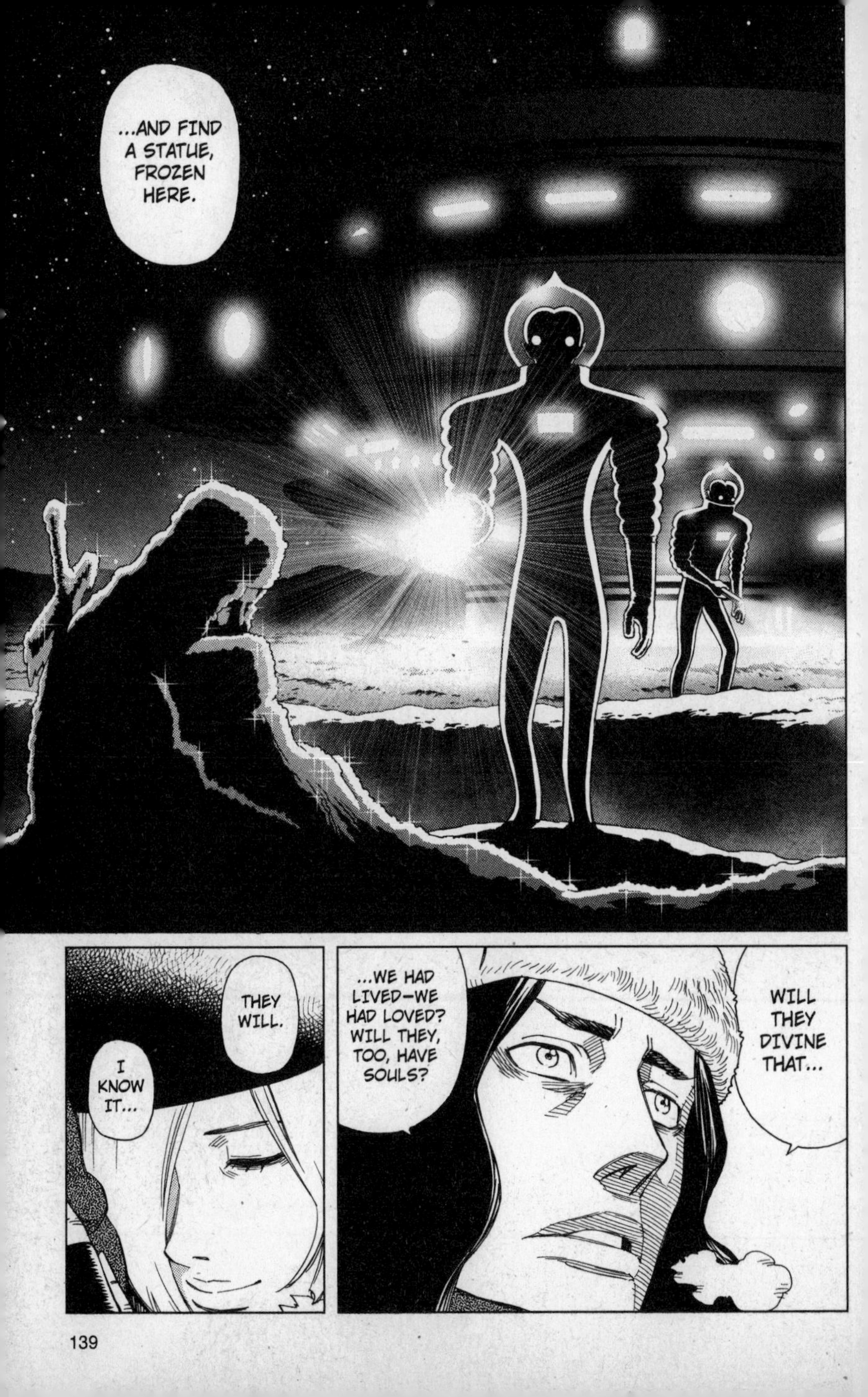
...AND FIND A STATUE, FROZEN HERE.
WILL THEY DIVINE THAT...
...WE HAD LIVED—WE HAD LOVED? WILL THEY, TOO, HAVE SOULS?
THEY WILL.
I KNOW IT...

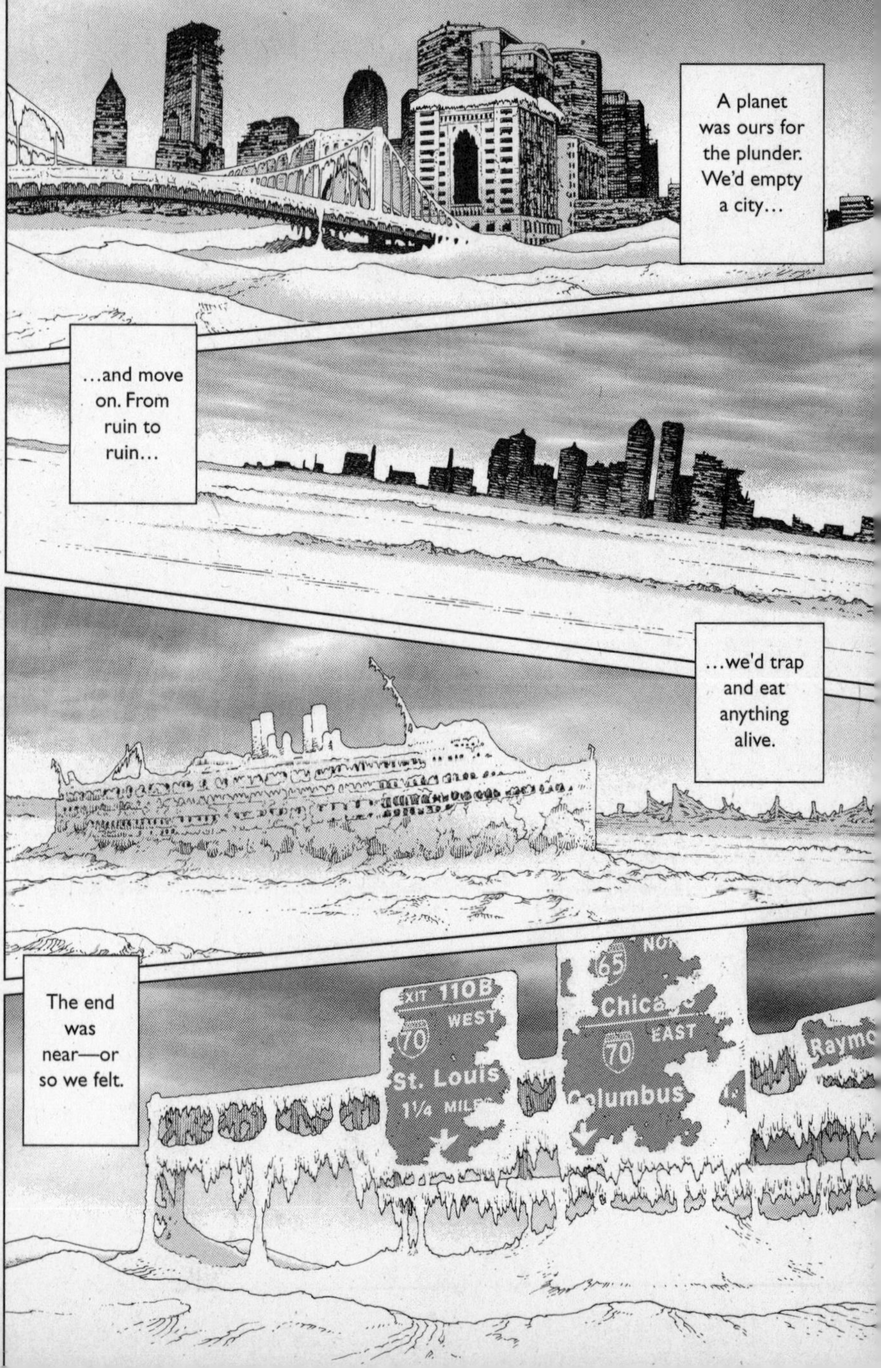
A planet was ours for the plunder. We'd empty a city…
…and move on. From ruin to ruin…
…we'd trap and eat anything alive.
65
EXIT 110B
WEST
70
St. Louis
EAST
70
The end was near—or so we felt.

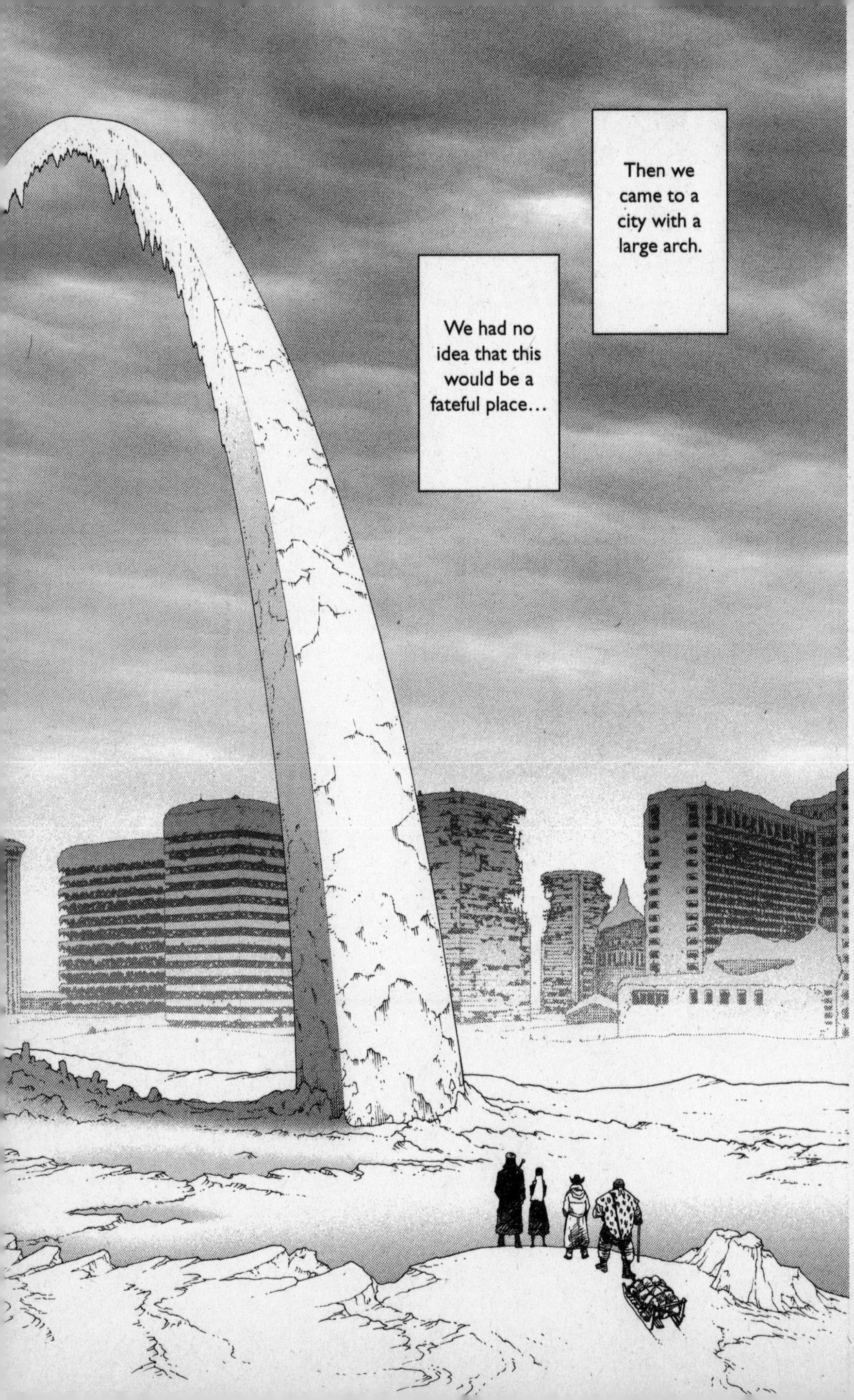
Then we came to a city with a large arch.
We had no idea that this would be a fateful place...

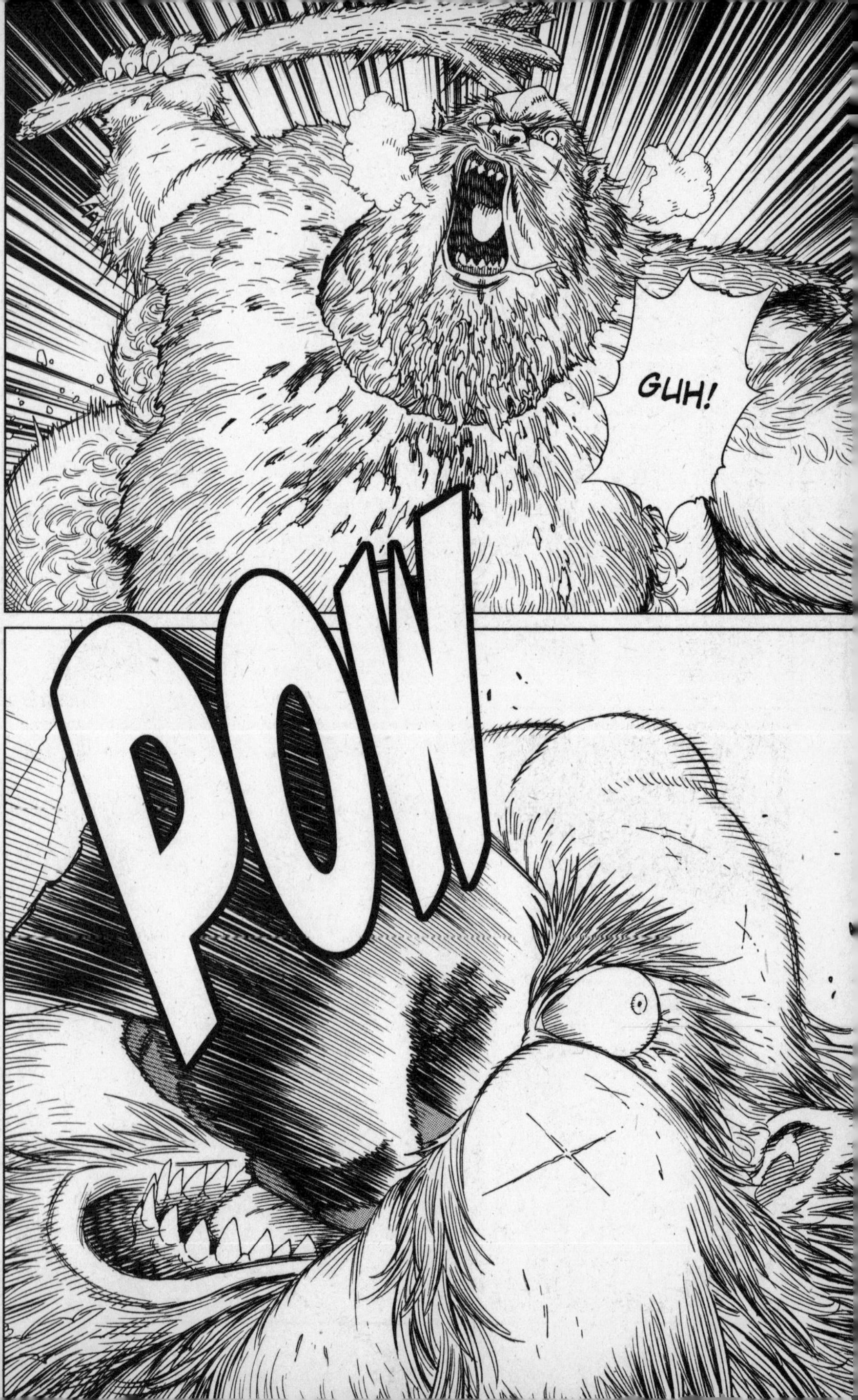
GUH!
POW

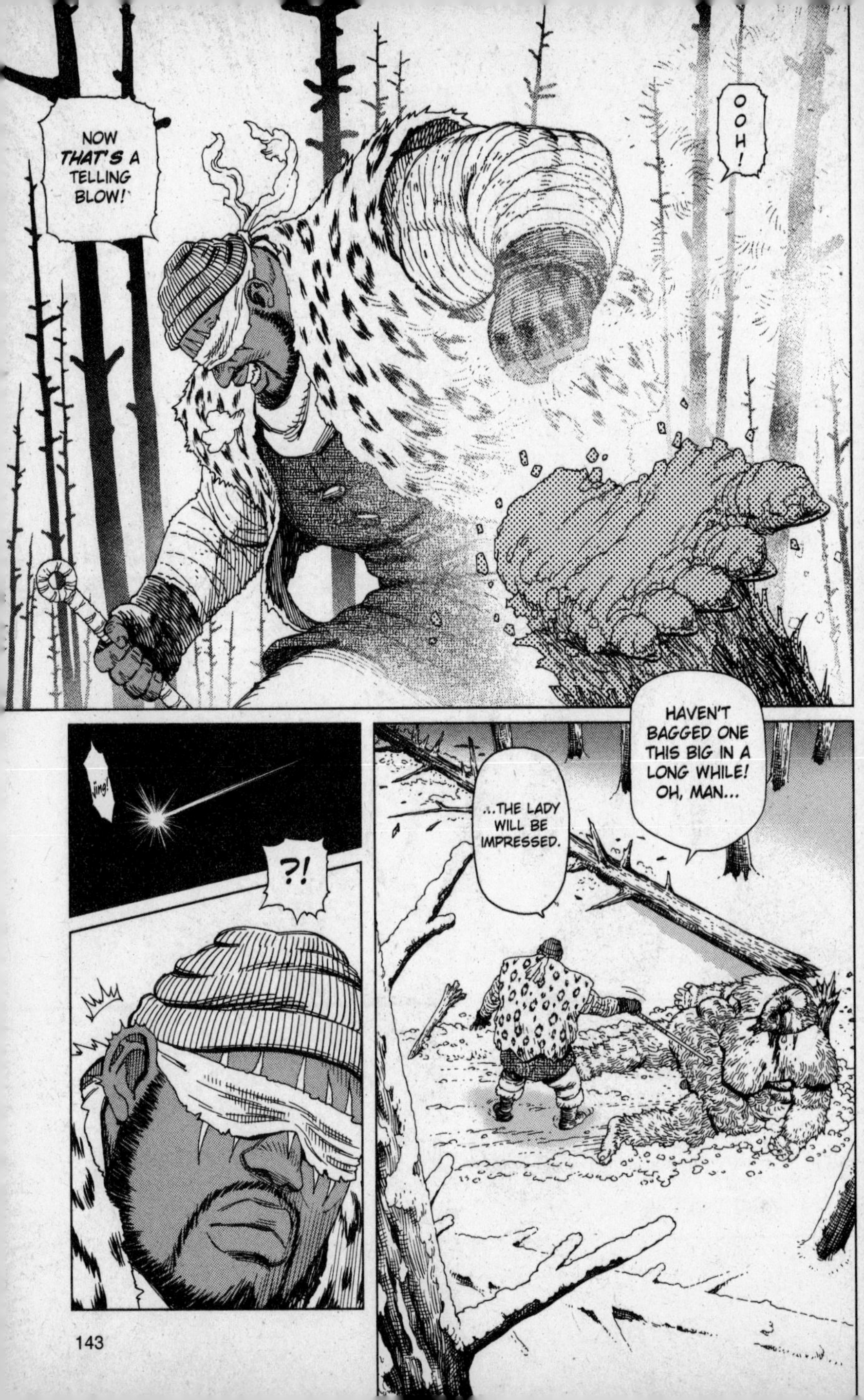
OOH!
NOW *THAT'S* A TELLING BLOW!
HAVEN'T BAGGED ONE THIS BIG IN A LONG WHILE! OH, MAN...
...THE LADY WILL BE IMPRESSED.
jing!
?!

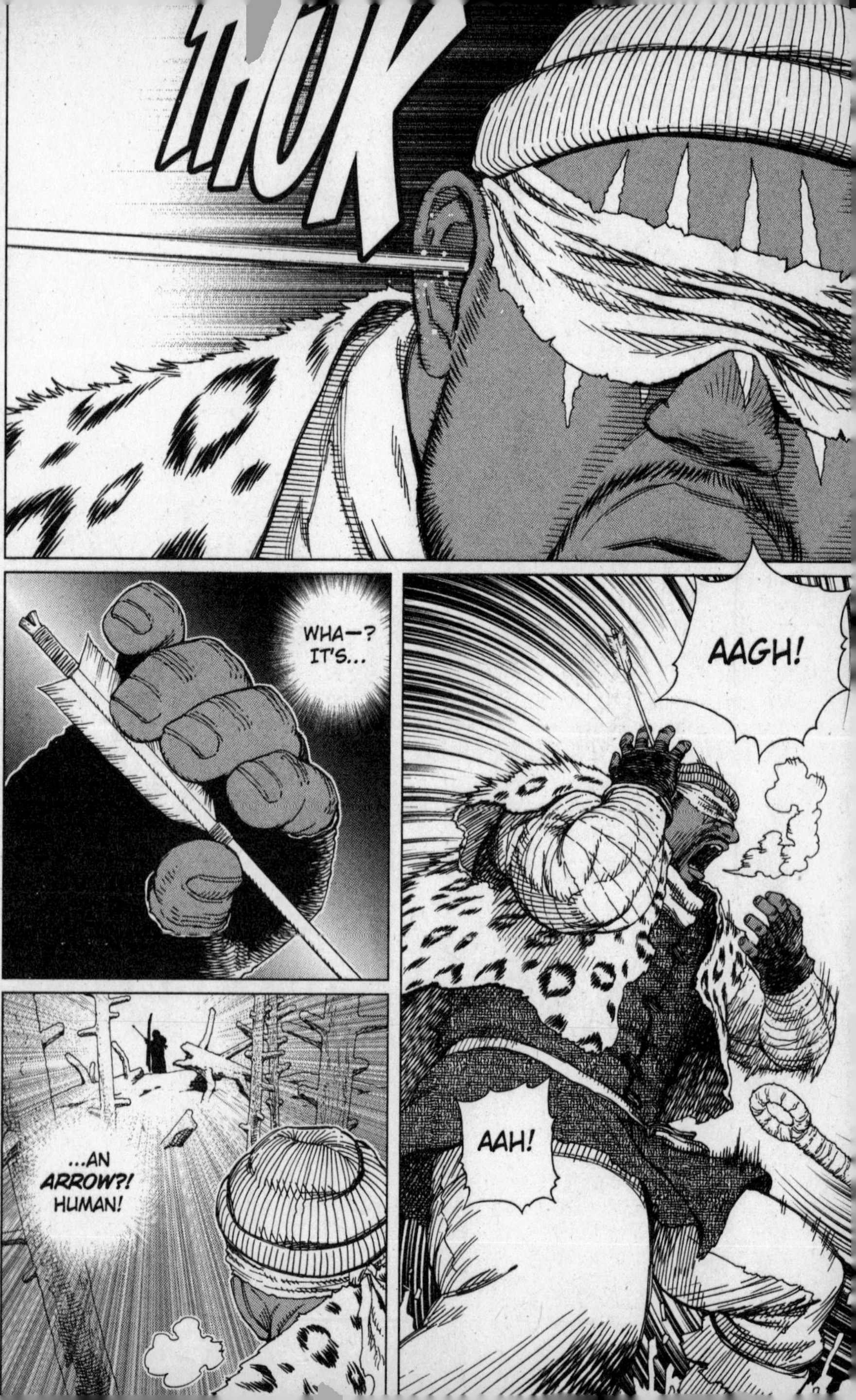
THOK
AAGH!
AAH!
WHA—? IT'S...
...AN *ARROW?!* HUMAN!

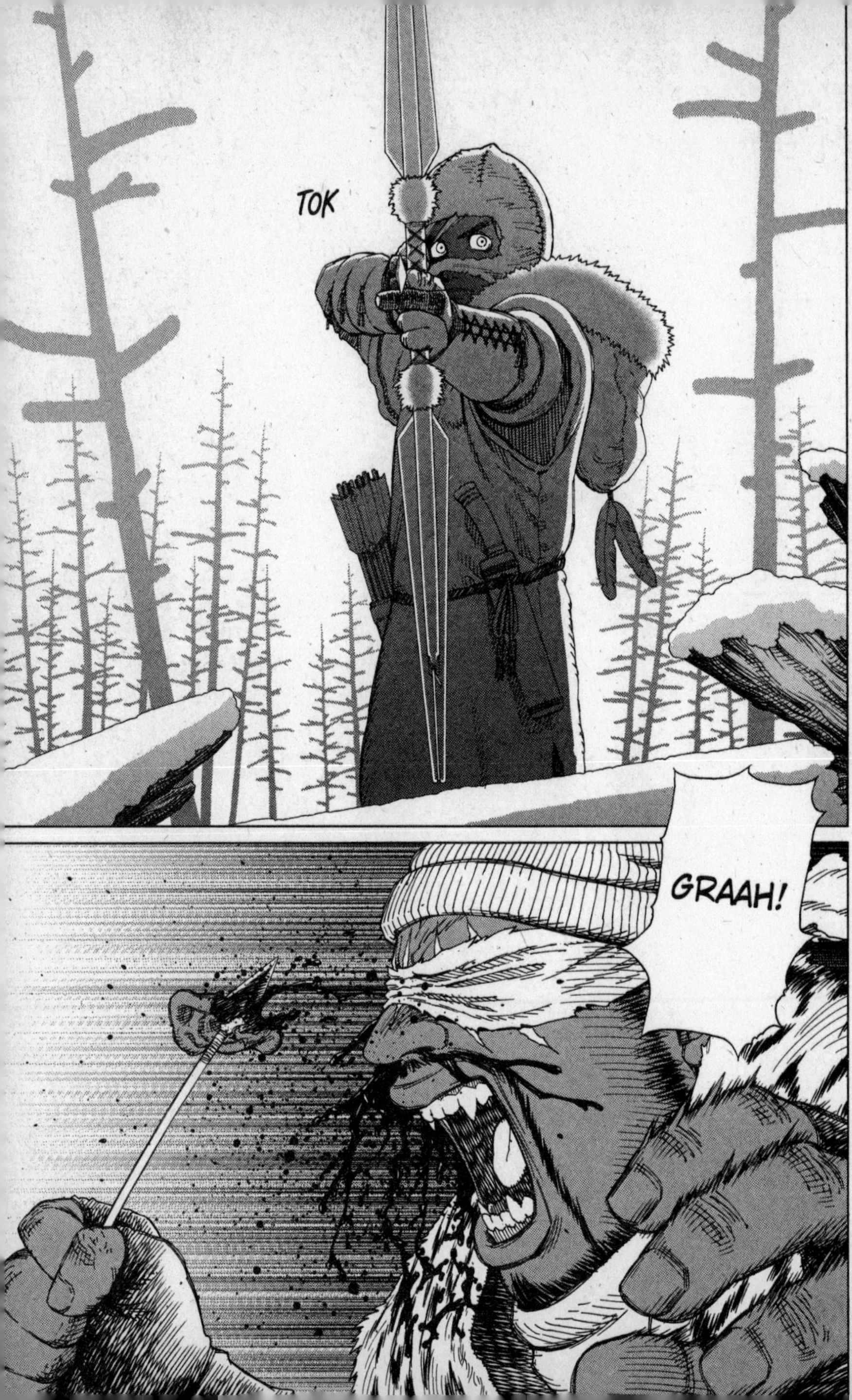
TOK
GRAAH!

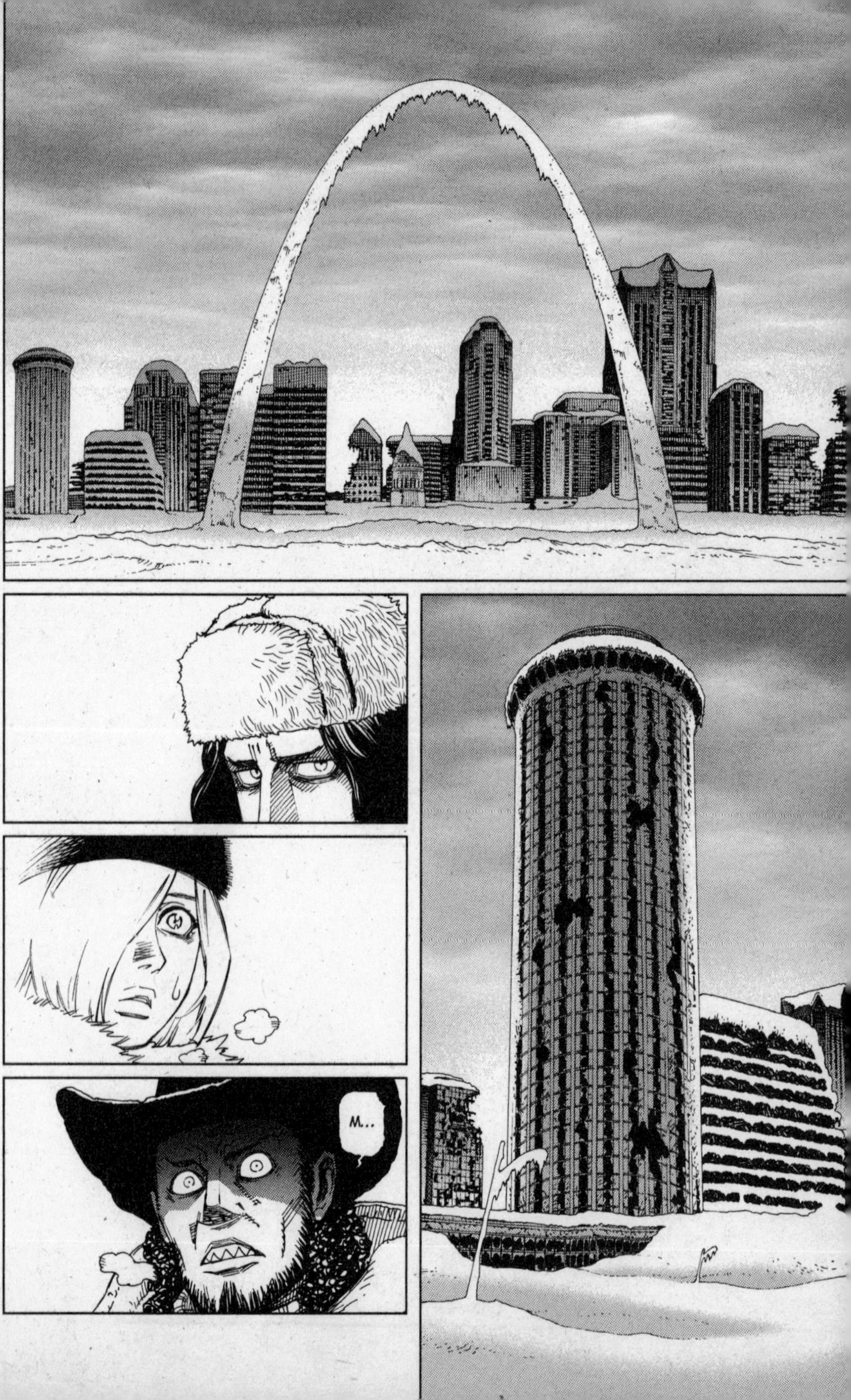
M...

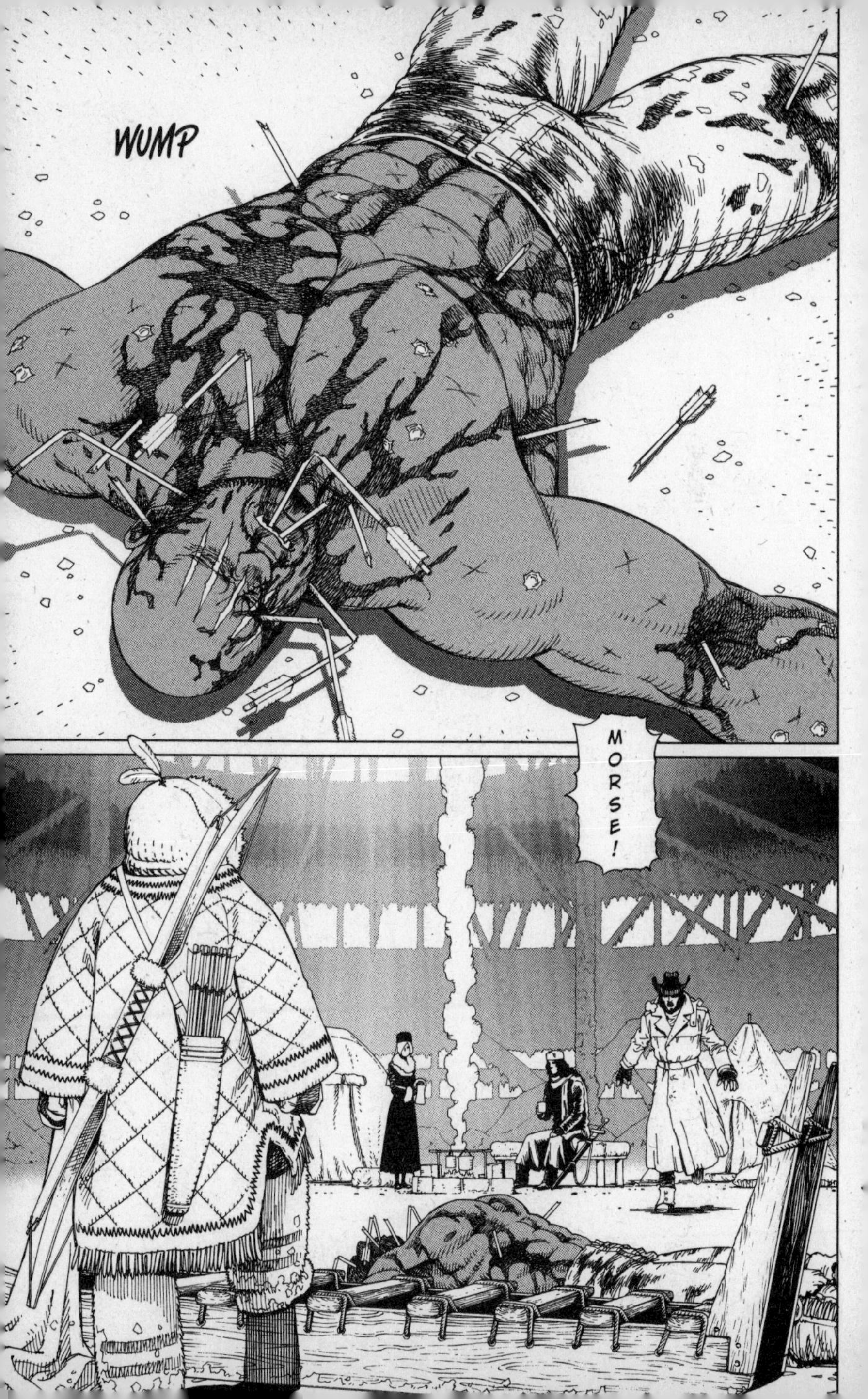
WUMP
MORSE!

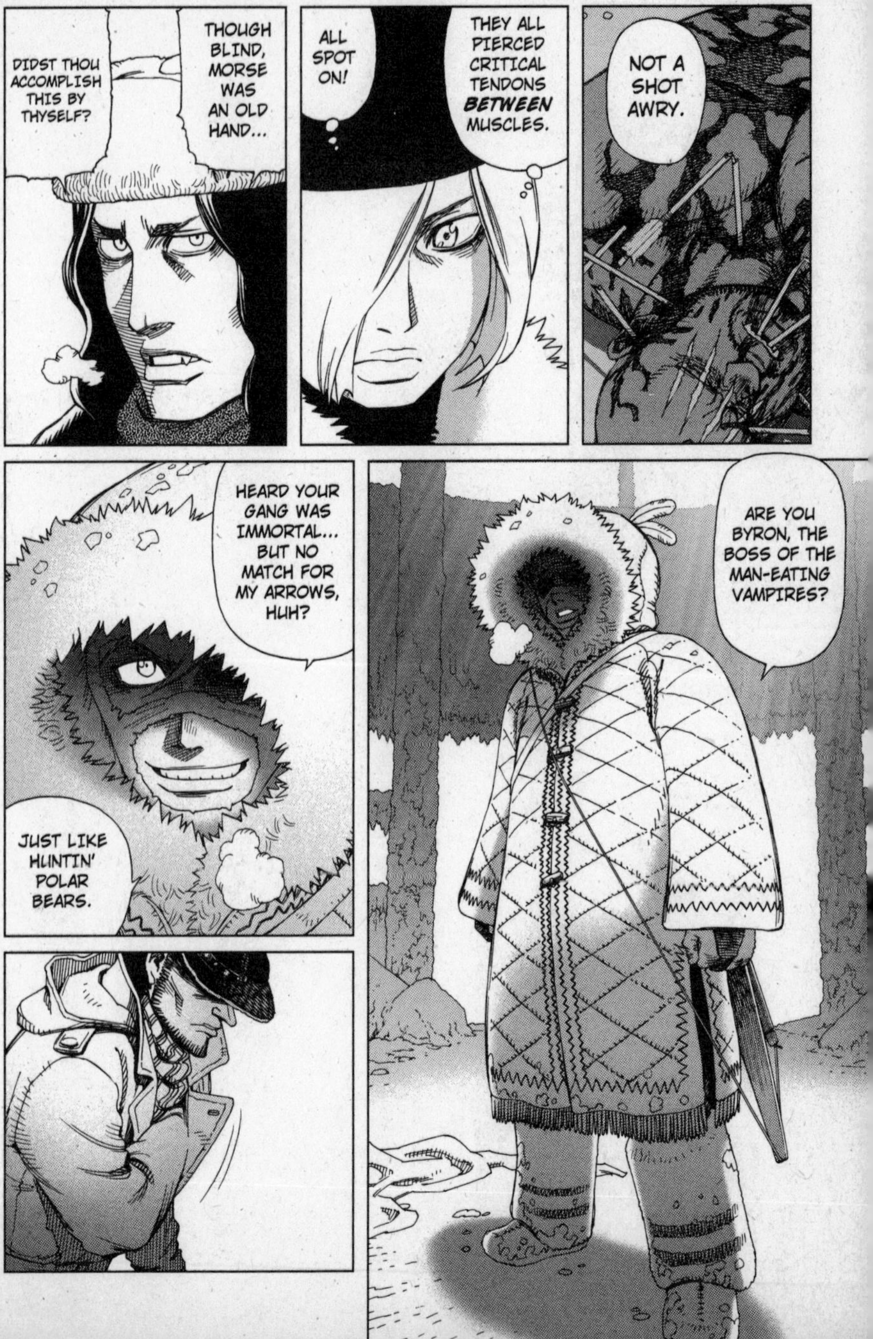
NOT A SHOT AWRY.
THEY ALL PIERCED CRITICAL TENDONS *BETWEEN* MUSCLES.
ALL SPOT ON!
THOUGH BLIND, MORSE WAS AN OLD HAND...
DIDST THOU ACCOMPLISH THIS BY THYSELF?
ARE YOU BYRON, THE BOSS OF THE MAN-EATING VAMPIRES?
HEARD YOUR GANG WAS IMMORTAL... BUT NO MATCH FOR MY ARROWS, HUH?
JUST LIKE HUNTIN' POLAR BEARS.

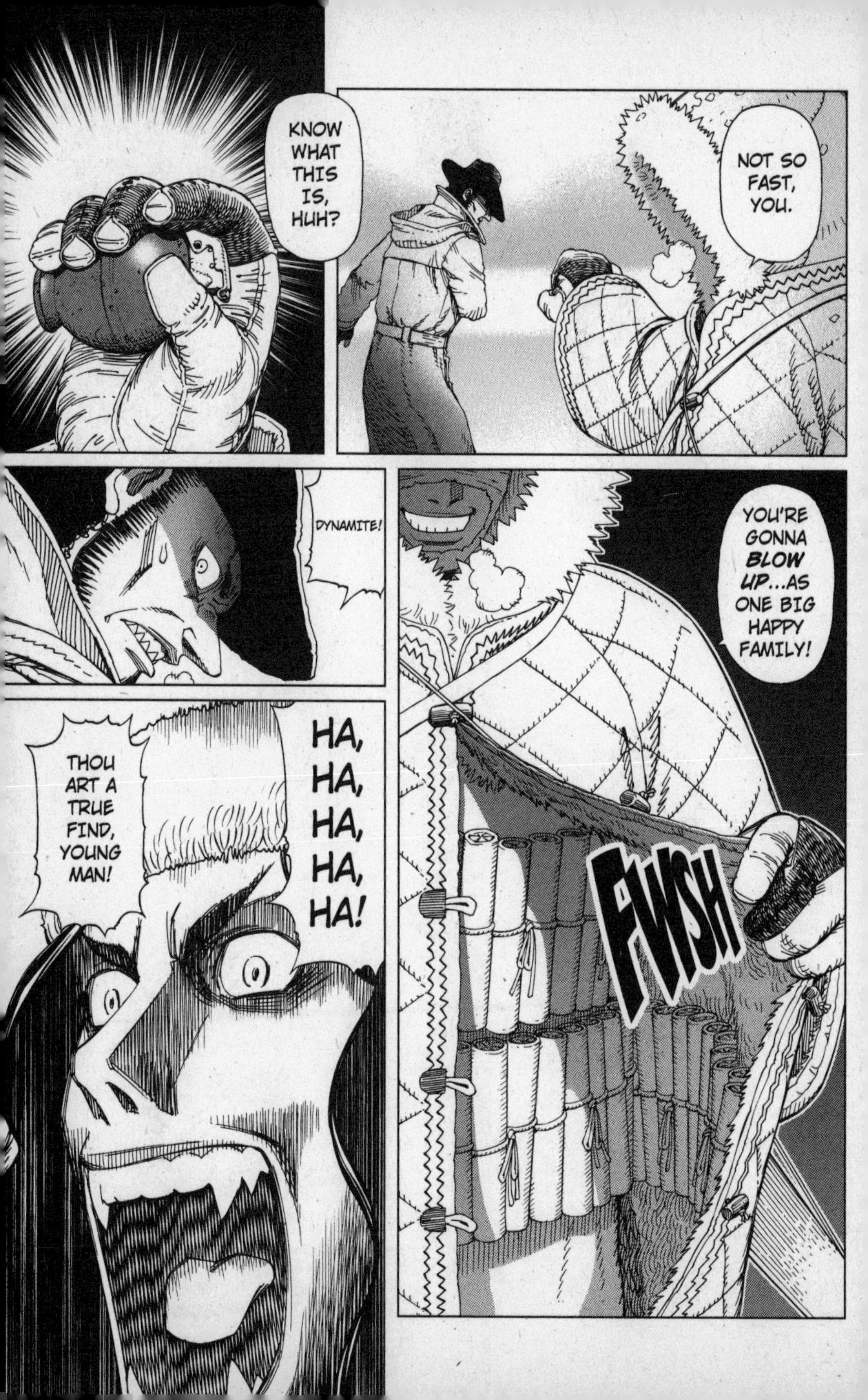
NOT SO FAST, YOU.
KNOW WHAT THIS IS, HUH?
YOU'RE GONNA *BLOW UP*...AS ONE BIG HAPPY FAMILY!
FWISH
DYNAMITE!
HA, HA, HA, HA, HA!
THOU ART A TRUE FIND, YOUNG MAN!

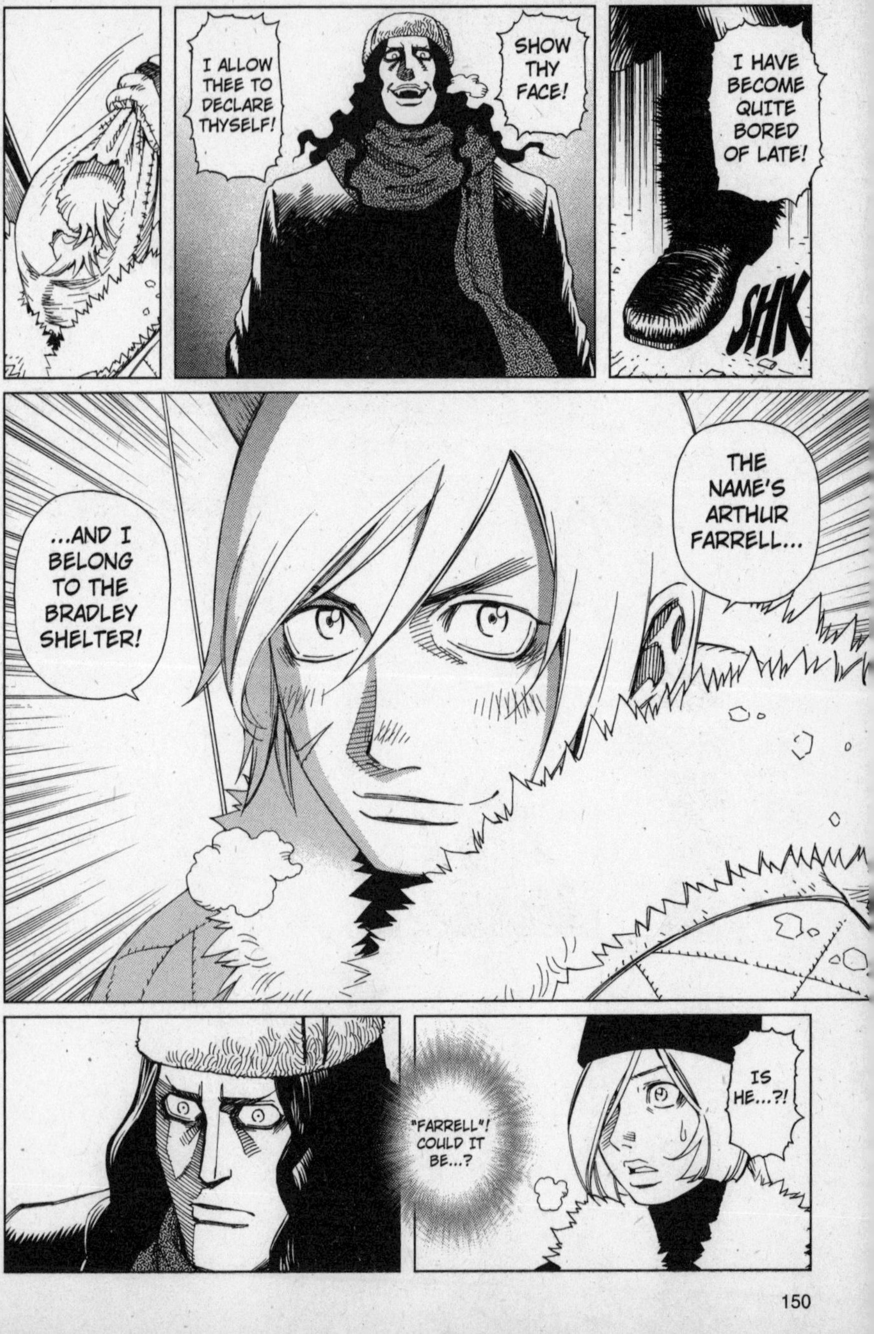
I HAVE BECOME QUITE BORED OF LATE!
SHK
SHOW THY FACE!
I ALLOW THEE TO DECLARE THYSELF!
THE NAME'S ARTHUR FARRELL...
...AND I BELONG TO THE BRADLEY SHELTER!
IS HE...?!
"FARRELL"! COULD IT BE...?

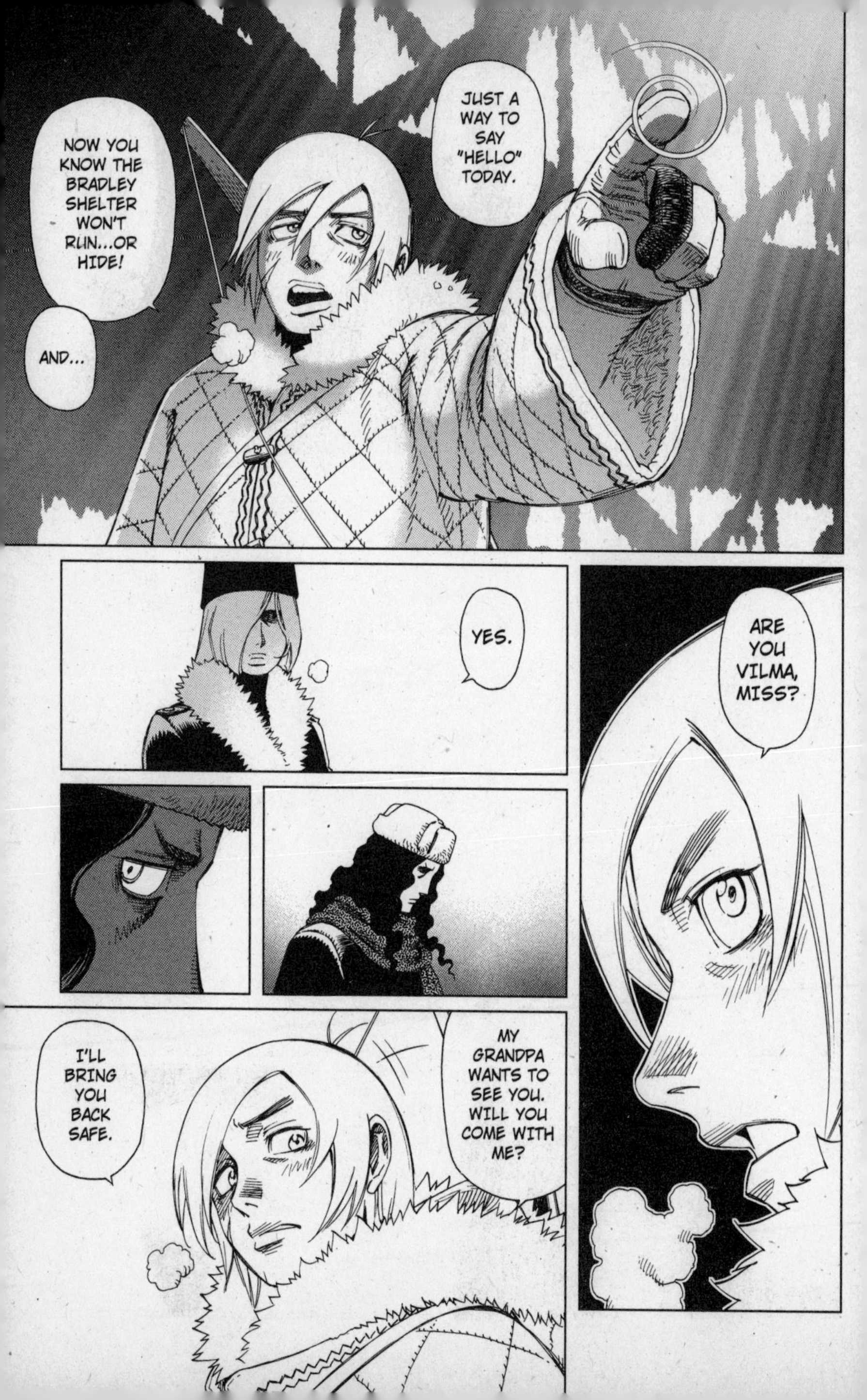
JUST A WAY TO SAY "HELLO" TODAY.
NOW YOU KNOW THE BRADLEY SHELTER WON'T RUN...OR HIDE!
AND...
ARE YOU VILMA, MISS?
YES.
MY GRANDPA WANTS TO SEE YOU. WILL YOU COME WITH ME?
I'LL BRING YOU BACK SAFE.

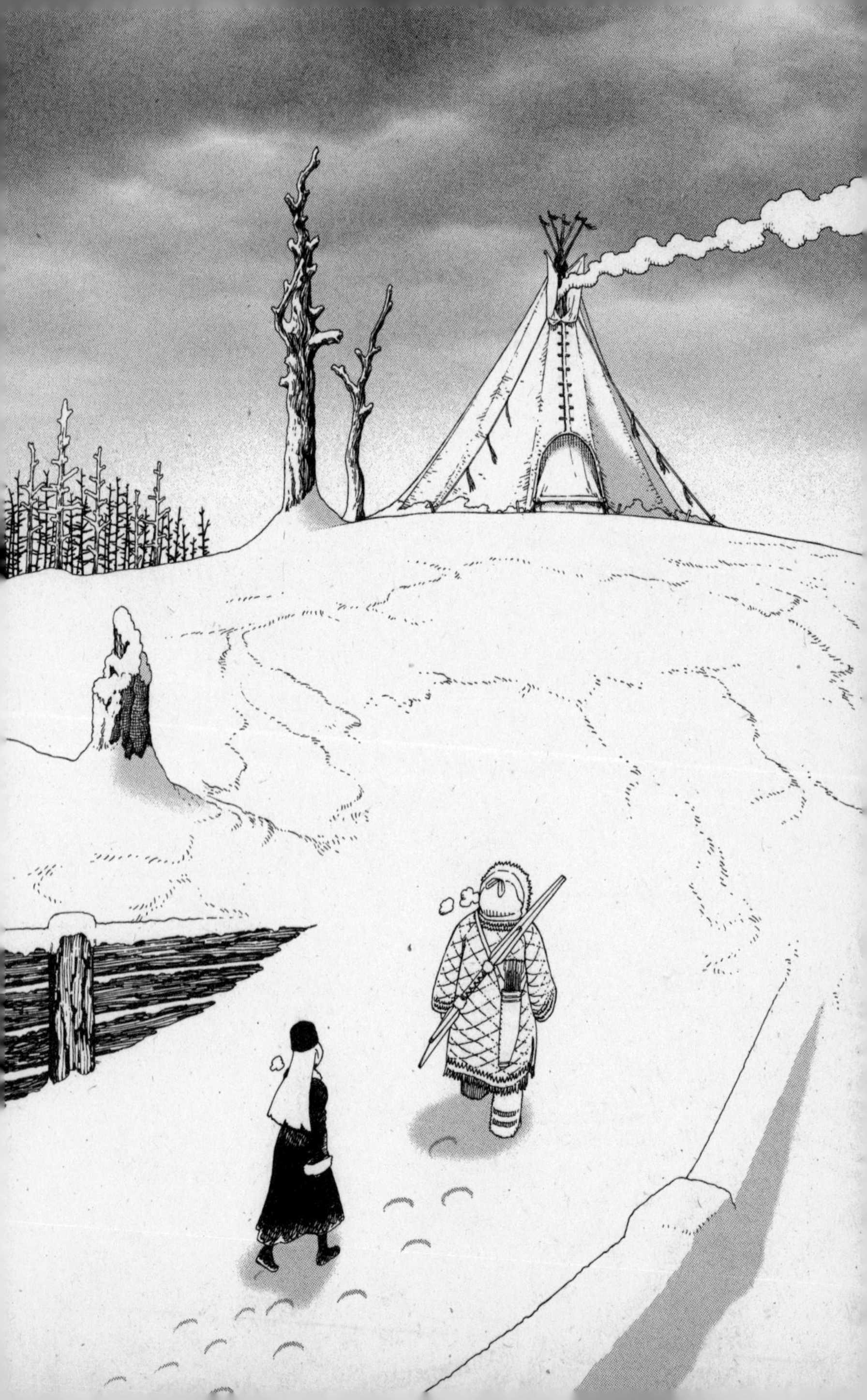

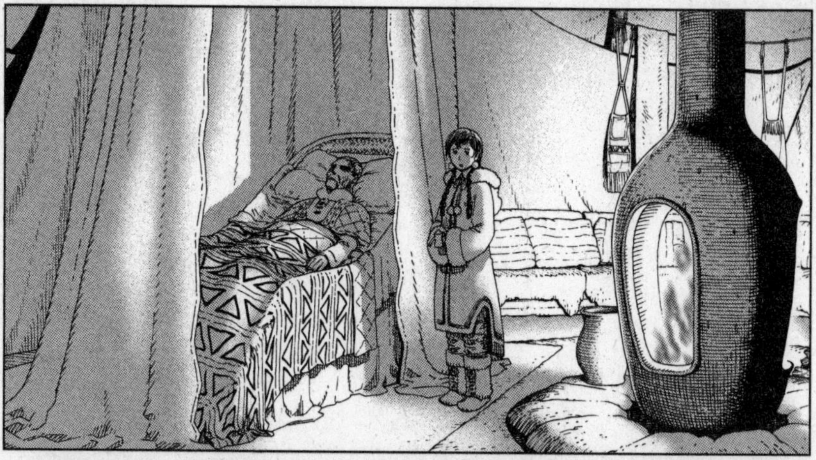

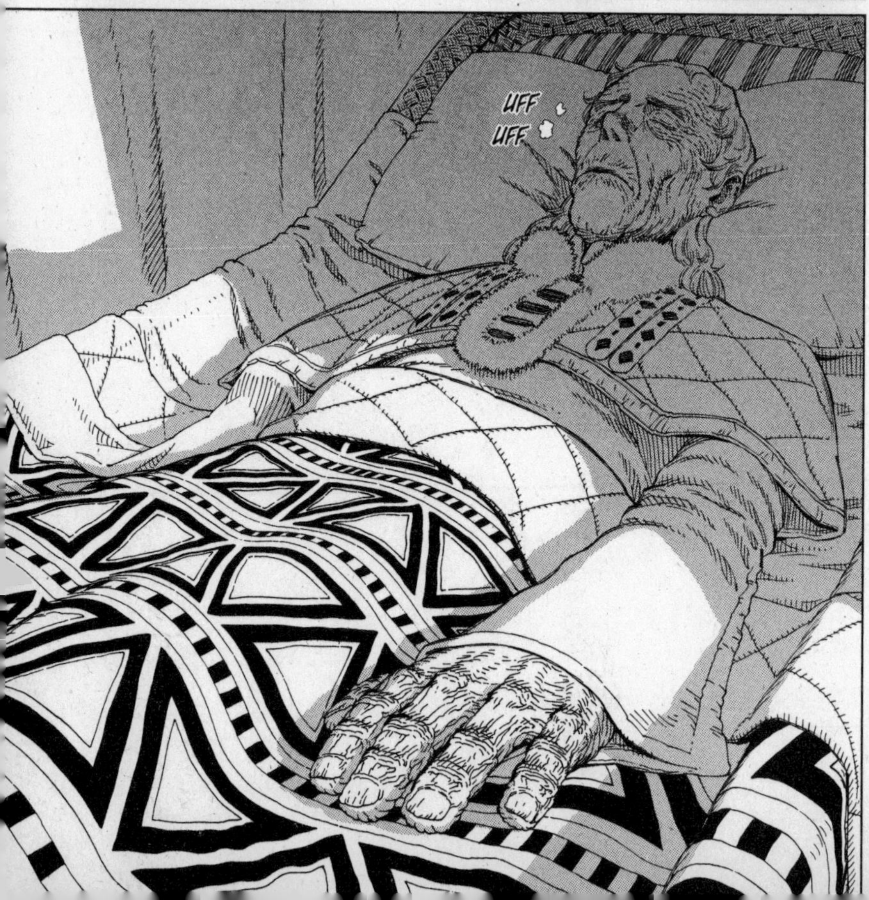
UFF
UFF

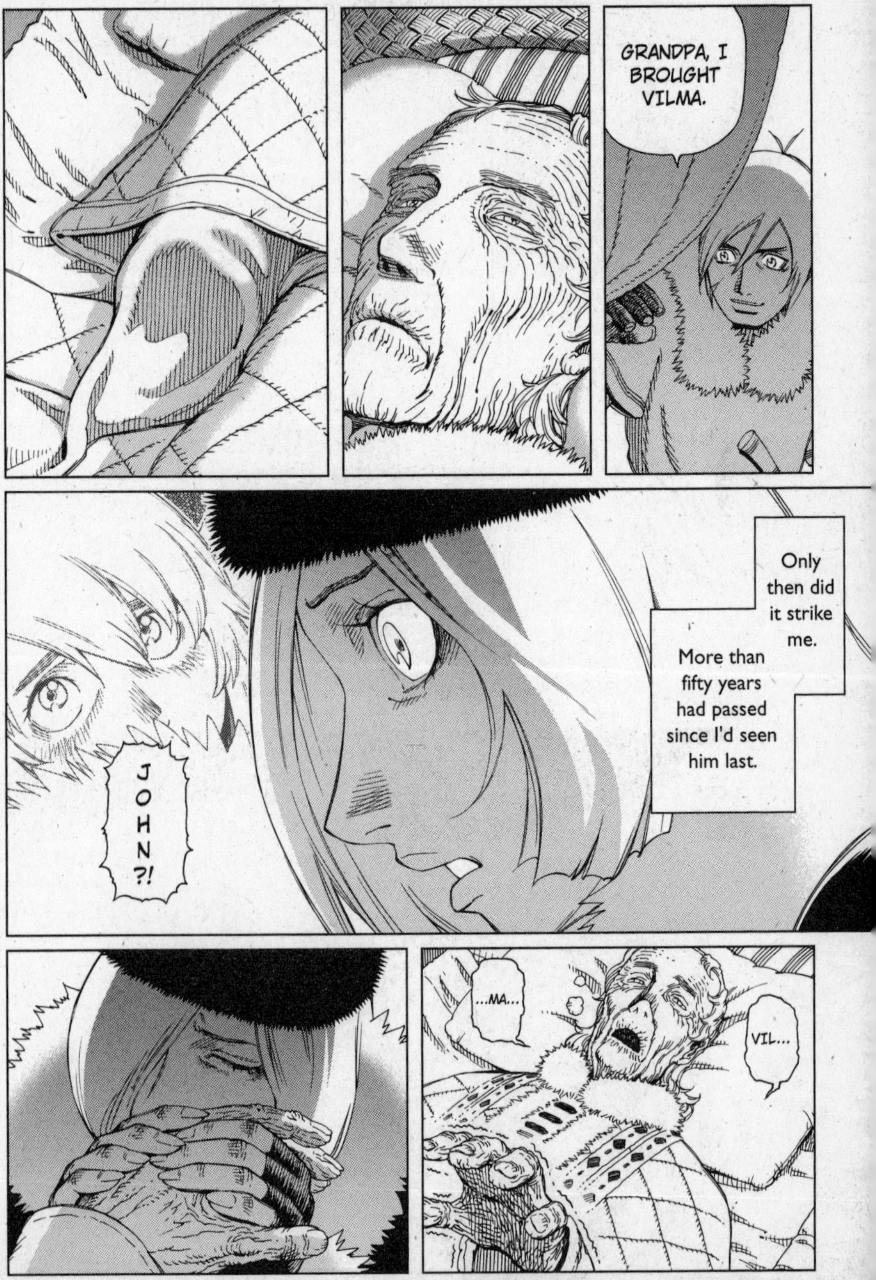
GRANDPA, I BROUGHT VILMA.
Only then did it strike me.
More than fifty years had passed since I'd seen him last.
JOHN?!
VIL...
...MA...

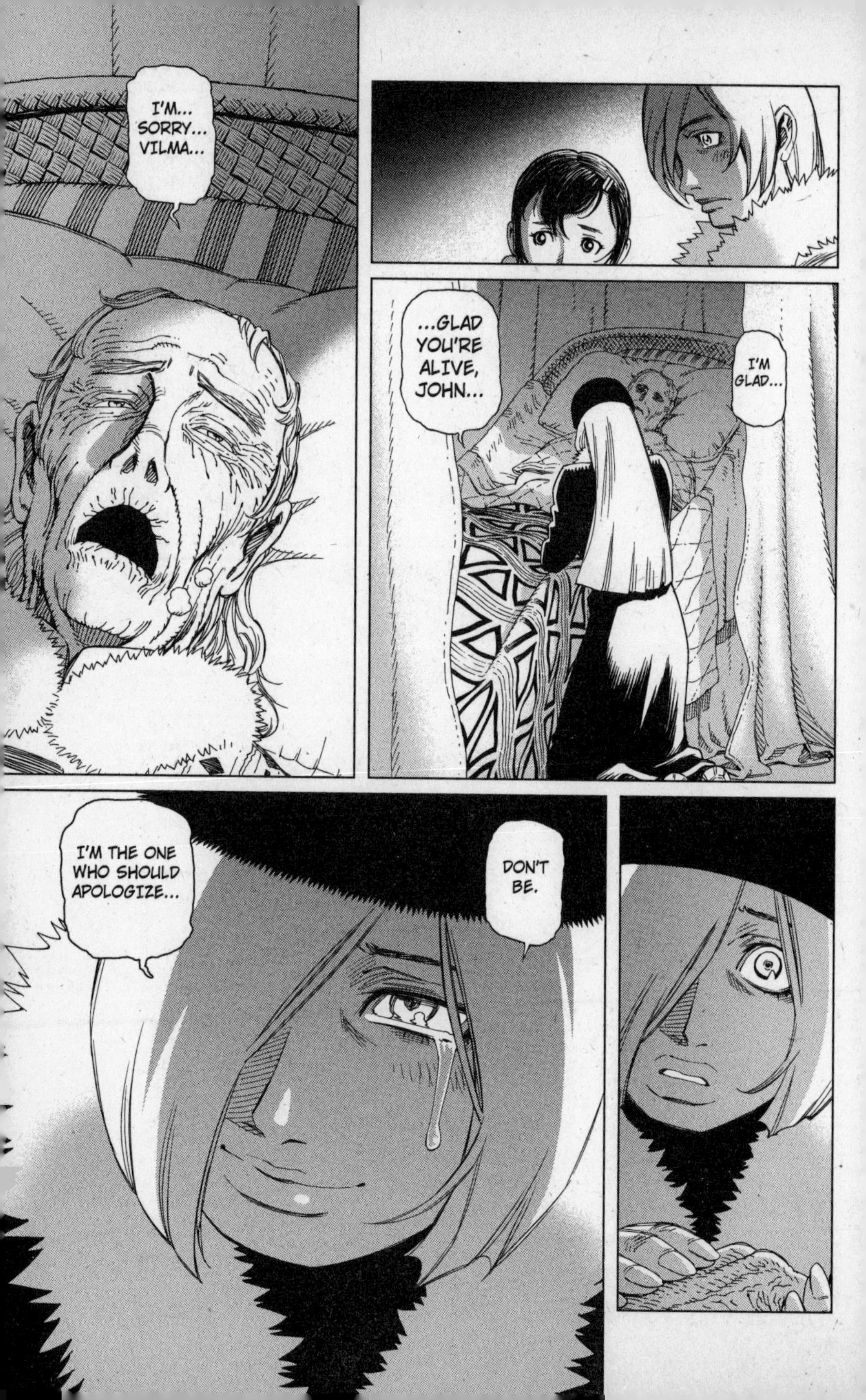
I'M GLAD...
...GLAD YOU'RE ALIVE, JOHN...
I'M... SORRY... VILMA...
DON'T BE.
I'M THE ONE WHO SHOULD APOLOGIZE...

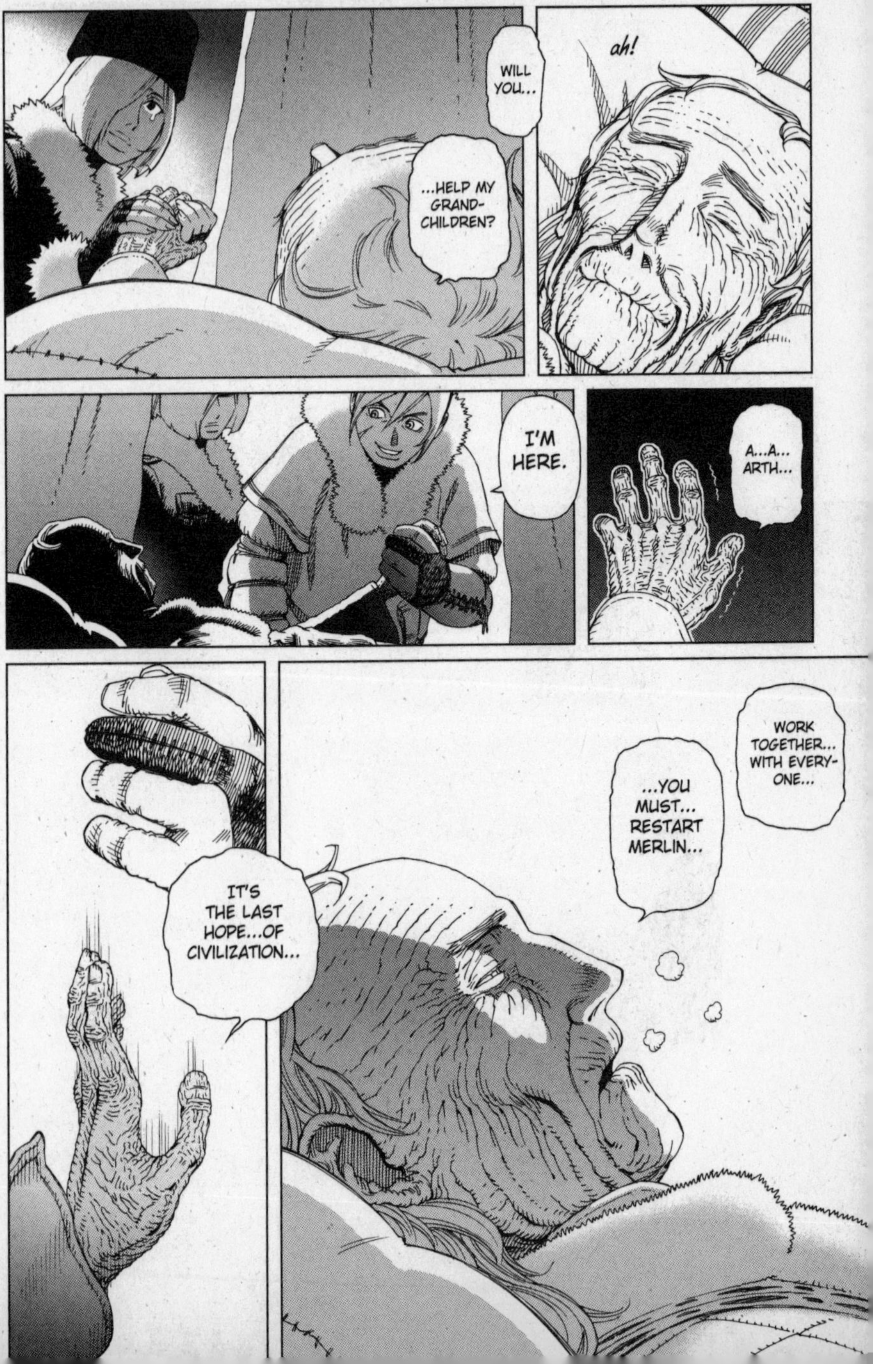
ah!
WILL YOU...
...HELP MY GRAND-CHILDREN?
A...A... ARTH...
I'M HERE.
WORK TOGETHER... WITH EVERY-ONE...
...YOU MUST... RESTART MERLIN...
IT'S THE LAST HOPE...OF CIVILIZATION...

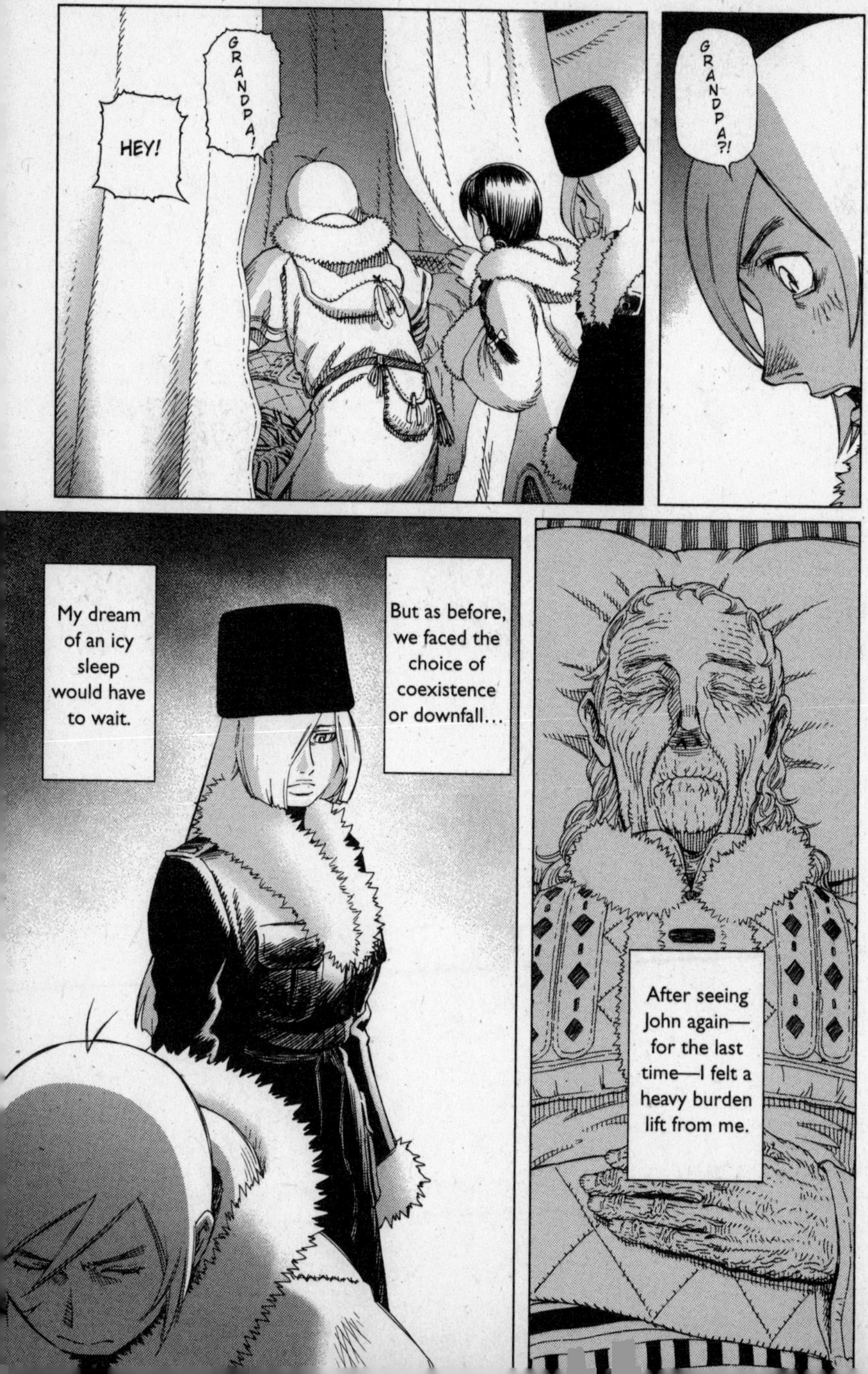
GRANDPA?!
GRANDPA!
HEY!
After seeing John again—for the last time—I felt a heavy burden lift from me.
But as before, we faced the choice of coexistence or downfall...
My dream of an icy sleep would have to wait.

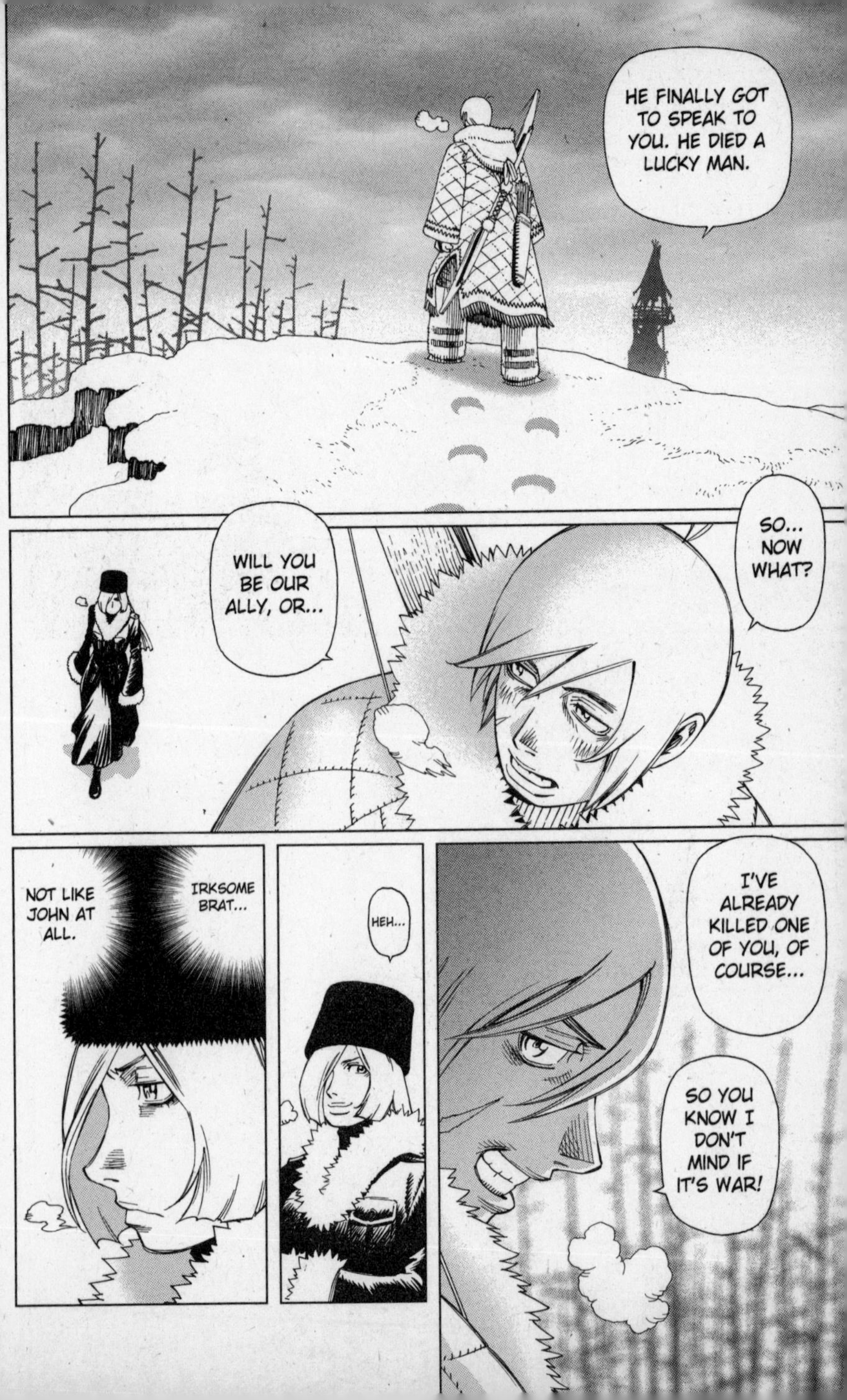
HE FINALLY GOT TO SPEAK TO YOU. HE DIED A LUCKY MAN.
SO... NOW WHAT?
WILL YOU BE OUR ALLY, OR...
I'VE ALREADY KILLED ONE OF YOU, OF COURSE...
SO YOU KNOW I DON'T MIND IF IT'S WAR!
HEH...
IRKSOME BRAT...
NOT LIKE JOHN AT ALL.

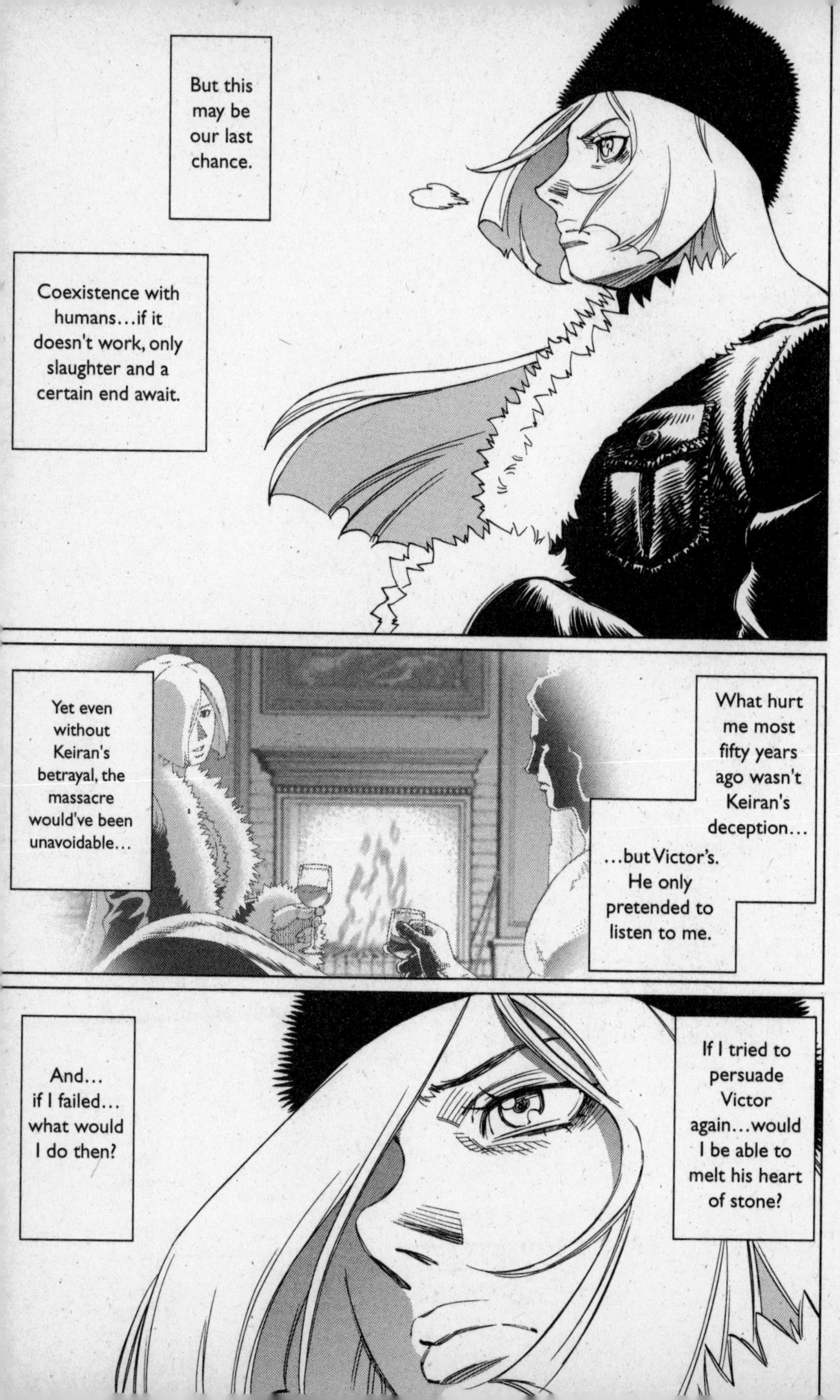
But this may be our last chance.
Coexistence with humans…if it doesn't work, only slaughter and a certain end await.
What hurt me most fifty years ago wasn't Keiran's deception…
…but Victor's. He only pretended to listen to me.
Yet even without Keiran's betrayal, the massacre would've been unavoidable…
If I tried to persuade Victor again…would I be able to melt his heart of stone?
And… if I failed… what would I do then?

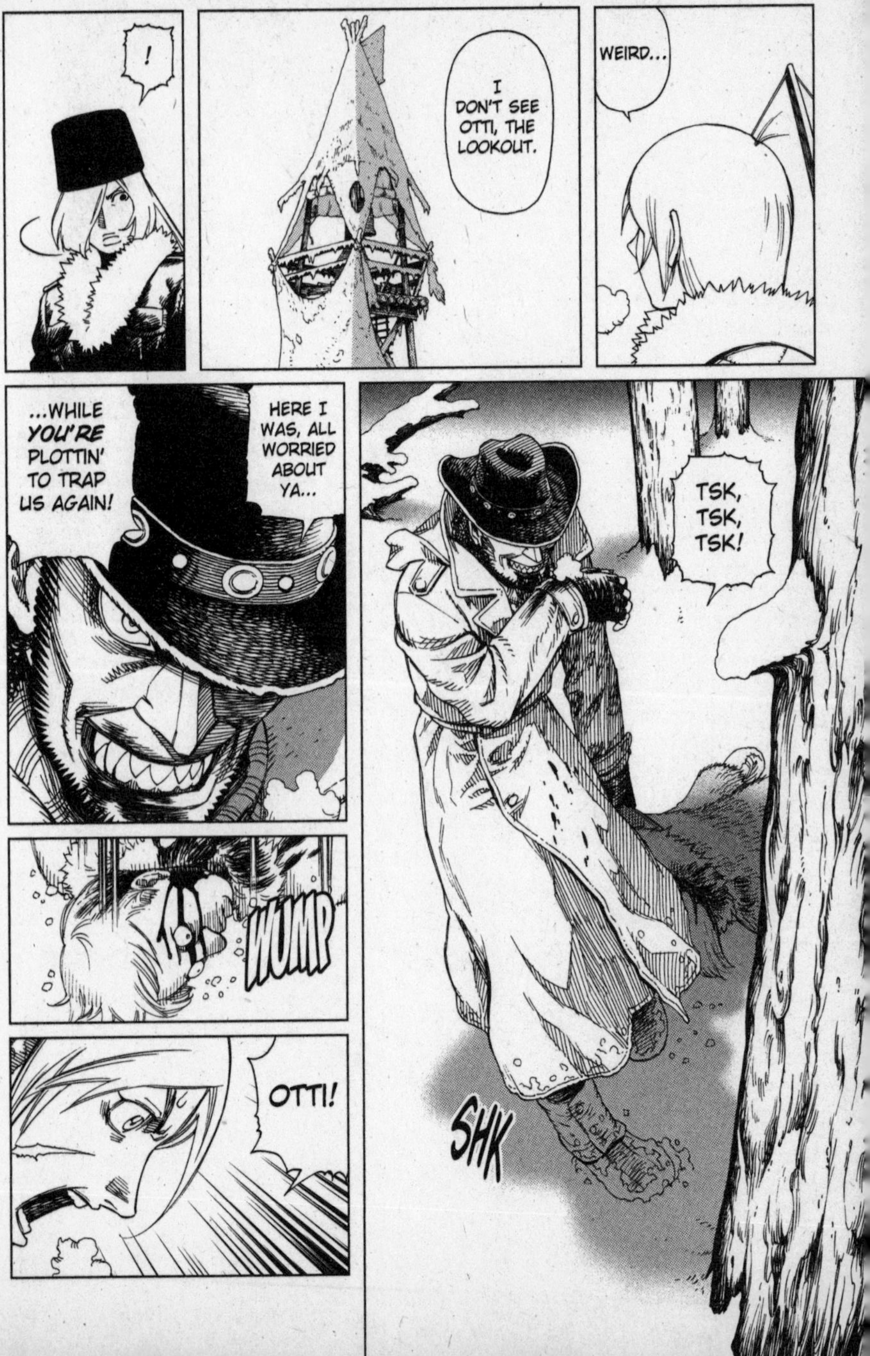
WEIRD...
I DON'T SEE OTTI, THE LOOKOUT.
!
TSK, TSK, TSK!
SHK
HERE I WAS, ALL WORRIED ABOUT YA...
...WHILE YOU'RE PLOTTIN' TO TRAP US AGAIN!
WUMP
OTTI!

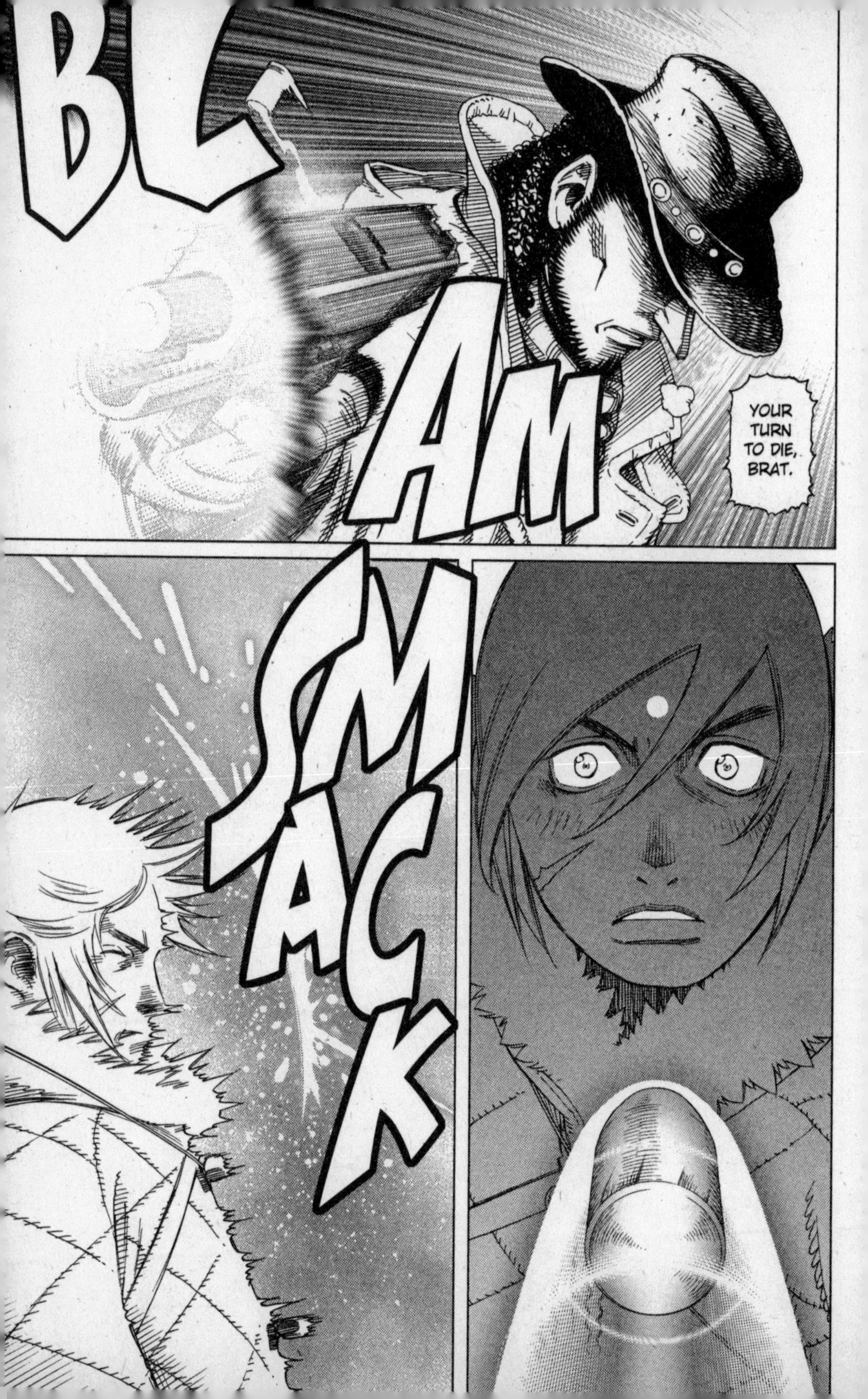
YOUR TURN TO DIE, BRAT.
BLAM
SMACK

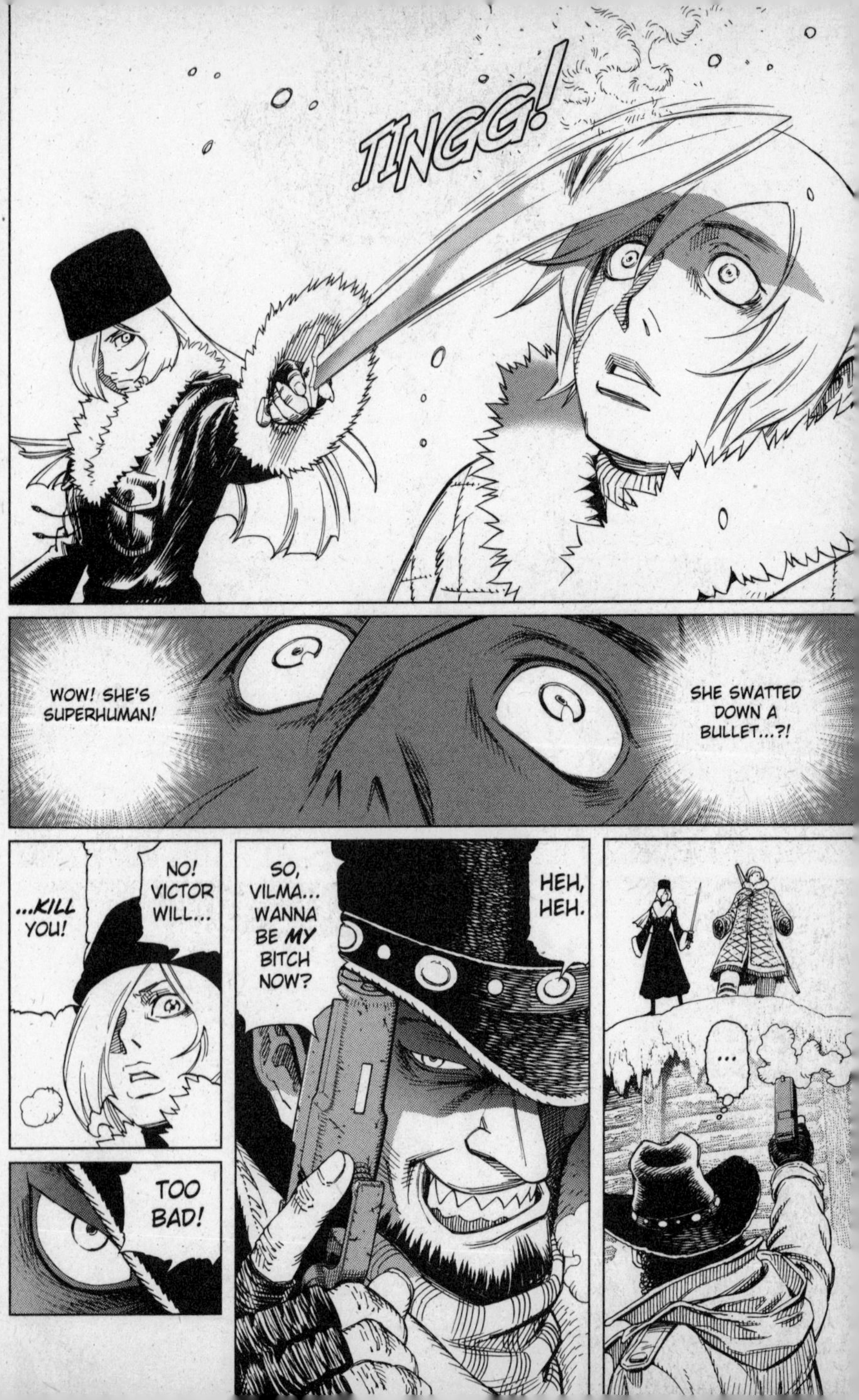
TINGG!
SHE SWATTED DOWN A BULLET...?!
WOW! SHE'S SUPERHUMAN!
...
HEH, HEH.
SO, VILMA... WANNA BE *MY* BITCH NOW?
NO! VICTOR WILL...
...*KILL* YOU!
TOO BAD!

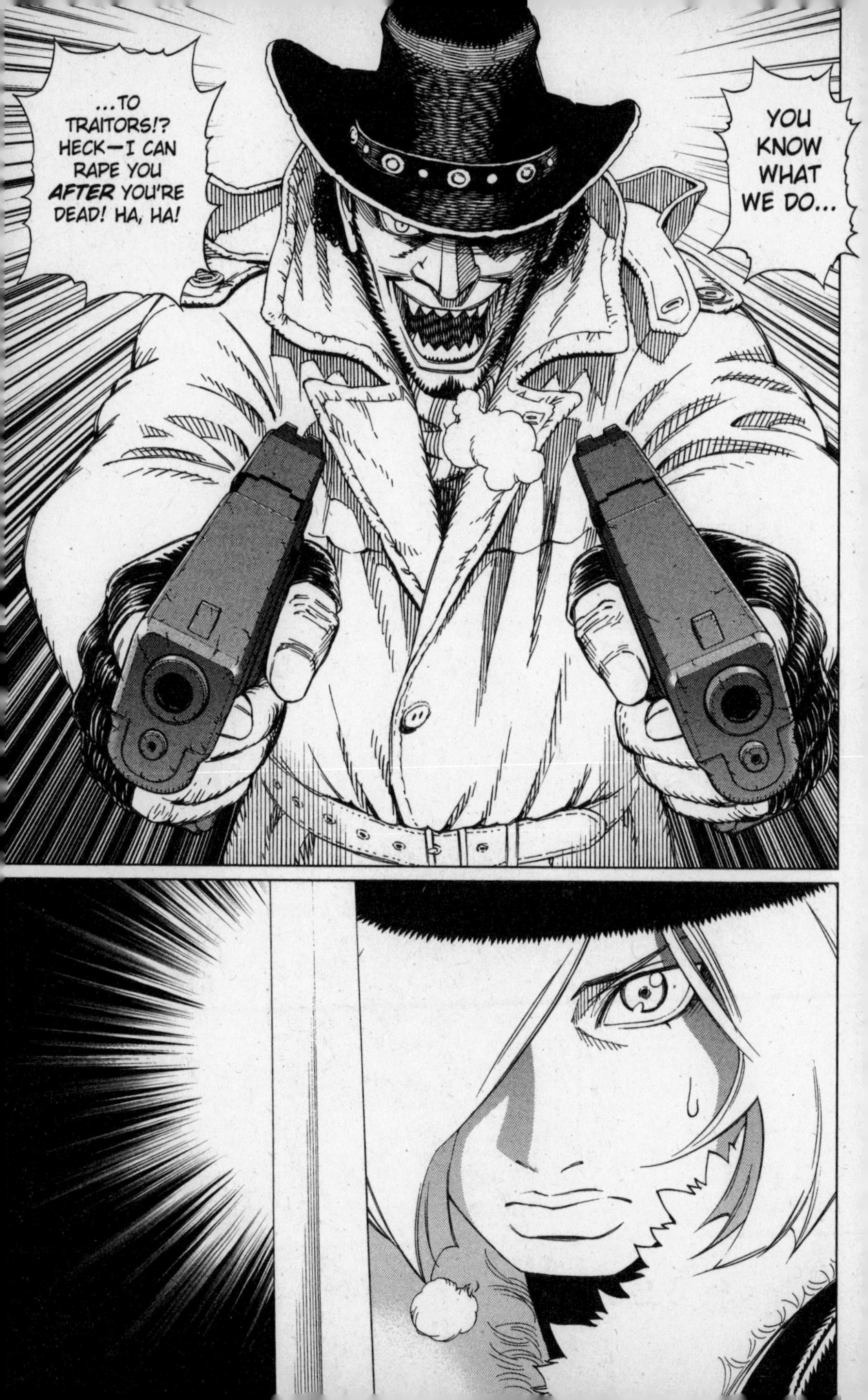
YOU KNOW WHAT WE DO...
...TO TRAITORS!? HECK—I CAN RAPE YOU *AFTER* YOU'RE DEAD! HA, HA!

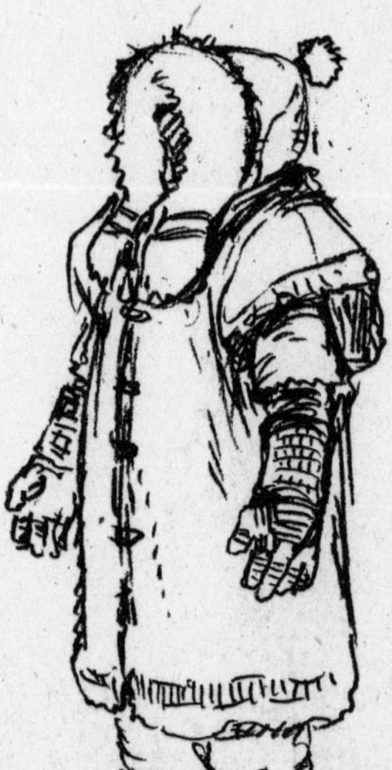
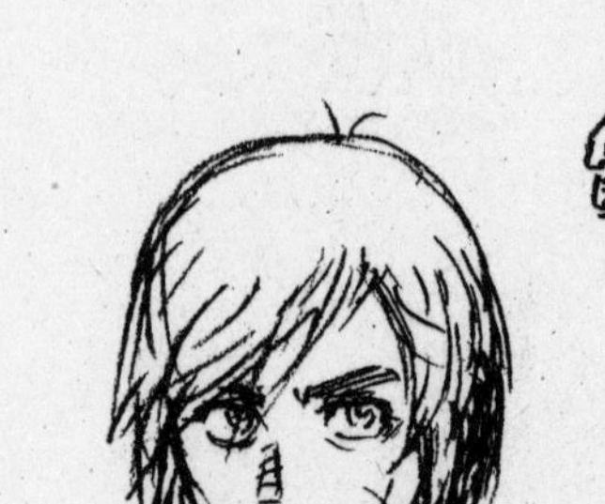

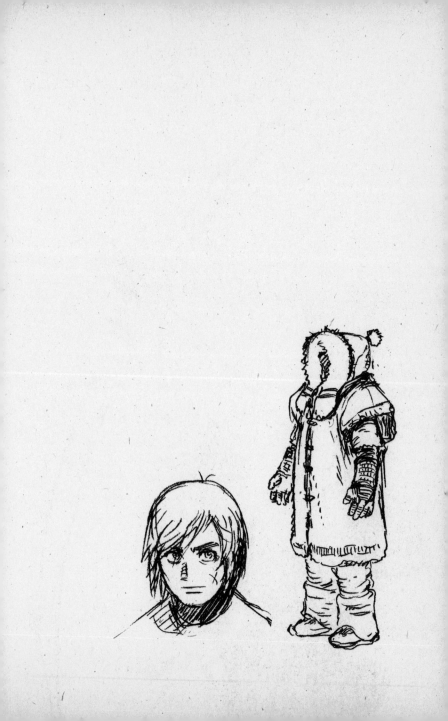

PHASE 49:
Punch Through the Thick Clouds One Day

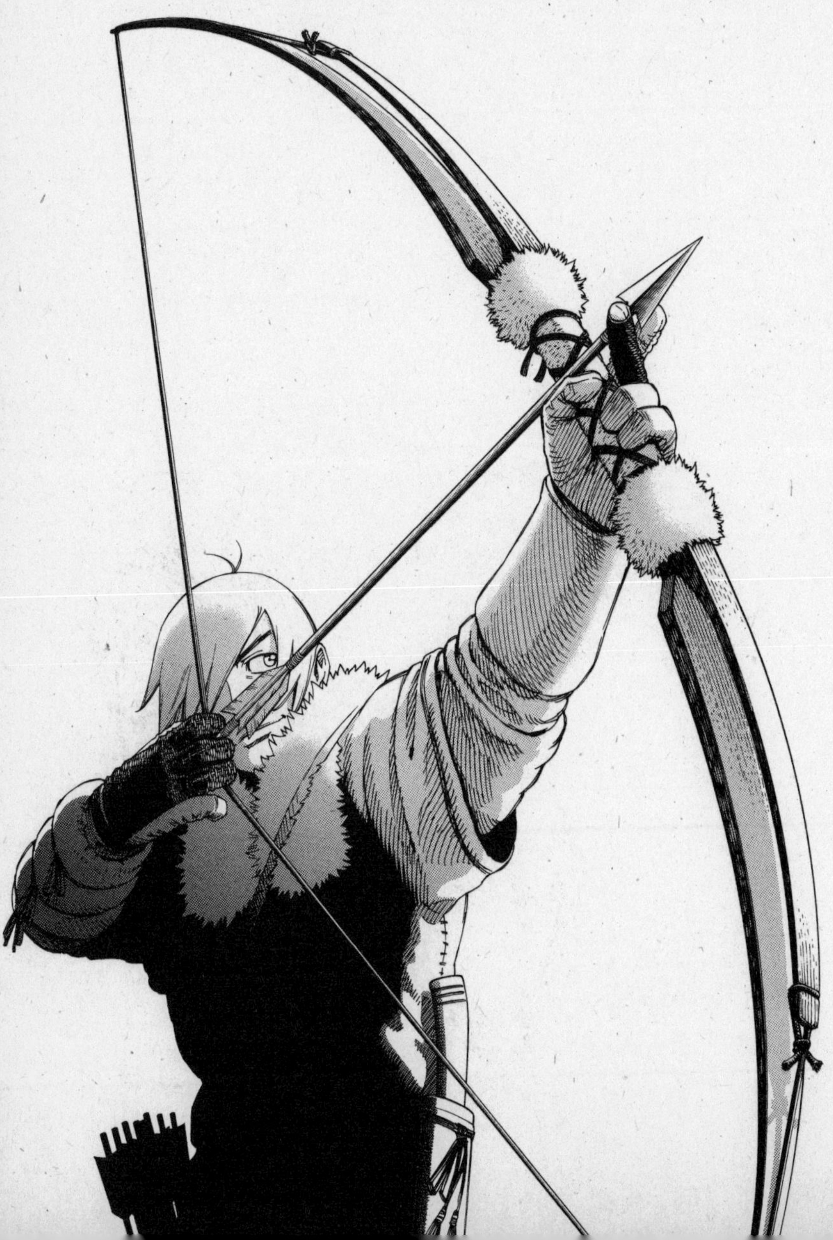

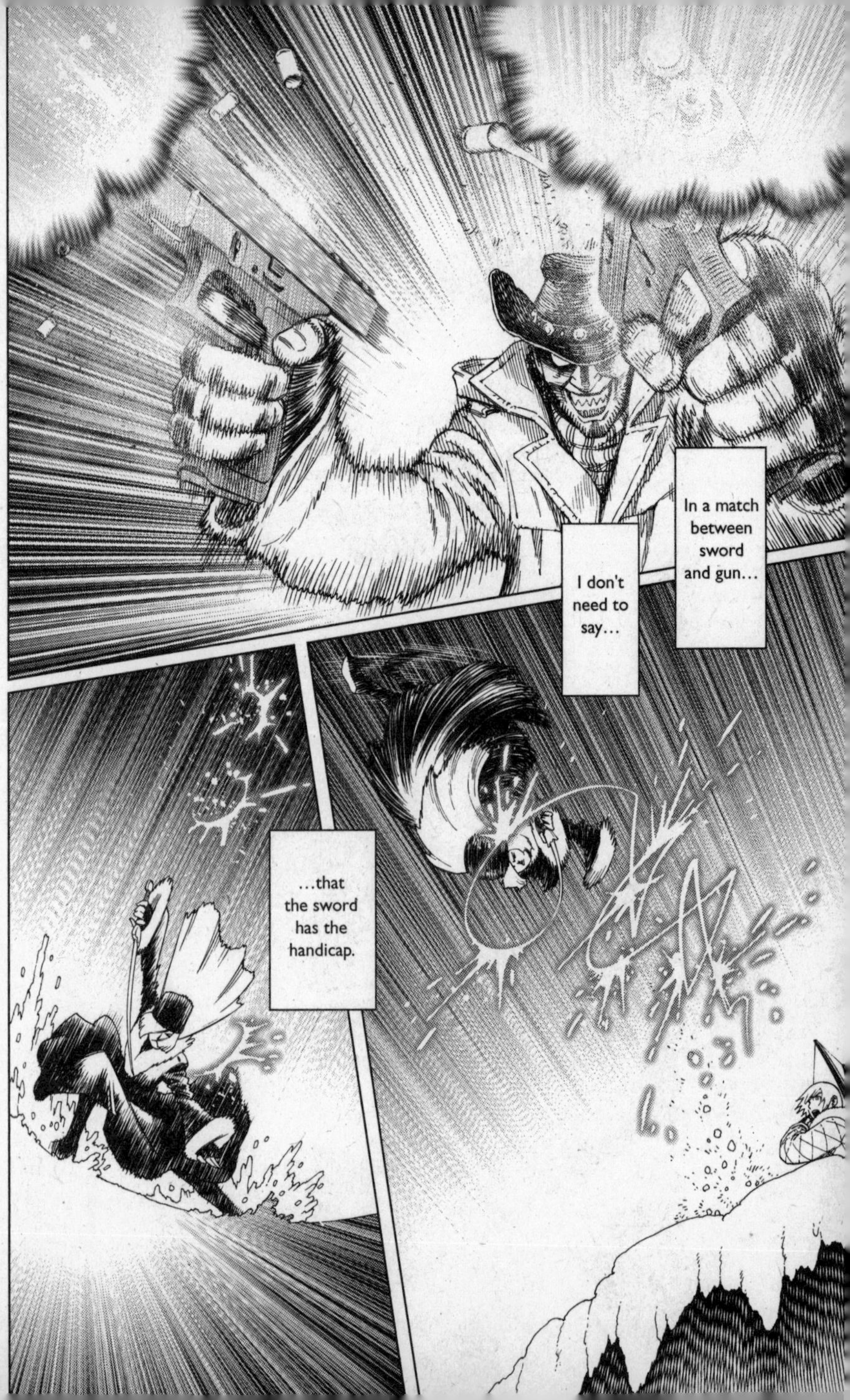
In a match between sword and gun...
I don't need to say...
...that the sword has the handicap.

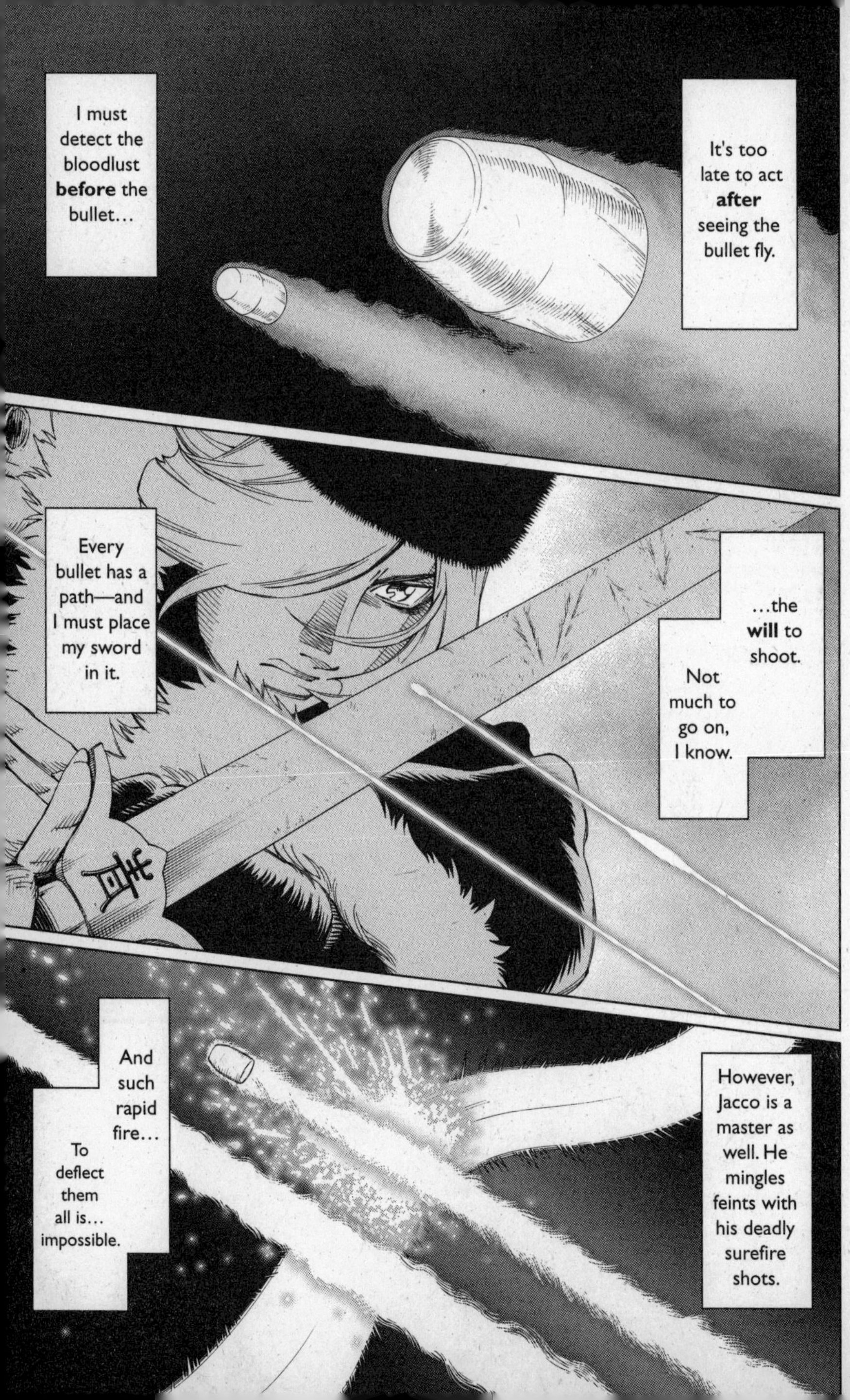
It's too late to act **after** seeing the bullet fly.
I must detect the bloodlust **before** the bullet...
...the **will** to shoot.
Not much to go on, I know.
Every bullet has a path—and I must place my sword in it.
However, Jacco is a master as well. He mingles feints with his deadly surefire shots.
And such rapid fire...
To deflect them all is... impossible.

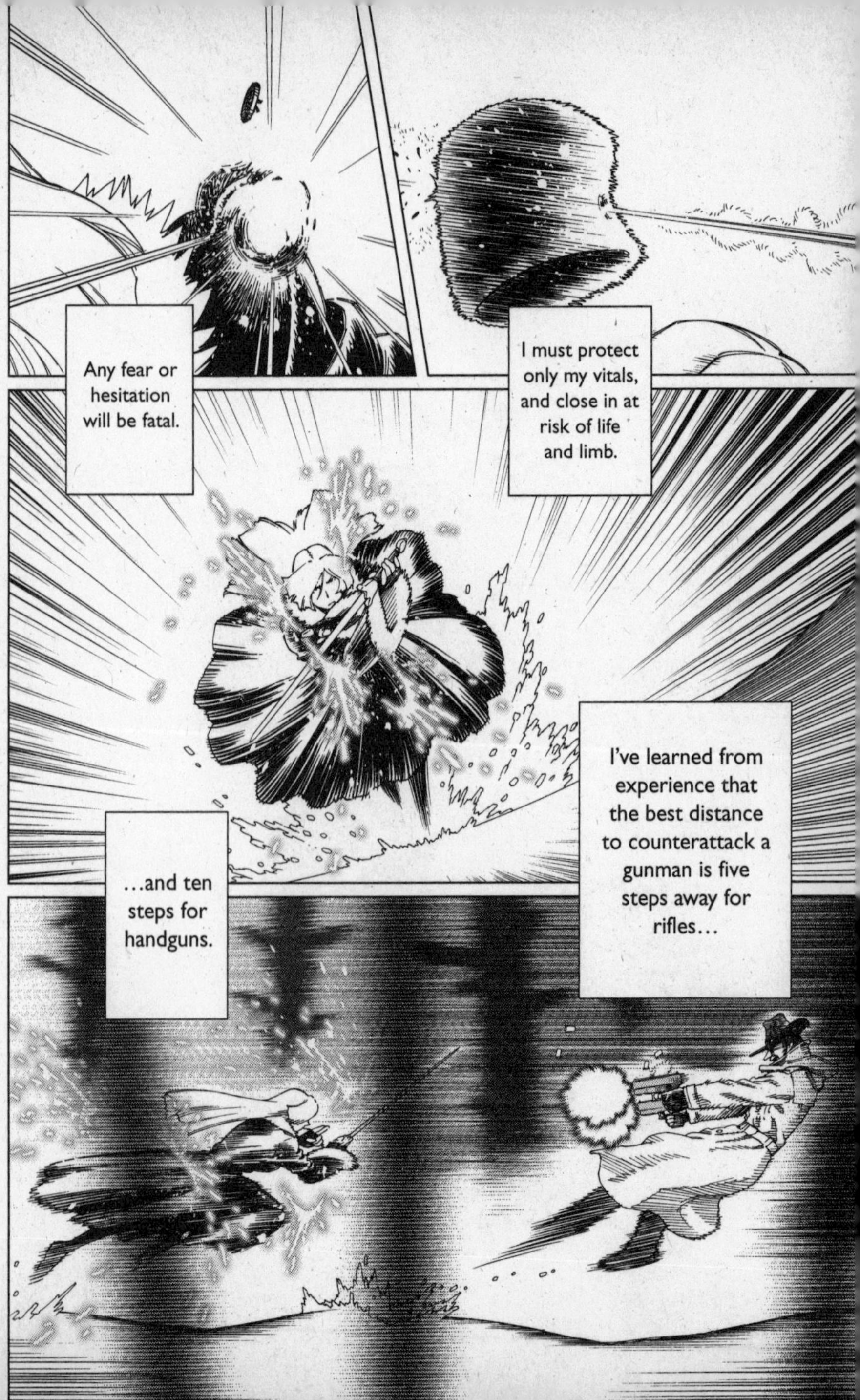
I must protect only my vitals, and close in at risk of life and limb.
Any fear or hesitation will be fatal.
I've learned from experience that the best distance to counterattack a gunman is five steps away for rifles...
...and ten steps for handguns.

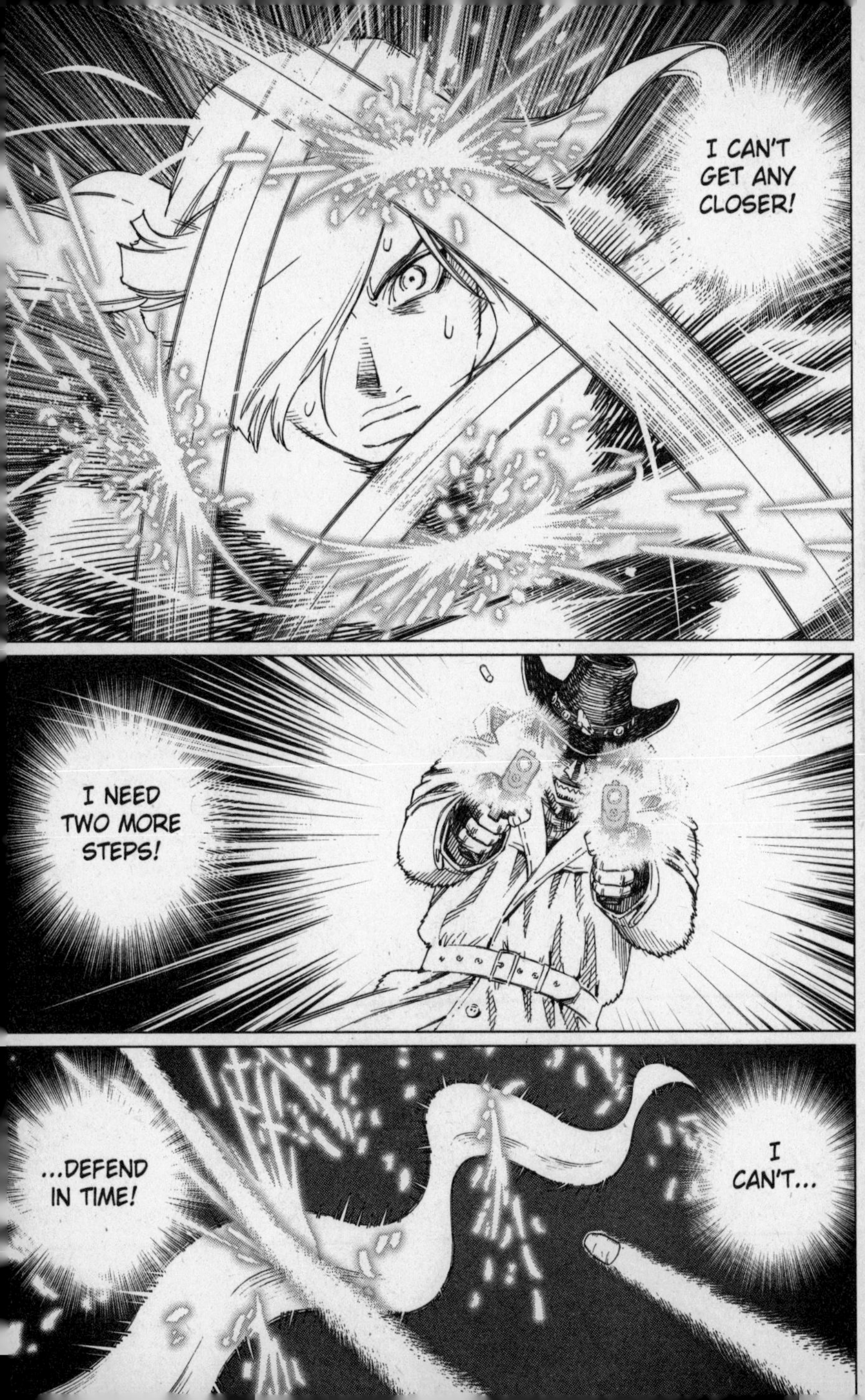
I CAN'T GET ANY CLOSER!
I NEED TWO MORE STEPS!
I CAN'T...
...DEFEND IN TIME!

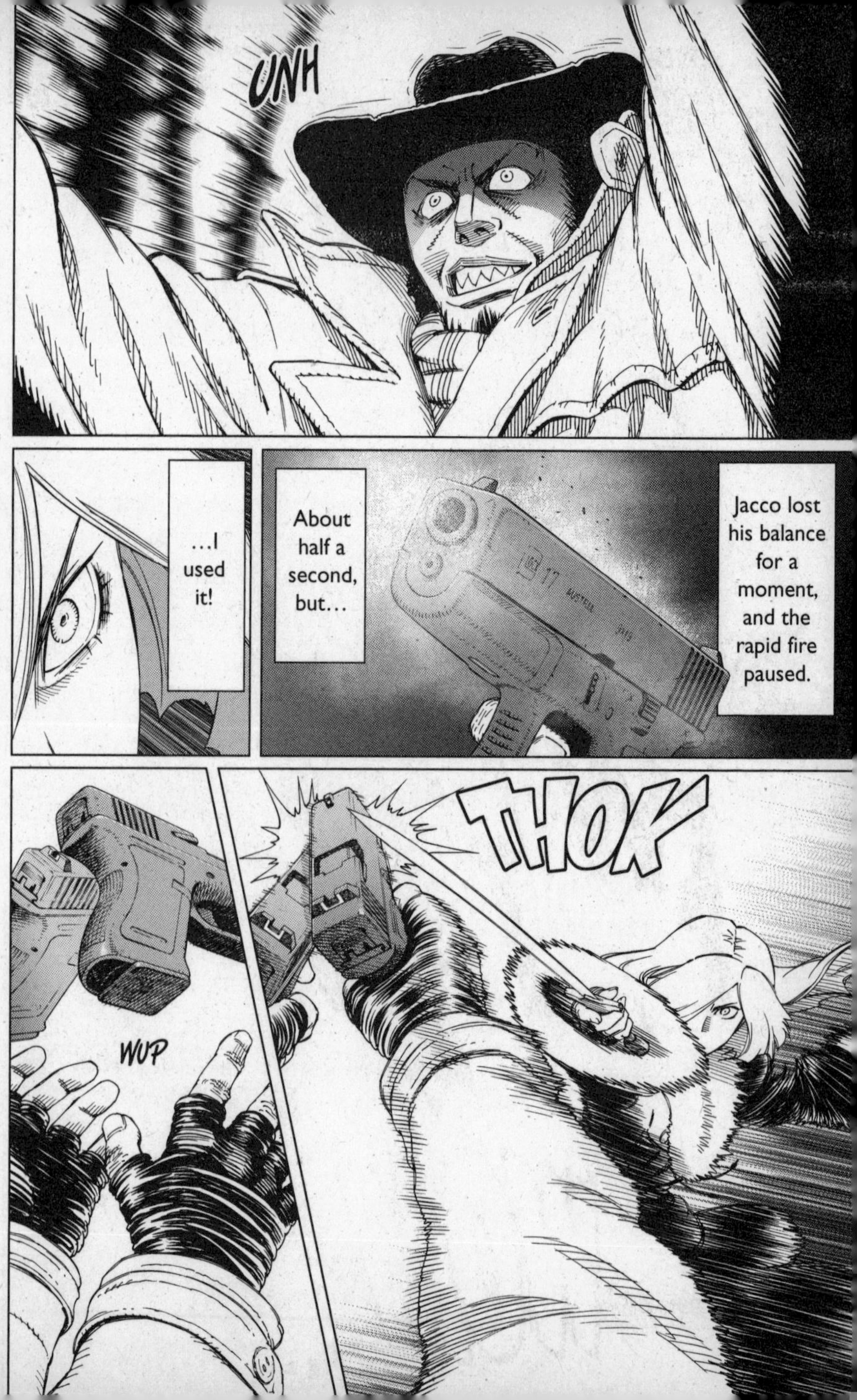
UNH
Jacco lost his balance for a moment, and the rapid fire paused.
About half a second, but…
…I used it!
THOK
WUP

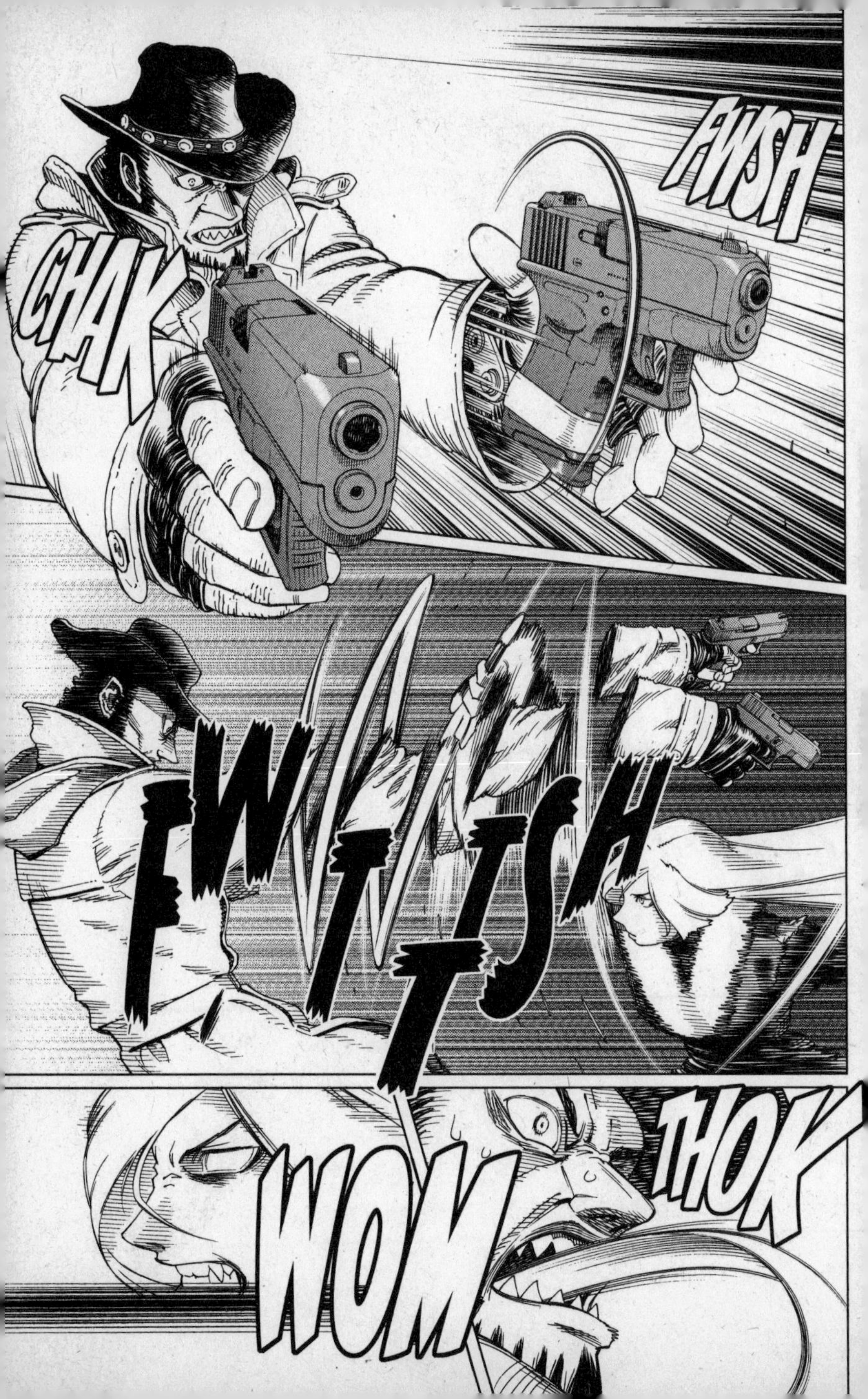
FWSH
CHAK
FWITSH
THOK
WOM

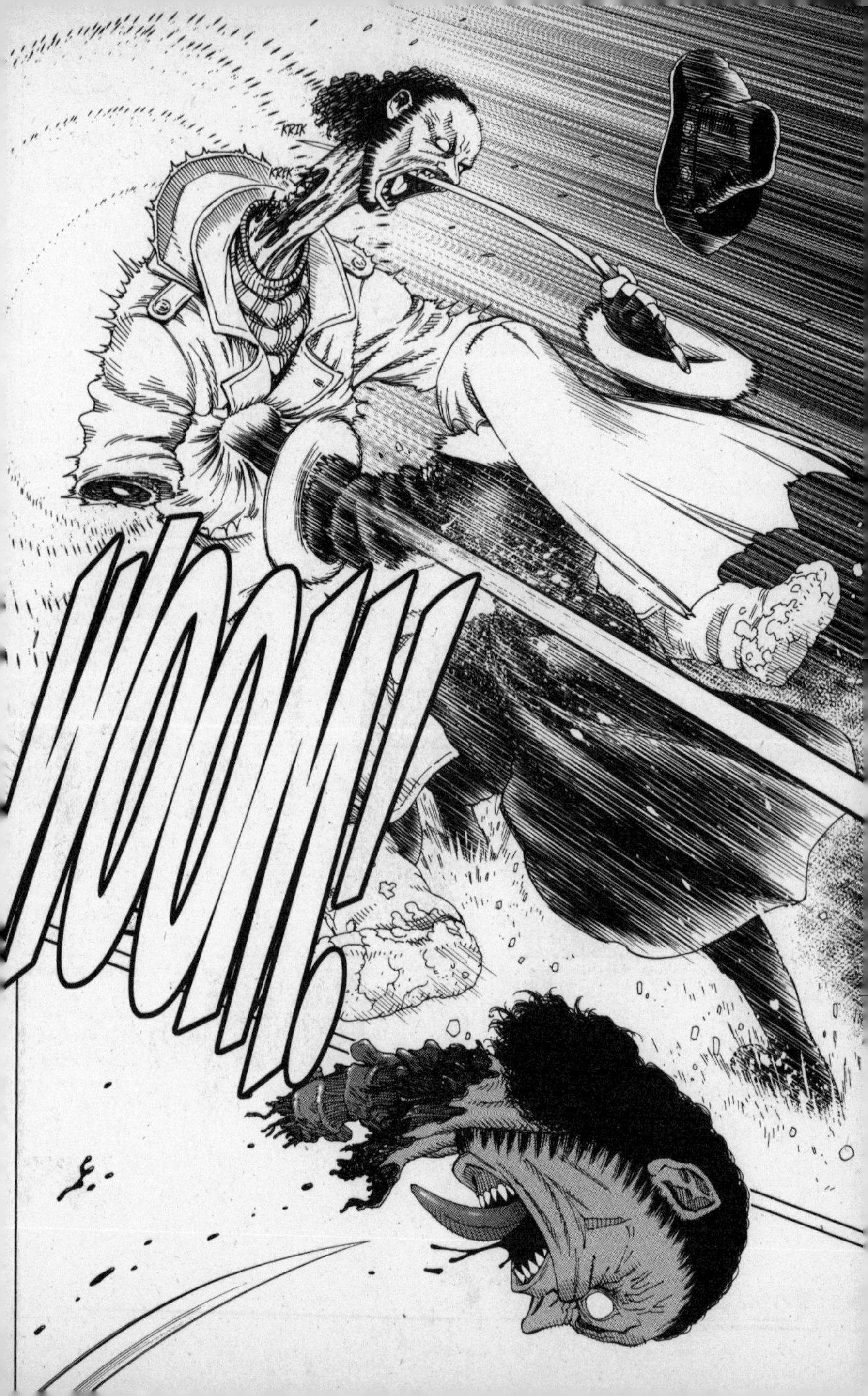
KRIK
KRIK
WOOM!

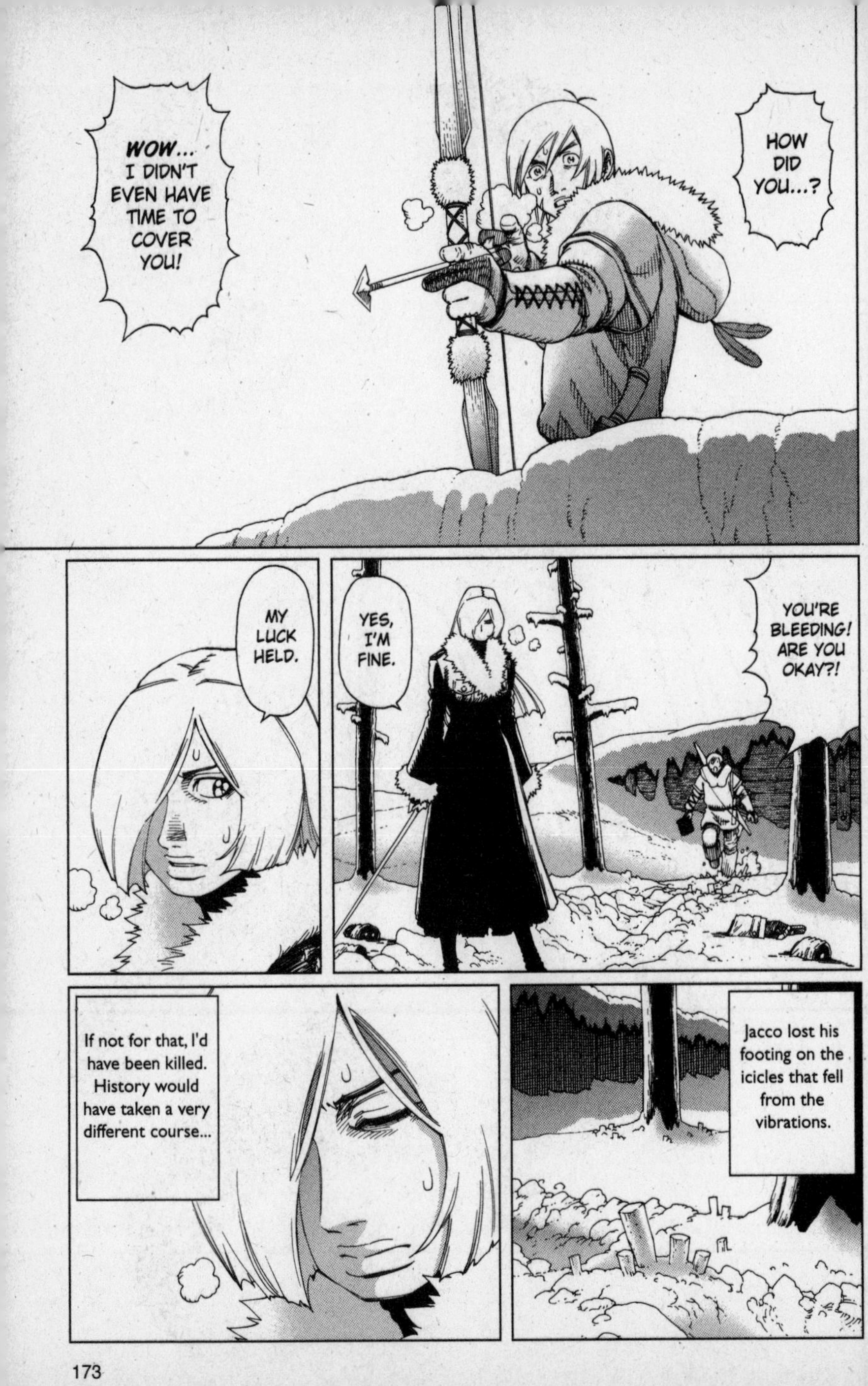
HOW DID YOU...?
WOW... I DIDN'T EVEN HAVE TIME TO COVER YOU!
YOU'RE BLEEDING! ARE YOU OKAY?!
YES, I'M FINE.
MY LUCK HELD.
Jacco lost his footing on the icicles that fell from the vibrations.
If not for that, I'd have been killed. History would have taken a very different course...

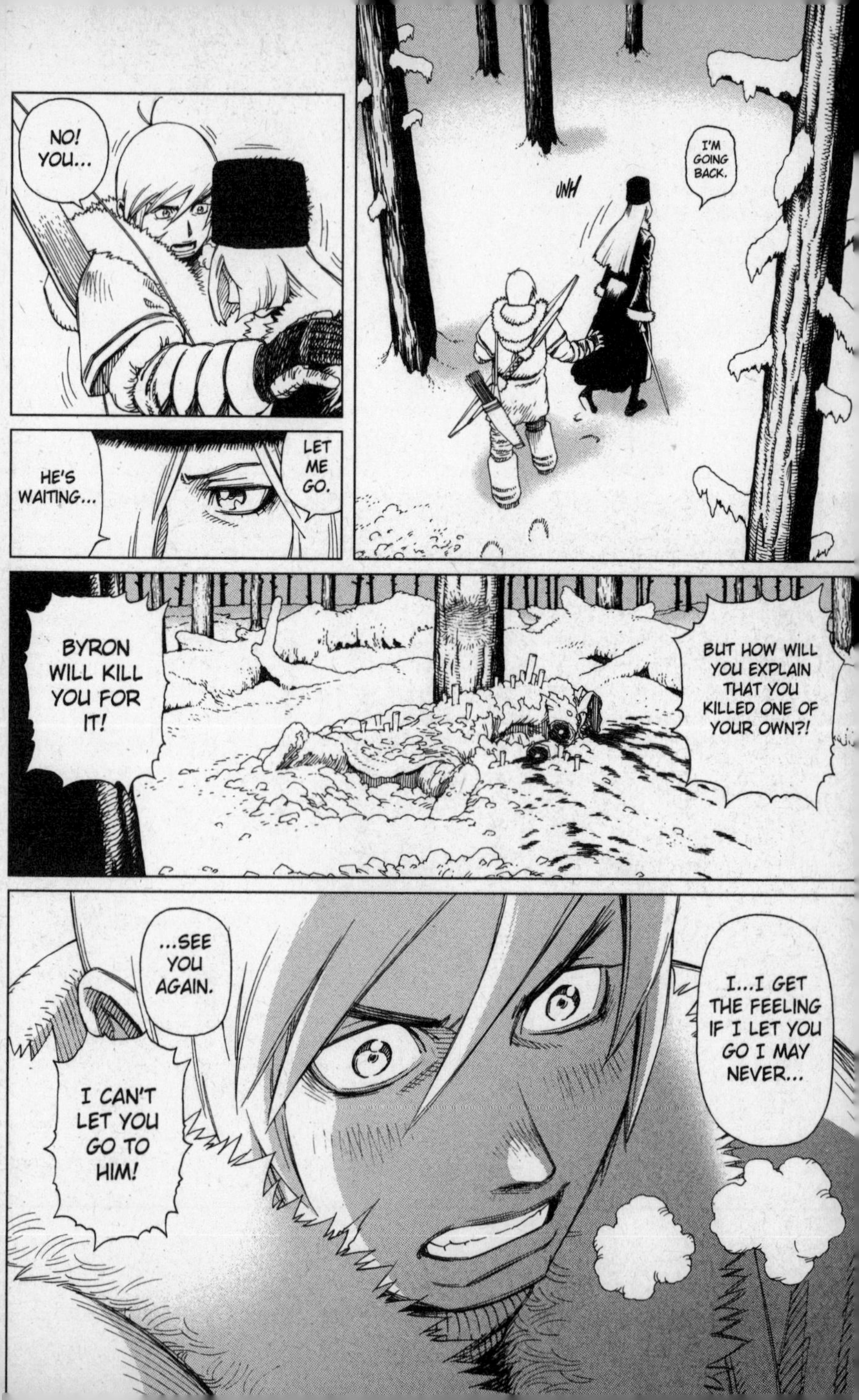
I'M GOING BACK.
UNH
NO! YOU...
LET ME GO.
HE'S WAITING...
BUT HOW WILL YOU EXPLAIN THAT YOU KILLED ONE OF YOUR OWN?!
BYRON WILL KILL YOU FOR IT!
I...I GET THE FEELING IF I LET YOU GO I MAY NEVER...
...SEE YOU AGAIN.
I CAN'T LET YOU GO TO HIM!

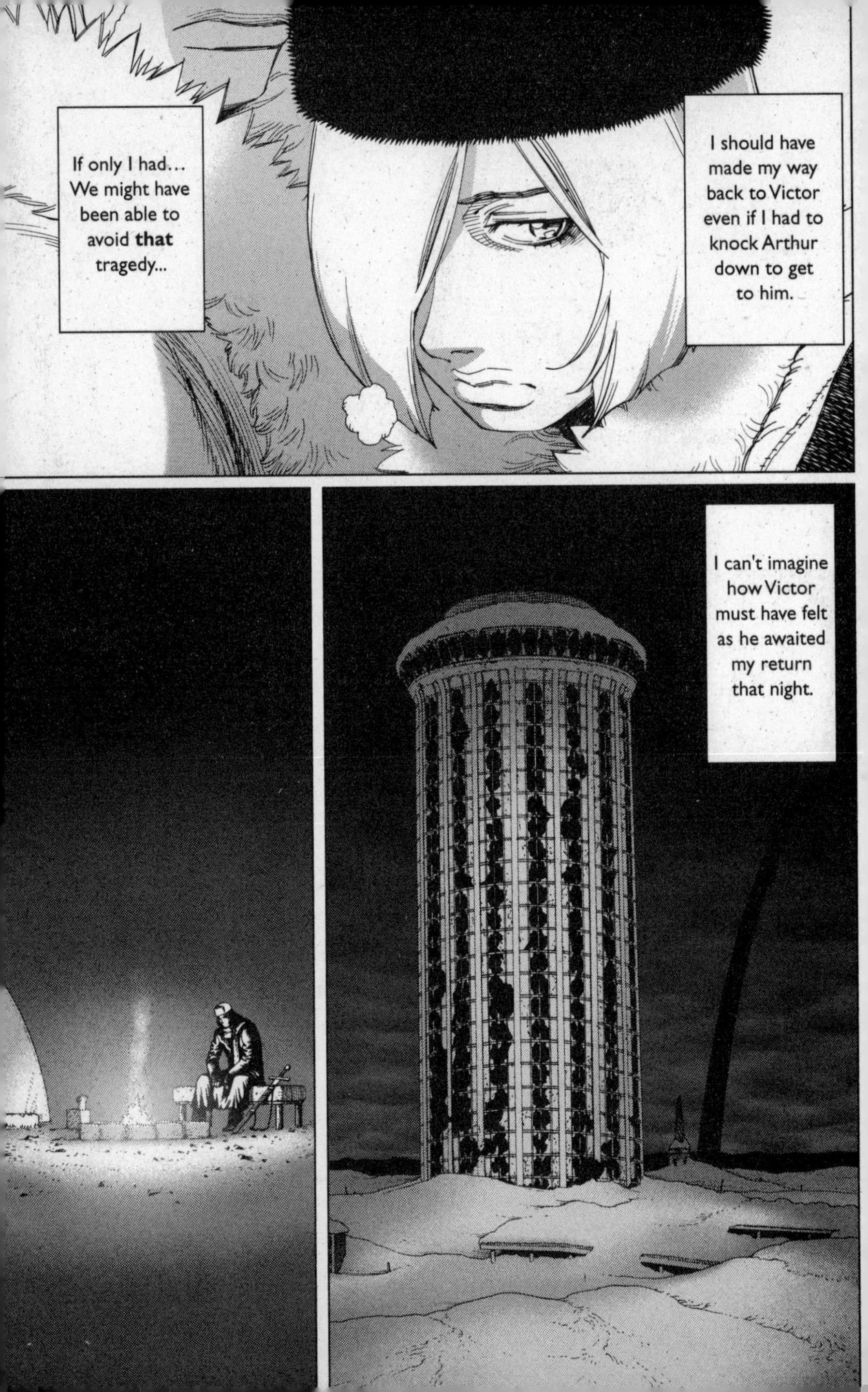
I should have made my way back to Victor even if I had to knock Arthur down to get to him.
If only I had... We might have been able to avoid **that** tragedy...
I can't imagine how Victor must have felt as he awaited my return that night.

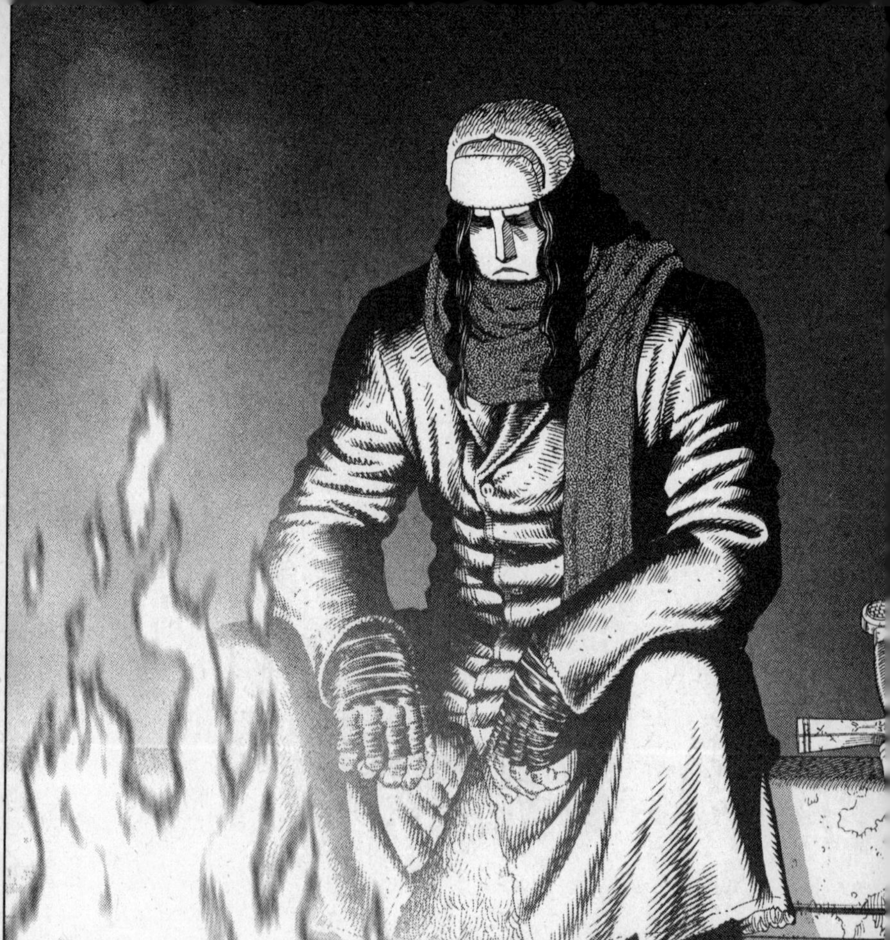
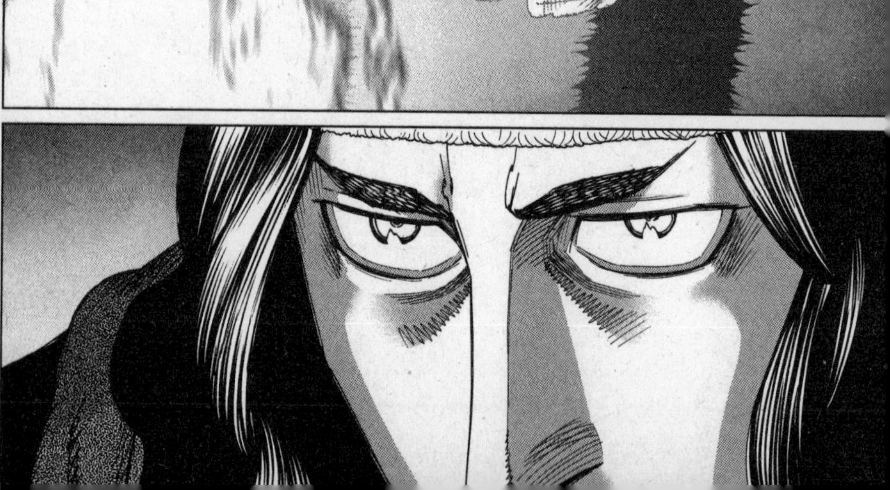

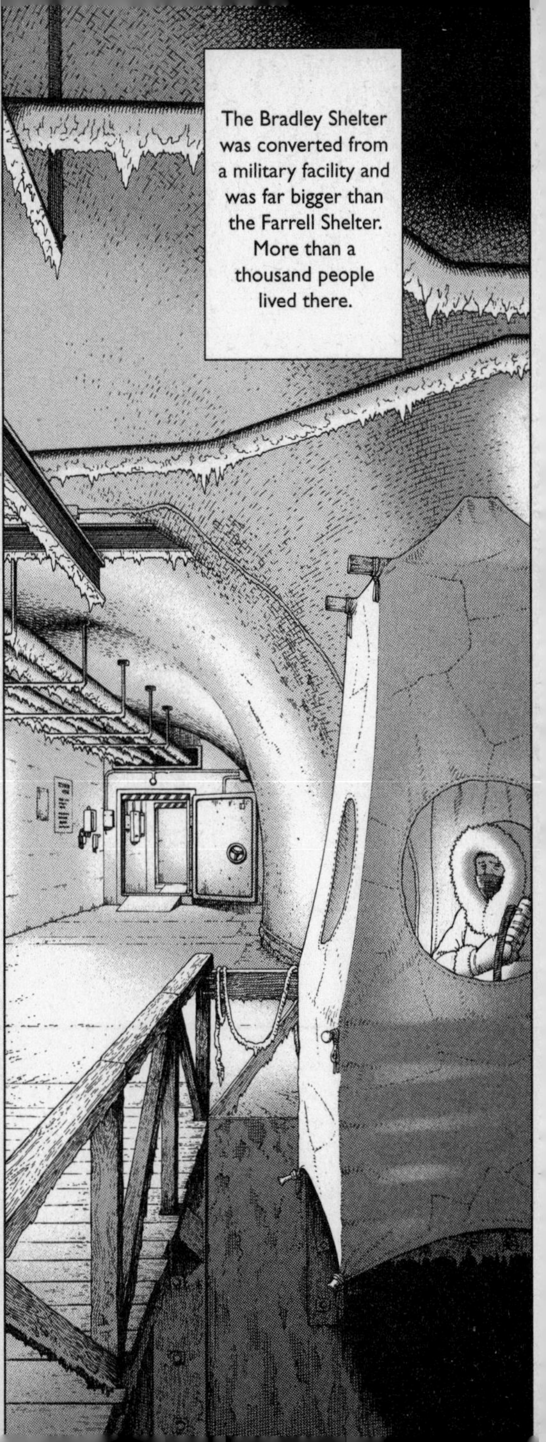
The Bradley Shelter was converted from a military facility and was far bigger than the Farrell Shelter. More than a thousand people lived there.
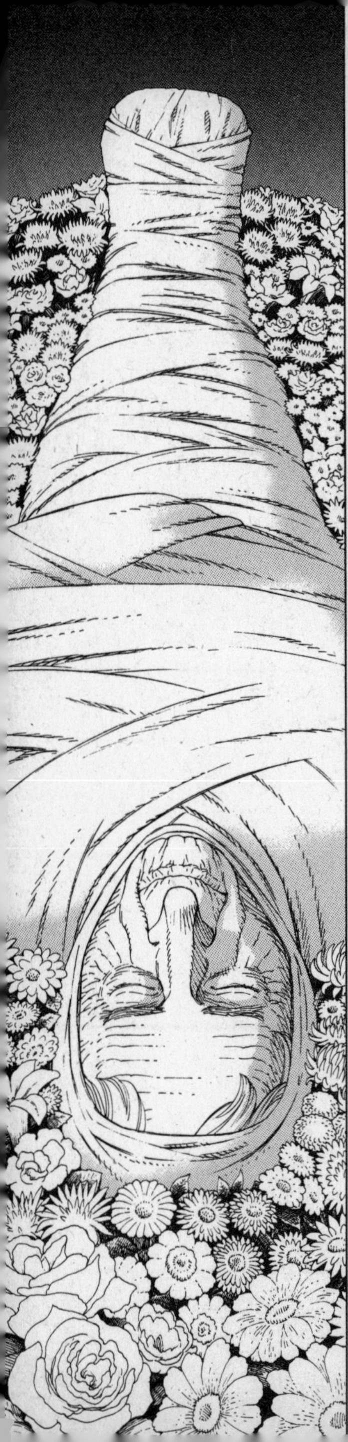

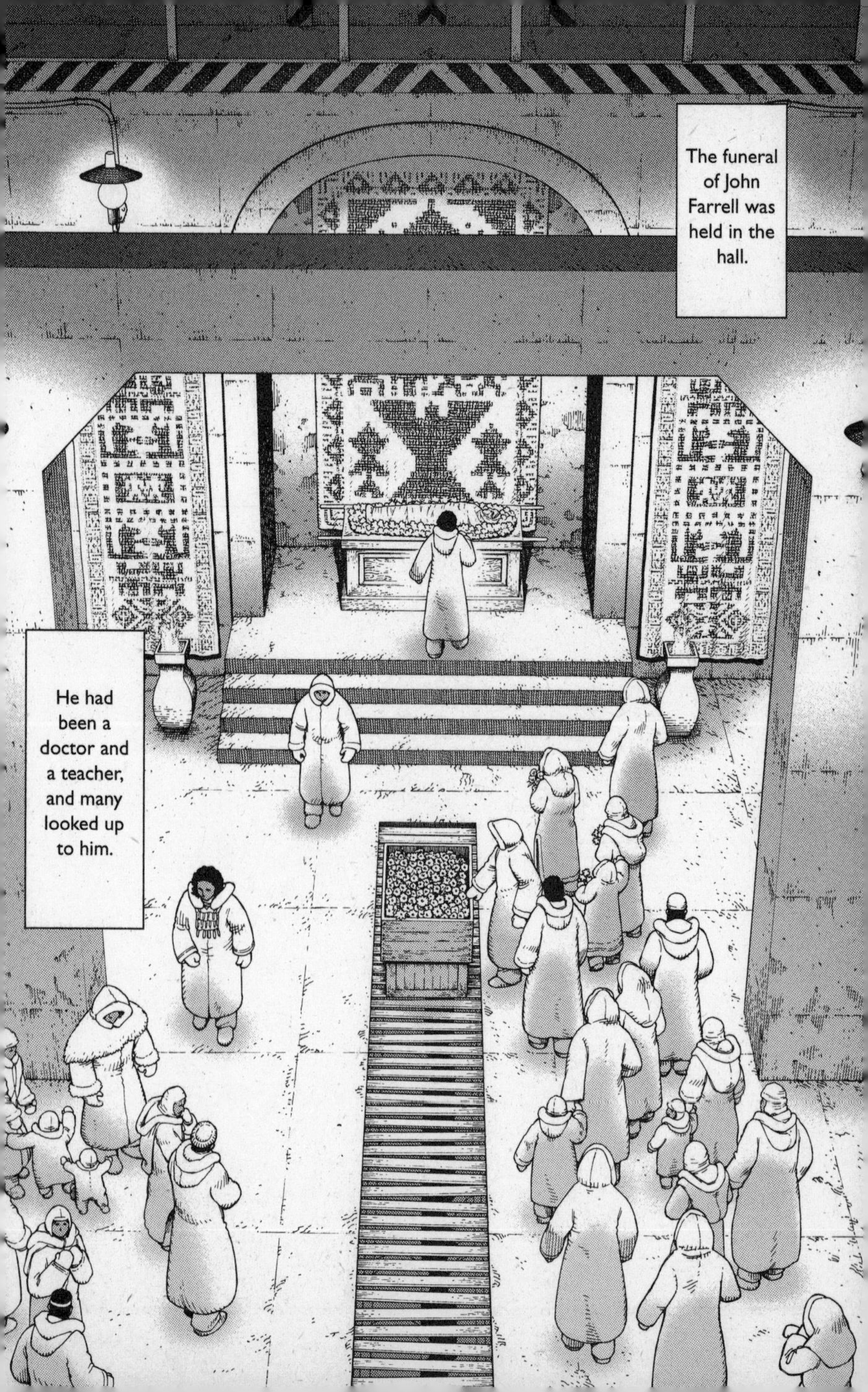
The funeral of John Farrell was held in the hall.
He had been a doctor and a teacher, and many looked up to him.

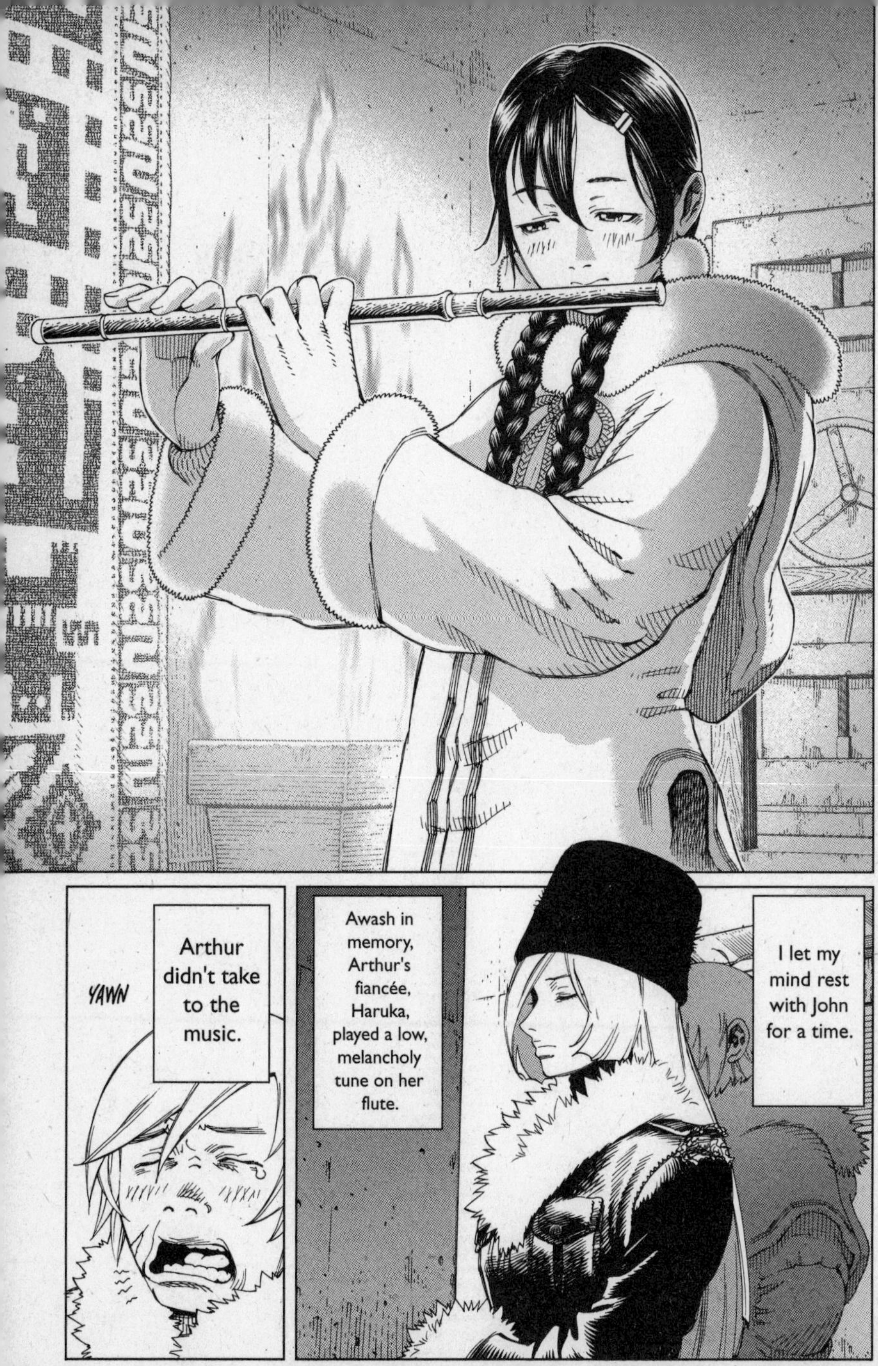
I let my mind rest with John for a time.
Awash in memory, Arthur's fiancée, Haruka, played a low, melancholy tune on her flute.
Arthur didn't take to the music.
YAWN

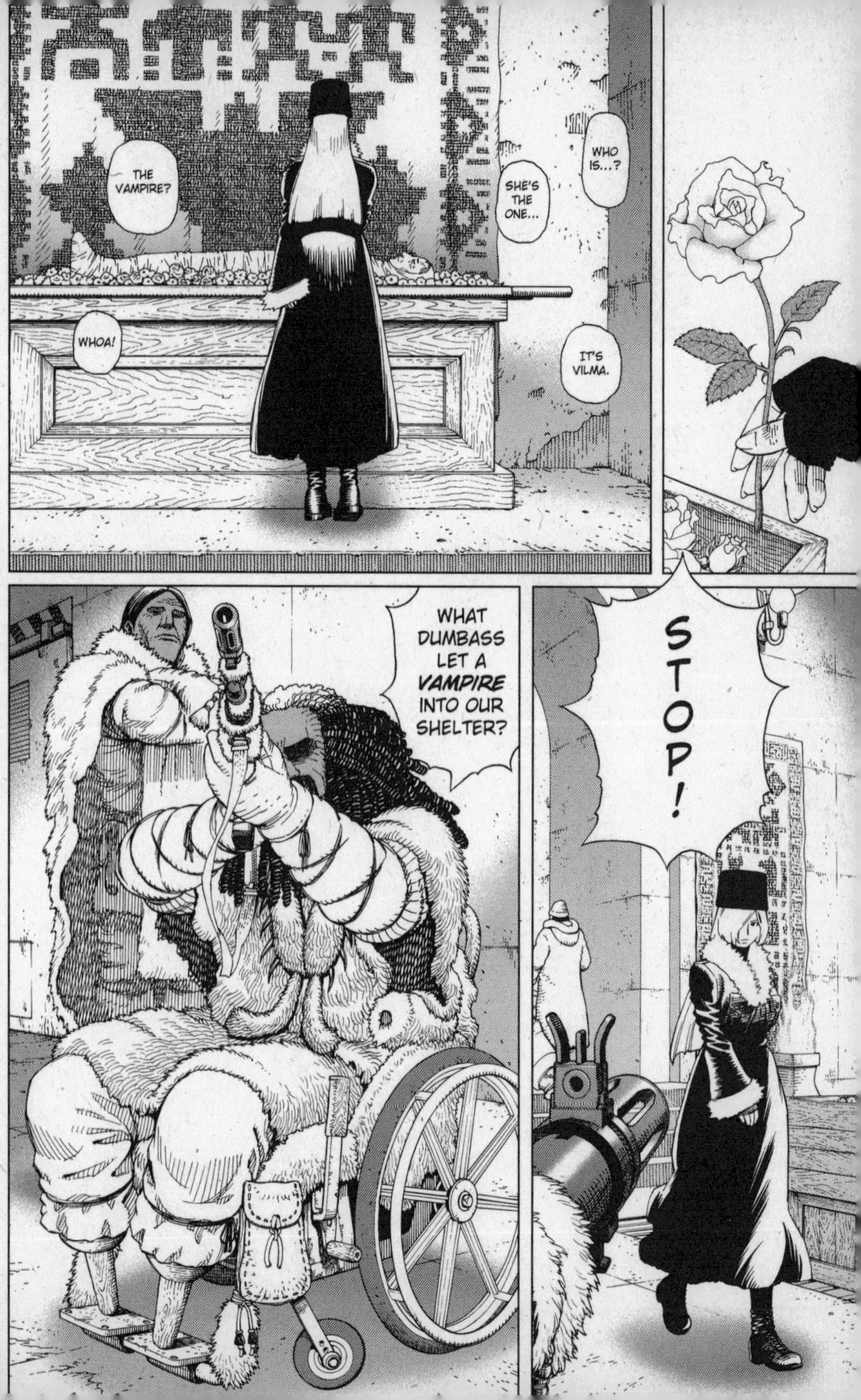
WHO IS...?
SHE'S THE ONE...
THE VAMPIRE?
IT'S VILMA.
WHOA!
STOP!
WHAT DUMBASS LET A *VAMPIRE* INTO OUR SHELTER?

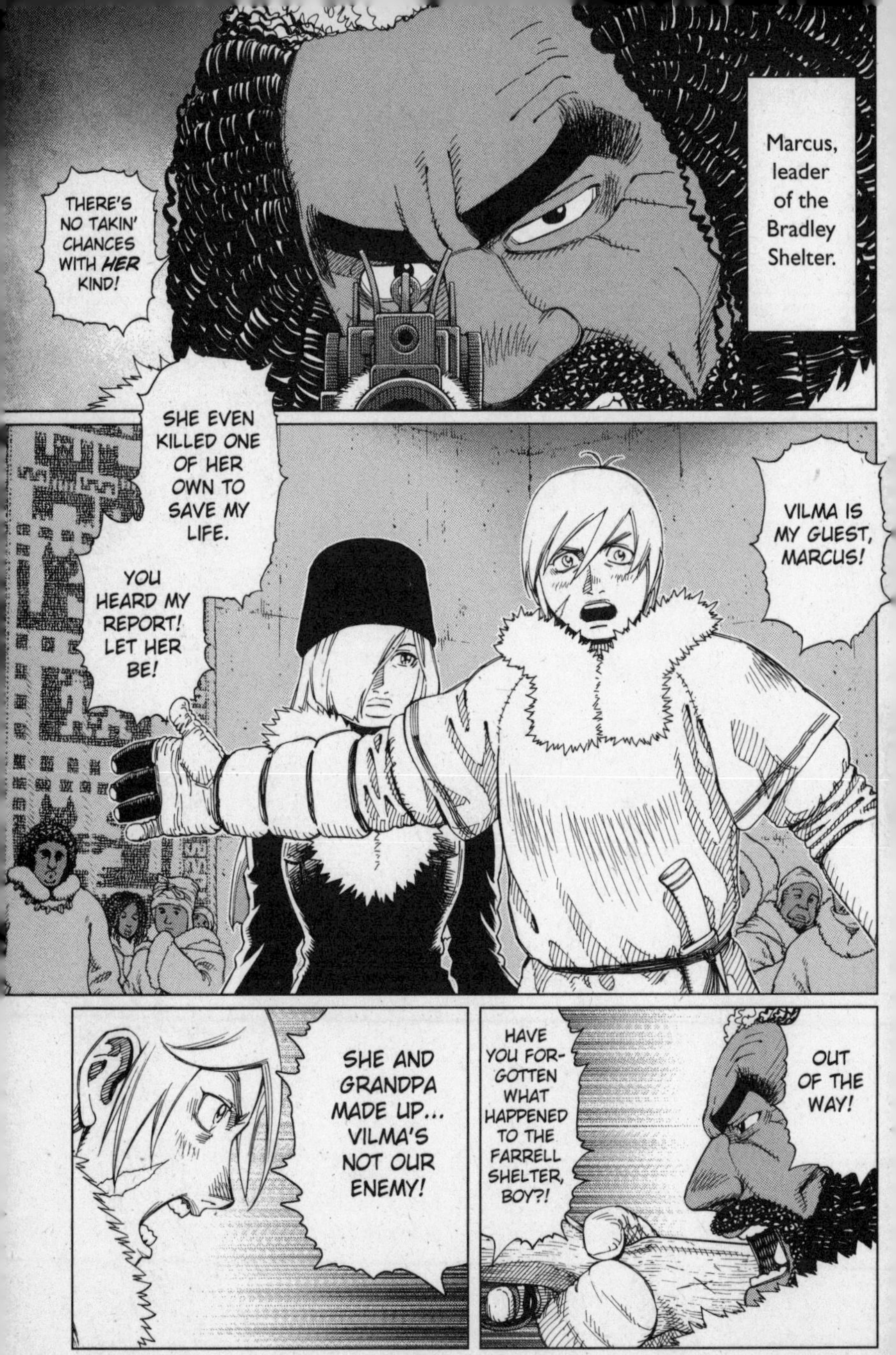
Marcus, leader of the Bradley Shelter.
THERE'S NO TAKIN' CHANCES WITH *HER* KIND!
VILMA IS MY GUEST, MARCUS!
SHE EVEN KILLED ONE OF HER OWN TO SAVE MY LIFE.
YOU HEARD MY REPORT! LET HER BE!
OUT OF THE WAY!
HAVE YOU FOR-GOTTEN WHAT HAPPENED TO THE FARRELL SHELTER, BOY?!
SHE AND GRANDPA MADE UP... VILMA'S NOT OUR ENEMY!

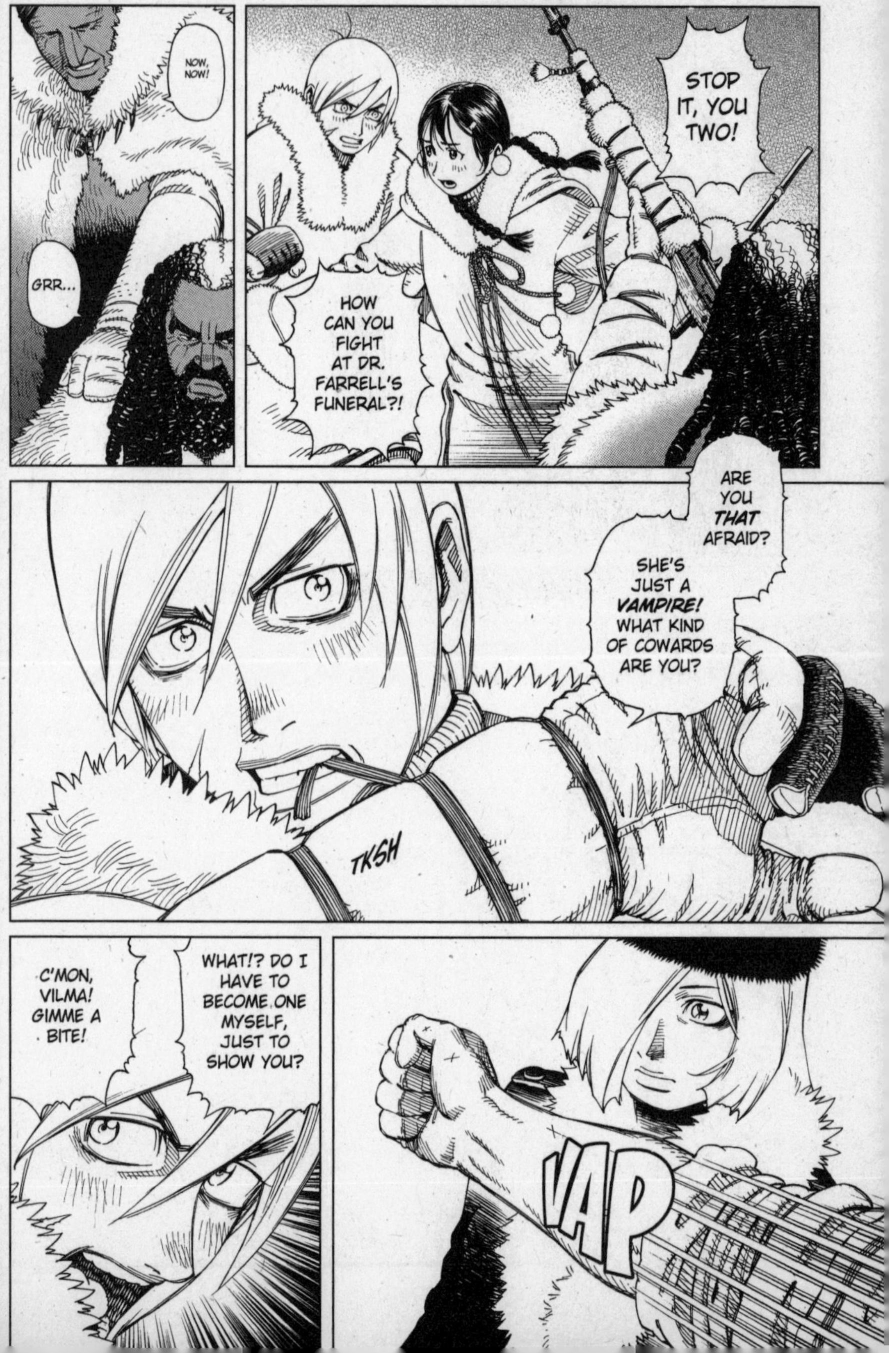
STOP IT, YOU TWO!
HOW CAN YOU FIGHT AT DR. FARRELL'S FUNERAL?!
NOW, NOW!
GRR...
ARE YOU *THAT* AFRAID?
SHE'S JUST A *VAMPIRE!* WHAT KIND OF COWARDS ARE YOU?
TKSH
VAP
WHAT!? DO I HAVE TO BECOME ONE MYSELF, JUST TO SHOW YOU?
C'MON, VILMA! GIMME A BITE!

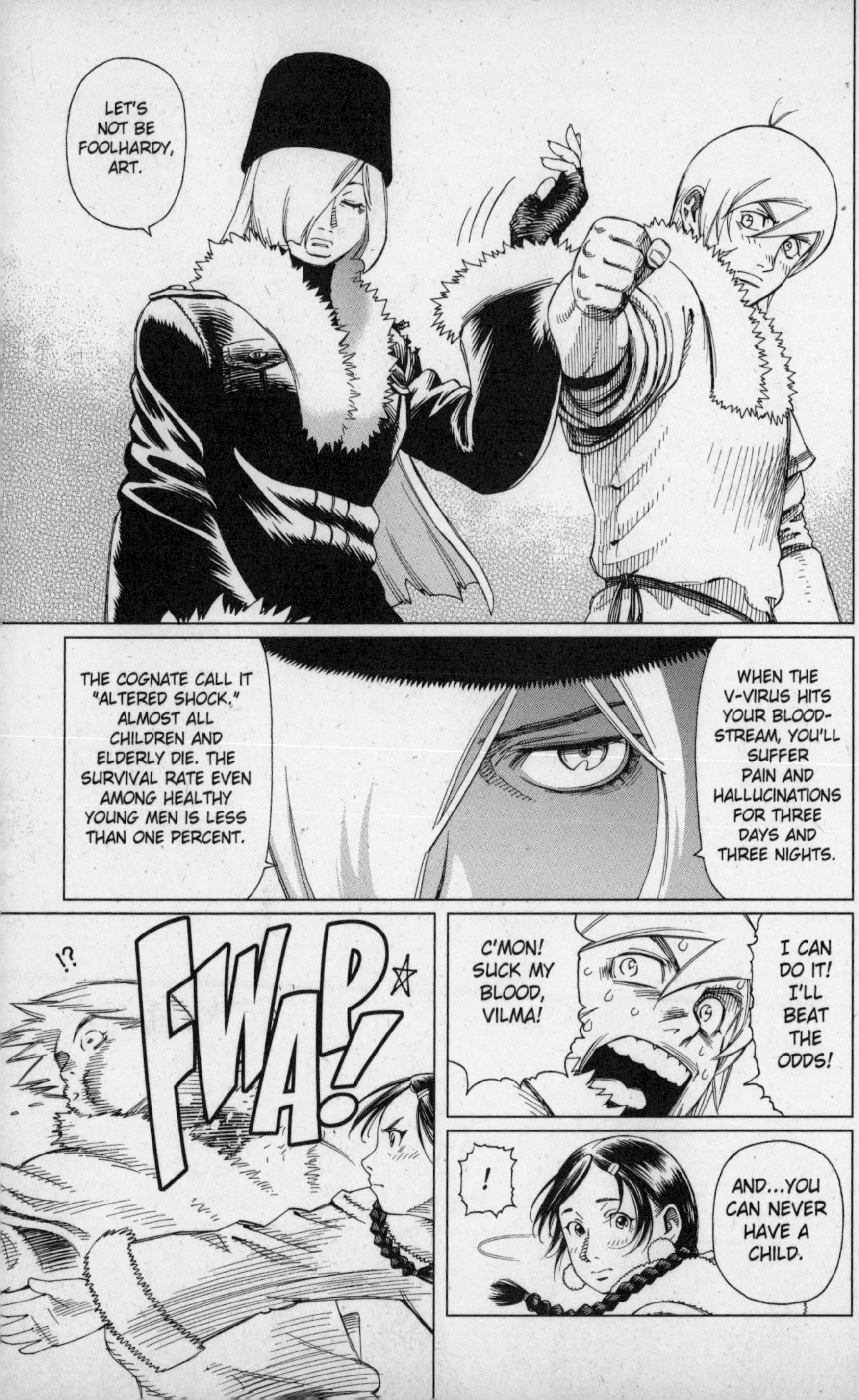
LET'S NOT BE FOOLHARDY, ART.
WHEN THE V-VIRUS HITS YOUR BLOODSTREAM, YOU'LL SUFFER PAIN AND HALLUCINATIONS FOR THREE DAYS AND THREE NIGHTS.
THE COGNATE CALL IT "ALTERED SHOCK." ALMOST ALL CHILDREN AND ELDERLY DIE. THE SURVIVAL RATE EVEN AMONG HEALTHY YOUNG MEN IS LESS THAN ONE PERCENT.
I CAN DO IT! I'LL BEAT THE ODDS!
C'MON! SUCK MY BLOOD, VILMA!
AND...YOU CAN NEVER HAVE A CHILD.
!
FWAP!☆
!?

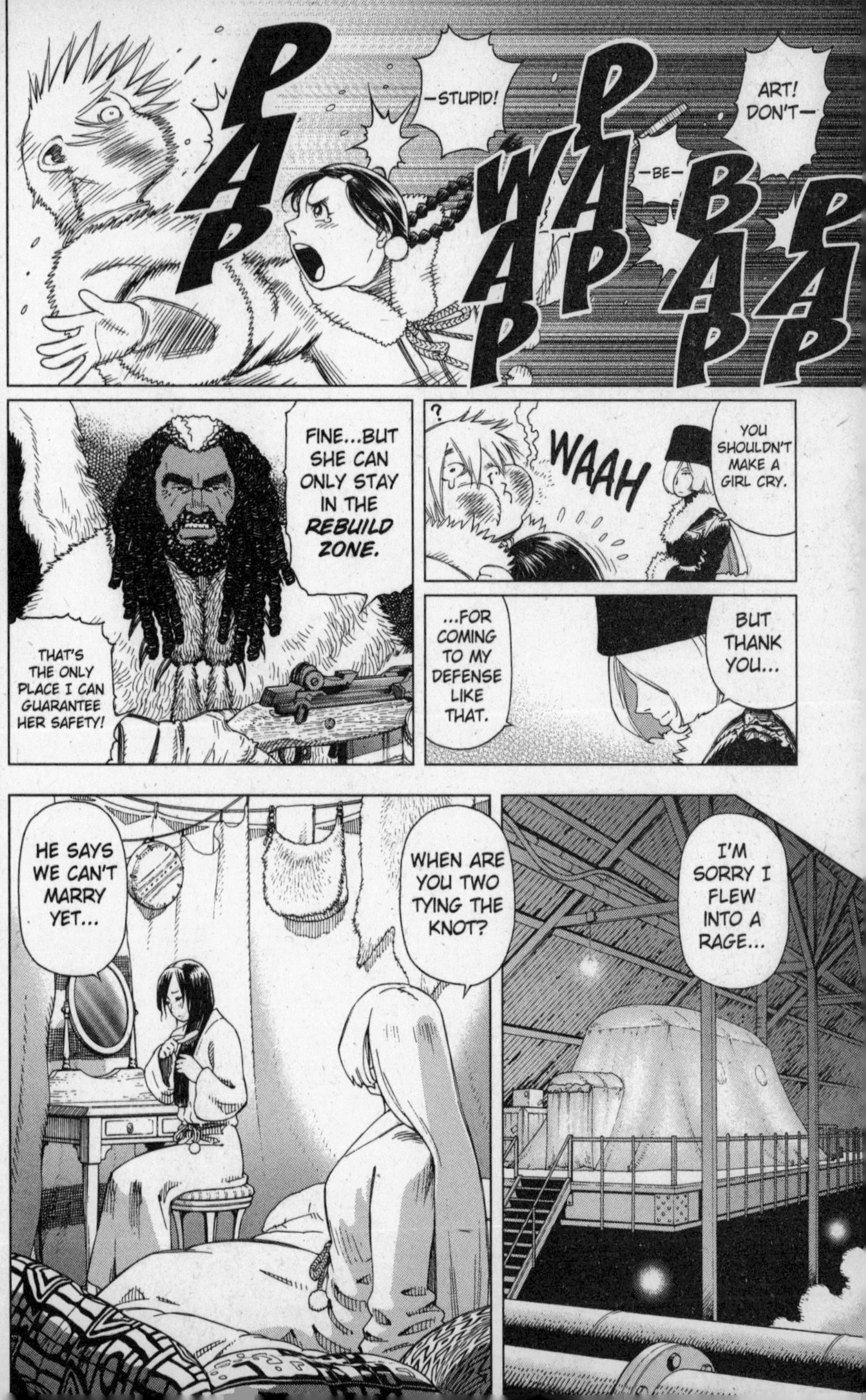
ART! DON'T—
—BE—
—STUPID!
PAP
BAP
PAP
WAP
PAP
YOU SHOULDN'T MAKE A GIRL CRY.
WAAH
?
BUT THANK YOU...
...FOR COMING TO MY DEFENSE LIKE THAT.
FINE...BUT SHE CAN ONLY STAY IN THE *REBUILD ZONE.*
THAT'S THE ONLY PLACE I CAN GUARANTEE HER SAFETY!
I'M SORRY I FLEW INTO A RAGE...
WHEN ARE YOU TWO TYING THE KNOT?
HE SAYS WE CAN'T MARRY YET...

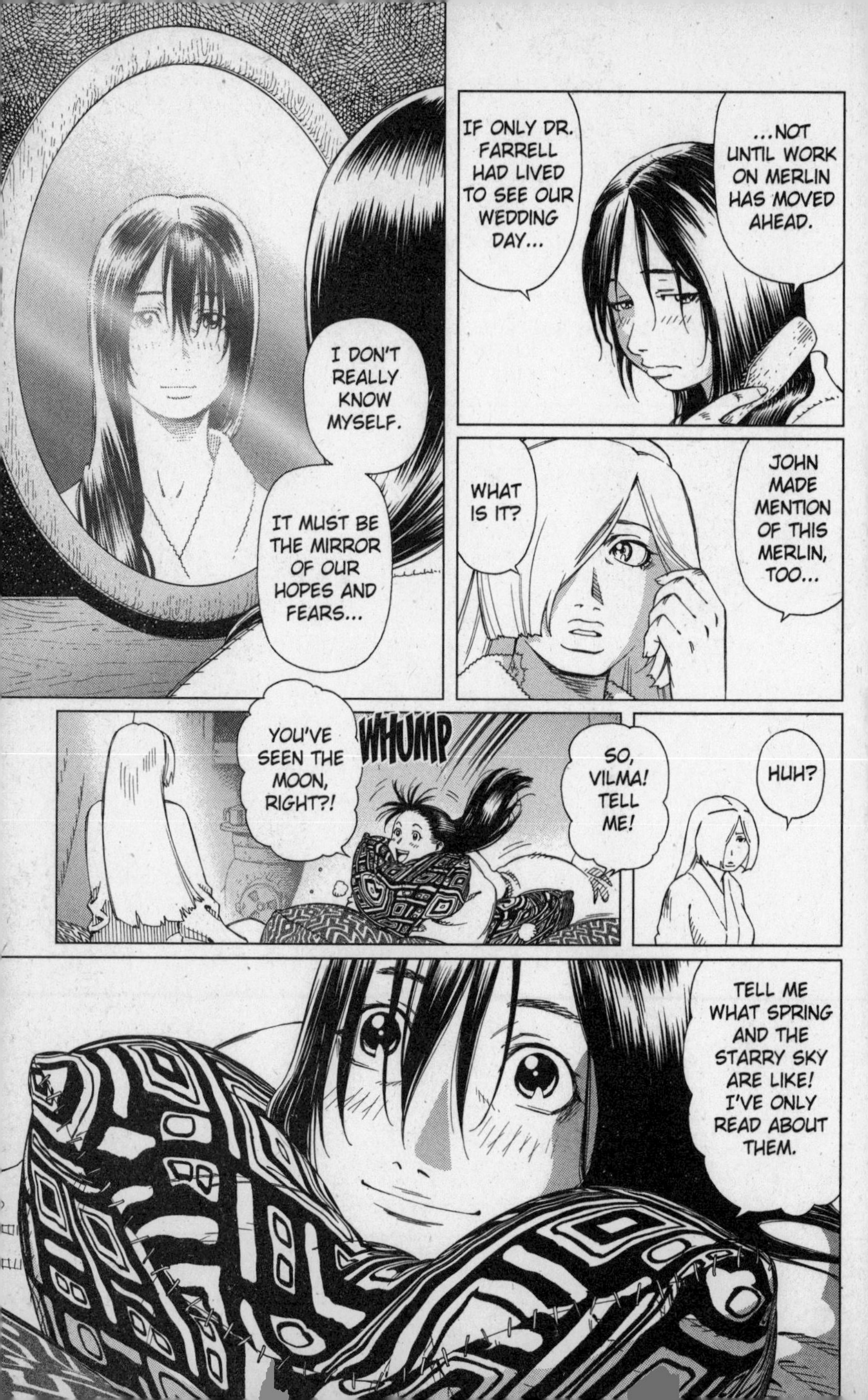
...NOT UNTIL WORK ON MERLIN HAS MOVED AHEAD.
IF ONLY DR. FARRELL HAD LIVED TO SEE OUR WEDDING DAY...
JOHN MADE MENTION OF THIS MERLIN, TOO...
WHAT IS IT?
I DON'T REALLY KNOW MYSELF.
IT MUST BE THE MIRROR OF OUR HOPES AND FEARS...
HUH?
SO, VILMA! TELL ME!
WHUMP
YOU'VE SEEN THE MOON, RIGHT?!
TELL ME WHAT SPRING AND THE STARRY SKY ARE LIKE! I'VE ONLY READ ABOUT THEM.

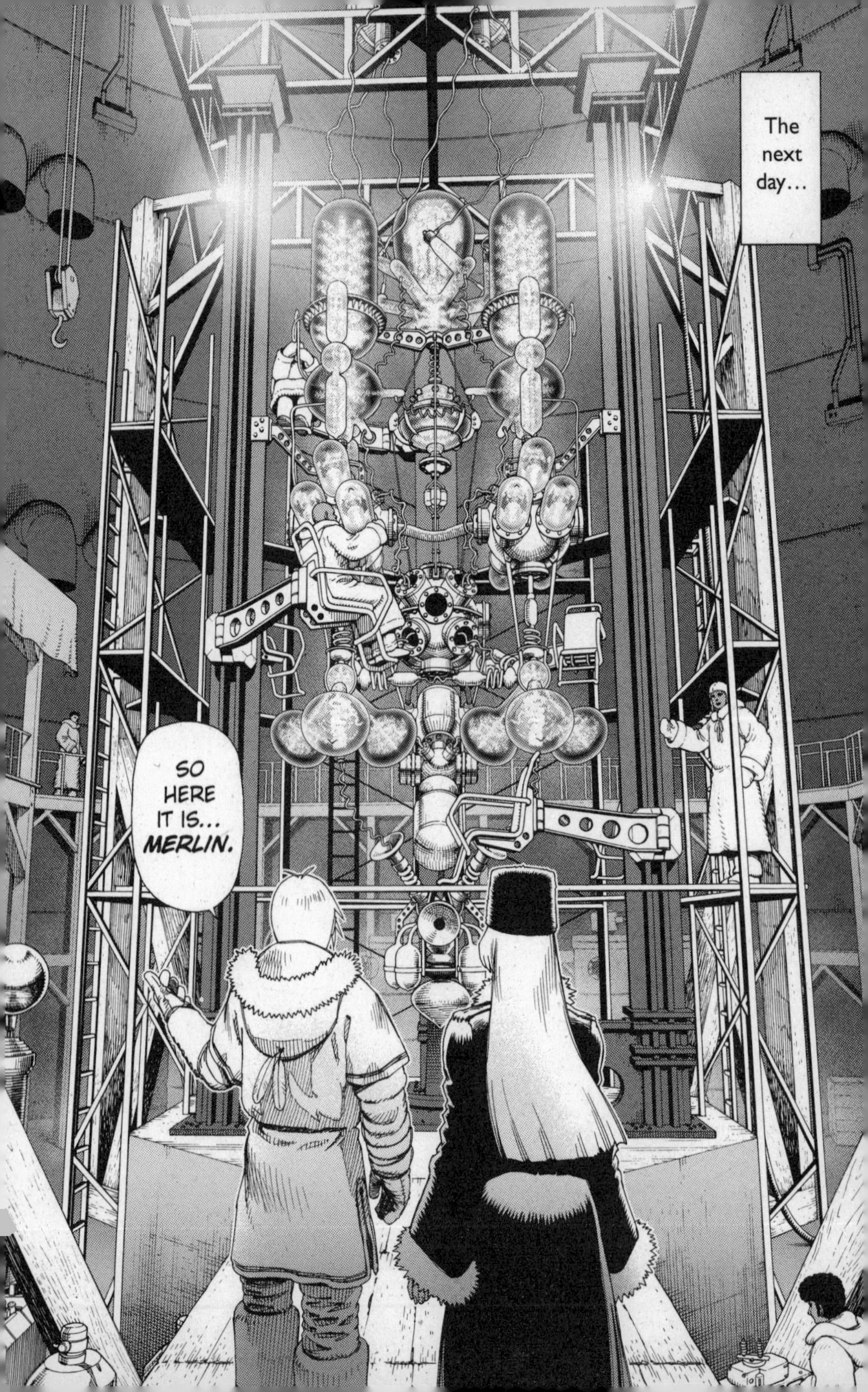
The next day…
SO HERE IT IS… MERLIN.

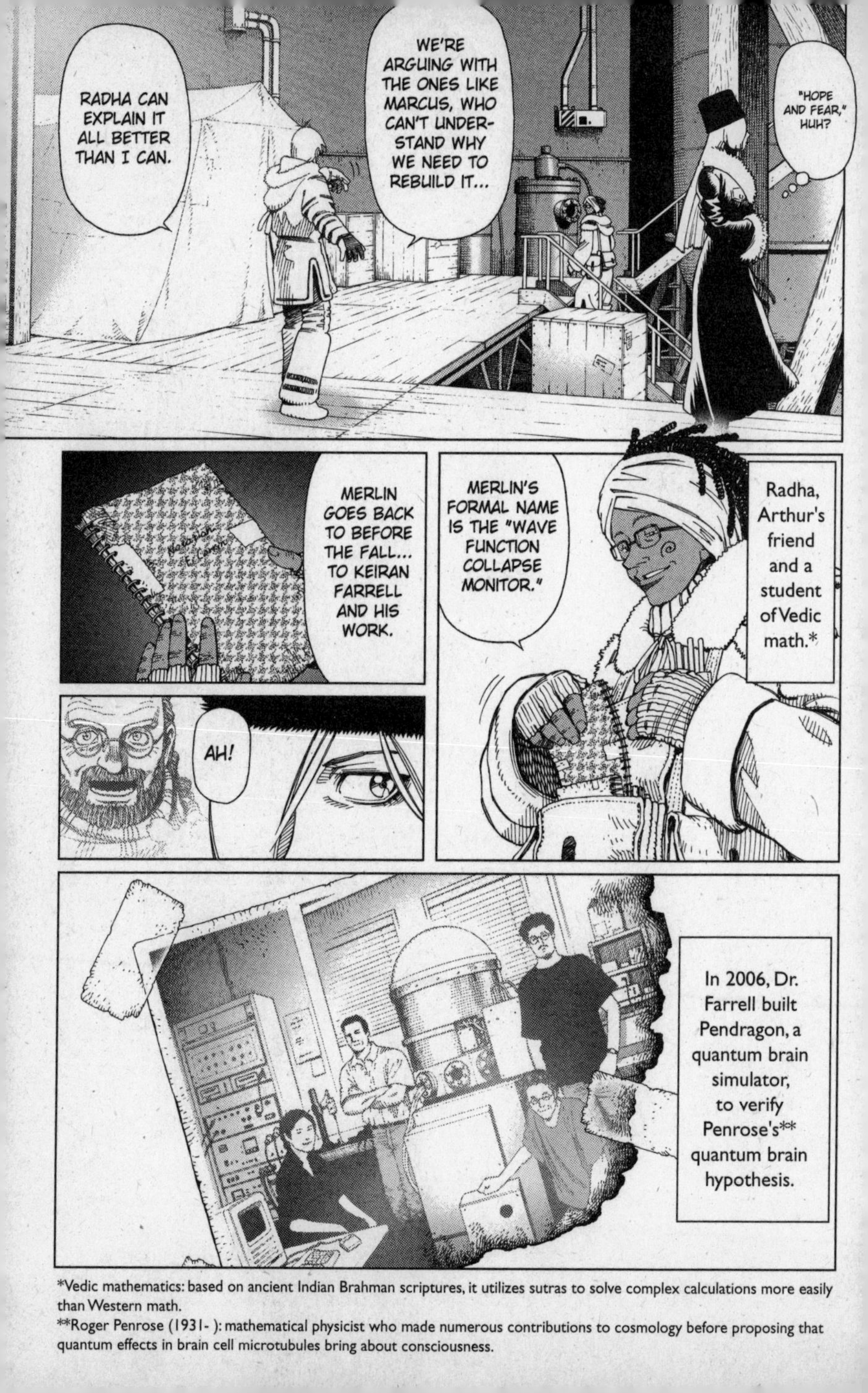
"HOPE AND FEAR," HUH?
WE'RE ARGUING WITH THE ONES LIKE MARCUS, WHO CAN'T UNDER-STAND WHY WE NEED TO REBUILD IT...
RADHA CAN EXPLAIN IT ALL BETTER THAN I CAN.
Radha, Arthur's friend and a student of Vedic math.*
MERLIN'S FORMAL NAME IS THE "WAVE FUNCTION COLLAPSE MONITOR."
MERLIN GOES BACK TO BEFORE THE FALL... TO KEIRAN FARRELL AND HIS WORK.
AH!
In 2006, Dr. Farrell built Pendragon, a quantum brain simulator, to verify Penrose's** quantum brain hypothesis.

*Vedic mathematics: based on ancient Indian Brahman scriptures, it utilizes sutras to solve complex calculations more easily than Western math.

**Roger Penrose (1931-): mathematical physicist who made numerous contributions to cosmology before proposing that quantum effects in brain cell microtubules bring about consciousness.

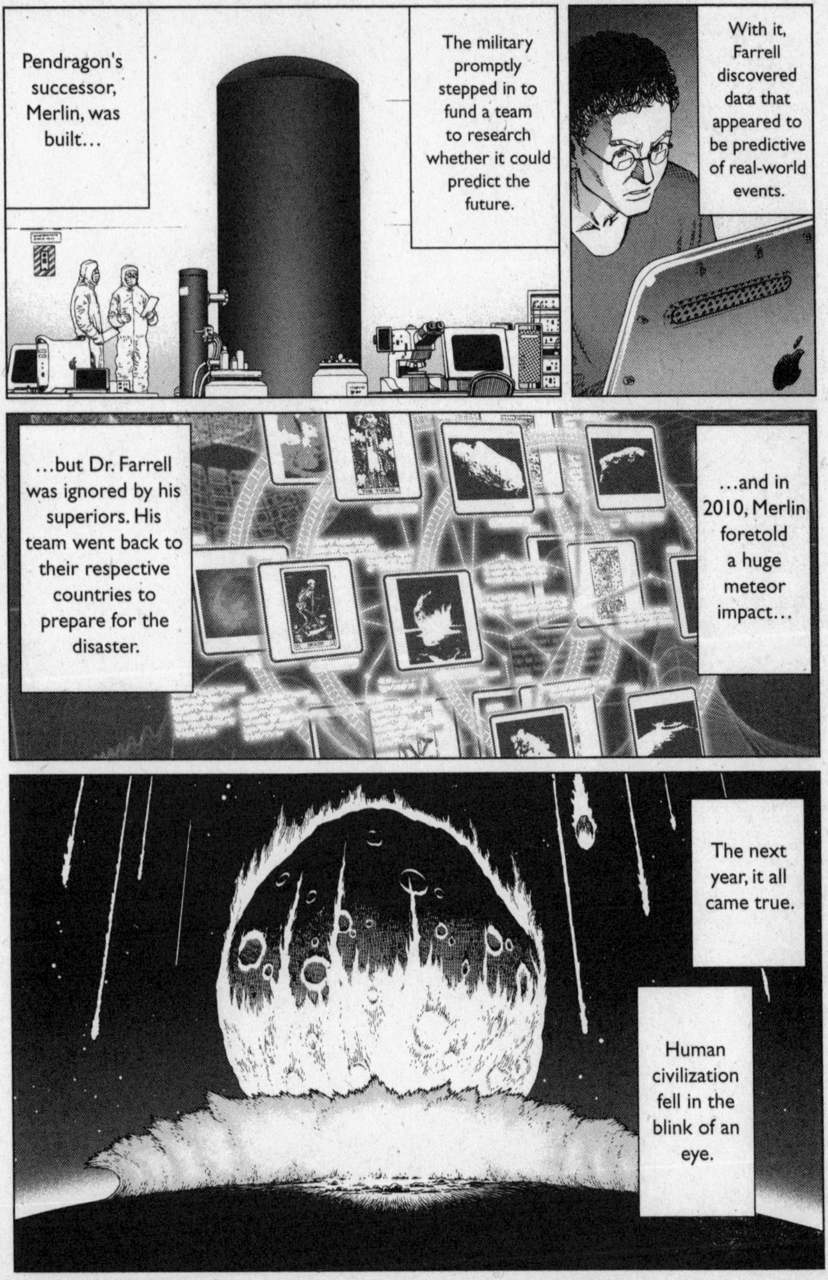
With it, Farrell discovered data that appeared to be predictive of real-world events.
The military promptly stepped in to fund a team to research whether it could predict the future.
Pendragon's successor, Merlin, was built...
...and in 2010, Merlin foretold a huge meteor impact...
...but Dr. Farrell was ignored by his superiors. His team went back to their respective countries to prepare for the disaster.
The next year, it all came true.
Human civilization fell in the blink of an eye.

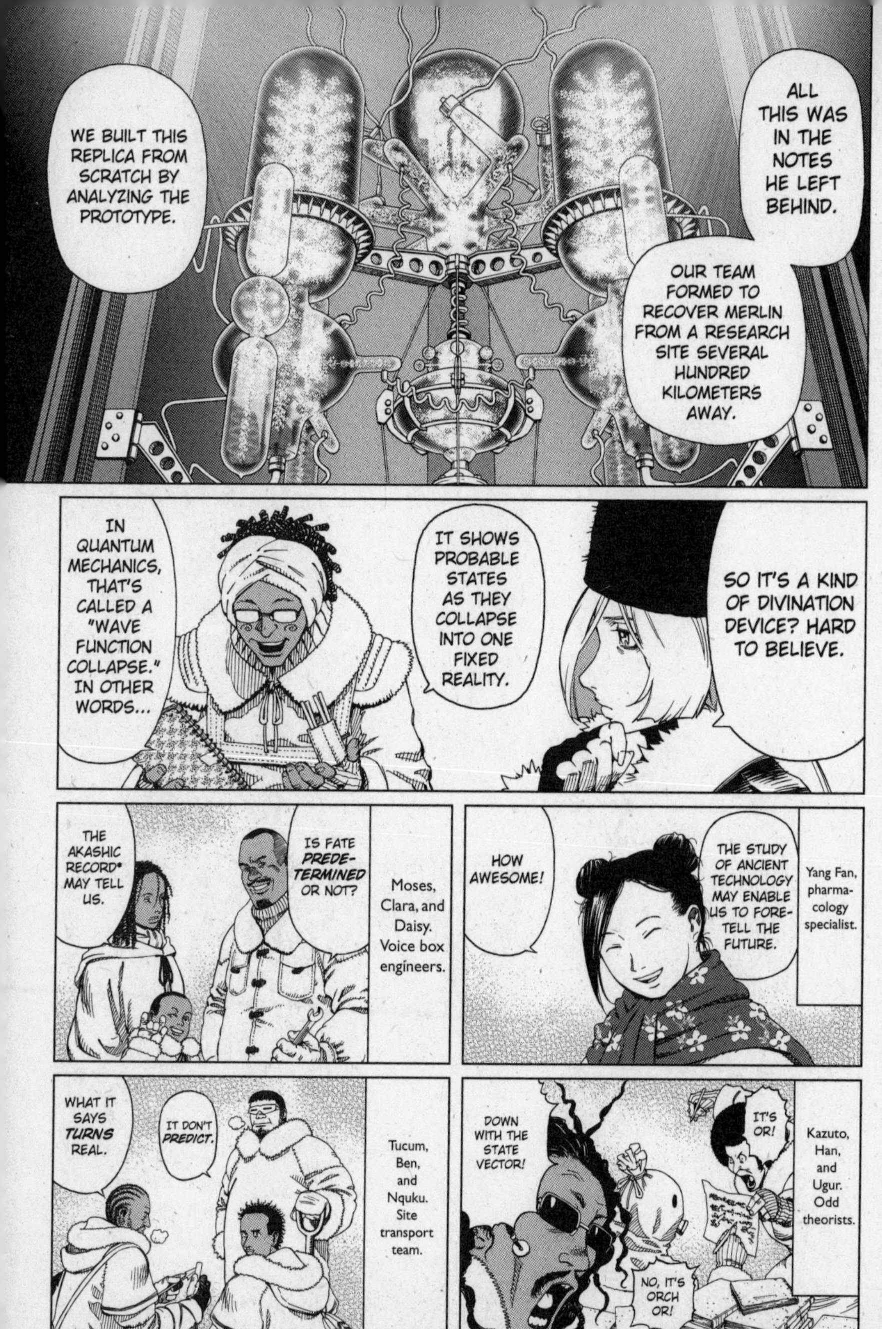
ALL THIS WAS IN THE NOTES HE LEFT BEHIND.
OUR TEAM FORMED TO RECOVER MERLIN FROM A RESEARCH SITE SEVERAL HUNDRED KILOMETERS AWAY.
WE BUILT THIS REPLICA FROM SCRATCH BY ANALYZING THE PROTOTYPE.
SO IT'S A KIND OF DIVINATION DEVICE? HARD TO BELIEVE.
IT SHOWS PROBABLE STATES AS THEY COLLAPSE INTO ONE FIXED REALITY.
IN QUANTUM MECHANICS, THAT'S CALLED A "WAVE FUNCTION COLLAPSE." IN OTHER WORDS...
Yang Fan, pharmacology specialist.
THE STUDY OF ANCIENT TECHNOLOGY MAY ENABLE US TO FORETELL THE FUTURE.
HOW AWESOME!
Moses, Clara, and Daisy. Voice box engineers.
IS FATE *PREDETERMINED* OR NOT?
THE AKASHIC RECORD* MAY TELL US.
Kazuto, Han, and Ugur. Odd theorists.
IT'S OR!
DOWN WITH THE STATE VECTOR!
NO, IT'S ORCH OR!
Tucum, Ben, and Nquku. Site transport team.
IT DON'T *PREDICT*.
WHAT IT SAYS *TURNS* REAL.

*Akashic record: an eternal etherical library of past, present, and future, a concept espoused by Rudolf Steiner, Edgar Cayce, Max Heindel, and many theosophists.

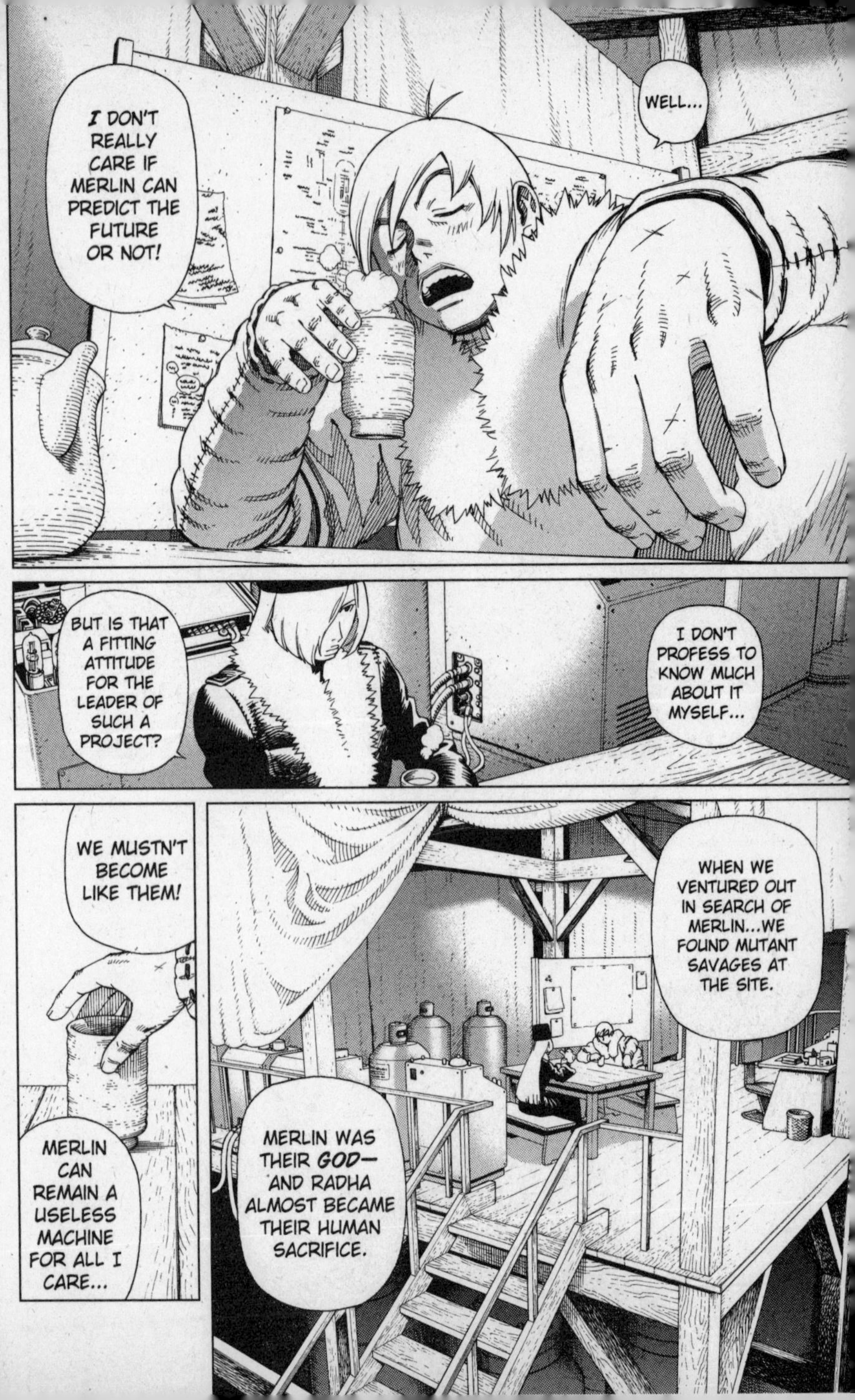
WELL...
I DON'T REALLY CARE IF MERLIN CAN PREDICT THE FUTURE OR NOT!
I DON'T PROFESS TO KNOW MUCH ABOUT IT MYSELF...
BUT IS THAT A FITTING ATTITUDE FOR THE LEADER OF SUCH A PROJECT?
WHEN WE VENTURED OUT IN SEARCH OF MERLIN...WE FOUND MUTANT SAVAGES AT THE SITE.
MERLIN WAS THEIR GOD—AND RADHA ALMOST BECAME THEIR HUMAN SACRIFICE.
WE MUSTN'T BECOME LIKE THEM!
MERLIN CAN REMAIN A USELESS MACHINE FOR ALL I CARE...

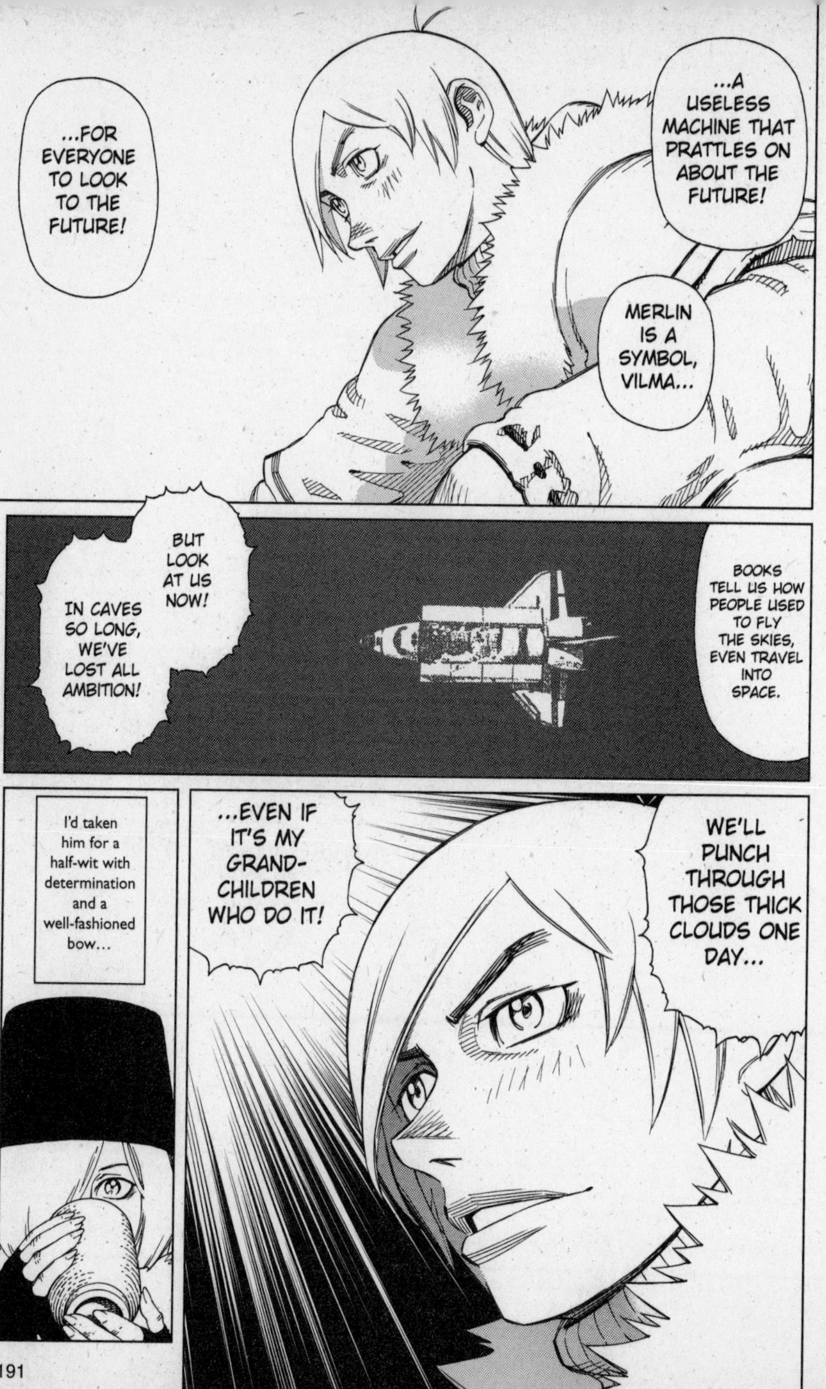
...A USELESS MACHINE THAT PRATTLES ON ABOUT THE FUTURE!
MERLIN IS A SYMBOL, VILMA...
...FOR EVERYONE TO LOOK TO THE FUTURE!
BOOKS TELL US HOW PEOPLE USED TO FLY THE SKIES, EVEN TRAVEL INTO SPACE.
BUT LOOK AT US NOW!
IN CAVES SO LONG, WE'VE LOST ALL AMBITION!
WE'LL PUNCH THROUGH THOSE THICK CLOUDS ONE DAY...
...EVEN IF IT'S MY GRAND-CHILDREN WHO DO IT!
I'd taken him for a half-wit with determination and a well-fashioned bow...

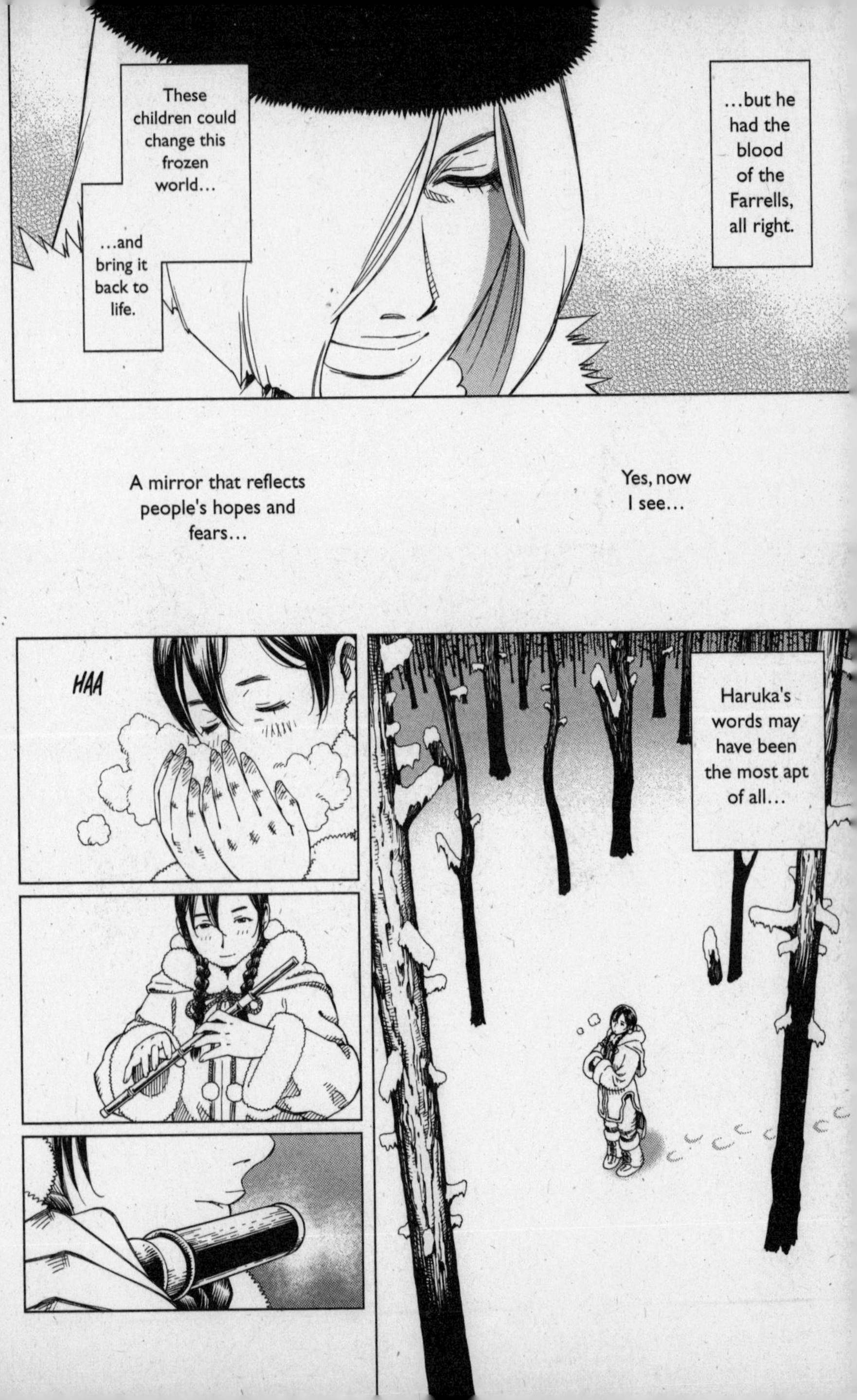
...but he had the blood of the Farrells, all right.
These children could change this frozen world...
...and bring it back to life.
Yes, now I see...
A mirror that reflects people's hopes and fears...
Haruka's words may have been the most apt of all...
HAA

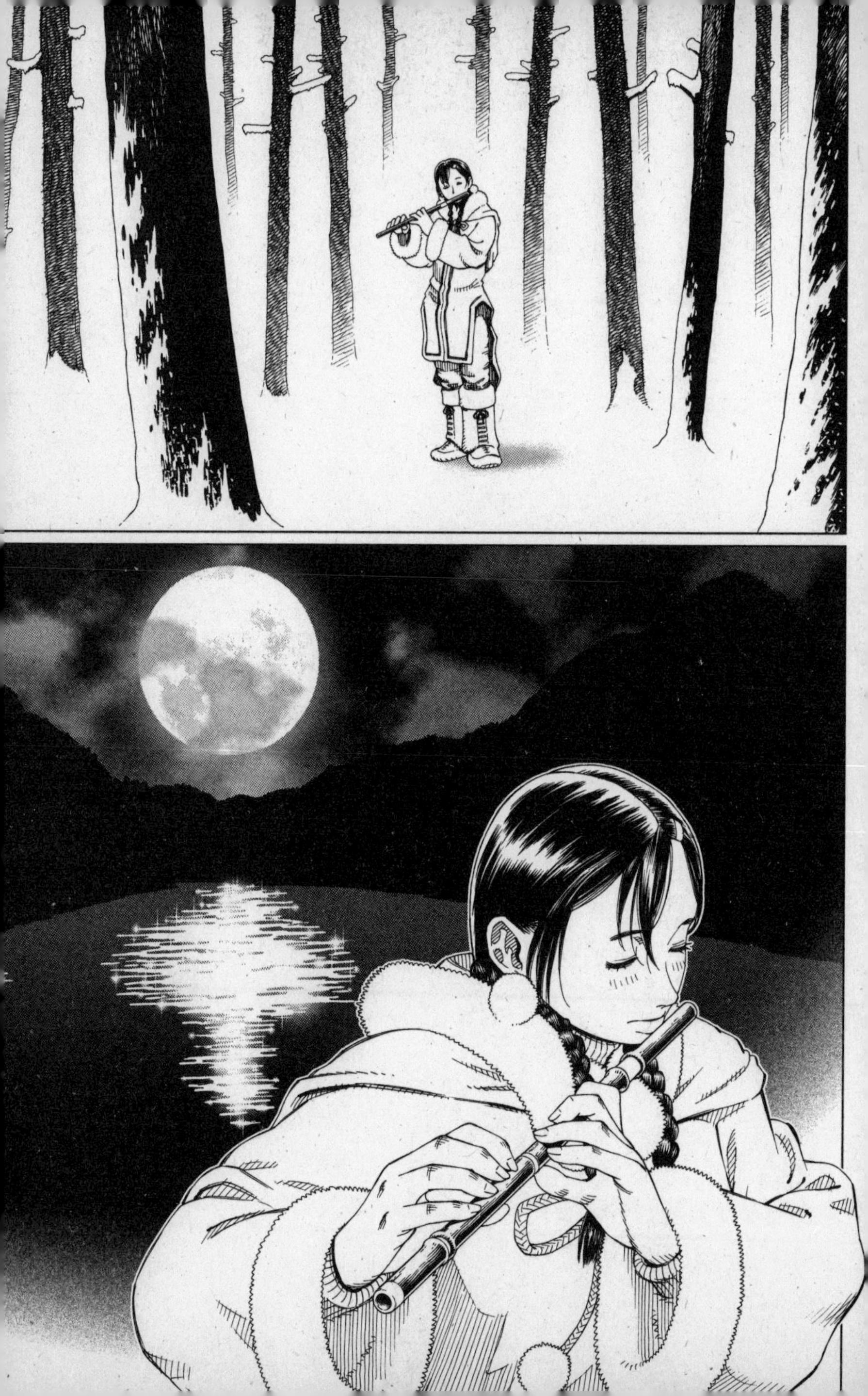

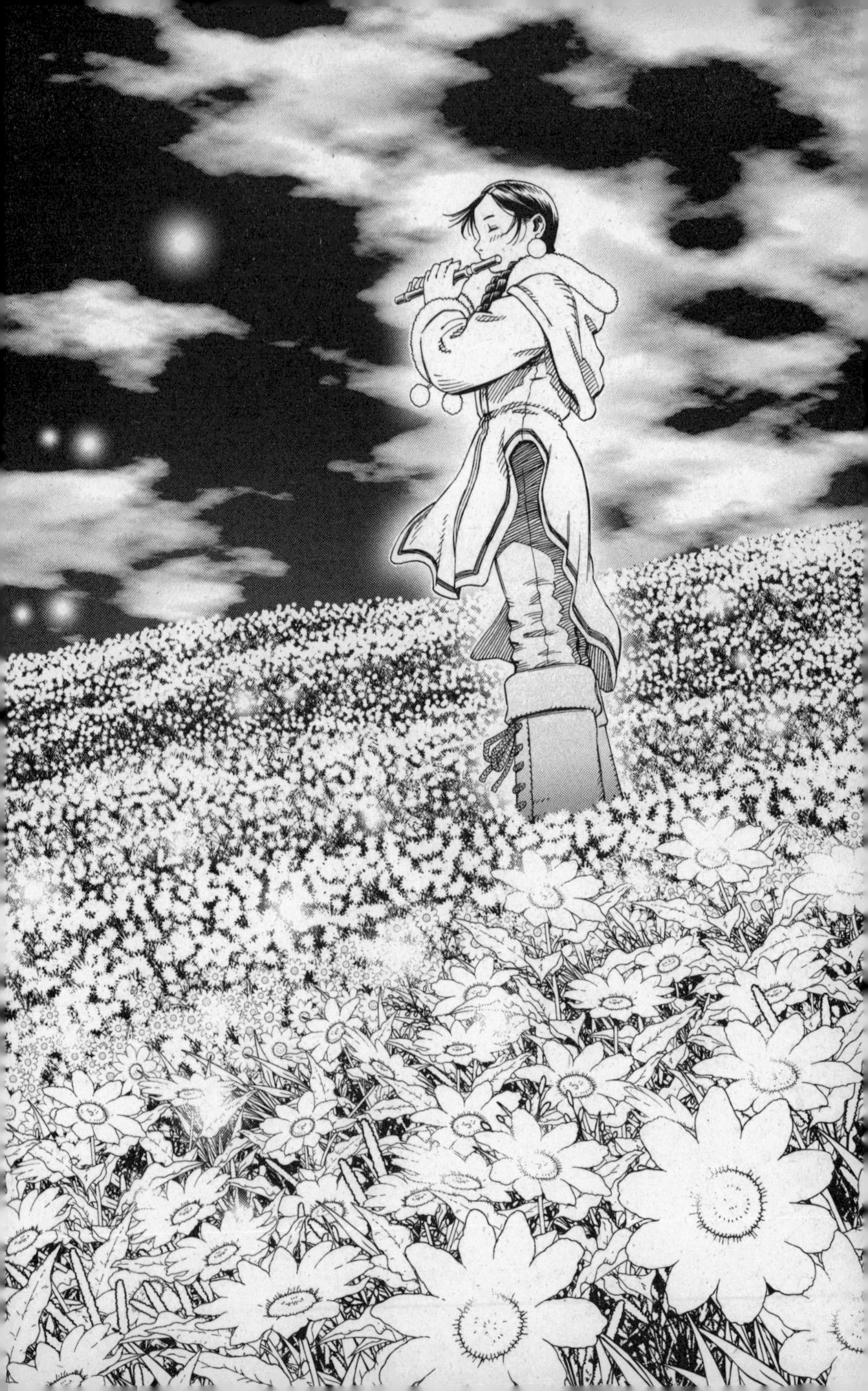

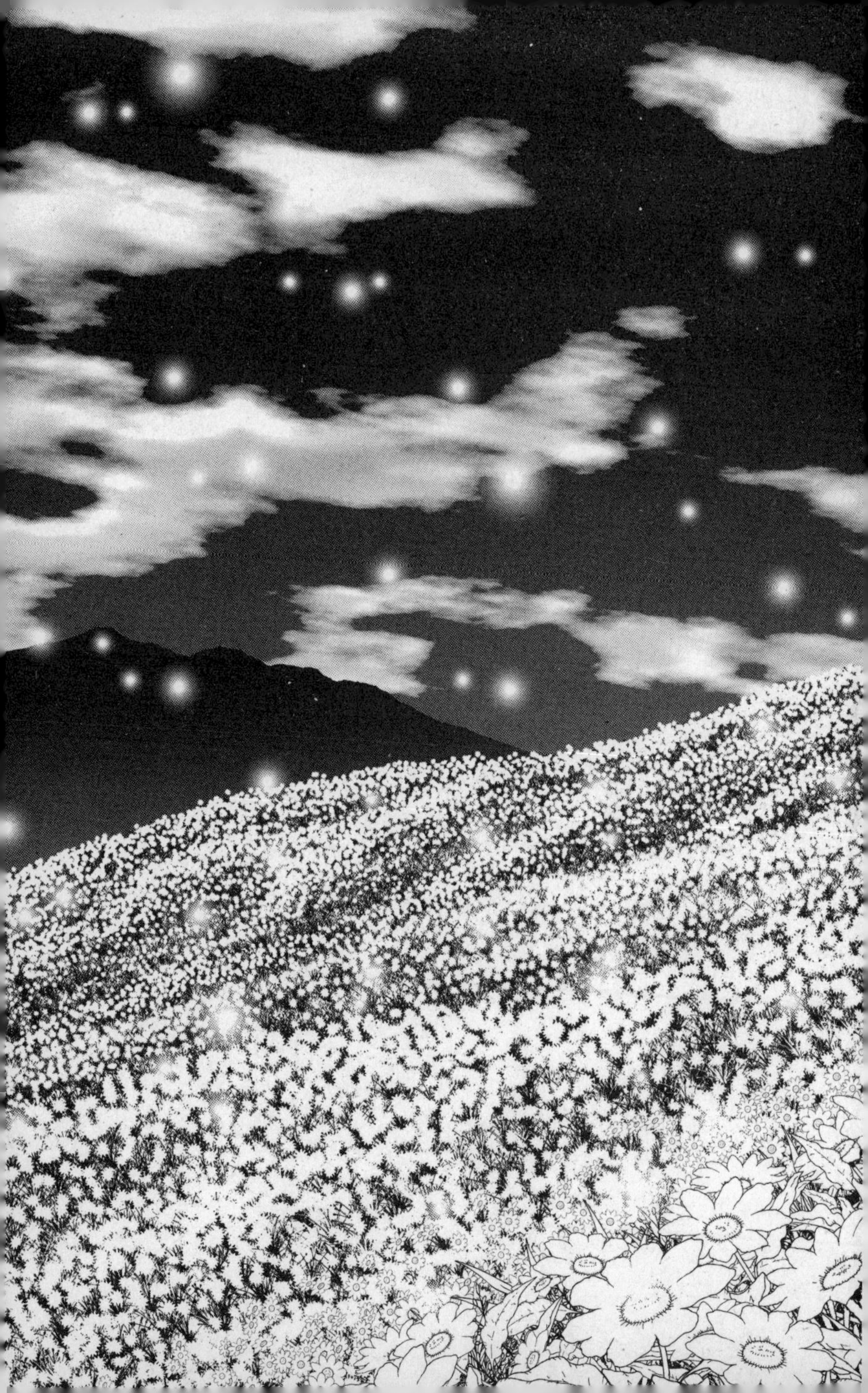

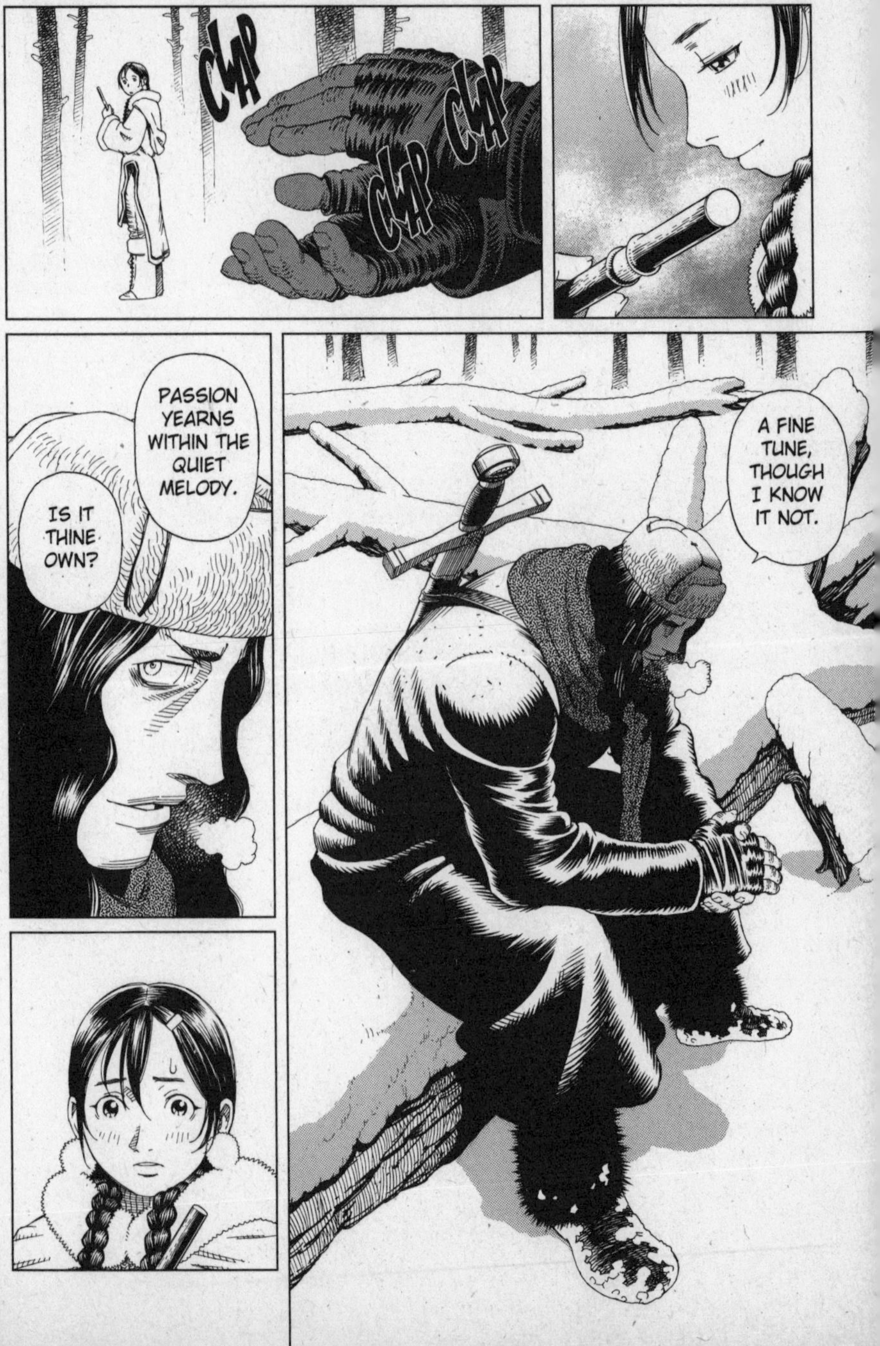
CLAP
CLAP
CLAP
A FINE TUNE, THOUGH I KNOW IT NOT.
PASSION YEARNS WITHIN THE QUIET MELODY.
IS IT THINE OWN?

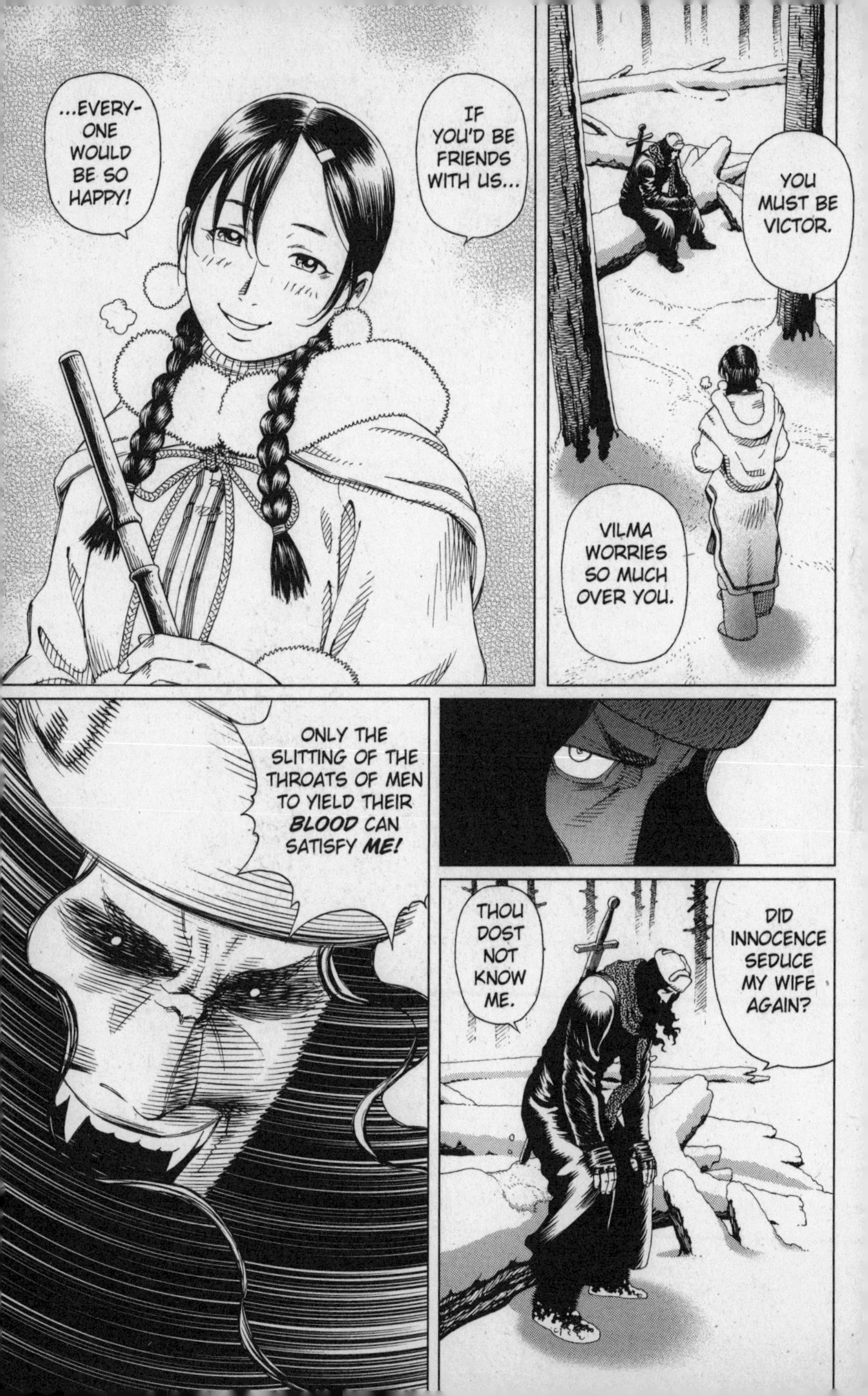
YOU MUST BE VICTOR.
VILMA WORRIES SO MUCH OVER YOU.
IF YOU'D BE FRIENDS WITH US...
...EVERY-ONE WOULD BE SO HAPPY!
DID INNOCENCE SEDUCE MY WIFE AGAIN?
THOU DOST NOT KNOW ME.
ONLY THE SLITTING OF THE THROATS OF MEN TO YIELD THEIR *BLOOD* CAN SATISFY *ME!*

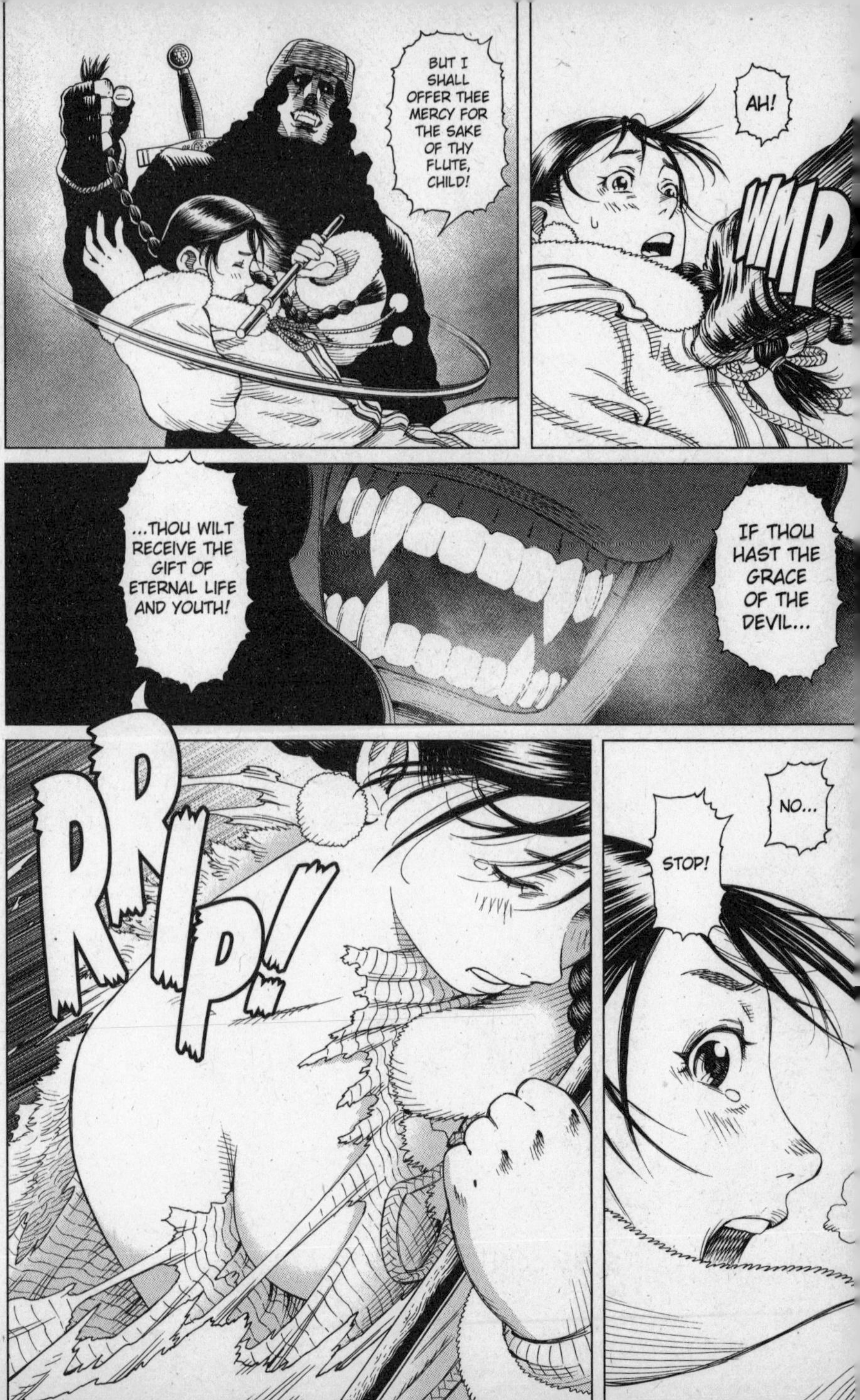
AH!
WMP
BUT I SHALL OFFER THEE MERCY FOR THE SAKE OF THY FLUTE, CHILD!
IF THOU HAST THE GRACE OF THE DEVIL...
...THOU WILT RECEIVE THE GIFT OF ETERNAL LIFE AND YOUTH!
NO...
STOP!
RRIP!

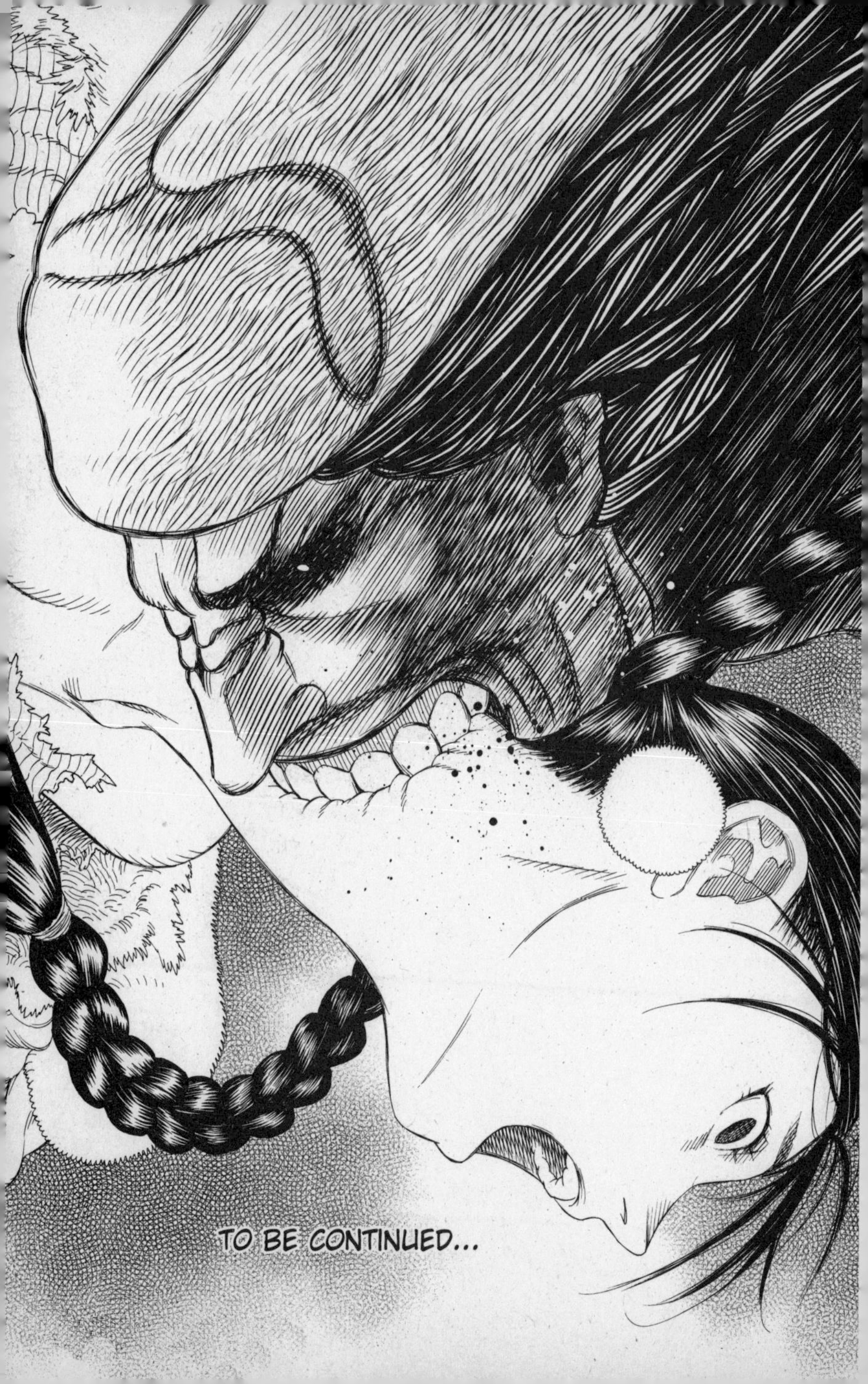
TO BE CONTINUED...

REVEALED!

VAMPIRES IN THE WORLD OF BATTLE ANGEL ALITA

The supernatural creatures known as vampires have been feared throughout history. Late 20th century advances in biology showed that they are indeed formerly human, mutated via infection with the retrovirus known as the "V-virus." Carriers of the V-virus are called "Type-V mutants."

HISTORY

Tired of being oppressed by the Christian community in medieval Europe, Type-V mutant elders assembled in the 17th century to found a secret organization known only as "The Society." Type-V mutants across the globe were united, taught to refrain from excessive violence, and integrated with humans into a system of coexistence.

The Society considers the word "vampire" a derogatory term, and prefers to refer to themselves as "The Cognate."

	Vampires (in folklore)	Type-V Mutants
Suck Human Blood	Y	Yes, but they also eat normal food
Eternal Youth	Y	Y
Immortal	They can only be killed by exploiting their weaknesses	Recuperative powers are exceptional, but they do die
Paranormal Abilities	Can transform into bats or puffs of smoke, etc.	N
Special Abilities	Y	Physical strength, heightened senses, and individuals may have even greater unique powers
Pass on vampirism through bites	Y	Yes, but victim's survival rate is less than 1%
Reproductive capacity	?	Both males and females lose the ability to reproduce
Are warded off by a cross	Y	No, but if they were devout Christians, could form stigmata
Have no reflection in reflective surfaces	Y	N
Will die with a stake through the heart	Y	Well, yeah–anyone would
Reduced to ash by sunlight	Y	They don't turn to ash, but can get sunburned
Hate Garlic	Y	Depends on individual taste

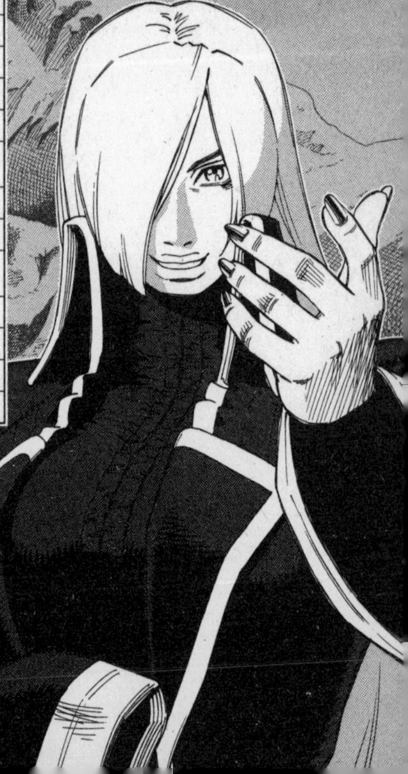

ALTERED SHOCK

The V-virus can only be transmitted through bodily fluids. Once infected, the body goes into a reaction called "Altered Shock." Symptoms—including a drop in blood pressure, agonizing pain, hallucinations, stupor, convulsions, and muscle rigidity—continue for about 70 hours. Most die. Survival rates are thought to be correlated to levels of growth hormones and sex hormones.

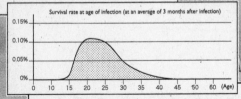

Survival rate at age of infection (at an average of 3 months after infection)

The temperature at the onset of symptoms is also thought to have a significant impact. Some data imply that survival rates decrease when the temperature goes above 25°C—perhaps explaining why there are few Type-V mutants in the tropics.

THREE MAIN CAUSES OF DEATH

SUICIDE

Getting over Altered Shock doesn't mean the coast is clear. The victim then faces psychological anguish. Carnivorous aggression (the so-called "thirst for blood") increases. If victims did not wish to be infected, they may try to suppress the thirst for moral or religious reasons, and often cannot accept the change that has come over them. The suicide rate within ten years of infection may be as high as 60%. Only someone who thinks nothing of taking a life will easily adapt to being a Type-V mutant.

MURDER

If a Type-V mutant finds too much pleasure in killing, and The Society is unable to shelter or confine him, a reckless escalation of crimes may ensue, leading to retaliation or police action. However, once the Type-V gains the skill and experience to attack proficiently (or a desire not to rock the boat) only conflict within the Cognate itself leads to such a murderous end.

DISEASE

Type-V mutants are exceptionally resilient against injury, but are surprisingly prone to disease, especially cancer. This is likely related to the mechanism of ageless cell division. The rate of cancer within 50 years of infection is 30 times that of normal. However, the rate drops again 100 years after infection. The Society superstition has it that once one manages to survive 200 years, the likelihood of death is practically zero—except in power struggles with other Cognates.

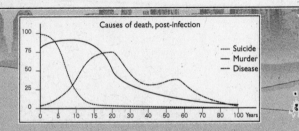

Causes of death, post-infection

----- Suicide
—— Murder
- - - Disease

The above data was gathered by The Society prior to the Catastrophe. The Society had enough clout to have a say in human politics, mainly in Europe. However, the Catastrophe destroyed their organization, along with the rest of civilization.

THE LOCAL JAPANESE VARIETY... URBAN LEGENDS!

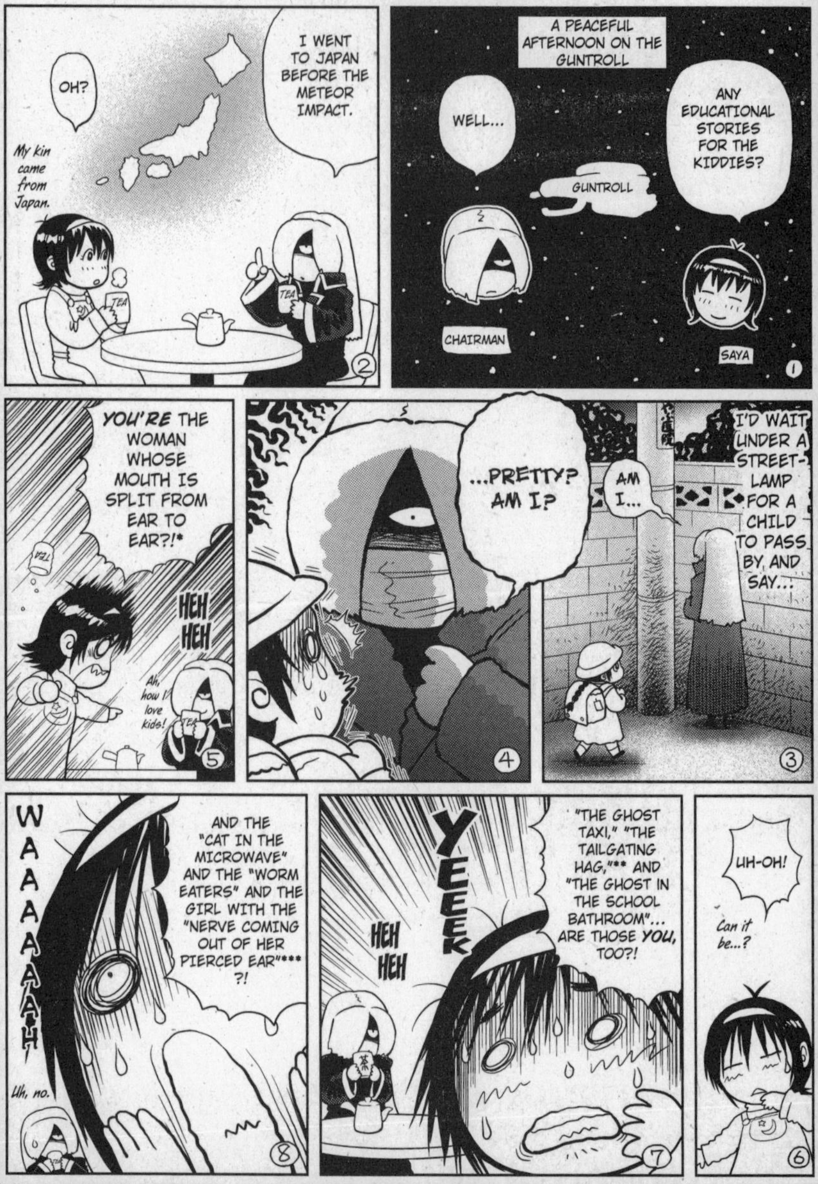
A PEACEFUL AFTERNOON ON THE GUNTROLL
ANY EDUCATIONAL STORIES FOR THE KIDDIES?
WELL...
GUNTROLL
CHAIRMAN
SAYA
I WENT TO JAPAN BEFORE THE METEOR IMPACT.
OH?
My kin came from Japan.
TEA
TEA
I'D WAIT UNDER A STREET-LAMP FOR A CHILD TO PASS BY, AND SAY...
AM I...
...PRETTY? AM I?
YOU'RE THE WOMAN WHOSE MOUTH IS SPLIT FROM EAR TO EAR?!*
HEH HEH
Ah, how I love kids!
TEA
UH-OH!
Can it be...?
YEEEK
"THE GHOST TAXI," "THE TAILGATING HAG,"** AND "THE GHOST IN THE SCHOOL BATHROOM"... ARE THOSE YOU, TOO?!
HEH HEH
AND THE "CAT IN THE MICROWAVE" AND THE "WORM EATERS" AND THE GIRL WITH THE "NERVE COMING OUT OF HER PIERCED EAR"*** ?!
WAAAAAAAH
Uh, no.

NO GHOST STORIES, NO LIFE!

NEXT TIME: GRAVEYARD CHAIRMAN!

* [Japanese urban legend: a woman wearing a mask asks passing children if she is pretty, then reveals a mouth split from ear to ear. She kills you if you reply "yes" or "no," so you should answer "average."—translator's note.]

** [Urban legend of the "tailgating hag": an old driver pursues you until you cause an accident.—translator's note.]

*** [Urban legend: a girl got her ears pierced, then noticed a string-like thing coming out of the hole, so she cut it off. It turned out to be her optic nerve, and she went blind.—t.n.]

WANTED! BATTLE ANGEL ALITA: LAST ORDER

NEW CHARACTERS/NEW COSTUMES

We're accepting ideas for reader-designed characters and new costumes for Alita! Here's your chance to see Alita wear clothes you designed, or for your own characters to find life in Battle Angel Alita: Last Order!

USED FOR ALITA: LAST ORDER, VOL. 8

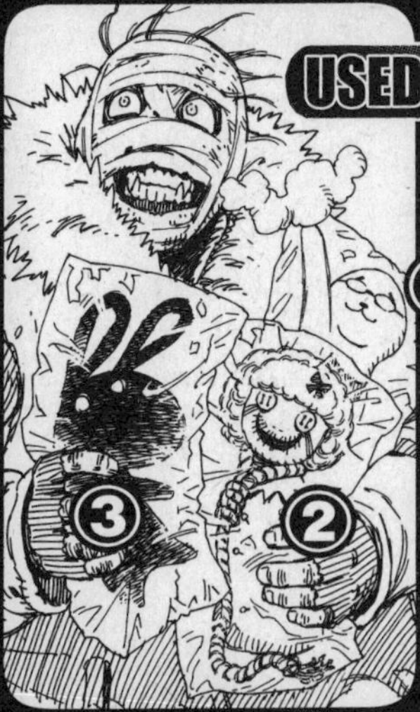

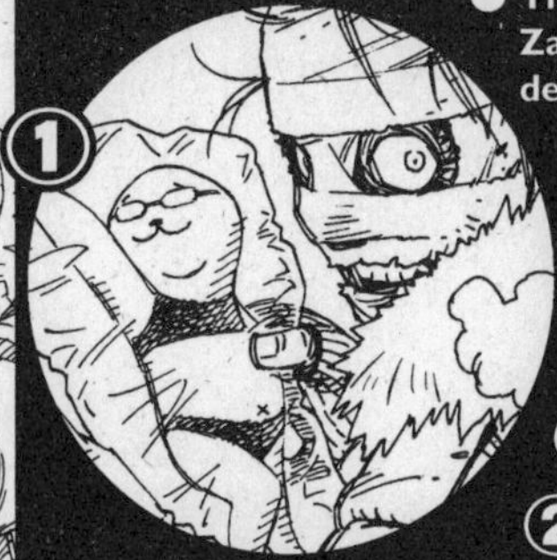

● The three dolls Zapolska found were designed by readers.

① Mr. Yamauchi

② Death Doll

③ Remmie

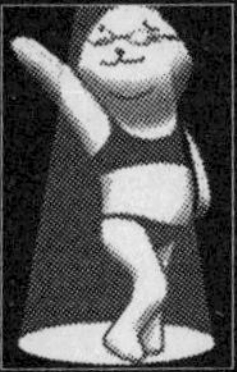

Mr. Yamauchi
By Suzakumaru
(from Tokyo)

He's gay and looks like a stuffed animal. He loves muscular dudes. His favorite phrase is "Train yourself!"

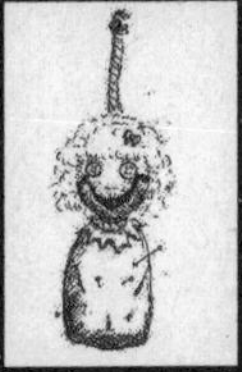

Death Doll
By poly
(from Kanagawa)

A new mascot. But it's actually a bomb. Horrible, but cute.

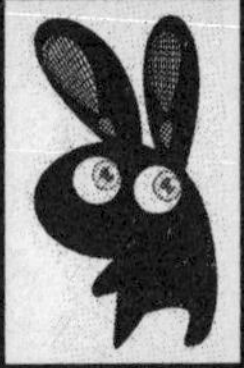

Remmie
By Ken-chan
(from Saitama)

An emergency sleep device modeled after the tapir that eats nightmares for you.

SEND YOUR ENTRIES HERE!

- Please draw with an ink pen, ballpoint pen, or a marker.
- Please include your address, name, handle, title of your work, and comments about the manga.
- Please do not send works drawn in pencil. Entries cannot be returned.
- We are no longer accepting new characters for the Z.O.T Tournament.
- Copyright for all works used in the manga are the possession of Yukito Kishiro.

Entries will be disposed of after a certain period of time, so please make a copy before you send it! Please specify if you'd rather be kept anonymous.

We're accepting entries via the Internet! Yukitopia is full of artwork and information on Yukito Kishiro! All fans should check it out!

http://www.yukito.com/

Fullmetal Alchemist Profiles

Get the background story and world history of the manga, plus:

- Character bios
- New, original artwork
- Interview with creator Hiromu Arakawa
- Bonus manga episode only available in this book

Fullmetal Alchemist Anime Profiles

Stay on top of your favorite episodes and characters with:

- Actual cel artwork from the TV series
- Summaries of all 51 TV episodes
- Definitive cast biographies
- Exclusive poster for your wall

Everything You Need to Get Up to
Fullmetal Speed

Get the who's who and what's what in Edward and Alphonse's world—buy these *Fullmetal Alchemist* profile books today at store.viz.com!

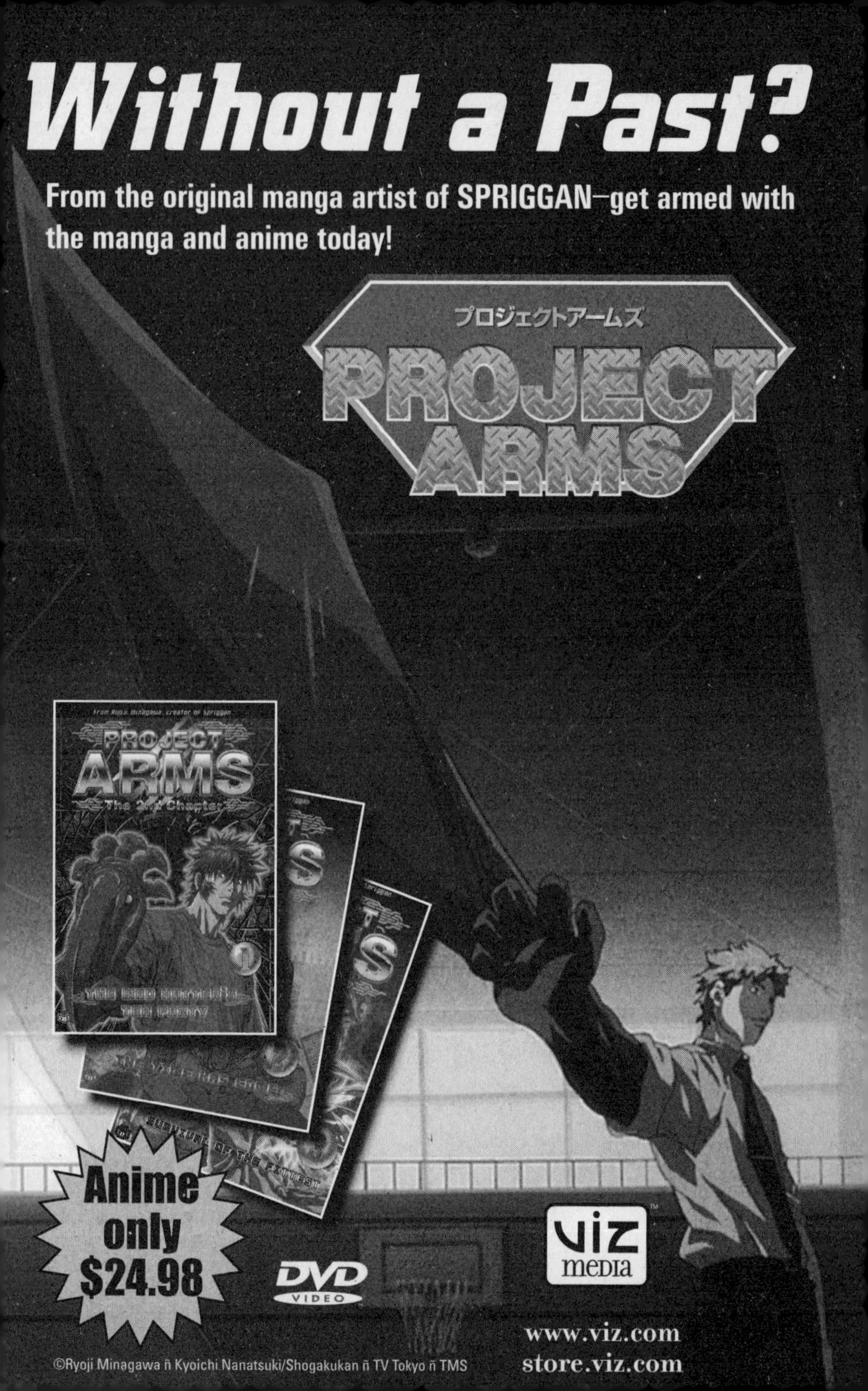
Without a Past?
From the original manga artist of SPRIGGAN—get armed with the manga and anime today!
プロジェクトアームズ
PROJECT ARMS
PROJECT ARMS
The 2nd Chapter
Anime only $24.98
DVD VIDEO
viz media
www.viz.com
store.viz.com
©Ryoji Minagawa ñ Kyoichi Nanatsuki/Shogakukan ñ TV Tokyo ñ TMS

What's a Future

Ryo thought he was normal until he learned his arm was secretly replaced with a powerful weapon. But he soon learns that there are others—teens like him—with mechanical limbs and no idea how the weapons were implanted. Now a secret organization is after the only living samples of this technology and wants to obtain their power by any means possible...

Manga only $9.95